Performing South Africa's Truth Commission

CATHERINE M. COLE

Performing South Africa's Truth Commission

Stages of Transition

INDIANA UNIVERSITY PRESS
Bloomington and Indianapolis

This book is a publication of

Indiana University Press
601 North Morton Street
Bloomington, IN 47404-3797 USA

www.iupress.indiana.edu

Telephone orders	800-842-6796
Fax orders	812-855-7931
Orders by e-mail	iuporder@indiana.edu

♾The paper used in this publication meets the minimum requirements of the American National Standard for Information Sciences—Permanence of Paper for Printed Library Materials, ANSI Z39.48-1992.

Manufactured in the United States of America

Library of Congress Cataloging-in-Publication Data

Cole, Catherine M.
Performing South Africa's Truth Commission : stages of transition / Catherine M. Cole.
    p. cm. — (African expressive cultures)
  Includes bibliographical references and index.
  ISBN 978-0-253-35390-0 (cloth : alk. paper) — ISBN 978-0-253-22145-2 (pbk. : alk. paper)
  1. South Africa. Truth and Reconciliation Commission. 2. Television broadcasting of news—Social aspects—South Africa. 3. Discourse analysis—South Africa. 4. Reconciliation—Social aspects—South Africa—History. 5. Apartheid—South Africa. 6. Post-apartheid era—South Africa. 7. South Africa—Politics and government—1994– I. Title.
  DT1974.2.C65 2009
  968.06—dc22   2009025619

1   2   3   4   5   15   14   13   12   11   10

For Kwame and Aaron

Contents

Preface and Acknowledgments

My life existed somewhere in the liminal space between that which is recorded officially and that which remains officially off the record. I cannot begin to explain the pain of living a life with no record, where one breathes but there is no existence.

—Yazir Henry

I come from an island within an island, which lies within another island, South Africa, severed from the continent, surrounded on three sides by ocean, and on the fourth by desert (Namibia), sparsely populated farmland (Botswana, Zimbabwe), the Limpopo River, and dense subtropical vegetation (Mozambique). To these natural barriers, white settlers added their own multitude of thorny hedges, walls and electrified fences, cleaving the country from its continent till it might just as well have been called "South of Africa." . . . In the 1990's, the country has begun its drift back to the continent, while swelling numbers of its poor, and those of many other African countries, come pressing against the bulwarks of its inner island-cities.

—Denis Hirson

This is a book about South Africa's transition from authoritarian to democratic rule and the forum it used to help accomplish that transformation, the Truth and Reconciliation Commission (TRC). Like the subjectivities described above by South African political activist Yazir Henry and expatriate poet Denis Hirson, the TRC was neither here nor there, located somewhere between the islands of the past and an imagined future of integration—integration for the races, of course, but also integration for South Africa itself within both the continent and the larger world from which it had been severed through years of cultural and economic boycotts.

The TRC also occupied a liminal space between performance and the law. "The trial is preeminently a theatrical form," said Susan Sontag.[1] Yet to say that theatre and the law share an affinity is to say nothing new. "From the earliest Greek tragedies to the *Farce de Maistre Pierre Pathelin* to Arthur Miller's *The Crucible* to the contemporary cinematic *Retour de Martin Guerre*," Jody Enders observes, "the exposition and resolution of juridical proceedings have always had latent if not blatantly manifest dramatic value."[2] The uses to which theatre and performance have been put within the nascent field of transitional justice in the late twentieth and early twenty-first centuries, however, *are* new.[3] As the trial of

Adolf Eichmann in 1961 made clear, performance, in its convergence with legal formats devised to address gross violations of human rights and crimes against humanity, had gained new potency, much to the dismay of critics such as Hannah Arendt.[4] In the field of transitional justice that arose in the wake of the Eichmann and Nuremburg trials, performance has become central. One can see its importance in, for instance, Slobodan Milošević's theatrics before the International Criminal Tribunal for the former Yugoslavia in 2002; in Argentinean efforts to make visible the many people "disappeared" during the Dirty War; in the appropriation of traditional rituals called *gacaca* for reconciliation in postgenocide Rwanda; and in the overlapping theatrical and legal testimonies of those who appeared before the UN-backed Special Court for Sierra Leone.[5]

Transitional justice is an "invented tradition" of the late twentieth century.[6] Devised as a way to cope with the aftermath of systematic and large-scale violations of human rights, transitional justice has achieved its most notable impact via truth commissions. Such commissions grapple with the ultimate failure of traditional jurisprudence in the face of contending demands for justice, reparation, acknowledgement, mourning, healing, reconciliation, and the promulgation of public memory. Can the law punish individuals and former state operatives while at the same time honoring victims and educating the public so that crimes against humanity happen never again, *nunca más*? Frustration with the limits of law and retributive justice in the face of such demands led to the formation of transitional justice as a field as well as to its attendant notion of "restorative justice," which focuses on restoring humanity to both perpetrator and victim.

The "transition" in transitional justice denotes the transformation of a nation-state from authoritarian to democratic rule. South Africa is one of the most significant, most celebrated, and most discussed examples of state transformation in the late twentieth century. When South Africa held its first democratic elections in 1994, voters of all races, ethnicities, religions, sexualities, abilities, and creeds waited for hours in lines that snaked around buildings, through fields, and down roads. As these ballots were cast, the country ended over forty-five years of rule by the National Party, thirty-four of which had seen the grimmest days of apartheid. The state's violations of human rights were legendary. For instance, after the Sharpeville massacre of 1960—during which police fired into a crowd that was protesting restrictive pass laws, killing and wounding hundreds of Africans—prisoners could be held for weeks without trial and were routinely tortured and denied access to legal counsel. Prison was just one site of oppression, but it was the center of apartheid's vortex, a vast system propelled by an obsession with race, segregation, and socially engineered inequality. The chief instrument of apartheid was the dreaded passbook, otherwise known as "*dompas*," or dumb pass. South Africa's black majority had to carry this 96-page booklet at all times, for it inscribed the performative capacities of its bearers—where they could live, work, and travel. The hubris of a system that so fastidiously tried to script lives via a single text was evident in the passbook's administrative failure: government records were often wrong. At times the government's backlog of movement and tax data was so great that it took nine months to get a response to attempts to bring passbooks up to date. It was not uncommon for multiple books to be issued to one person, and an attendant fingerprinting system degenerated into chaos.[7] Yet the inefficiencies of the passbook did not inhibit its power—rather, they enhanced it. "Out-of-order" books meant more opportunities to arrest. As historian Keith Breckenridge writes, "By 1962 the Dompas had duly become the key instrument of a brutally enforced white supremacy—a mechanism of capricious policing, mass arrest and imprisonment. . . . There is a macabre symmetry in the figures for monthly registrations in the 1950s and monthly arrests in the 1960s."[8] In 1957, pass-law offenses accounted for 1,000 arrests per day; by 1962, that figure had risen to over 1,600 per day.[9] Passes effectively criminalized large portions of the population. "A black man stay out of trouble? Impossible, Buntu. Our skin is trouble," Sizwe Bansi aptly observes in the famous anti-apartheid play *Sizwe Bansi Is Dead*.[10]

With a vast legacy of human rights abuses, South Africa faced overwhelming challenges in reinventing itself in 1994 as a liberal democracy that respected those rights. Penning one of the most progressive constitutions in the world was a visionary and provocative first step. But texts in and of themselves do not reality make. In order to take effect, texts—whether in the form of passbooks or constitutions—require performance. One must "do things" with words. As performance studies has shown, there must be a connection between *saying* something and *doing* something for words to construct reality.[11] South Africa's process of reinvention and its performative realization of its new constitution took many forms. Even as the constitution was being drafted, the country was faced with questions that nearly all transitional societies confront. In her influential survey of truth commissions globally, Pricilla Hayner articulates the myriad problems occasioned by state transition:

> What should be done with a recent history full of victims, perpetrators, secretly buried bodies, pervasive fear, and official denial? Should this past be exhumed, preserved, acknowledged, apologized for? How can a nation of enemies be reunited, former opponents reconciled, in the context of such a violent history and often bitter, festering wounds? What should be done with hundreds or thousands of perpetrators still walking free?[12]

To address such questions, South Africa decided to create a truth commission, an entity that would realize the imperatives articulated in the new constitution. The mandate authorizing the TRC—Act No. 34 of 1995, the Promotion of National Unity and Reconciliation Act—specified the following goals: to investigate past gross human rights violations, grant conditional amnesty, give victims a place to "relate the violations they suffered," take measures toward restoring human dignity, report to the nation at large about its findings, and make recommendations aimed at preventing gross violations of human rights in the future.

This act was a highly demanding script—to the point of being (some would say) unproducible. How could one commission accomplish so many things? Yet with the energy and euphoria of a newly liberated state and the innovation and charisma of key producers, the show of the truth commission opened, beginning with its first public hearings in April 1996. By all accounts the TRC was an epic production, transpiring over nearly a decade that lasted from those first hearings to the presentation in 2003 of the last installment of its seven-volume summary report. The commission was epic in content, given its mandate to investigate gross violations of human rights committed during a 34-year period of South African history (1960 to 1994). We can also say the TRC was epic in form, made up of exhausting, daylong hearings in which many discrete narratives were woven into larger narratives that when written down and published consumed over eleven inches on a bookshelf. And yet this was not an epic of a solitary and legendary hero of high status. Rather, the TRC represented the deeds and stories of a wide range of people, from the most elevated to the lowly in society, those that Archbishop Desmond Tutu, chairperson of the TRC, often referred to as the "little people." The TRC put the voices and words of thousands of "ordinary" people into the public record, an extraordinary feat both in South African history and in African history in general.[13] As David William Cohen and E. S. Atieno Odhiambo argue, records of commissions and trials, especially in Africa, have a contingent power "to open views of otherwise thinly documented, poorly understood, or weakly represented worlds."[14] I would contend that the TRC archive has precisely such capacities as a historical record, yet they have gone largely untapped because the commission's historiography to date has been driven by questions of efficacy and positivism.

There were sixteen truth commissions in the world before South Africa's, but the TRC was the first to take place in the public eye. Previous truth commissions were conducted behind closed doors and became known to the public through the publication of a final report.[15] But South Africa's Truth and Reconciliation Commission was held in front of two sorts of audiences: the crowds that assembled in the town halls, churches, and public venues throughout the country where the public hearings were held over roughly two years from 1996 to 1998 and the spectators and listeners who tuned in via television and radio. Hearings were broadcast throughout the country, and the performative iterations of the TRC's decision to "go public" reverberated outward to ever-larger circles of witnesses. For many South Africans, these public hearings *were* the commission. This deceptively simple observation has profound implications, as I shall argue throughout this book. The TRC embraced performance—that is, embodied enactment before an audience—as a central feature of its operations. What were the consequences of this decision?

The word "stages" in my title has both spatial and temporal significance. The TRC happened quite literally on stages, usually raised platforms in town halls, schools, and churches. The public proceedings of the commission were both seen and heard; they used aural and visual signification. Like theatre, the hearings were a time-based practice, and also like theatre, the hearings were retained in individual and collective memories in unique ways, at once ephemeral and enduring. As Edith Hall argues, via Kierkegaard, the moment of human apprehension of performance "transcends time" because "the images it leaves on the mind are uniquely powerful and indelible. This moment is in a sense lost forever, but it can also be held in remarkable detail in consciousness until death."[16] Walter Benjamin goes even further, suggesting that memory itself is a theatre: "Language shows clearly that memory is not an instrument for exploring the past but its theatre. It is the medium of past experience, as the ground is the medium in which dead cities lie interred."[17] The complexity and theatrical dimensions of memory are enduring themes of this book. In particular, I am interested in the relationship between time-based public enactments and the archives, repertoires, and memories they leave behind.

Performing South Africa's Truth Commission also considers the temporal dimensions of South Africa's transition from apartheid to democracy. I depart from the tendency within the field of transitional justice to refer to societies like South Africa's as "post conflict," which seems to suggest that the conflicts of the past have been resolved. As this book goes to press, South Africa has erupted into a conflagration of xenophobic violence unlike anything the country has seen since the end of apartheid fourteen years ago. From Cape Town to Mpumalanga, Gauteng to Durban, "foreigners" (meaning fellow Africans from Zimbabwe, Mozambique, Malawi, Botswana, Rwanda, Nigeria, and Somalia—indeed, from all over the continent) are being assaulted by angry mobs, robbed of their possessions, stabbed, and burned alive. In May 2008, sixty two people were killed and more than 100,000 immigrants displaced, many of whom sought refuge in police stations or left South Africa altogether. This violence diminishes the country's global reputation and tarnishes the often-rosy image the world has held of the "new" South Africa, an image largely based upon the perceived success of the Truth and Reconciliation Commission.

Is the recent violence symptomatic primarily of persistent socioeconomic discrepancies between rich and poor, which are indeed profound? Or is this violence a restored behavior of apartheid, a replication of apartheid's repertoire of inhumanity honed over so many decades but reenacted now with a slight adjustment in the cast of characters—with "foreigners" as the target of abuse rather than specific races? The recent violence raises questions about the dominant rhetoric that post-apartheid South Africa has become a "rainbow nation," a unified state of many races, languages, religions, and ethnicities that is tolerant of all differences. Former president Nelson Mandela and Desmond Tutu, the former chairperson of the Truth and Reconciliation Commission, were the key proponents of the rainbow-nation image. During the recent xenophobic violence, the ever-prescient cartoonist Zapiro of the *Mail & Guardian* depicted in full color Mandela and Tutu gaping at an enormous South African flag dripping with blood. At this historical moment, the post-apartheid rainbow that the TRC itself helped create seems to have evaporated. In May 2008, just as during the days of apartheid, poor people in townships were necklaced with tires, doused with petrol, set alight, and burned alive. Once again the government deployed troops and sharpshooters in townships to quell unrest. Once again the country saw large-scale displacements of people. But these forced removals, unlike the ones of apartheid days, were perpetrated not by the state but by neighbors and fellow residents in the townships. And unlike the police stations of apartheid, which were sites of

torture or of shootings of innocent civilians who had gathered to peacefully protest pass laws (recall Sharpeville in 1960), police stations in the new South Africa
are seen as places of refuge for the most vulnerable members of society—
immigrants from elsewhere in Africa who have become targets of mob violence.
The present-day backdrop to the story of the truth commission brings into sharp
relief my contention that South Africa is certainly not a "post-conflict" society
but one still very much in transition. The Truth and Reconciliation Commission
was an early stage in an ongoing process.

The international impact of South Africa's TRC has been remarkable. In the
words of scholar Christopher Colvin, South Africa's truth commission was "the
most publicized and celebrated post-conflict transition process undertaken in
the last fifty years."[18] It has consequently generated a veritable cottage industry of
publishing. Commissioners, investigators, and journalists who covered the TRC
have penned memoirs; legal scholars, political scientists, anthropologists, and
historians have written appraisals; and human rights activists and bureaucrats in
nongovernmental organizations have assessed South Africa's commission for the
purpose of establishing similar commissions elsewhere in the world.[19] In 2004,
just eight years after the commission began its work, the South African History
Archive at the University of Witwatersrand compiled a "Guide to Archival Sources
Relating to the Truth and Reconciliation Commission" that lists in its "select"
bibliography over ninety books and monographs published about the TRC.

With so many books already written on South Africa's Truth and Reconciliation Commission, why does the world need yet one more? While the secondary
literature on the TRC is vast, scholars have yet to grapple with a fundamental
aspect of the commission—its public, performed dimensions. Inasmuch as South
Africa's truth commission has become a model for transitional justice throughout
the world, we must understand the implications of its decision to be so overtly
public in its operations. *Performing South Africa's Truth Commission* not only
tackles this subject but also departs from the evaluative mode that has dominated much scholarship on the commission. The literature on the TRC often
remains at a general and comparative level, offering assessments of the successes and failures of the TRC as a human rights and/or historical project or
quantitative analyses of patterns of violence or theoretical investigations of the
TRC's use of concepts such as truth, justice, amnesty, and reconciliation. Both
the tone and approach of this literature tends to replicate the TRC's discursive
positioning. The commission sought to establish "as complete a picture as possible of the causes, nature and extent of the gross violations of human rights committed" during a 34-year period.[20] Very often scholars have interpreted "complete" to mean "broad,"[21] and in order to paint the broad picture, many have
painted with broad strokes. What is gained by macronarrative approaches is an
overall understanding of national, regional, and historical patterns of violence
as well as valuable assessments of the efficacy and utility of truth commissions
for transitional justice. What is sacrificed are complexity and specificity—
essential qualities for rendering and deciphering the profound truths the TRC
brought to light.

Richard Wilson argues that global human rights discourse, of which South Africa's Truth and Reconciliation Commission is very much a part, combines scientism, legal positivism, and human rights in order to rationalize information. Wilson finds the human rights forms of investigation and documentation "too legalistic for adequately recording and reflecting upon past violations. The instrumental rationality of law and rights systematically transforms the life-world, rather than being a sensitive device for listening to subjectivity on its own terms."[22] The TRC's Human Rights Violations Committee (HRVC) gathered over 21,000 statements, the majority of which were tightly constrained within statement-taking protocols.[23] However, in the 2,000 testimonies given at public hearings, the unruliness and specificity of the lifeworlds this testimony represents—as well as the idiosyncrasies of individual subjectivities—had a fuller expression in the TRC process.

Performing South Africa's Truth Commission offers a radically alternative view of the commission. How did the TRC's performative conventions, modes of address, and expressive embodiment shape the experience for both participants and spectators? By what means did people experience the hearings, through what levels of mediation, of telling and retelling? How did the medium shape the message? How did public storytelling conveyed by witnesses, governed by commission protocols, and mediated by simultaneous language interpreters, journalists, and television influence public perceptions? While South Africa's Truth and Reconciliation Commission was designed to contain and make manageable the effects of atrocity, the magnitude of that atrocity constantly exceeded the commission's bounds and thus it was the domain of performance that was called upon to cope with this excess. The "completeness" of the vision of the apartheid past, which was mandated in the act that authorized the commission, can be discerned as vividly through in-depth analysis of performed testimony as it can through macronarratives that calculate in quantitative terms apartheid's national dimensions, as the commission's summary report attempts to do. The integrity of victims—which was supposed to be paramount within the TRC's "victim-centered" approach to restorative justice—surely requires this level of attention to testimony. Whatever the victims' intentions toward or expectations of the commission, their words and embodied expressions are now in the public record, and this material deserves to be closely analyzed.

To grapple with the commission's public enactment, one must analyze not just what witnesses said before the commission but how they said things and how the event itself was scripted, produced, rehearsed, stage-managed, and represented. Why and by whom were certain individuals chosen to give public testimony? By the time witnesses appeared before the TRC, they had already told their stories to the commission several times through the statement-taking, investigative, and hearing-preparation processes. *Performing South Africa's Truth Commission* examines the radiating layers of performance: from witness to interpreter to journalist to audience. Repetition was structured into the commission most directly by the simultaneous interpreters who translated the hearings into South Africa's eleven official languages. Like actors, these interpreters repeated in the first person the testimony of perpetrators, witnesses, and survivors as well as that of commissioners and lawyers. They had to embody the voice of the other, walking the careful line between representation and personal appropriation of traumatic narrative as they shifted between languages, with all the perils such on-the-spot translation entailed. Journalists likewise mediated the story, repeating and revising tales from the commission. They too made selections, and they reshaped, retold, and augmented testimony, providing "the stories behind the stories," as the most celebrated weekly television program on the commission, the South African Broadcasting Corporation's *TRC Special Report,* claimed in its motto. Testimony on television—as at the hearings—was embodied. Television reproduced the TRC's enactment as an event that was both seen and heard by its public.

In performance studies, such embodied tellings and retellings are called "restored behavior," a concept that cuts to the heart of defining exactly what is meant by the term performance. "Performance means: never for the first time," says theorist Richard Schechner. "It means: for the second to the *n*th time. It means 'twice-behaved behavior.'"[24] A child of anthropology and theater studies, performance studies opens the frame of analysis beyond the realm of theatre and the realm of the aesthetic to consider the presentation of self in everyday life.[25] To say that people performed before the truth commission is not to say they were actors in a theatrical performance. Nor is it to suggest that what witnesses did or said was fictional, fake, untrue, or manipulative. An attorney who heard me sum up this work as a study of the performative dimensions of the commission interjected, "Well, that must mean you take a very dim view of the truth commission," to which I answered, "On the contrary: your comment suggests you take a very dim view of performance." My listener's negative assumptions about the word "performance" reflect a widespread antitheatrical prejudice and a common assumption that to call the TRC performance is to judge it.[26]

In looking at the TRC through the lens of performance I neither see the commission negatively nor do I valorize it with romantic notions about the miraculous, cathartic, healing potential of performance. I simply assert that the commission *was* a performance and that we need to understand how its performative dimensions operated: how the commission used restored behavior, expressive embodiment, storytelling and retelling; how it called into being different audiences and arenas of witnessing; how it functioned as a ritual for addressing a massive breach in the social fabric; how it drew upon existing genealogies of performance, particularly as the disempowered came into contact with the law in judicial or quasi-judicial arenas; how, in sum, the TRC served as a literal and figurative stage for South Africa's political transition. *Performing South Africa's Truth Commission* deploys the vocabulary, methods, and theory of performance studies to analyze a principal feature of the TRC: its public enactment. The TRC's public hearings constitute what Diana Taylor might call its "repertoire"— the performed, embodied expressions of the endeavor that stand in contrast to the many traces the TRC left behind in transcripts, photographs, videotapes, and audio recordings in the archive.[27] One also sees in the public hearings the complex genealogies of performance that informed the TRC, a kind of rainbow genre that was part law court, part Christian ritual, and part psychological "talking cure," all of which was fully invested in the establishment of a new nation state.[28]

As a performative act, the TRC had multiple and ambiguous meanings. Scholars have not begun to perceive the complexity of these meanings, despite the very large bibliography on the TRC. That bibliography, I suggest, has perhaps been generated too close to the TRC both temporally and geographically. The tendency to make an evaluative pronouncement about the effectiveness of the commission is incredibly persistent in the scholarly literature and in public discourse. At nearly every public presentation on this subject I have given during the past six years, someone asks a variant of the question Was the TRC "good" or "bad," effective or not? While I understand that people ask this question either because they care about the efficacy of transitional justice or because they may wish to know that apartheid is wrapped up neatly and over, I see the question itself as an intellectual cul-de-sac, certainly from a historian's point of view. Imagine how impoverished the historiography of Europe or America would be if scholars examined the Spanish Inquisition or Joseph McCarthy's House Committee on Un-American Activities solely in order to determine whether these endeavors were good or bad, successful or not. What if the only aspect of the trial of Ethel and Julius Rosenberg deemed relevant for scholarship was whether they were, in fact, communists? Historians David William Cohen and E. S. Atieno Odhiambo in their book on the death of Kenyan political figure of John Robert Ouko found themselves similarly hounded by "Who done it?" questions as they attempted instead to read the event as a window onto the complex cultural and social history of Kenya and postcolonial Africa.[29] Of course, to mention the TRC in the same breath as the Spanish Inquisition, McCarthyism, the execution of the Rosenbergs, or the murder of a famous Kenyan politician is not to say that I view the commission in a negative light but rather to suggest that even if one did decide with the benefit of historical hindsight that the TRC was profoundly misguided or even immoral, this conclusion would not make the TRC's archive unworthy of sophisticated, nuanced, and sustained analysis, a robust scholarship that moved far beyond evaluative assessment.

If we step outside of the Truth and Reconciliation Commission's logic—if we move beyond asking utilitarian and operational questions about efficacy—and instead look at the commission as a multifaceted oral history and archival project that put into the public record via testimony information that previously had been excluded, censored, and repressed in apartheid South Africa, we will find many, many other stories and insights that have yet to be analyzed by scholars. The picture that emerges from an analysis attentive to performance is complex, full of details that both confirm and resist the dominant narratives of the past and of the TRC's mission. We also see how individuals performed within the commission the particular truths they were trying to achieve. In the disjunctions between participants' performances of truth *they* wished to perform and the commission's public iteration of the truths *it* wished to perform, we come closest to perceiving the complexity of the knowledge the TRC brought into being. *Performing South Africa's Truth Commission* moves beyond the narrow juridical frame of culpability and redress to explore the larger issues of cultural memory and its many guises of performance. It provides not a broad picture of the TRC but a narrow one, focusing on certain testimonies, particular tellings and retellings, and reading these deeply with a respect for the ambiguity of language, the importance of the coherence of testimony, and the subtle capacities of embodied expression.

Performing South Africa's Truth Commission is also distinctive in its commitment to primary sources. The book is based upon close readings of sources, including new translations of African-language testimony and analysis of raw video footage of TRC hearings now housed at the National Archives (the only part of its TRC holdings that are fully open to public access); interviews with over twenty-five individuals (including TRC commissioners, researchers, lawyers, and staff; those who gave testimony; translators; and journalists, archivists, and artists who have worked on the TRC material); and extensive use of previously overlooked sources, such as the enormously important television documentary series *TRC Special Report*. This is also the first book to focus prominently on the role of TRC interpreters as central mediators and interlocutors in the public life of the commission.

The bulk of the Truth and Reconciliation Commission archive, it should be noted, is still locked away, largely inaccessible to researchers as well as to those who testified before the commission. The National Archives and Records Service in Pretoria, South Africa, is the custodian of the collection, but the Department of Justice is the owner. Although technically the records are accessible to researchers who complete a request and invoke entitlements granted by the Promotion of Access to Information Act of 2000, in actuality this process bumps against obstacles of Kafkaesque dimensions at every turn. The TRC worked feverishly to capture and document the information it unearthed, and it produced great reams of documentation. To be precise, the TRC generated three kilometers' worth of printed material, not including the transcripts from public hearings, which are available online. Since only one in ten human rights violations cases were chosen for public hearing, nonpublic statements given by the remaining 90 percent of witnesses are located in this larger archive, which also houses all of the background research done on each human rights and amnesty case by the TRC's Investigative Unit. Yet this vast archive of material is essentially closed.[30]

Throughout its tenure, the TRC upheld the premise that a new human rights culture could be built only on a foundation of truth, transparency, and freedom of information. Censorship is entirely contrary to the goals of the Truth and Reconciliation Commission, an enterprise that privileged the production of information over the administration of justice.[31] So why is the TRC's archive now locked away in the "new" South Africa? As with anything in South Africa, the answer is complex. Shortly after the TRC finished its work, public access to its archive was challenged by lawsuits that claimed that the information that was revealed about some of the persons named in nonpublic statements was too sensitive to be public. Subsequent legal decisions affirmed that the TRC archive should be open. Yet in practice it is not. We know that the files were moved at the conclusion of the TRC from its headquarters in Cape Town to the National Archives. The staff there has been instructed to refer all requests for information to the Department of Justice, which retains control over access to TRC information. The person at the Department of Justice to whom I was directed never responded to my inquiries over three years. I tried to work through other representatives at the Department of Justice but got nowhere. I then began contacting other researchers of the TRC to see if any had been successful either in submitting a request to the Department of Justice or in gaining access. So far, I have met no researchers, other than those who work for the Department of Justice, who have successfully gained access to the classified portions of the archive, which are in fact the majority of it.

In 2006, the TRC archive was the subject of a lawsuit brought against the Department of Justice by the South African History Archive on behalf of filmmaker David Forbes. He is making a documentary about the well-known Cradock Four, activist community leaders who were murdered by the state during the apartheid era.[32] The Pretoria High Court ruled in 2006 that Forbes could get access to the relevant files for thirty days. But the story did not end there. Nomonde Calata, the wife of Cradock Four member Fort Calata and a participant in the lawsuit, received a phone call from her local municipality in Cradock saying that "some people" from Pretoria wanted to see her about her request. Mrs. Calata agreed to a meeting the next day, for she assumed the officials would need time to fly to Cradock from Pretoria. Much to her surprise, not twenty minutes later several men in suits emerged from state-issued vehicles and descended on her house.[33] "Are you Mrs. Calata? Can we see you privately?" She took them into her living room, where they explained that while David Forbes had requested access to the TRC files, there was some "sensitive information" in the files. They asked her, "Do you want to see these files?" They took out a "bunch of bags" and opened them. "Do you want to see the files?" they repeated. Mrs. Calata recalls

> And at that moment I was not ready to see the files. I don't know when will I be able to be ready to see those files, because what I think, whatever is in those files, I don't want to see it. I want to remember my husband as I know him. Because I heard at the inquest about how he was beaten by dogs, his fingers were off, his tongue was pulled, his hair was pulled. I don't . . . I don't want to see those things. OK, I heard it. But I don't want to SEE it. Because I only want to remember my husband the way he was. So these people made us to sign affidavits and things like that.[34]

Pressured, intimidated, and emotionally manipulated, Mrs. Calata signed an affidavit the men had already prepared that rescinded her request on behalf of Forbes to see the TRC files. She had wanted the information there to be given to Forbes because she believed his documentary was "a good thing, it's for the community." But as a traumatized widow, she could not bear to look at what the files held. In an interview with me and Liza Key, Mrs. Calata said she most feared the likelihood of viewing graphic, gruesome images of her husband after he had been tortured. For her, there would be no benefit in having these images seared into her thoughts, eclipsing happier memories of Fort Calata as a robust, healthy young man. The experience of having government officials suddenly descend on her home was haunting, reminiscent of the old apartheid state. Home invasions were a routine part of her married life with Fort:

> The way they came here, it really reminded me of the old days when the security branch used to come to my house, you know, coming into your house without expecting them to come to your house, because I thought maybe the lady from the municipality phoned, neh?, and maybe they are going to phone and confirm [a meeting] time, and ask me when am I going to be ready to see them so that I can prepare myself to see them. I didn't know that they are going to instruct the people from the municipality to phone me and all of a sudden, here they come. You know? And it shocked me in this . . . in this new era that people are still acting in that same way. I was surprised.[35]

After the state officials left her house, Mrs. Calata consulted with family members and lawyers, and she eventually completed a second affidavit granting David Forbes the right to see the TRC files relevant to her husband's case. Yet the episode dramatizes how fraught the content of the TRC archive remains, even when derived from cases that were highly publicized and had open hearings, so that in the new—as in the old—South Africa even the victims and prominent witnesses who appeared before the TRC cannot look at their own records. I have heard various speculations about the reasons for this situation: that the TRC archive contains information that would be embarrassing or even incriminating to people who are currently in office or hold prominent positions in society, that there is a concern to maintain the integrity of evidence should there be prosecutions in the future, that the Department of Justice simply does not have the capacity—meaning money, staff, or trained personnel—to go through the messy process of vetting individual access request. We might even consider the degree to which the civil service sectors of the society in the new South Africa are staffed with lifetime employees of the old order who are still operating according to the protocols and zeitgeist of the old regime of secrecy, despite the fact that they now work side by side with new employees who perhaps embrace greater transparency in public institutions. Suffice it to say that the inaccessible archive is yet more proof that the TRC was just one stage in an ongoing process of political transition, a process that will surely take decades.

The audiences for this book are multiple. They include scholars not only in the fields of Africa in general and South Africa in particular but also in performance studies, legal studies, trauma, transitional justice, media studies, and postcolonial culture and literature. Moving beyond its specific treatment of South Africa, this book contributes to a larger conversation about performance and transitional justice. How are the notions of performance, embodiment, and public enactment being used in the larger areas of transitional justice and human rights law? Given that performance is being embraced by many researchers as well as artists, composers, and actors as a means to assimilate traumatic history into public memory, it is of paramount importance that we understand more fully the implications of this convergence. *Performing South Africa's Truth Commission* offers an empirically rich study of one particularly notable truth commission in order to provide a basis for such comparative research on performance, human rights, and transitional justice globally.

In addition to addressing multiple academic fields, I have tried to make my analysis accessible to an intellectually curious reading public beyond the ivory tower. I believe that such public engagement is essential to the health of both the academy and the greater civil society. This claim holds especially true in North America, where I live and work, a place where, as Kitty Calavita (the past president of the Law and Society Association) asserts, "'book learning' is a derisive epithet, and 'Everything I Need to Know I Learned in Kindergarten' is a national bestseller, and too much intelligence is arguably a handicap in national presidential elections."[36] The need for public intellectuals is even more pressing in South Africa, for in countries with totalitarian pasts, intellectuals have not uncommonly been complicit.[37] In the recent book *At Risk: Writing on and over the Edge of South Africa,* a number of prominent academics break convention and speak in a style and tone accessible to those outside the academy. At this book's launch, the celebrated poet and memoirist Antjie Krog noted the compelling need for such writing in South Africa. "In a fast growing and complex country like ours," she said, "we can't afford to have the best brains in our country talking only to the best brains of elsewhere, in incomprehensible language, debating from their well ensconced positions in the wrought-iron corners of cyberspace and badly-designed journals."[38]

I write this book as a public intellectual. My goal is not to form policy but rather to stimulate informed public debate and advance a discourse about a subject that matters.[39] Speaking to multiple audiences—those in different geographical, disciplinary, and professional domains—has been one of the biggest challenges in writing this book, compounded by the sprawling nature of the TRC itself as well as South Africa's continually morphing "status quo." An unavoidable consequence is that some readers will come to this book already knowing a great deal about South Africa and some may know very little. Some readers will be experts in performance studies or transitional justice, but many others will encounter these fields here for the first time. I beg your indulgence, reader, when you come upon material that for you is "old hat," for it is likely that some other reader needs this information in order to make sense of this book and of the TRC.

Performing South Africa's Truth Commission adds yet one more layer to the TRC process, in which stories passed from witness to translator, from translator to lawyer, from commissioner and deponents (the actors) to live audiences, and, finally, from live hearing to television and radio audiences. This book is one more interlocutor, and unlike all of the above, what you hold before you is a text and hence a representation that lacks the kinetic, sonic, and visual registers of embodied communication that made the TRC so distinctive. What I hope this book can accomplish is an interlocution of another sort, one that takes us into a deeper analysis of the commission and inspires well-informed debates about the legacy of the TRC in South Africa, the role of performance in transitional justice, and the rich capacities of archives and repertoires generated by commissions such as the TRC for writing social and cultural history.

The move toward more accessible writing in the academy has taken many forms over the past few decades, and feminists and people of color in the United States were among the first to cross the line from using the impartial third person to the more subjective first person. For these constituencies, unmasking the particularities and biases of the supposedly objective third person has been about decolonizing the alliance between knowledge and power. To acknowledge "the politics of location" or "positionality," writers often identify exactly where they stand and for whom they speak. While wishing to avoid the solipsistic excess of self-reflexivity, this book requires a brief statement about my motivation for writing it. When I first started this project, the TRC was one of the least politically correct subjects in South Africa, and I encountered there deep ambivalence, suspicion, and even anger toward the foreign researchers who have descended on the country. Ambivalence was manifest in subtle ways, such as a quick change of subject when I explained, in casual conversation, why I was visiting. At times apprehensions were blatant. For instance, one night during a dinner party a white Afrikaner woman goaded me, asking repeatedly about my country, my president (then George W. Bush), and America's appalling behavior in the world at that moment. Finally, leaning close to me while swirling her gin and tonic, she demanded, "Why are you here.... I mean *really*, why the fuck are you here!!" Such questions, even when crudely or rudely stated, demand an answer.

I can date the inspiration for this book to the summer of 1967 in Detroit, to a day I lay hidden on the floor of a rusted grey Studebaker. My mother careened through the turbulent streets of downtown, then gripped by the infamous race "riots" of that blistering July, as she headed for the Henry Ford Hospital. I had a raging fever, as I routinely did when I was small, and my mother was taking me to the emergency room in the hospital where I was born. She clung to the steering wheel, blurting commands for me to stay down. From my vantage point on the floor I could see plumes of black smoke, could smell burning wood and plastic, and could taste my mother's fear of the people she referred to (based on her own warped upbringing in working-class upstate New York) by a word I will not publish here. I knew my city was in flames, but I didn't know why. I knew that skin color had something to do with it, but I didn't know how. My childhood experience of segregation, racial isolation, a city deeply scarred by engineered inequality, and widespread denial in my all-white subculture that anything was wrong— all shaped me profoundly. To reach the hospital, for instance, my mother and I traveled from our all-white suburb of Dearborn, a city positioned on the doorstep of Henry Ford's River Rouge assembly-line plant, where thousands of black workers who had fled America's South in search of upward mobility now worked in horribly alienating and dehumanizing conditions. Dearborn's notoriously racist mayor, Orville Hubbard, pioneered a public project that placed white rocks at boundary points and declared on public trash cans, "Let's keep Dearborn clean," a motto with a hidden racist message more explicitly enacted through the city's obstruction of African Americans who tried to buy property within city limits. Such surroundings helped shape what I did with my life, my choice to go to graduate school, and the questions I asked in my research once I got there. Ultimately these experiences led me to this particular project on South Africa.

Like many Americans, I have been drawn to South Africa for its seeming affinities with the United States, in particular the resemblance of apartheid to Jim Crow segregation. While there are many parallels between South Africa and the United States, these parallels readily break down upon closer inspection. South Africa is exceptional in many regards, as any South African will tell you. And yet when one compares Johannesburg with Detroit—the City of Gold with the Motor City—the parallels go a bit further, the affinities resonate more deeply. Both began as single-industry towns built upon the exploitation of migrant black labor, both engineered extreme racial segregation and depended upon systematic economic inequality. Both experienced a sudden and cataclysmic decline (Detroit after the riots of '67, Johannesburg after the elections of '94) that eventually resulted in white flight from the urban center and left the city pockmarked with vacant neighborhoods—five-star hotels and block-long department stores boarded up and abandoned. When I first visited Johannesburg in 2002, I felt quite viscerally that I *knew* the place, or at least knew something quite important about it.

The inspiration for this book also came from my life in New York City in 1989, when I was preparing for my first trip to Africa—to Ghana, the country where Kwame Braun, the man I eventually married, was born and raised. We were at the time struggling artists in the Big Apple, I in theatre and Kwame in film. Our reason for journeying away from the cosmopolitan yet provincial island of Manhattan was personal. It was a trip home for Kwame, a return to the place where he spent the first eighteen years of his life. For me it was a journey to the unknown. The image of Africa promulgated in American schools and media is so distorted that famine, safaris, "tribes," war, and disease are the only words most Americans know to describe a continent so vast that it is three times the size of the United States; a place so diverse that over one-third of the world's living languages are spoken there. Despite my elite college education, I was no exception. At age 25, I knew little (and almost nothing accurate) about Africa. Shortly after we returned from our trip, on 11 February 1990, Nelson Mandela walked through the gates of Victor Verster Prison in the Western Cape of South Africa, free for the first time in twenty-seven years. The world watched, still reeling from the recent fall of the Berlin Wall and the bloody protests of Tiananmen Square, riveted to their televisions as Mandela's long walk to freedom finally reached its destination, or so we all hoped.

By complete chance, I had tickets that night to see a production of the legendary South African play *Woza Albert!* in a community center on the Upper West Side. The play's irreverent humor, rousing song, and incisive critique of the apartheid state's supposedly Christian foundations had drawn international audiences for years and did not need an historic event like the freeing of Mandela to attract crowds. But on this night the performance was mobbed with South

African expatriates from the greater New York area, the atmosphere electric. At play's end, the actors resurrect dead anti-apartheid heroes, calling each by name to "*woza!*" or "rise up!" As the litany of dead heroes went on, the audience grew irrepressible; they ululated and cheered, rejoicing in the fact that one of the greatest heroes of the struggle had indeed risen, not from the grave but from the death of decades-long imprisonment. The post-show applause spilled over into a spontaneous celebration on stage. Though I barely understood what I was experiencing, I was deeply transformed. That night started me on a path that led to graduate school in African studies, a Ph.D. from Northwestern University, writing a book on popular theatre in West Africa (*Ghana's Concert Party Theatre* was a finalist for the 2002 Herskovits Award from the African Studies Association), and eventually to my current subject.

Between writing the Ghana book and this one, I battled and survived cancer, losing my leg in the process. My illness was diagnosed four months after I gave birth to my son, even as my father entered the last phase of his own unsuccessful bout with cancer. So I commenced this book during a period of intense personal transition, a time when I, like South Africa, was figuring out an entirely new way to function in the world. While I do not confuse my trauma with South Africa's—mine was a loss with "natural" causes, the traumas heard before the truth commission were perpetrated by other human beings—I have nevertheless drawn upon my own experience of suffering, loss, and transition to a new life as a grounded point of entry into this difficult subject.

The significance of my shift in research from West to South Africa during the past six years has been profound. Although they share the same continent, Ghana and South Africa could not be more different. South Africa is an exceptional and complicated place, one that even people whose families have lived there for generations rarely claim to understand. During the post-apartheid years of transition, this complexity has only compounded. As Malcolm Purkey, the artistic director of The Market Theatre in Johannesburg, once said, "Whatever thing you think you know about this place, you don't know it. All bets are off."[40] South Africa has a rich intellectual tradition of producing gifted writers who have tried to understand the country or to explain it or at the very least to represent its breathtaking extremes of beauty and inhumanity. I am humbled to add one more text that library. I do so as an outsider—a tenuous position, especially in light of the country's history of isolation. At a time when foreigners are feeling particularly unwelcome in South Africa, I wish to articulate a perspective on the country that is admittedly an outsider's point of view. I have tried to get the details right, for the devil is always in the details. My perspective will no doubt suffer from blindness and omissions, though I have strived mightily to identify and address these. Finally, I would suggest that outsiders can potentially have insights that would be much harder to achieve for one fully immersed in a rapidly transforming and highly polarized society such as South Africa.

South Africa is a state in transition, and transition is a messy and imperfect process.[41] It has no clear beginning or end and no shortage of contradictions.

Stated aims may not conform to reality. Invented rituals do not always work, or work fully. New reconstruction is thoroughly intermixed with old habits of obstruction. Yet what we see in South Africa's Truth and Reconciliation Commission, despite all of its imperfections, is a rich utilization of South Africa's performative genealogies, of its potent embodied enactments before an audience, and a continuation of its repertories of public storytelling, even many years after the TRC's conclusion.

This book is structured around the genealogies and genres of performance that inhabited the TRC process. The first chapter provides a conceptual and theoretical framework, examining the relationship of transitional justice to performance and how their confluence had particular manifestations within the TRC's public operations. Chapter 2, "Justice in Transition: Political Trials, 1956–1964," looks at the performative genealogy of the TRC, finding its origins several decades ago in three important political trials of the late 1950s and mid-1960s: the Treason Trial, the Incitement Trial, and the Rivonia Trial. I contend that in order to understand how the TRC—which was a quasi-judicial forum—participated in a transition from authoritarian rule to democracy, we must also understand how the South African state used legal forums such as show trials to promote and make manifest to the public a regime change of a very different sort, a regime change *to* authoritarian rule. From the perspective of South African history, the decision to have the TRC take place in public and embrace performance drew upon long-standing South African repertories of how performance encountered the law.

Chapter 3, "Witnessing and Interpreting Testimony: Live, Present, Public, and Speaking in Many Tongues," focuses tightly on a few human rights violations hearings, paying close attention to what people actually said and how interpreters served as central interlocutors. Mark Sanders contends that the truth commission "revealed more than expected."[42] I contend that scholars' expectations of the commission have often been so narrow that the full significance of the commission's revelations has yet to be appreciated, acknowledged, or indeed even perceived. If we move beyond the commission's focus on soliciting evidence of gross violations of human rights, we see also demands for revenge, articulations of grief, descriptions of everyday life under apartheid, and breaches of human rights that did not fit into the TRC's mandate of "gross" violations but were nonetheless damaging narratives about pass laws, prohibitions against women owning property, and the fragmentation of families. We also see through testimony a view into the interior realm of subjectivity under apartheid: the dissociation of trauma and the simultaneous and conflicted urges to both remember and forget.

The next chapter, "Eyes and Ears of the Nation," focuses on the South African Broadcasting Corporation's weekly television series *TRC Special Report,* a rich archive of eighty-seven weekly episodes that because it was produced by a capable team of journalists far surpasses any other chronicle of the truth commission in factual density, vivid imagery, contextual information on the "stories behind the stories," and many-sided perspectives. While much has been written about the shortcomings of the TRC's summary report, I argue that few have actually read this tome and that we should consider media representations such as *TRC*

Special Report as being more truly those by which the general public learned about and participated as witnesses in the commission process. This chapter also makes clear that many of the assumptions about media coverage (in particular about television coverage) of the TRC (that it sensationalized, provided no context, was racially polarizing, dichotomized victims and perpetrators, and tended to focus on victims rather than "survivors," suffering rather than agency) do not, in fact, hold up to scrutiny.

My last chapter, "Dragons in the Living Room: Truth and Reconciliation in Repertoire," leaps forward in time to 2006, a full decade after the TRC began its work. This chapter examines how the commission is not just remembered but performatively reenacted through a repertoire that exists in contrast with the TRC's sequestered archive. "Dragons" grapples with viewing the TRC in retrospect, and it focuses on the creation of an artistic work by composer Philip Miller, a cantata for voice, tape, and testimony called *REwind*. Finally, the epilogue reflects on the implications of the South African example of a highly public transitional process for those studying transitional justice globally.

A research project of this magnitude relies profoundly on the assistance, generosity, insight, and support of many individuals and institutions. For their generous funding of the project, I am indebted to the National Humanities Center (for granting me a John Hurford Fellowship), the National Endowment for the Humanities, the University of California Regents' Humanities Faculty Fellowship, and the University of California, Santa Barbara's Interdisciplinary Humanities Center and Academic Senate. I am indebted to the American Society for Theatre Research for awarding me the 2009 ASTR McNamara Publication Subvention Grant, which helped subsidize photographic reproductions in this book. The final phases of the book received financial support from the University of California, Berkeley, my new academic home. I am especially grateful to Dean David Marshall at the University of California, Santa Barbara and Dean Janet Broughton at the University of California, Berkeley for their tireless support.

For granting interviews and sharing information in South Africa, I wish to thank, among others, John Allen, Kate Allen, Zenariah Barends, George Bizos, Mary Burton, Nomonde Calata, Max du Preez, Mrs. Edward Juqu, Sello Hatang, Verne Harris, Yazir Henry, Janice Honeyman, Mahlubi "Chief" Mabizela, Gerhard Marx and Maja Marx, Philip Miller, Eunice Miya, Mrs. Plaatjie, Wendy Orr, Nicky Rousseau, Angela Sobrey, Yasmin Sooka, Peter Story, Jane Taylor, and Tony Weaver. Director Michael Lessac organized an unprecedented retreat with former TRC interpreters as part of his research for his play *Truth in Translation,* and he kindly shared with me transcriptions from this event. I also had the good fortune to cross paths with filmmaker Liza Key as she worked on a documentary about Philip Miller's TRC cantata, and she not only allowed me to accompany her during filming but also to fully participate in interviews.

Earlier versions of chapters were presented in seminars at Duke University, Emory University, the National Humanities Center, Northwestern University, Yale University, the University of Michigan, the International Federation for Theatre

Research, the African Studies Association, Performance Studies International, the American Society for Theatre Research, and the University of California's Multicampus Research Group in International Performance and Culture. I am especially thankful for these invitations and to the colleagues in attendance who provided thoughtful and substantive feedback. For their consultation and responses to the work, I would particularly like to thank Catherine Admay, Paul Berliner, Keith Breckenridge, Catherine Burns, Leo Cabranes-Grant, James Campbell, David William Cohen, John Conteh-Morgan, Erik Doxtader, Jody Enders, Isabel Hofmeyer, Michael Levine, Stephan Miescher, Louise Mentjies, Tejumola Olaniyan, Joseph Roach, Tom Seller, Diana Taylor, Richard Wilson, and William B. Worthen as well as the anonymous readers commissioned by *Theatre Journal* and Indiana University Press.

At the National Archives in South Africa, I benefited from the capable and patient assistance of Zahira Adams and Natalie Sokolo. At the National Humanities Center in Research Triangle Park, North Carolina, the library staff of Betsy Dain and Eliza Robertson worked tirelessly to locate sources for me. Translators Sizwe Satyo and Thuleleni Mcanda at the University of Cape Town provided an invaluable service, as did Galen Sibanda at the University of California, Berkeley. Without Bianca Murillo's diligent research assistance, chapter 2 would not have been possible. To my editor Dee Mortenson at Indiana University Press, who believed in this project from the beginning, I extend my heartfelt thanks. Polly Morrice's careful editorial attention to the manuscript during the final phases of revision was of pivotal importance, and copyeditor Kate Babbitt has made this a better book. Any remaining errors are solely my responsibility.

Portions of this book draw upon two earlier publications: Catherine M. Cole, "Performance, Transitional Justice, and the Law: South Africa's Truth and Reconciliation Commission," *Theatre Journal* 59, no. 2 (2007): 167–187; and Catherine M. Cole, "South Africa's Truth and Reconciliation Cantata," *Theater* 38, no. 3 (2008): 80–105.

South Africa is a very long way from California, and I benefited from the hospitality extended by many in that country, including Catherine Burns and Keith Breckenridge, Isabel Hofmeyer and Jon Hysop, Malcolm Purkey, Liza Key and Janice Honeyman, and Anne Mager. During a research trip to Madison, Wisconsin, I was fortunate to be hosted by Laurie Beth Clark and Michael Peterson. My many research trips meant prolonged periods away from my family, which my husband Kwame Braun endured with incredible fortitude and grace as he shouldered the responsibilities of caring for our son, Aaron Braun Cole, who himself has grown at an astonishing rate during the writing of this book. Kwame has supported me at every stage of this project, read and responded to drafts of chapters, and journeyed with me intellectually, physically, and emotionally during the several years of this book's gestation. To him I extend my most profound thanks of all.

Performing South Africa's Truth Commission

1. Spectacles of Legality: Performance, Transitional Justice, and the Law

Athena addresses the Furies, "We will change your job description. You will no longer be the Furies. You will be the Eumenides. You will spread good will among men and bless the crops." So this is a theatrical example of putting an end to the blood feud by actually changing—whether you change the prosecutors or persecutors or whether you change society, the main motive is to put an end to the blood feud. And if I were to speak to Palestinians and Israelis, I would actually tell them to read the *Eumenides*.

—South African anti-apartheid attorney George Bizos

The trial was understood as an exercise in the reconstitution of the law, an act staged not simply to punish extreme crimes but to demonstrate visibly the power of the law to submit the most horrific outrages to its sober ministrations. In this regard, the trial was to serve as a spectacle of legality, making visible both the crimes of the Germans and the sweeping neutral authority of the rule of law.

—Lawrence Douglas on the Nuremburg Trial

Lawrence Douglas's use of theatrical language in the epigraph above—the words "act," "stage," and "spectacle"—is no accident. Such language is ubiquitous in the discourse of transitional justice. Political scientist Deborah Posel speaks of South Africa's truth commission as "theater." Literature scholar Shoshana Felman writes of the Holocaust trials as "theatres of justice."[1] And who can forget Hannah Arendt's extended use of theatrical metaphors to critique the Eichmann trial?[2] Though she notes that the judges eschewed anything theatrical in their conduct, the 1961 trial happened on a stage, the remodeled Beit Ha'am municipal theatre in Jerusalem.[3] Arendt sees theatre in opposition to the law: "No matter how consistently the judges shunned the limelight, there they were, seated on top of the raised platform, facing the audience as from the stage in a play."[4] The trial had a villain, Eichmann, and an audience of spectators in the theater, which Arendt contends stood in for the world, and a stage manager, Israeli prime minister Ben-Gurion. Yet as theatrical as the trial was, "it was precisely the play aspect of the trial that collapsed under the weight of the hair-raising atrocities," writes Arendt.[5] While Arendt's critique of the trial is, in part, that true justice is incompatible with the theatre's limelight because justice "demands seclusion," her analysis ultimately leads us toward recognizing that the real problem with the Eichmann trial may have been that it was bad theatre.[6] The scope of the play (the "huge panorama of Jewish sufferings") was too great and the action (the Holocaust) too horrific, unimaginable, colossal, and unspeakable.[7] Moreover, the Eichmann trial lacked theatrical suspense. Its outcome was inevitable from the beginning: Eichmann would be convicted and executed.

Hannah Arendt viewed the trial of Adolph Eichmann as "one example among many to demonstrate the inadequacy of the prevailing legal system and of current juridical concepts to deal with the facts of administrative massacres organized by the state apparatus."[8] She argued that Eichmann's alleged crimes were not large-scale murders but rather an entirely new crime: "Politically and legally . . . these were 'crimes' different not only in degree of seriousness but in essence."[9] Such crimes, the argument goes, demand not only that the judicial process determine individual responsibility and mete out appropriate punishment but also that the law serve didactic functions of national proportions, extending far beyond the courtroom. Crimes of unprecedented nature and magnitude required new legal principles. The concept "crimes against humanity," for instance, was first articulated in the charter of the International Military Tribunal that authorized the Nuremberg trials held in post–World War II Germany.[10] Without a doubt, the Nuremberg trials are the epicenter for both transitional justice and international criminal justice, "the precedent upon which all ensuing developments are based," in the words of Stephen Landsman.[11] Yet transitional justice departs from international law by suggesting that traditional jurisprudence has limited value when faced with crimes against humanity. Transitional justice is a field that, according to Louis Bickford, focuses on "how societies address legacies of past human rights abuses, mass atrocity, and other forms of severe social trauma, including genocide or civil war, in order to build a more democratic, just, or peaceful future."[12] Resulting from a convergence of the human rights movement and international law, transitional justice not only formulates a relationship between political transition and the law, it also addresses the unique challenges that a history of state-sponsored atrocity presents *to* the law.

When addressing crimes against humanity, the law is often called upon to place those crimes into the public record; to convey to the public both the facts of what happened and the historical context of those crimes; and finally, to perform the restoration of the rule of law. International law in the wake of the Nuremberg trials has traditionally assumed that "both didactic and individual goals can be met in the same proceeding," says Landsman.[13] Yet it is precisely this conjunction of personal responsibility and didacticism on a national scale—and the theatrical devices used to accomplish grand didactic ends—that makes critics such as Hannah Arendt most acutely uncomfortable. "The purpose of a trial is to render justice and nothing else," she argues, elaborating that even the noblest of ulterior motives for making a historical record of Nazi crimes "can only detract from the law's main business: to weigh the charges brought against the accused, to render judgment, and to mete out due punishment."[14] The need to memorialize, dramatize, and document crimes against humanity is enormous and of paramount importance. But trials, according to proponents of transitional justice, may not be the best forums to accomplish these goals. Further, when the law is asked to serve such purposes, and especially when it exploits theatrical devices to do so, the paradoxical result may be a travesty of justice rather than the very necessary restoration of the rule of law.[15]

If the desired goal is to establish consensus and memorialize "controversial, complex events," writes Martha Minow, "trials are not ideal. Even if they were adequate to the task, the theatrical devices and orchestration required threaten the norms of law that are a crucial part of the lesson, at least in societies committed to the rule of law."[16] Mark Osiel contends that "what makes for a good 'morality play' tends not to make for a fair trial. And if it is the simplifications of melodrama that are needed to influence collective memory, then the production had best be staged somewhere other than in a court of law."[17] These criticisms by Arendt, Minow, and Osiel suggest that although the law may be preeminently a theatrical form, theatre and the law may also be ultimately incompatible when yoked together to address crimes against humanity.[18] To use the trials of particular individuals as a vehicle for documenting and promulgating a larger history is morally and legally problematic, for it saddles individual defendants with responsibility for crimes beyond those they are charged with committing. And while it may seem counterintuitive, trials that address crimes against humanity can be particularly debilitating and disempowering for victims. In tribunals that address such crimes, as in all trials, the rules of the court cast victims in a passive rather than active role, allowing them to speak only when spoken to by an agent of the court and even then to speak only on certain terms and topics, subject to cross-examination that may be adversarial in nature.[19] In addition, the principles of evidence and truth that operate in the court are often woefully inadequate to grapple with the psychological complexity of trauma, especially trauma perpetrated on a massive scale.[20] The role of the victim in the prosecution of crimes against humanity is vexing.[21] At the Nuremberg trials, which were largely based upon the evidence of atrocities that was documented in the Nazi's own records, the victims were generally absent altogether. The Eichmann trial tried to redress this absence by bringing a parade of victims to testify. Yet much of their testimony had no direct relevance to the particular case of Adolph Eichmann. The result was a corruption of justice, for one perpetrator was made to stand in for a whole state apparatus of genocide.

Thus, in the face of the twentieth and twenty-first centuries' breathtaking capacity for genocide, state-sponsored torture, and systemic violations of human rights, the inherited mechanisms for restoring the rule of law have proven inadequate. Crimes against humanity require new means of redress, a mechanism that records hidden histories of atrocity, didactically promotes collective memory, and gives victims a place of respect, dignity, and agency in the process. Such purposes are not well served by traditional jurisprudence. What forum other than trials could serve such complex needs? Enter the "truth commission," a new genre of international law and a defining form of the field of transitional justice.[22]

Designed as an alternative to trials, a truth commission is "a body charged with the duty of uncovering the truth about certain historical events rather than prosecuting specific defendants."[23] According to Priscilla Hayner's exhaustive and invaluable comparative study of twenty-one truth commissions, Uganda's 1974 Commission of Inquiry into the Disappearances of People was the first such commission, and South Africa's TRC, which began in 1995, was one of the largest, most complex, most sophisticated, most well funded, and most successful.[24]

Willingly or not, deliberately or not, the Nuremberg and Eichmann trials were drawn into the domain of performance. Like the attraction of a moth to a flame, this attraction proved fatal, at least according to some critics. Does performance hold the same force of attraction for truth commissions? And if so, is this attraction as morally or legally problematic as some find it to be in human rights jurisprudence? Or are performance and theatre embraced by the creators of truth commissions because they are seen as effective and appropriate means to accomplish particular ends? As a point of entry into addressing such questions, we must explore how performance is being used within specific truth commissions. I turn to the case of South Africa's TRC: How was performance used in this particular and highly celebrated example of transitional justice?

The Power to Make Visible

South Africa's TRC was a product of a negotiated settlement by which South Africa transitioned from apartheid to nonracial democracy.[25] The commission began its work in December 1995 and concluded with the formal presentation of the last two installments in its seven-volume report to President Thabo Mbeki in 2003. During the intervening years, the commission became known to the public of South Africa largely through its hearings. These were of two main types: Human Rights Violations Committee (HRVC) hearings, in which victims told "narrative truths" about their experiences, and Amnesty Committee hearings, in which perpetrators came forward in the hope of being granted amnesty. In order to be granted amnesty, perpetrators had to fully disclose the gross violations of human rights they had committed and prove that their deeds were both politically motivated and proportionate.[26] Within the structure of the TRC these two committees were kept institutionally separate, and their rules of decorum and procedure as well as their performance conventions were entirely distinct. Generally speaking, the HRVC hearings were more improvisational and victim-centered. Their function of creating collective memory was explicitly didactic. The Amnesty Committee hearings, which were run by judges and in which the question of legal amnesty hung in the balance, tended to function much more like a court of law.

While the commission's design was quite different from that of the paradigmatic trials of the Holocaust—the Nuremberg and Eichmann trials—the TRC's two core committees are clearly genealogical descendents of these famous trials.[27] The Amnesty Committee hearings shared the perpetrator-centered character of the Nuremberg trials. By way of contrast, the HRVC hearings descended from the victim-centered impulse of the Eichmann trial. Thus, the TRC combined both approaches into one commission but kept them institutionally distinct. The division between the Human Rights Violation and Amnesty committees circumvented many of the most egregious problems that had riddled the Nuremberg and Eichmann trials. Victim testimony was unmoored from prosecution and was thus unfettered by the protocols and epistemologies of a court of law. Perpetrators in the Amnesty Committee hearings, drawn by the "carrot" of amnesty, came forward *of their own volition* to confess their crimes. These acts were quite different from the defensive positions in which criminal proceedings would have placed them. What this meant for the TRC was that the public heard stories about murder, torture, and other gross violations of human rights from the mouths of perpetrators themselves, speaking of their own free will.

South Africa's was the seventeenth truth commission in the world, and it departed from precedent in two significant ways. First, it was empowered to grant conditional amnesty to those who gave full disclosure about gross violations of human rights perpetrated for political motives. Second, the TRC was the most public and publicized truth commission the world had seen, then or now.[28] Not only were hearings performed live, before spectators who assembled in the halls, churches, and other public venues where the TRC was enacted, but they also transpired on stages and raised platforms. The TRC toured like a traveling road show, beginning on 15 April 1996. But the audiences for the TRC extended far beyond these physical spaces; they included ever-widening circles of radio listeners and television viewers as well as newspaper readers. Of the extensive media coverage the TRC enjoyed, the commission's deputy chairperson Alex Boraine has written:

> Never in my wildest imaginings did I think that the media would retain its insatiable interest in the Commission throughout its life. Not a day passed when we were not reported on radio. We were very seldom absent from the major television evening news broadcasts, and we were, if not on the front page, on the inside pages of every newspaper throughout the two and a half years of our work. . . . Unlike many other truth commissions, this one was center stage, and the media coverage, particularly radio, enabled the poor, the illiterate, and people living in rural areas to participate in its work so that it was truly a national experience rather than restricted to a small handful of selected commissioners.[29]

While public hearings were truly the center stage of the commission, every appearance in them represented countless hours spent behind closed doors, where the commission staff busily prepared and investigated, researched and interviewed. In addition, the witnesses who spoke before the public represented only a fraction of those who gave statements to the commission. For every case heard before the HRVC, nine others were not selected. This was a situation of expedience—it was simply not possible to have a public hearing for every case of abuse, killing, or torture.[30] Thus, as emblematic as the public hearings became of the commission, one must remember that they in fact represented a small fraction of the commission's work.

So successful were the public hearings at making the truth commission visible and accessible to the nation and so saturated was the media coverage they received that for many people, both inside and outside South Africa, they became synonymous with the truth commission. In the words of Commissioner Wendy Orr, who also believes that the hearings came to symbolize the commission, they were "an absolutely core part of the TRC process. . . . You know, the whole reconfiguration of what had happened, the rewriting of history, the . . . bringing into the public domain what for so long had been hidden, the hearing what for so long had not been heard, the public acknowledgement of what for so long had been denied—all of this was accomplished in these public hearings."[31] For a country that had censored its journalists for decades, the extent and nature of media coverage of the TRC hearings was astonishing. Under apartheid, the state had repressed information at every stage at which it was produced. With powers to detain without trial, for instance, the former regime forbade the press from mentioning the names of prisoners. The government also tightly controlled the right to speak publicly, to organize collectively, to move freely around the country, and to gain access to official information.[32] The state enforced such censorship through a full arsenal of means, including detention, house arrest, banning individuals, and a proliferation of legislation aimed controlling pubic information. Censorship laws were at once extensive and vague, which consequently promoted self-censorship because journalists felt they were walking blindly through a minefield.

Against this backdrop the Truth and Reconciliation Commission performed the antithesis: here was a public airing of information that would have been forbidden under the old order; here was a multiracial public gathering that would also have been forbidden (or perhaps would have led to surveillance, interrogations, imprisonment, and quite possibly torture); here was public acknowledgement of acts of atrocity that had long been denied, unseen, unpublished, and sequestered from public view. The power of the Truth and Reconciliation Commission was its ability to make visible that which had been unseen. This power is the very essence of theatre: the word "theatre" is derived from the Greek *theatron*, or θέατρον, meaning "place of seeing." The TRC staged and remade the past through a complex dynamic of watching, seeing, testifying, and bearing witness. As important as seeing was to the commission, its public enactment was also was about people speaking and being heard. This was a commission of words and voices, speaking and listening, interacting face to face. Because of the hearings' focus on embodiment and the implicit assumption of authenticity and veracity of first-person accounts, the TRC public hearings were of paramount importance to achieving the commission's didactic aim—far more so, I would argue, than was the TRC's summary report.[33] (I favor the term "summary" over "final" since the report came out in segments over a five-year period and ultimately could not encapsulate the commission's work. For instance, the "final" report does not—rather astonishingly—publish the amnesty decisions.)

One of the commission's primary functions (as articulated in the authorizing legislation, the Promotion of National Unity Act of 1995) was to "prepare a comprehensive report which sets out its activities and findings, based on factual and objective information and evidence collected and received by it or placed at its disposal."[34] The first five volumes appeared in October 1998 and the final two were published at the conclusion of the amnesty process in 2003. Such reports are quite common in the world of truth commissions, as they are the usual means by which commission's work is made public. Perhaps most famously, Argentina's National Commission on the Disappeared published a condensed version of its 50,000-page findings in 1984 as a book entitled *Nunca Más*. This text became "an immediate and enduring bestseller" in Argentina and provided detailed descriptions of the state's methods of abduction, detention, torture, execution, and, ultimately, disposal of bodies during Argentina's Dirty War.[35] Its introduction calls *Nunca Más* "a report from Hell," yet this label did not deter readership. Between November 1984 and May 1986, thirteen editions were published.[36] In contrast, South Africa's report has had a very limited readership and distribution. The seven volumes are long, heavy, and unwieldy, and the text is likewise sprawling. The product of multiple unnamed authors, the report lacks the clarity of authorial voice evident in *Nunca Más*. Besides being unreadable— not to mention inaccessible to those many South Africans who do not read the language in which it was published—the TRC report is expensive, costing more than 1500 rand (approximately US$250 in 1999), far beyond what most South Africans can afford.[37] A concise popular version of the TRC report was prepared in the late 1990s but was never published in South Africa. Hence, as Piers Pigou contends, "The vast majority of South Africans, including those who directly engaged the commission, have . . . never seen what the commission actually found and why."[38]

Much scholarship on the TRC examines the final report as though it were the preeminent representation of what the commission was or did or was perceived to be. This focus on the report is misguided. Millions of South Africans experienced the commission not through its summary report but through its hearings, more specifically through representations of hearings via the media.[39] Very few people have read the report, including those who worked for the commission whom I interviewed. Even the report's chief editor, the TRC's director of research Charles Villa-Vicencio, suspects that "few critics read it in its entirety from the first cover to last. As I listen to people suggesting that something has been left out or ought to have been included, I find myself wanting to assist them in their search, while not wanting to sound too defensive."[40] Three researchers who helped prepare the report are also quite modest about the claims of their text. Janet Cherry, John Daniel, and Madeleine Fullard contend that while the report was a necessary conclusion to the TRC, it was just one component of process, one they admit is likely to have far less impact than televised testimony: "The reality is that the testimony of a single victim relayed to the country by the media will ultimately have had more of an impact upon the national consciousness than any number of volumes of the report. The enduring memory of the Commission will be the images of pain, grief and regret conveyed relentlessly, week after week, month after month, to a public that generally remained spellbound by what it was witnessing."[41] In contrast to the TRC report's relative obscurity, the media both acted in what scholar Ron Krabill calls "the TRC drama" and served as "the stage on which much of the drama has been performed."[42] Journalism functioned in some ways as an extension of the commission, or, in the case of the TV weekly digest *TRC Special Report,* it sometimes operated as a kind of shadow or alternate commission, conducting its own interviews, undertaking its own investigations, making findings, and even provoking the commission, through criticism or praise, to conduct its affairs in particular ways.

Thus, hearings (and television and radio coverage of them) were the "public face of the commission"[43] in a way that the TRC's summary report never came close to achieving. But what did that public face look like? How did the hearings work? How were they called into being, organized, structured, physically laid out, cast, and enacted? Were the hearings performative—that is, something that *did something,* that changed reality through performance? What insights into the TRC public hearings do the terms and theories of theatre, performance, ritual, and drama enable?

Staging the Commission

The movie *Red Dust* (2006, HBO; dir. Tom Hooper), based on Gillian Slovo's novel about the TRC, begins with a majestic image of a convoy of white trucks traversing the Great Karoo, a spectacular arid South African landscape. Looking like the road crew for a touring musical, this convoy is the TRC's advance team arriving in the fictionalized town of Smitsrivier as children and onlookers stir with excitement. When Commissioner Yasmin Sooka saw the movie, she said to herself, "Actually, why didn't we do that?"[44] Like other commissioners I interviewed, Sooka stressed that the TRC was not as organized as many people presumed. While its operations were on a massive scale, they had to be launched with little planning time and no precedent. As a site-specific performance event, the commission took the process to the people, moving throughout the country and invading particular communities for several months at a time. According to Sooka, there was usually an eight-week cycle in any particular location. This began with an advance team that briefed the community, made logistical arrangements, and organized the statement-taking process. A few days before the public hearings, the commissioners would arrive in the town to be briefed and to meet witnesses and community leaders. The eight-week cycle would culminate in the public hearings.[45]

Wendy Orr, one of those charged with advance planning, writes in her memoir of the TRC that "preparing for a hearing is not unlike preparing for a major stage production," inasmuch as one had to attend to so many dimensions:

Security, parking, catering, seating arrangements, media facilities (requiring the installation of telephone and fax lines, audio and video feeds, TV lighting etc.), computers, printing and photocopying facilities, debriefing rooms, facilities for emergency medical care, . . . translation (we usually had at least three-way, simultaneous translation at every hearing), sound—and this was just what needed to be provided at the venue![46]

In selecting a venue, the TRC was intervening in a history and performatively enacting a new social order. The commission often reclaimed spaces that under the old apartheid regime had excluded blacks. In her interview with me, Sooka recalled:

> Your first choice was the town hall, because you knew that black people were not allowed into the town hall or to see the town hall as something they could use. So it was an important step for the commission to arrive in town, to appropriate that space. And then to imagine the power of giving that space over to people who were excluded and telling them, "You have a chance to tell your story in that space."[47]

If the HRVC hearings were a major stage production, then the protagonists were those who gave testimony. And the commission served as the casting director, choosing which victims would have the opportunity to appear in public. All persons who gave a statement to the commission were asked if they would be willing, if invited, to appear at a public hearing. Most said yes. Once TRC investigators had verified that the statement was essentially true, the HRVC members held a meeting to select cases. Thus, the process involved three groups—investigators, commissioners, and Human Rights Violation Committee members. The commission had the difficult task of deciding which testimonies would be chosen for a public hearing. Through this selection, it orchestrated a particular vision of the past for public consumption.

In each venue, there were on average three days of hearings. In that short span, the TRC had to convey the types of injustice that had happened in that particular community and cover the thirty-plus years that the TRC had mandated were to be vetted. So the pressure to have historical coverage was enormous. Testimonies about events in the 1960s were rare, so when someone came forward with a tale from that era, Commissioner Mary Burton told me, "we pounced on that."[48] The commission tried to get a fair distribution of men and women, different races and ethnicities, abuses perpetrated by the state and those committed by people in the liberation movements, extreme atrocities and less serious violations. The approximately twenty people chosen to testify would, it was hoped, "somehow reflect the totality of the experience of that particular region or that particular city," said Burton.[49] Mahlubi "Chief" Mabizela, a TRC researcher, explained that he and his team were responsible for determining key events and patterns of violence in an area before the selection meeting.[50] Mabizela claimed that someone's ability to tell a story in public (performance competence) was not a factor in the selection process. Commissioner Sooka noted, however, that the "newsworthiness" of a person's story was considered relevant. "You kind of look through a whole lot of shootings, you kind of looked for the one that would *resonate* the most with people."[51]

Victims who were chosen to have a public hearing were given on average about thirty minutes to speak, and they spoke uninterrupted. They could speak in any one of South Africa's eleven official languages with simultaneous interpretation over headphones available for all participants, including the audience and commissioners. Victims were not subjected to cross-examination, although commissioners could and often did ask questions for clarification at the end of their testimony. The aim of these hearings was to establish, in the words of the TRC's constitutional mandate, "the truth in relation to past events as well as the motives for and circumstances in which gross violations of human rights have occurred, and to make the findings known in order to prevent a repetition of such acts in [the] future."[52] The audience was not, one might argue, primarily the commissioners assembled at a table next to and sometimes in front of the victims but rather the public, spectators who attended the hearings in person and, by extension, those who witnessed the proceedings through the media. This was perhaps why the weekly television series *TRC Special Report* (the subject of chapter 4) rarely cut away from victims giving testimony to the attentive commissioners; rather, cutaways focused on anonymous spectators in the auditorium, many of whom listened intently to testimony via headsets.

The hearings were unpredictable. Much as the commission tried to impose protocols and constraints, there were always surprises. Yasmin Sooka sees these improvisational elements as coming directly from the TRC's theatricality and its resonance with African cultures:

> You always have to be prepared for the unexpected . . . once you put [people] under the glare of a camera and audience. It's an interesting thing—African people, this is part of their culture, the theatre of the village. It ties in so much with the cultural pattern of oral testimony, and the way history is passed down. Only this time the audience is very different and the medium is very different. But it's so much about people enjoying the theatre. I mean what I was always struck by was how once a hearing started you could control very few of the things.[53]

So while the hearings were an enormous production, involving many of the same logistics as a traveling theatre show, and while the content was orchestrated by the commission in terms of selection of deponents and the manufacturing of a certain narrative about a particular place and the nature of the atrocities that happened there, the deponents—the victims themselves—had substantial agency. They could say what they wanted when they got in front of the audience. Unpredictability was a cause for great consternation. For instance, a witness could decide to start naming names of people never mentioned in a prior statement, to the surprise of those who had been given no advance warning that public accusations would be made about them before the TRC. The commission tried to make sure that anyone who was to be named before the commission was forewarned before the hearing. In the end, at least some commissioners felt they had no control, that one just had to be prepared for surprises. And it was this very unpredictability—this improvisational uncertainty—that made the HRVC hearings, in the words of Yasmin Sooka, "the theatre of this decade. I don't think anything will ever come close to it."[54]

"You Come Out Here and Perform!"

A cartoon published in the *Natal Witness* depicted the ambiguity of the TRC as a genre. Chairperson Tutu appears as a lion tamer in a circus (fig. 1.1). Whip in hand, Tutu shouts into a cavernous pen where the wild beast of the apartheid past, the "Great Crocodile" ("Die Groot Krokodil")—Botha himself—resides. "I don't care what you think the TRC is—You come out here and perform!" Tutu exhorts.[55] The artist conveys the underlying imperative to perform that drove the commission. Even if no one could agree on exactly what genre of performance the commission was—circus, ritual, drama, bioscope, show—participants had to perform, and they had to perform in a certain way. The cartoonist succinctly captures the multifaceted meanings of "performance" that are operative both in the TRC and in my study of the commission. These meanings include the following: to accomplish an act, to make a public presentation, to use embodiment as a central instrument of communication, and to simulate or represent (i.e., to "act"). As Mary Strine, Beverly Long, and Mary Francis Hopkins have argued, performance is an essentially contested concept,[56] and I do not propose here to reiterate or resolve that contestation. Rather, like the cartoonist Stidy, I deploy these multivalent meanings and embrace the heuristic potential of simultaneity. Often the most dynamic moments during the TRC proceedings represent a convergence of one or more of these definitions of performance.

Early on in the hearings, when witness Nomonde Calata broke into a loud wail during her testimony, this disconcerting cry became an emblematic moment in public memory. The importance of this sound—a wail that transcended language and, in doing so, captured something elemental about the experience of gross violations of human rights—indicates the degree to which physical expression was central to the TRC process, even though this aspect of the commission is rarely, if ever, given much notice in the TRC's summary report or in the burgeoning secondary literature on the TRC. The research of Kay McCormick and Mary Bock of the University of Cape Town is an exception. They use discourse analysis as a method for transcribing from videos of the hearings the embodied, performed meanings expressed by witnesses, and they analyze extralinguistic communication through breath, cadence, pauses, eye contact, and gestures.[57]

In a recent article on the rise of the terms "performance" and "performativity" in cultural analysis, Julia Walker argues that the metaphor of performance has come to the fore in critical theory in order to address "the problematic role of individual agency."[58] She argues that performance, both as physical practice and as a metaphor, gives access to vocal and pantomimic/kinetic signification in addition to textual or verbal signification. Because performance resonates simultaneously in several different registers—including reason, emotion, and experience—it is more capacious than the culture-as-text metaphor in cultural analysis. The public and embodied signification expressed through the performative aspects of the HRVC hearings of South Africa's TRC potently resonated in the affective and

Figure 1.1. TRC Chairperson Desmond Tutu trying to coax the Great Crocodile P. W. Botha to appear before the truth commission. Courtesy of Anthony Stidolph (Stidy) of the *Natal Witness*.

experiential registers of human experience. These aspects of communication combined with the actual words spoken were an essential vehicle for communicating the density of the profound experiences of human suffering that the TRC brought to light.

The TRC was never specifically framed as "theatre." Though there were many moving, poignant, and even beautiful moments, the hearings were not self-consciously aesthetic events. Nor was the commission conceived to be pleasurable. In fact many public hearings were entirely lacking in what is known in the theatre world as "production values." Mark Gevisser, who was one of the first to write about the theatricality of the TRC, noted that the commission's "hundreds of hours of testimony have been, almost by definition, banal and routine rather than heightened and dramatic. The halls are drafty and echoing; neon lighting flattens all contours; amplified sound deadens voices and simultaneous translation renders testimony affectless."[59] Unlike performers in a play, those who participated in the TRC were not overtly impersonating another character or promulgating a fiction—though there were cases in which the integrity of particular individuals was highly questionable or their narratives seemed invented and implausible. The many, many narratives heard before the commission—whether discrete and individualized or an interlocking of cases and multiple parties or cumulative when told in succession as some kind of macronarrative of the past—were so sprawling that they made *Nicholas Nickleby* seem like a haiku. For all their innate theatricality, the TRC proceedings were driven more by storytelling than by action. With rare exceptions, not much beyond talking actually *happened* at the TRC hearings. There was little in the way of *dramatic action*. But the stories conveyed were often dramatic and touched upon profound themes: love, pain, evil, resentment, hate, heroes, villains, violence, bravery, cruelty, prejudice, patriotism, and jealousy. The event was meant to both teach audiences something about the past and induce empathy.

For all these dissimilarities with theatre, the Truth and Reconciliation Commission nevertheless holds compelling affinities as well. Among these are emotional expressiveness and volatility; communication through the dense registers of embodiment; and moments of direct conflict and confrontation between perpetrator and victim—conflict being one of the central features of genre of drama. The hearings were also theatrical in the sense of being aural and visual. They were highly structured in terms of being rehearsed, cast, and produced, but at the same time they were open to the vagaries and surprises of improvisational interventions of key performers. In the manner of the western proscenium theatre, the TRC had a bicameral spatial separation of actors and audience. Often the witnesses and commissioners were placed quite literally on a stage, facing out toward the audience. High personages were metaphorically brought low, as in tragedy, and persons of low status were also transformed into highly esteemed ones. The live audience served as a kind of Greek chorus. Its members did not just witness but also often commented on the action. Sometimes their vocalizations during a hearing indicated a change of heart about a particular witness or perpetrator. For the famous resistance lawyer George Bizos, who appeared often before the TRC, the resonances between the audience of the TRC and the chorus of ancient Greek theatre were particularly strong. During my interview with him, Bizos (who is Greek) recalled his study of *Antigone* and how the chorus changes its view during the course of the play. It starts off with praise of Creon,

> this great leader who saved the city from invasion, and the killing of the traitor brother that he ordered, saying that he should not be buried but be food for the wild birds and dogs. And they start off like most people when tyrants are in control: embattled. They praise him. But as things change, when he orders the death of Antigone, and particularly when the tragedy strikes the family as a whole, then Creon becomes a real pitiful figure. The chorus changes. They say . . . I remember the words well in translation: "Out of the world's greatest virtue, moderation is the best of all, and the wise man is moderate and remembers to respect the gods." So you know, this is a chorus that really responds to a situation.[60]

During the trials of resistance leaders in the apartheid days, audiences were small and intimidated. According to Bizos, they were "terrified that they would be asked to produce their documents or, as they were exiting the court, would be interrogated as to why you were there to witness a trial of a terrorist." But at the

TRC, black spectators came "heads high, they knew that they had won. They knew that their oppressors were in retreat. And they made that known."[61] The audience as chorus was thus newly empowered at the TRC, enjoying a status and prestige unknown during the old regime.

The public hearings were highly theatrical events in terms of their dramatic revelations of information, emotional displays, improvisational storytelling, singing, weeping, and ritualistic lighting of candles.[62] But what of their performativity? Did they contain effective utterances—that is, speech acts that were performative in the sense described by J. L. Austin? In other words, speech acts that "did things" either of an illocutionary or perlocutionary nature?[63] The actual administrative *power* of the HRVC wing of the TRC—its ability to do, to act, to *perform* in a way that would change the lives of those who testified—was limited. The HRVC could only recommend reparations for victims. It had no authority beyond being able to determine which individuals of the 21,000 who gave statements would be given a public hearing and which would be named as a "victim" of gross violations of human rights in the final report and hence be eligible to receive whatever reparations the government (not the commission) ultimately provided.[64] The judges who presided over the Amnesty Committee hearings, on the other hand, were empowered with the capacity to grant amnesty. So in these hearings something was at stake judicially—profoundly so. At the end of the process, the fundamental legal status of the perpetrator could be changed forever through the findings and pronouncements of the commission. If granted amnesty, a perpetrator was free from civil and criminal prosecution (for certain crimes) for the rest of his or her life. In some instances, persons were freed after having already been prosecuted or imprisoned.

Interestingly, Amnesty Committee hearings, while they had performative capacity that far exceeded the Human Rights Violation Committee hearings, were generally *not* as theatrical as the HRVC hearings in terms of emotional expressiveness (with notable exceptions). Amnesty hearings were much more constrained by courtroom protocol, with lawyers and advocates making presentations to judges. There were "objections," cross-examinations, and requests to approach the bench. Often the perpetrators who came forward were affectless and subdued in their testimony, reporting heinous, grotesque acts of inhumanity in unwavering, flat tones. Yet the revelations had an innate drama, not so much because of how they were expressed but because of who was speaking and what they were saying. "You're hearing it from those who did it, and that brings a different kind of theatricality to it," says Yasmin Sooka.[65] Significantly, the commission did not require perpetrators to express contrition or remorse. Rather, the priority of the TRC was truth, the production of information, the full disclosure of deeds: who did what to whom, who gave the orders, and where the bodies were buried. There was no incentive or encouragement for those who appeared before the Amnesty Committee to "perform" in the sense of projecting any particular demeanor, emotion, or attitude. In this regard, the South African TRC was quite different from Sierra Leone's truth commission, which during its proceedings in 2003 pressured perpetrators to publicly apologize to the community. As Tim Kelsall has shown, this led to much public discussion about how genuinely contrite particular perpetrators appeared; that is, how "good" (i.e. authentic, sincere, or convincing) the perpetrators' performances of remorse were.[66] Pumla Gobodo-Madikizela, a psychologist who served on the Human Rights Violations Committee, contends that despite the emotionless narration of perpetrators of acts of cruelty at the hearings, a complex transfer of inner realities between the killer and the relatives of the victims was taking place. She claims that for victims, the manner in which the words were conveyed was less significant than their content. "The killer's words are, in a sense, performative utterances, almost palpably potent instruments that accomplish the reorganization of the survivor's inner reality even as they come out, regardless of how flat, shifty, or uninspired they may sound."[67] While affective expressiveness of testimony was evident during parts of the TRC hearings, at other points this element was given far less priority. Yet still the face-to-face presence, the confession and witnessing between perpetrator and survivors, enabled a performative transformation of self.

Some analysts have read the TRC through the lens of ritual. Embodied storytelling that is witnessed live and with a group in community has a potential for transformation that often far surpasses that of a textual report or record. Belinda Bozzoli has written on hearings in Alexandra Township through the perspective of Durkheim's theories of ritual. The TRC can be seen as a rite that (at least in theory) "created and recreated beliefs and sentiments, caused new beliefs to come into existence, and strengthened existing ones."[68] This ritual was a public one that was intended to facilitate transformation through acts of confession, mourning, and public expression of private emotion. It was meant to mark transformation at both the individual and communal levels. Bozzoli concludes that that the TRC did create for South Africa a new public realm, one that held the possibility of ending the "seclusion of the poor." And yet at the same time the commission performed a paradoxical *new* silencing and seclusion of this same constituency. This suppression happened through what wasn't said at hearings or through partial appropriations of what was said, particularly within the TRC's nationalist discourse. In considering the TRC as a ritual, we should also keep in mind Victor Turner's theory of "social drama," which identifies four phases of public action: 1) a *breach* of regular norm-governed social relations; 2) *crises*, during which the breach widens; 3) *redressive action* "ranging from personal advice and informal mediation or arbitration to formal juridical and legal machinery"; and 4) finally, "*reintegration* of the disturbed social group, or of the social recognition and legitimation of irreparable schism between the contesting parties."[69] Placed within Turner's structure of social drama, South Africa's truth commission attempted redressive action. Yet as Bozolli's analysis also concludes, the result was partial: the breach in social relations the TRC was designed to "redress" was a chasm so enormous, long-standing, and violently enacted it is no wonder the commission failed to achieve either truth or reconciliation to the degree that many would have wished.

Though not framed as theatre, the TRC was often explicitly described as such both by participants and the media. Some used theatrical metaphors to speak in laudatory terms about the TRC process. Commissioner Pumla Gobodo-Madikizela, for instance, touted the public hearings because they put the victims "center stage" within a state-sponsored investigative process.[70] Deputy Chairperson Boraine praised the public hearings as both "dramas" and "rituals." He vividly recalled the first hearings, held in East London: "At last the curtain was raised. The drama which was to unfold during the next two and half years had witnessed its first scene. The ritual, which was what the public hearings were, which promised truth, healing, and reconciliation to a deeply divided and traumatized people, began with a story."[71] Boraine views the TRC as both dramatic and cathartic, walking the line between theatre and ritual that performance studies has also long transgressed.[72] "Here we are, the actors on the stage," said George Bizos, adding "it's unusual to have a judicial proceeding on a stage."[73] The theatrical qualities of the TRC, the way it literally *staged* truth and reconciliation, were occasionally cause for great distress. The first Amnesty Committee hearings, for instance, were delayed for hours because the judges worried about the symbolism of having perpetrators sit on the same raised platform as the judges. They also fretted about where the victims should sit: Should they be on the stage or down among the audience? Should they face the commissioners or face outward toward spectators? "The judges are used to such matters being resolved by the architecture of the courtroom," writes journalist Antjie Krog. "Now they have an ordinary hall, and it seems from the human rights hearings that you make a Statement with your seating arrangement"—as any theatre director could have told them.[74]

Not all participants in the TRC embraced its theatrical manifestation. At the East London TRC hearings, chairperson Archbishop Desmond Tutu struggled to subdue unruly spectators by admonishing: "We have been given a very important task: this is not a *show* what we are doing. We are trying to get medicines to heal up our wounds."[75] Tutu substituted a medical metaphor (the healing of wounds) for a theatrical one (a "show"). In his view, the entire success of the commission—and indeed of the new democratically elected nonracial South African government—rested on public perceptions of the TRC as evenhanded and effective. Spontaneous expressions of emotion from the audience would undermine the legitimacy of the commission by turning it into a "show." Using his characteristic rhetorical signature of speaking in a mix of South African languages, Tutu elaborated, first in Xhosa: "Do not make us a laughing stock, because people will say, 'Because these things [i.e., state-sponsored commissions] are now being run by blacks, now everything is turned into a bioscope.' [In English]: I will not tolerate that please."[76] This masterful code switching, typical of Tutu's style when he presided over the commission, made his message clear: the TRC was not entertainment, it was not a movie, it was not a show. But in Tutu's vociferous protestations one can perhaps sense his conflicted relationship to the theatricality of the TRC. He was, after all, the unquestioned master of ceremonies, a brilliant showman. Without his talents, it could be argued, the commission would surely have broken down at several particularly fraught junctures. His ability to stage-manage, to orchestrate contending forces, to shift abruptly the tone, style, language, and mood of the proceedings kept the audience and all participants slightly off guard. This proved efficacious for moving the ritual forward, for keeping the show on the road, for better or worse.

While theatrical metaphors surrounding the TRC were ubiquitous, these metaphors were deployed for a wide range of purposes and with many meanings. They carried a tone of derision as often as they did praise. Thus we see Boraine embracing the TRC as a ritual and a drama, while Tutu guards against the proceedings became a "bioscope" (in South African English, a movie theatre). This is in keeping with theatre's historically fraught relationship with truth: theatre has been both lauded for its truthful rendering of the complexities of the human condition and condemned for being at core a lie, a fabrication. Tracy C. Davis and Thomas Postlewait contend that since antiquity, "the critique of theatre has focused on both its tendency to excess and its emptiness, its surplus as well as its lack. In this critique, performance is characterized as illusory, deceptive, exaggerated, artificial and affected."[77] The Inkatha Freedom Party (IFP), which resisted and was largely uncooperative with the TRC, took particular issue with chair Archbishop Desmond Tutu and depicted him in derogatory theatrical terms. As IFP leader Manqaqa Mncwango put it, "The TRC has become a sensationalist circus of horrors presided over by a weeping clown craving for the front stage spotlight."[78] Another prominent South African invoked a similar metaphor as part of his spectacular refusal to appear before the commission at all. The former prime minister and state president of South Africa, P. W. Botha, rejected the commission's summons by calling the proceedings a "circus," which inspired the cartoonist Stidy to further amplify this comparison (see fig. 1.1).[79]

Whether seen as ritual, drama, theatre, and/or performance, the TRC hearings fully embraced the theatricality that Arendt rejected in the Eichmann trial. The commission's public hearings—with their gestures, their weeping, their silences, their demonstrations of "wet bag" torture techniques, their confrontations between former torturers and those they tortured, the wails and the moments that transcended language—defined the commission for many and hence deserve our careful analysis of the ways in which they performatively operated.

The TRC was devised to express events and experiences that ultimately are unspeakable. This is one of its core paradoxes. Gross violations of human rights unmake the world. As Elaine Scary has shown, pain is a condition defined by its unsharability, its resistance to language. "Intense pain is world destroying," she says.[80] This inexpressibility has political consequences, particularly when pain is inflicted through torture. If gross violations of human rights unmake the world, as Scarry contends, the advocates for the TRC wished to remake that world by restoring certain extreme experiences and unspeakable deeds to language. The performative dimensions of public hearings facilitated this objective of the TRC—to express the inexpressible and to humanize people's experiences of extreme dehumanization. Sometimes the most potent moments of truth occurred when the commission failed to follow its own protocols and mandates, when the densely congealed layers of truths and untruths became unglued. The dramatic, unruly, ephemeral, and performed aspects of live hearings strongly expressed both the power of the TRC and its limits for truly grappling with the magnitude of the violations of human rights in South Africa's past. In the next section and in subsequent chapters, I offer examples of the kinds of analysis and history that draw attention to the many dimensions of performance can yield.

The Case of the Guguletu Seven

On 3 March 1986, seven alleged agents of the military wing of the African National Congress (ANC) were killed in a violent shootout in the township of Guguletu outside Cape Town.[81] The cause of the incident was investigated during two inquests by the apartheid state in 1986 and 1989 as well as in a criminal trial of a journalist in 1987. Yet these investigations failed to determine who was responsible for instigating the shootout or for the deaths. Much about the case, which was known as that of the Guguletu Seven, remained shrouded in mystery.[82] There were many inconsistencies that the authorities did not pursue, that still haunted the survivors: Why had all seven men been shot dead? Was this truly necessary for police self-defense? Why were there no injuries among the police? What accounted for the discrepancies between the official police version of the story and that of eyewitnesses, who reported that some of the men had been shot in the back, execution style, even when their hands were raised in the air in a posture of surrender? With so many unresolved questions, the mothers of the Guguletu Seven came forward in 1995, responding to the call for truth-telling from the TRC. They wanted answers. Instead, the TRC asked them many, many questions. One of the mothers, Cynthia Ngewu, said during the first day of public testimony: "We cannot see that drama again. We . . . cannot re-life [sic] this whole experience."[83] And yet that is exactly what the TRC's HRVC hearings asked her and the other mothers to do—to relive the drama of their trauma again and to do so in front of an audience.

The case of the Guguletu Seven was unusual in many regards. It was considered a "window case" (a case identified by the truth commission as representative of broader patterns of abuse) for the Western Cape. The dedicated TRC investigative team had managed to seize documents and link evidence that exposed to an unprecedented degree the corrupt inner workings of the apartheid state at a high level. Among TRC cases, this one threaded through the hearings of both the Human Rights Violations and Amnesty committees to an unusual degree. Several mothers of young men who were killed testified in the Human Rights Violations Committee hearings, and two of the perpetrators came forward to seek amnesty. The Guguletu Seven hearings also witnessed one of the few moments of genuine dramatic action in the TRC, when the commission moved beyond its familiar mode of storytelling and even beyond the occasional moment of demonstration, such as when amnesty applicant Jeffrey Benzien *showed,* in a now-infamous incident, just how to use a wet bag to torture someone.[84]

The first Guguletu Seven hearing was held on 23 April 1996 in the Western Cape township of Heideveld. Four mothers of the deceased testified: Cynthia

Ngewu, mother of Christopher Piet; Irene Mxinwa, mother of Simon Mxinwa; Eunice Miya, mother of Jabulani Miya; and Elsie Konile, mother of Zabonke John Konile. Each woman approached the public forum with a distinctive tone, style, and set of stated objectives.[85] Cynthia Ngewu was the most forthright. She narrated the events before and after her discovery of her son's murders in chronological order, and she enumerated what she wanted from the TRC in clear and specific ways. Mrs. Konile's testimony, on the other hand, was far more fragmentary. She described her discovery of her son's death as a period of moving in and out of consciousness. She dreamed of a goat (a bad omen) when a young man came to lead her to the "houses belonging to the comrades." She told of being seized by tremors as the man took her to Cape Town "to see her son" and of then being taken to a hospital and given pills and injections. Later, Mrs. Konile discovered that the house of the comrades was, in fact, the mortuary, and there she saw her son Zabonke so disfigured she could identify him only by his feet. She told the commission, "When I looked at him, his body, I couldn't see his body. I didn't want to look at his body. One of his eyes was out, there was just blood all over. He was swollen, the whole head was swollen. I could only identify his legs, because they were just thrown all over the place, one of his eyes was out. His whole head was swollen." Afterward, she lost consciousness again. "When I woke up, I felt like I was just getting out of bed. And there was a continuous cry that I could hear. It felt like I was going down-down-down. When I looked, I was wet-wet-wet—I was wet all over the place."[86] Mrs. Konile's testimony poignantly expresses the disorientation and physical toll of trauma. Dream and reality merge. Sometimes, the passage of time seems quite finite—a few hours—but at other times infinite.

The testimonies of the four mothers were distinctive and yet all shared certain themes: contentious encounters with police; trauma that exacted both a physical and psychological toll; the media as a locus of trauma, for television and newspaper coverage of the Guguletu Seven case was a prime means by which the women learned of their sons' deaths; and official state inquests and police interrogations, which compounded the trauma and suffering. The TRC itself risked reproducing trauma, for it, too, was both an official state inquiry and a highly televised media event. Eventually, the TRC process discovered that the police—specifically Vlakplaas, a secret unit of the security apparatus squad named for its farm headquarters near Pretoria—had infiltrated the comrades, entrapped the seven young men into plotting a crime, and then brutally executed them, staging their deaths to look like the results of a shootout. At the time of the murders, the police shot and edited a video at the scene that showed the dead bodies. Ten years later, when this video was played during the TRC hearings, the spectacle of violence intensified and refracted. The media spectacle of violence provoked live spectacle. The result was dramatic and explosive.

Mrs. Ngewu closed her testimony in April 1996 by demanding that "these boers must be put in front of us, in front of this Commission." Her wish was granted. In November 1996, police officers responsible for the entrapment and killing of the Guguletu Seven appeared before the commission for a Section 29 hearing, the number of the section of the law authorizing the TRC that gave it formidable, if ultimately underutilized, powers of subpoena. Technically, the November hearing was held under the auspices of the HRVC, but instead of focusing exclusively on victims, it heard testimony from the nine police who had been subpoenaed and who were suspected of perpetrating the murders. This particular hearing was thus more like a legal proceeding than were typical Human Rights Violations Committee or Amnesty Committee hearings: the alleged perpetrators came to it involuntarily and both the accused and the relatives of their victims testified in the same arena.

At the hearing, the police, along with an audience, commissioners, and the mothers of the deceased, sat watching the videotape that had been shot shortly after the murders of the Guguletu Seven. Originally created as propaganda, the video was part of a larger effort by the police involved to convince superiors of their unit's effectiveness in stopping so-called communist subversives and to justify new budget requests. Portions of the video had been released to the media and broadcast on national television at the time of the killings in order to prove the veracity of National Party claims about ANC violence and insurrection.[87] The video was a prop in the apartheid government's expansive war on terror. It contained gruesome footage, including close-up images of the dead, one of whom the police were dragging with a rope.

Viewed ten years later within the context of the TRC hearings, this same video became part of a very different sort of enactment of governmental authority and identity—a commission that sought to legitimize the new democratic state by putting the atrocities of the old apartheid government on public and publicized view. State-making through spectacle is a global and transhistorical phenomenon, but what is striking about the Guguletu Seven case is its complexity. A video created by the police as a vehicle for the apartheid state to justify its oppression and killing of young black men later became evidence of the culpability of the police (and the state).[88] The police officers subpoenaed to appear at the TRC hearings sat like Claudius and Gertrude watching the play-within-the-play of *Hamlet*. They posed as innocent witnesses, watching a video depicting the aftermath of brutal murders that they had, in fact, committed. The mothers of the Guguletu Seven watched like the brooding Hamlet, haunted by the specters of the dead. They watched both the representation of the murders (the video) and the police officers, whom they knew (but could not yet prove) to be the murderers.

The spectacle of this TRC hearing did not end with these enactments. During the video screening one of the surviving family members hurled a single shoe across the room.[89] This projectile decisively struck two of the accused police officers and completely disrupted the hearing. This dramatic action shifted the focus from the gruesomeness of the video and the impassivity of the accused perpetrators to the presence of mothers of the dead who sat several rows behind them. According to the *Cape Argus*, when the video showed the police putting a rope around the dead body of Christopher Piet, "One of the mothers jumped to her feet, shouting hysterically, 'Why a rope? Why a rope?'"[90] The others began, one after the other, to wail. Professional "debriefers," members of the TRC staff, surrounded the distraught women, offering handkerchiefs and physical support. Slowly the mothers were ushered out the door. The subpoenaed police officers fled the auditorium and reportedly took shelter in the press room. TRC transcripts record that advocate Dumisa Ntsebeza said, "Can we stop there—stop the video—we'll take a break now, if you would just stop the video right at this moment."[91] Perhaps betraying the transcriber's desperation, the record then reads, in capital letters, "PEOPLE ARE HYSTERICAL—CRYING AND SCREAMING."

The TRC hearings followed explicit rules of decorum and rationality. Although it was not a court of law, the TRC borrowed heavily from juridical protocol. Commissioners began each session by stating ground rules that tried to ensure that the subject of the hearings would be discussed and (in the case of the Guguletu Seven) viewed in a rational manner. The commission took great pains to "prepare" the mothers for the psychological experience of watching the video, even offering them the option of not viewing it, but the mothers insisted that they wanted to see and know what had happened to their loved ones. Whatever the motivation of the woman who tossed the shoe during the hearing on 28 November 1996, the effect of her missile was to completely disrupt the session. Whether planned or spontaneous, the women's responses of standing, throwing their arms over their heads, and wailing in grief effectively upstaged the video. The bereaved mothers asserted themselves as active agents of performed live spectacle rather than passive consumers of a video spectacle.

When the session resumed, Ntsebeza publicly regretted the theatrics of the women and said commissioners had been concerned about screening the video. Before the session, he said, the women "were told that it might not be in their interest to see the video, precisely because it might lead to this sort of *scenes* [sic] that we have seen which we *regret* as a Commission."[92] Ntsebeza then gave an extensive exhortation, using the TRC's juridical vocabulary of truth-finding, directed at the crime of the thrown shoe. Regarding "an allegation that a shoe or a similar like missile was thrown at Mr. Kleyn and Mr. Knipe presumably by one of the witnesses," Ntsebeza said:

> I did not see it, I don't know who saw it, clearly the gentleman also didn't see who it was, because obviously the missile came from behind their backs. I don't want to make a finding about this matter. I need merely say if it happened, it is something we take a very dim view of, we understand emotions of people who come to this proceedings [sic] carrying the sort of trauma that is commensurate with a loss that they obviously have. But it must be emphasized—it must be emphasized very strongly and in the strongest terms that the Commission has a task to perform which must be performed in circumstances where it's [sic] integrity and reputation will not be undermined. The entire aim and the broader aims of the Commission is to achieve not only the exposure of truth, but reconciliation. And the test, the acid test is going to be moments like this—at moments where no version of the truth as we are trying to achieve it, should be suppressed because witnesses are not made comfortable to testify.[93]

Ntsebeza's concern that the TRC proceedings be conducted fairly and safely for all participants was understandable. Indeed, it was his duty as acting chair of the commission that day to ensure such fairness and to ensure that the TRC performed restorative justice, not acts of retribution. Yet in light of the ways rationalization fueled the apartheid government's organized murder and torture of black people—rationalization so evident in the Guguletu Seven case—perhaps something other than a calm rational viewing of videotapes of murder was necessary in post-apartheid rituals of truth and reconciliation. The Guguletu mothers provided a visceral, emotional, and physical response that officially had no place in the TRC hearing. Why was their response regrettable and the calm, impassive viewing of a video of murder by the murderers somehow *not* regrettable theatrics? The police officers' behavior was far more of a "performance" than that of the mothers, as their demeanor at the hearing was a masquerade, a disguise. They performed as passive spectators of the atrocity, when in fact (as the TRC eventually revealed), they had actually been its perpetrators.

In Ntsebeza's words, the commission not only "has a task to perform," but its task had to be performed in a certain way. In order to maintain the TRC's integrity and reputation, spectators and participants also had to perform, and perform in a certain way. Ntsebeza's exhortation recalls Stidy's cartoon (fig. 1.1). While South Africa's Truth and Reconciliation Commission was designed to contain atrocity, the scale and extreme nature of such atrocities constantly exceeded its parameters. The Guguletu Seven hearings contained one moment when a state-sponsored spectacle was derailed and transformed by the volatility of the experiences it was designed to manage. Ntsebeza was right to identify this moment as an acid test of the truth "as we are trying to achieve it."

The Holocaust trials that are the TRC's genealogical ancestor also saw spectacular disruptions via the use of media and unexpected expressions of emotion. The screening of the gruesome video of the Guguletu Seven crime scene evokes the screening of the film *Nazi Concentration Camps* at the Nuremberg trials. "By providing a visual register of extreme atrocity," Lawrence Douglas writes, "the film crossed a threshold of representation from which there was no turning back."[94] Likewise, the mothers' emotional outburst evokes the collapse of writer Yehiel Dinur on the stand at the Eichmann trial.[95] These earlier moments haunted the Guguletu Seven event hearing, reminding us of the performative genealogy of the TRC and the degree to which the experiences that transitional justice forums are intended to manage are on some level unmanageable.

There are other ghosts as well: those of the Guguletu Seven. Ntsebeza refers to the shoe thrown at the police officers as a "missile," an interestingly martial reference, and he notes that part of what made the incident so appalling is the fact that this missile was thrown from behind. We might read this moment as a symbolic dramatization of reversal: several of the Guguletu Seven were shot from behind, execution style, their hands raised in a posture of surrender, with no chance to see their attackers, no chance to respond, no chance to negotiate.

Finally, there are the "ghosts" of the hearing that might have been, the hearing that would have happened if Dumisa Ntsebeza had not been in charge that day. The TRC was a "rainbow" commission, comprised of leaders from many different professional backgrounds, including medicine, psychology, ministry, and the law. The character and profession of the person chairing a particular hearing dramatically shaped the tenor and nature of the proceedings. If a different commissioner who (like Ntsebeza) was a lawyer had been in charge—Denzil Potgieter, Richard Lyster, Yasmin Sooka—he or she may well have been inclined to guide the Guguletu Seven Section 29 hearing as Ntsebeza did, using language and modes of address drawn from the courtroom. However, had Mary Burton, the former leader of the Black Sash, been at the helm,[96] or Pumla Gobodo-Madikizela, the psychologist and HRVC member, there may have been a greater emphasis on empathy.[97] When Gobodo-Madikizela led testimony, she preferred to speak to witnesses in Xhosa, especially when they were older African women, calling them deferentially "Mama" and asking how it *felt* to have some particular thing or event happen. In the face of affectless perpetrators, such as the policemen subpoenaed to the Guguletu Seven Section 29 hearing, Gobodo-Madikizela could be censorious, as she was at the Bisho massacre hearings.[98] Stung by the alleged perpetrators' lack of remorse, she chastised them.[99] TV journalist Max du Preez found Gobodo-Madikizela's performance at the Bisho hearing so inappropriate that he offered on his program *TRC Special Report* the following editorial rebuke:

> We think it is legitimate to ask the truth commissioners tonight, is it your role to force suspected bad guys to eat humble pie, to humiliate them in public? Is it not more important to elicit the truth than to try and force people to say how sorry they are? Commissioners should be very careful not to undermine the credibility of the TRC.[100]

Du Preez was provoked not only by Gobodo-Madikizela's conduct at the Bisho hearing but also by that of commissioner and psychologist Mapule Ramashala, who appealed to Brigadier Oupa Gqozo during his testimony to look at the families of victims sitting in the first rows of the audience and "to speak from the heart." She prompted Gqozo, who was accused of instigating the Bisho massacre, to make a formal apology, though this was not officially part of the TRC's mandate.

The Bisho massacre hearing shares many similarities with the Guguletu Seven hearing: both were "event hearings" that were singled out by the TRC as window cases; both aroused highly emotional spontaneous outbursts of grief from surviving family members in the audience; and both hearings tried to bring together victims and perpetrators in a way that privileged neither party, for the event was the focus of the hearing rather than the people involved.

What is interesting to note in comparing the Bisho and Guguletu event hearings is the degree to which the characters, interests, and interventions of commissioners shaped the proceeding. Had the charismatic and multilingual chairperson Desmond Tutu been running the Guguletu Seven event hearing, he might have responded to the shoe-throwing incident by leading everyone in prayer or in the singing of hymns. He might have engaged in the sort of direct conflict mediation for which he is universally famous, for Tutu is a man who directly intervened with an angry mob trying to kill a man suspected of being a police informer and who once fearlessly led protesters to kneel before a phalanx of riot police.[101] Tutu might have exhorted participants at the Guguletu Seven hearing to calm down by appealing to morality, to a shared history, or to the concept of *ubuntu*.[102] He might have used the force of admiration to gain compliance, as he did with Winnie Madikizela-Mandela, when, after many days of a hearing in which Mrs. Mandela refused to accept any responsibility for misdeeds carried out by members of her Mandela United Football Club, Tutu praised her role in the struggle, her greatness, and then exhorted her that her greatness would be magnified if she could only admit that "something went wrong" when young activists mysteriously died in her home.[103] Tutu was prone to end victims' testimonies with homilies in which he thanked God for the witnesses' honesty and for the role they had played in making the new nation. Tutu's expansive repertoire of rhetorical strategies certainly made the TRC hearings over which he presided interesting. During unexpected moments—occasions that required an improvised response—Tutu was in his element. TRC commissioners Alex Boraine and Bongani Finca were also Christian ministers, and they shared Tutu's penchant for spontaneous homilies during hearings. Yet their conduct was generally more restrained and modulated, not prone to Tutu's idiosyncratic combination of sobriety and impishness, gravitas and irreverence.

In imagining how the Guguletu Seven event hearing might have transpired differently had someone else been chairperson that day, my point is not to suggest that Ntsebeza's conduct was inappropriate. Rather, I suggest that hearings were contingent and susceptible to the interests, proclivities, and professional background of those in charge. The commission lacked precedent—there was no rule book or case history on how to handle the wide variety of situations in which commissioners found themselves. As Commissioner Wendy Orr writes of her experience, "There were no precedents to fall back on, no policies to guide decisions. We learned by making mistakes—and boy, did I make mistakes."[104] Commissioners and staff often had to improvise on the fly. But unlike in successful musical improvisations, the key players might not agree on the dominant key or rhythm or the defining melodic lines.[105]

Richard Wilson contends that in the HRVC hearings, commissioners laid a redemptive template across testimonies as they responded to victims' stories, linking individual stories to a larger narrative of nation building:

> The commissioners' responses to HRV testimony were formulaic and predictable, regularly containing the following stages: a recognition of suffering, the moral equalizing of suffering, the portrayal of suffering as a necessary sacrifice for the liberation of the nation, and finally the forsaking of revenge by victims. There was a progressive movement built into these stages, from individual testimony towards the collectivity and the nation and finally back to the individual, all in order to facilitate forgiveness and reconciliation.[106]

While such a pattern could certainly be discerned, my reading of commission transcripts indicates that there was in fact far more variance among commissioners' reactions. As scholar Annelies Verdoolaege summarizes, when victims came forward at HRVC hearings to testify, the reception of their testimony could take a number of forms: "psychotherapeutic discourse, with an emphasis on the cathartic power of storytelling; religious discourse, with an emphasis on the redemptive power of forgiveness and confession; and to a lesser extent also courtroom discourse, with an emphasis on individual testifying but also on questioning by the HRV committee members."[107] To these Verdoolaege adds the discourse of reconciliation.

The Guguletu Seven event hearing is of particular note not only because it reveals how contingent hearings could be on the responses and professional backgrounds of particular commissioners but also because it was an occasion when the procedures of the commission broke down. On this day, the TRC did *not* perform—or, to be more precise, it did not perform according to script. Such occasions reveal the uncertainties and indeterminacies that were as much a part of the TRC's production of truth and knowledge as were the sweeping narratives it generated in its summary report. Such moments also reveal the potency of performance with its ambiguity, embodiment, and ability to convey the affective dimensions of human experience as well as to portray dramatic action. Although the Guguletu mothers' expression of rage was suppressed at the hearings, the commission's format did allow the mothers to demand that the entire command structure of the metropolitan police force responsible for the murders of their sons be summoned to answer for their crimes in public. And the live nature of the public hearings allowed the women agency of expression even while the commission tried to censure it. The shoe-throwing incident at the Guguletu Seven hearings demonstrates that while some truths could be contained within the commission's mandate and procedures, other truths constantly erupted in the live experience of public hearings. Yes, everyone had to perform, and they had to perform a certain way. But the structure and format of live hearings also allowed room for those moments when individual agents took charge in unscripted and unexpected ways. In such moments, the TRC performed multiple truths most potently. Such moments revealed that the truth could not be tightly packaged, it could not be fully regulated by protocol, and it could not—and perhaps should not—be calmly and passively viewed on television.

Conclusion

The truths promulgated by the TRC hearings were of many types: factual, forensic, theatrical, emotional, subjective, and narrative. The HRVC hearings enabled people who had previously been voiceless in the official documents and discourse of the South African nation to place their stories in the public record. Live testimony given at TRC hearings also provided a corrective to the narrow epistemologies of truth-telling that were operative in venues like the Nuremberg and Eichmann trials. As Deborah Posel says of the TRC:

> The theatre of these public hearings produced—necessitated—very different genres of truth-telling from those of the more scientific efforts at fact-finding. The hearings gave space for many people to tell their own stories, versions of events that often

conflicted with others told in the same forum or which, on closer inspection, were internally inconsistent. Yet none of this seemed to detract from the truth-telling. Truth lay in the emotional power of individual stories and the capacity of the hearings to uncover seemingly pristine, uncorrupted narratives of past brutalization.[108]

While the compellingly theatrical and emotional nature of the public hearings appeared to provide unmediated access to authentic truth, in actuality these public hearings were highly mediated. The commission itself served as "casting director," determining which 10 percent of victims would tell their stories in public hearings. For its part, the media selected which portions of each daylong hearing would be broadcast on television and radio or splashed across the newspaper headlines.[109] But no matter how mediated or orchestrated the hearings were, their projection in the public eye provided spectators with a palpable connection with victims—victims of all races—and with the larger history that their individual stories, when told in succession, represented.

Posel contends that the public hearings made for "good theatre, but bad history," inasmuch as the conceptual premises and faults of the commission and its report (such as its wobbly definitions of truth, simplistic bifurcation of victims and perpetrators, lack of quality control in data collection, and absence of explanatory narrative) were deeply flawed.[110] Yet I would argue that the "good theatre" of the TRC does not *necessarily* have to lead to bad history. That may have been what the final report produced.[111] But the good theatre of the live hearings, with their compelling, densely meaningful embodied testimonies, if analyzed rigorously and with methodological creativity and attention to linguistic and performed nuance, can potentially produce good history. The archive is rich and yet largely neglected. It is worth noting here that the video and audio recordings of the TRC hearings are the only aspect of the truth commission's archive that is readily available. The National Archives and Records Service of South Africa in Pretoria has a collection of 10,446 hours of audio recordings and 14,202 hours of video recordings of the TRC public hearings. The video collection alone is so enormous that if one researcher worked eight hours a day for seven days a week, it would take over four-and-a-half years to view the collection in its entirety. Yet hardly any researchers are using this valuable resource.[112]

As David William Cohen and E. S. Atieno Odhiambo have argued, records of commissions and trials, especially in Africa, have a contingent power "to open views of otherwise thinly documented, poorly understood, or weakly represented worlds."[113] Cohen and Odhiambo's model for reading African trials and commissions suggests that scholars must read these records "against the grain" of their own internal logic. The massive work of South Africa's Truth and Reconciliation Commission is worth a much more empirically rich analysis than we have seen so far. Most studies have evaluated the successes or failures of the TRC—whether it, in fact, produced truth or reconciliation or good history or bad social science. Performance studies and other qualitative humanistic fields can contribute close readings of testimony in all its richness that open up precisely those contingent powers to which Cohen and Odhiambo refer.

While the law has always been innately theatrical, as we have seen, gross violations of human rights and crimes against humanity present unique challenges to this relationship. Does performance hold the same force of attraction for truth commissions? It certainly did for South Africa's truth commission, as this chapter has begun to demonstrate. The TRC's embrace of performance and of making its proceedings visible via widespread media coverage meant that deeds that had been unseen were made visible, deeds that seemed to be unspeakable were given language and an audience. I have argued that scholars have focused far too much on the TRC's summary report as a representation of the commission's work when in fact the hearings were the domain where the public participated in the commission as an exercise in memorializing, dramatizing, and documenting complex and controversial events from the past. Thus, these hearings demand far more analytic attention than they have so far received. Performance, theatre, ritual, and performativity operated in these hearings in dynamic, layered, and complicated ways: the hearings were both highly structured and unpredictable, planned and improvised, emotional and affectless. The TRC performatively remade public spaces where the hearings took place by making them open and welcome to people of all races. Theatre staged face-to-face encounters in which all participants—including television audiences—served as chorus and witnesses. The theatrical dimensions of the hearings made them emotionally affective, while at the same time the commission's affective dimensions were used by detractors to ridicule the hearings.

While no one seemed to be able to agree on exactly what *genre* of performance the TRC was—ritual, theatre, drama, bioscope, or circus—most seemed to agree that it *was* a performance. The ambiguity of the TRC's identity as a genre goes back much further than 1996, when the hearings commenced. To understand why South Africa embraced such a public enactment of regime change, we must look farther back in history—specifically, to 1960, another time of regime change when the country had also written a new constitution and had used quasi-judicial proceedings to make that regime change manifest to the country and the world. Three prominent trials of the late 1950s and early 1960s that are important genealogical roots of the TRC are the subject of the next chapter.

2. Justice in Transition: Political Trials, 1956–1964

Apartheid: a harsh, mean word that resounds in one's ears like a trapdoor opening beneath a gallows.

—Michel Leiris

And before June 12, 1964, there was November 7, 1962. And before November 7, 1962, there was March 21, 1960, and before the day in Sharpeville and before and before there was December 1952, and before the trial for treason there was 1948, and before the infamous apartheid laws there were so many befores. And Nelson was born July 18, 1919. And afterward there was Wednesday, June 16, 1976. And after the day of Soweto, there was September 1977. And after the death of Steve Biko, there had been . . .

—Hélène Cixous

There have been so many milestones in the history of resistance to apartheid in South Africa that when one tries to speak on the subject, one often feels the impulse to provide a litany of dates and laws or to hurry, breathlessly, back and forth in time as Hélène Cixous does in the text that opens this chapter.[1] Taken from Cixous' fictional imagining of the life together (and mostly apart) of Nelson and Winnie Mandela, the passage lurches in time, disrupts chronological order, and moves from the realm of the individual to that of the national, from the birth of Mandela to the death of Black Consciousness Movement activist Steven Biko. "And before . . . and before . . . and before . . . ," the sentence runs on. The narrator then shifts to an "afterward," a time for which there is no conclusion, just a trail of ellipses. Cixous wrote this story in the mid-1980s, before Nelson Mandela was released from prison in 1990, before the passage of the interim constitution in 1993, before the first democratic elections in 1994, and before the commencement of the Truth and Reconciliation Commission in 1995–1996.

This chapter focuses on three occasions Cixous referred to: the long-running Treason Trial held from 1956 to 1961, a 1962 proceeding against Nelson Mandela that I will call the Incitement Trial,[2] and the Rivonia Trial of 1964. While it may seem strange to begin a book on the Truth and Reconciliation Commission with an analysis of three important political trials in which Nelson Mandela, among others, stood in the dock, I do so for two reasons. In part, scrutinizing these trials allows me to introduce historical context, and of course the stories of the TRC are incomprehensible without some knowledge of South Africa's past. However, this point of entry is more than an expositional device: it is germane to my thesis. By analyzing both the verbal and the extralinguistic, physical aspects of discourse surrounding the early political trials, I address one of the book's larger questions: Why and to what effect did transitional justice in South Africa as manifested in the Truth and Reconciliation Commission take the idiosyncratic and unique form that it did? That the TRC was so performative—placing a high priority on public presentation, spoken individual narrative, physicalized speech acts, emotional expressiveness, and even singing and chanting—was no accident or departure from protocol. Rather it was a continuation of performance traditions that are associated with South African law as it emerged around moments of state transition.

Finally, our definitions of "transition" must be more inclusive than the particular regime changes implied by the field of transitional justice, which focuses only on transitions from authoritarian to democratic rule. As theorist of political justice Otto Krichheimer has said, "By utilizing the devices of justice, politics contracts some ill-defined and spurious obligations. Circumstantial and contradictory, the linkage of politics and justice is characterized by both promise and blasphemy."[3] While it may seem blasphemous to consider political trials staged by the apartheid state as sharing a genealogical heritage with the Truth and Reconciliation Commission, it is also accurate to say both share a heavy investment in the conjunction of politics and theatre.

The charges levied in the Treason, Incitement, and Rivonia trials ranged from treason, incitement, and sedition to attempting violent overthrow of the state. In each case, however, the accused and their counsel and anti-apartheid spectators transformed the proceedings by means of performance through songs, gestures, costumes, and speeches.[4] These performed dimensions of human behavior constitute what Diana Taylor calls the "repertoire"—the embodied expressions that stand in relation to historical traces left behind in transcripts, documents, and recordings in the archive.[5] Taylor's book The Archive and the Repertoire: Performing Cultural Memory in the Americas provides new terminology for old conundrums. Whereas in the past theatre and performance studies scholars tended to polarize text and performance in ways that were both artificial and rigid, Taylor's approach provides terminology that is more elastic and flexible. The archive consists of objects such as documents, letters, archeological remains, and maps—objects that seem "real," concrete, and able to transmit memory over space and time. The "repertoire," by way of contrast, is embodied memory: "performances, gestures, orality, movement, dance, singing—in short, all those acts usually thought of as ephemeral, nonreproducible knowledge."[6] Taylor posits the relationship between the archive and repertoire neither as a dichotomy nor as being sequentially related (first repertoire, then archive). Rather, the archive and the repertoire are parallel and overlapping realms. The repertoire *seems* less stable or concrete than the archive, though if we look further this contrast breaks down. As the history of the TRC archive makes abundantly evident, documents can mysteriously disappear, and the collection and classification process is intensely mediated, as is the process of requesting, granting, and denying access.

What *is* dichotomous between the realms of archive and repertoire are the biases and expectations people tend to bring to their reception: in scholarship, the archive is given pride of place. The archive is perceived as a rich repository of meaning that is worthy of precise and in-depth analysis, whereas the repertoire is not. The archive is seen as immutable, reliable, and unmediated. While intellectual bias tries to locate the repertoire only in the present, it too transmits knowledge from the past and into the future. The scholarly tendency, Taylor claims, is to banish the repertoire to the past, to see it as false, unreliable, and primordial—or worse, entirely devoid of meaning. "The dominance of language and writing has come to stand for *meaning* itself," according to Taylor, while embodied practices not based in literary codes are seen as having no claims to meaning.[7]

This chapter takes as a foundational assumption the idea that embodied practices *do* have significance and meaning and hence demand our analytical attention. While various studies have mentioned the repertoires enacted by the accused and their supporters at the South African political trials of 1956–1964 in passing, as sorts of colorful accents to the "real" story of the trials, I instead approach these performative repertoires as meaningful and coherent discourses in their own right. An examination of this repertoire gives a fresh perspective on the ways that performance and the law were deployed during a period of intense political transition. Justice and performance were used (and abused) in this era as South Africa devolved from following the rule of law into a police state. More than three decades later, justice and performance were deployed once again when the Truth and Reconciliation Commission enacted "transitional justice" as a means to restore the rule of law.

I argue that an intensity of meaning worthy of analytical attention occurs at precisely those moments when the archive and the repertoire explicitly converge, as they did during the political trials of the late 1950s and early 1960s. For example, the Treason Trial ended in acquittal in part because the police proved so spectacularly inept at documenting the live improvised speeches of African National Congress leaders at their political rallies, the content of which was alleged to be treasonous.[8] The problem of incoherent reportage came to light through the disparities between longhand and shorthand transcriptions. One of the accused, Helen Joseph, said that her fellow accused were most distressed by the longhand writers, who were, without exception, "White and non-reporters [whose] garbled, inadequate, reports drew scathing comment from the Judge President even during the trial." He testily chided the prosecution for its shoddy research methodology: "Sometimes the State employs shorthand writers, sometimes recording machines, sometimes Africans are sent who may or may not be qualified. Sometimes they are not qualified. *I* am not going to make people employed by the State qualified if they are not qualified."[9] Who would have predicted that the outcome of the largest and most high-profile trial in South African history would depend upon an arcane conundrum of performance studies: how to document live performance?[10]

The political trials of 1956–1964 must be seen as central to the performance genealogy of the TRC. The concept "performance genealogy" has its own intellectual heritage, with a lineage one can trace most directly to Joseph Roach, who in turn inherits from Nietzsche and Foucault.[11] Seeing political trials as part of the performance genealogy of the TRC is important not so we can discover an essence of form or clarify, once and for all, whether the TRC did, in fact, produce "real" truth or viable reconciliation, whether its justice was restorative or a travesty. Genealogy, in the Foucauldian sense, is not about getting to the bottom of things. Rather, performance genealogy provides a means for seeing the TRC's complex inheritance as multiple, contradictory, and more complex than has previously been understood. As Roach writes, genealogies of performance attend to "counter-memories" as well as to "the disparities between history as it is discursively transmitted and memory as it is publicly enacted by the bodies that bear its consequences."[12]

In South Africa prior to the TRC, the discursive practices of officially sanctioned history had been overwhelmingly logocentric while the practices of resistance had been largely located in performance—that is, in the realm of the body. This dichotomy was both racialized and racist, and the state was the chief agent in that racialization. The state passed a torrent of laws aimed at limiting, circumscribing, or eliminating altogether the discursive practices of those who most acutely bore the consequences of apartheid: nonwhites. Black cultures in South Africa had long-standing oral and performed traditions that far predated apartheid. But under apartheid, embodiment came to be linked to either resistance/transgression or to compliance. Hence, the trials staged, in essence, a confrontation between the archive and the repertoire. By the time of the TRC, thirty-five years later, the gap between the written record of history preserved in the archives and the countermemories recorded in repertoires had become a chasm. The Truth and Reconciliation Commission was intended to bridge this chasm, and it did so by drawing on many resources. Among these were the international traditions of transitional justice, the high-profile quasi-juridical events of the past such as political trials, and the repertoires of resistance cultivated by the anti-apartheid movement.

Befores and Afters

If we consider South Africa's Truth and Reconciliation Commission as a stage of transition *out* of a period of gross violations of human rights, when did that period begin? "Apartheid" is surely central to the answer. In addition to being "a harsh, mean word that resounds in one's ears like a trapdoor opening beneath a gallows," in Michael Leiris's phrase, apartheid is an Afrikaans word that means "racial apartness." Dr. Hendrik Frensch Verwoerd, the South African leader who is usually considered the architect of apartheid, once described it as a policy of "good neighborliness," a statement that was much parodied afterward.[13] The inception of apartheid is usually dated to the 1948 ascendancy to power of the Afrikaner National Party, which inaugurated an "avalanche" of security legislation.[14] The Prohibition of Mixed Marriages Act of 1949, the Population Registration Act of 1950, the Group Areas Act of 1950, the Suppression of Communism

Act of 1950, the Bantu Authorities Act of 1951—these and many related laws made apartheid ideology operational by tightly proscribing where nonwhites could live and work, whom they could marry and have sex with, what they could say, and what type of education they could receive.[15] Apartheid as an official policy was articulated and systematically enforced after 1948, though it was simply an extreme version of racial practices already in place. The fact that the African National Congress was formed in 1912 is a testament to the earlier need of blacks for representation, for even then land seizures and labor practices were racially driven. Under the post-1948 rule of the National Party, apartheid was made manifest performatively through passbooks, separate amenities, separate school curricula, and separate living areas, known as townships in cities and as homeland reserves in the country. The amount of legislation needed to bring apartheid into being was breathtakingly extensive, as evidenced by a huge wall—a monumental monolith—at the present-day Apartheid Museum in South Africa that is covered with plaques inscribed with acts of apartheid legislation. A "pathological proliferation of juridical prostheses," Jacques Derrida calls them.[16] Such prosthetics were necessary to prop up a state that had amputated morality from the law.

While state repression escalated and intensified in the 1950s, the early 1960s were a crucial turning point. Most important was the massacre at Sharpeville in March 1960, during which sixty-nine Africans were killed and another 180 wounded while peacefully protesting, brutally gunned down by the police during an anti–pass law demonstration. "Previously, nearly every ANC leader had been deeply committed to non-violence," says historian Leonard Thompson. "But nonviolence methods had achieved nothing except a series of defeats at the hands of a violent state."[17] The two leading anti-apartheid organizations, the African National Congress and the Pan Africanist Congress, were banned. The government declared a state of emergency and conducted mass arrests, facilitated by new legislation that permitted arrests without warrants and detention without trial. The prison populations exploded. Anti-apartheid activists began to call the years before 1960 "the legal days"; afterward, everything was illegal.[18]

For over fifty years the ANC had tirelessly and patiently fought oppression through nonviolent means. But after Sharpeville its policy changed. The ANC formed a military wing known as Umkhonto we Sizwe (MK, or "Spear of the Nation"), which endorsed certain acts of violence as part of the freedom struggle. In 1961, the South African government chose to leave the British Commonwealth and become the Republic of South Africa. The republic's first act was to pass a new constitution under which one-fifth of South Africa's people—its whites—determined the fate of the country's entire population, eighty-one percent of whom were not white.[19] Protesting against this new constitution—an unconstitutional constitution if ever there was one—landed Nelson Mandela in court for his Incitement Trial of 1962.

Not only does 1960 serve as a meaningful historical frame for understanding the period out of which the TRC was intended to be a transition, this year is also the historical frame for the TRC's mandate: the commission was charged with examining gross violations of human rights that took place after March 1960, the date of the Sharpeville massacre. Even at the time, many recognized Sharpeville as a historic watershed. "The old book of South African history was closed at Sharpeville," said Paul Sauer just two weeks after the shootings.[20] Thus, the Sharpeville massacre marks the beginning of the 34-year period the Truth and Reconciliation Commission was charged to investigate. Of course, gross violations of human rights did not *begin* in South Africa in 1960.[21] However, 1960 was seen by the authors of the interim constitution as a logical starting point for the Truth and Reconciliation Commission's investigations.[22]

South Africa in the Dock

The 1950s and early 1960s were a time of intense political change. As the government exerted increasing control over the domain of writing, anti-apartheid opponents responded by means of performance through songs, slogans, and codified gestures, traditions that would become defining features of the anti-apartheid movement during subsequent decades. The state passed repressive laws and Africans broke them. When Africans broke the law, they were put on trial. Yet, in Nelson Mandela's view, "Our appearances in court became the occasion for exuberant political rallies."[23] In the face of state repression and censorship, the anti apartheid struggle cultivated a rich and multifaceted repertoire of resistance. Embodied expressions, songs, gestures, dances, and speech acts were its weapons, especially in the early days of nonviolent protest before the ANC began throwing stones and wielding AK-47s. Performed repertoires of resistance attained national and international visibility during the political trials of 1956–1964 and were to remain a common feature of political trials during subsequent decades, much to the irritation of the state. How and what did anti-apartheid activists perform at political trials from 1956–1964, not just with words, but also with their bodies, voices, gestures, clothing, and use of physical space?

"Awful, wonderful, inspiring and boring beyond words," said defendant Hilda Bernstein of the Treason Trial, which began in 1956, when 156 people were arrested for treason and for planning to violently overthrow the government.[24] The accused, identified by the state as 105 blacks, twenty-one Indians, twenty-three whites, and seven coloreds, included the leaders of all the major resistance organizations, among them the African National Congress, the Coloured People's Congress, the Congress of Democrats, the South African Indian Congress, and the South African Congress of Trade Unions. (These organizations were collectively known as the Congress Alliance.) They faced charges of high treason and of setting up a countrywide conspiracy to topple the government and install a communist state. The trial droned on for nearly five years before ending in mass acquittals. Then, in 1962, Mandela alone was tried for inciting Africans to participate in a strike and for leaving the country without a passport. Found guilty on both counts, he was sentenced to five years in prison. Halfway through his sentence, he was again brought before a court, this time with several others, in the so-called Rivonia case. Their alleged crime was sabotage, which carried the threat of the gallows. The Rivonia Trial was Mandela's final appearance in court before he disappeared from public view for twenty-five years.

Although South African political trials transpired in what were ostensibly courts of law, the accused freedom fighters often argued that the courts in which they were tried were not, in fact, legal. In addition, the audience these courts addressed went beyond the judges, advocates, prosecutors, and spectators present in the room. The courts spoke also to an audience beyond the walls of the courtroom, to a national and, indeed, a global audience. L. J. Blom-Cooper, a British observer of the Treason Trial, remarked, "Not since the burning of the Reichstag in Berlin in 1933—with the notable exception of the special trials at Nuremberg—has a trial attracted such international attention."[25] South Africa's political trials were platforms, show trials, juridical events both inside and outside the law. They dealt with the law not just on an operational level but also on a philosophical one. The trials used semantic opacity, ephemerality, and locus in the body of performance to mediate between conscience and the law.

The Treason Trial

The state inaugurated the Treason Trial as a spectacle with a mass arrest at dawn of over 140 people. Lionel Forman, one of the accused, recalls the highly publicized event:

> One hundred and forty families were wakened that morning—Africans, Indians, Europeans, Coloureds; doctors and labourers, teachers and students, a university principal, a tribal chief. And if the names and occupations were analysed, here was a complete cross-section of South Africa. Afrikaaners, Englishmen, Jews, Zulu, Xosa, Basutho, Hindu, Moslem, young and old; sick and healthy; university graduate and illiterate.[26]

Specially arranged trains and military planes whisked the accused off to Johannesburg, where they were met by a squadron of soldiers "armed as for war."[27] The accused were shipped off to the Old Fort Prison In Johannesburg in a *kwela-kwela* van, and as they rode, they launched into performative repertoires that became characteristic of political trials.[28] Forman recalls, "Now we are swinging in the huge kwela-kwela towards the Fort. They are singing, and I am singing too: 'Izokunyathela iAfrika' . . . 'Afrika will trample you underfoot.' Unrepentant. People seen through the mesh: surprise and dawning understanding. The thumb raised in reply. 'Mayibu'ye iAfrika!'" The arrest was a spectacle orchestrated by the state, but those arrested and their supporters used song and gestures to transform military spectacle into a festival of resistance.

When the prisoners arrived at the Fort and assembled in a big hall, the atmosphere was one of elation and pandemonium. "It was like a great May Day picnic, or the most representative of national conferences," recalls Forman.[29] Anti-apartheid activists came together from Johannesburg, Durban, Cape Town, and Port Elizabeth, sometimes meeting for the first time. Forman writes,

> Warders wandered about with batons, not quite knowing what to do. White men and black men hugging each other. Black professors and doctors and lawyers. Ministers

of religion, a member of parliament. Men being introduced to one another and formally shaking hands as if they were at a braaivleis [barbeque]. Warders had never seen anything like this in the Fort before. They stopped wandering about and huddled together in a whispering group.[30]

This scene is emblematic of the dueling spectacles that characterized the Treason Trial. The National Party government tried to whip the public into a state of hysteria about "treason" and a "communist threat." The arrests at dawn, the secret military air flights, and the spectacular headlines in the press were all intended to dramatize the magnitude of this threat as well as the state's overwhelming capacity to suppress opposition. The trial was also implicitly a rationale for the state's increasing infringement on civil liberties—its intimidation and surveillance via the new Special Branch secret police. But the Treason Trial spectacle backfired. "It was the oddest paradox," writes Anthony Sampson, an editor of *Drum* magazine, an important voice in the anti-apartheid struggle, "that in the very court where they were being tried for treason, the Congress leaders were able to hold their biggest unbanned meetings for four years."[31] For the first time the opposition leaders had a central office—the Drill Hall, where the trial was held. This cavernous military building in Johannesburg was hastily fitted as a satellite court since no existing courtroom could accommodate 156 defendants in its dock. The accused were so numerous that the arrests and legal proceedings had the unintended consequence of fostering relationships among opposition leaders. Nelson Mandela notes, "Our communal cell became a kind of convention for far-flung freedom fighters. Many of us had been living under severe restrictions, making it illegal for us to meet and talk. Now, our enemy had gathered us all together under one roof for what became the largest and longest unbanned meeting of the Congress Alliance in years."[32] The great miscalculation of the political trials of 1956–1964 was that in seeking to break political opposition, the government instead succeeded in strengthening it.[33]

In the face of the state's escalating censorship of expression, the anti-apartheid movement developed an extraordinarily adaptable, enduring, and politically efficacious repertory of resistance. The freedom songs, the thumbs-up "Afrika! Mayibuye!" salute, and other, more subtle performed interventions in the drama of the trial were all means of protest that the state seemed incapable of regulating, a fact that was increasingly vexing to state officials. The protest repertory was deployed in myriad ways, and song was of primary and enduring importance throughout all three trials. As the musician Abdullah Ibrahim notes, South Africa's may well have been the first revolution ever conducted in "four-part harmony."[34] There was the "singing music box" that Forman and others describe— the vans that invariably rocked with freedom songs as they transported prisoners to and from the Treason Trial and later the Rivonia Trial as well. Helen Joseph remembers the latter days of the Treason Trial:

The men came pouring out of the goal gate and into the back of the van. I couldn't see them but I could feel the lorry rocking as they clambered in, and the singing started. The beautiful melodies and the incomparable harmonies as we rode through the streets of Pretoria. Our van was known as the "singing lorry" and the driver was so proud that he sometimes drove us round Church Square, "Sing up, sing up, chaps!" he shouted, "I'm taking you for a ride!"[35]

Joseph's story suggests the extent to which prisoners' singing of freedom songs affected onlookers, even the wardens directly charged with their imprisonment. What was this strange efficacy of song? Hilda Watts, wife of one of the accused, recalls the arrival of vans in Pretoria: "Soon there is a sound of singing, we look up—the buses have arrived! The songs, the raised thumbs, the spirit of courage and unity, all this arrives with the accused in their buses, just as it came with the *kwela* that morning more than a year and a half ago when they were first brought from the prisons to the Court."[36] Memoirs of political prisoners speak eloquently and often of the importance of song as a means of communication while in solitary confinement, as a way of creating a sense of community among individuals of disparate backgrounds, and as a way of knitting together moments in time during the long struggle for freedom.[37] During the 1962 Incitement Trial, the crowd that assembled each day often left the courtroom by breaking into song, reportedly "rocking" the courtroom as they spontaneously sang "Nkosi Sikelel i'Africa" ("God Bless Africa").[38] Even at the end of the Rivonia Trial, as the accused who had been sentenced to life in prison were being ferried away, Albertina Sisulu stood outside the court in traditional dress leading a crowd singing "Nkosi Sikelel i'Africa."[39]

Another technique of the repertoire of resistance was the manner in which the accused and their supporters performed courtroom protocol. When the Treason Trial defendants first arrived in the magistrates' court for their remands, they saw that a huge audience had gathered in the gallery. The spectators whispered slogans of support and raised their thumbs in the air, despite the magistrate's warning that such gestures could lead to charges of contempt.[40] As a way of expressing solidarity with the accused, the audience refused to sit even after the magistrate did so. In the spirit of improvised collective action, the accused spontaneously devised another and more subtle means of performed resistance, as Lionel Forman narrates:

> The prosecution called out the names one by one. The first few answered with a simple "yes" but then one responded in deep and formal Zulu and the idea caught on at once.
>
> In a variety of languages and in every form of subtle irony came the reply.
>
> "I am here if it may please your worship," said Archie Sibeko, Secretary of the Congress of Trade Unions in dignified si-Xosa.
>
> "My lord, I have the pleasure to be in court," said Cleopas Sibande in Sesutho.
>
> "Ich bin do," said Hymie Barsel in Yiddish.
>
> "Ndi Lapa"—"I am here"—said Chief Luthuli
>
> For a long time there was no Afrikaans, the language of [Prime Minister] Strijdom, but the morning was not to pass without a symbol that there are Afrikaners in the freedom movement too.
>
> "Ja, ek is teenwoordig," came the reply when Jan Hoogendyk's name was called, and the magistrate's head snapped up.
>
> Once again the roster had demonstrated that the "traitors" speak in all the voices of South Africa.[41]

This moment inaugurated the juridical space as a forum in which the agon between the apartheid state and anti-apartheid resistance would play out. Here we see a call-and-response that set the paradigm for much of what followed: the prosecutor calls the names of the accused and they respond in unexpected ways, their language and tone asserting individuality, difference, and irony. The audience is called to stand and they do so, but then they refuse to sit according to normal courtroom protocol. Spectators introduced hand gestures (the thumbs-up sign) and slogans ("Mayibuye") from another public sphere—the political rally.

The Treason Trial was a spectacle that attempted to respond most directly to a counterspectacle, the political rallies being staged throughout the country by the anti-apartheid movement. The political rally was what the political trials were intended to curtail. The charges of the Treason Trial largely resulted from an extraordinary gathering in Kliptown held in 1955, when a great tide of anti-apartheid delegates from across the country met to write the Freedom Charter, a document that would serve as a prototype for the future constitution. "There had been bigger political meetings in South Africa, but the Kliptown gathering was and still is unique in our history," according to Raymond Suttner and Jeremy Cronin.[42] "Seven thousand spectators watched the proceedings. This was certainly the most representative gathering there has ever been in South Africa. It was a real people's parliament, with one difference. It was not, of course, sovereign."[43] The political trials of 1956–1964 were an attempt by the state to stage a spectacle that would compete with and ultimately suppress the spectacles of political rallies, people's parliaments that were assembling with incredible force and magnitude throughout the country.

When the preparatory examination for the Treason Trial commenced, these two arenas of spectacle converged. A great throng of protestors pushed right up to the doorstep of the hearing. Thousands had assembled in the streets outside the Drill Hall. Yet they were not allowed in. Apartheid reigned inside the courtroom: only a third of the seats had initially been allocated to non-Europeans, and these were revoked when the European audience exceeded the hall's capacity. "The whites were allowed to take up all the seats meant for the blacks. And the thousands of Non-Europeans who stood patiently in long lines extended round several city blocks—who had stood there for many hours—were left to stand," recalls Forman.[44] When the accused were led into the courtroom, there was not one non-European in the audience. And yet somehow the masses of non-Europeans outside the hall knew with incredible precision what was happening inside the courtroom. The dueling spectacles had finally converged—the courtroom and the rally—and a disarming call-and-response ensued that momentarily connected the juridical space and the political rally. "How word got out to the streets is a mystery," Forman writes. "But the people out there knew of every move in the court as soon as it was made. They knew the moment the court orderly called out: 'Rise in court,' and the magistrate strode in. There was a hush outside, and with miraculous timing, just as he sat down there was a swelling sound of ten thousand voices singing 'Mayibuye, Afrika,' and then silence once more."[45] Once again we see a kind of oddly antiphonal structure, with the state initiating a "call" and Africans answering in unexpected ways. On this particular day, the rally outside the courtroom won the duel. Their booming voices combined with the horrendous acoustics of the Drill Hall, creating such a din that nobody inside the courtroom could be heard, and the court was adjourned until loudspeakers could be found.[46] The next day, the state erected a five-foot-high mesh cage for the accused and police dispelled the crowed with batons and gunshots.[47] "Everyone in the court stood up and the accused pushed forward in their cage," writes Forman, adding, "The police were shooting the people outside. The police were shooting the people," an alarming declaration that we can read in retrospect as a premonition of the state's new techniques of repression, for shooting into crowds gathered at rallies would eventually replace transcription of speeches at rallies as the state's primary technique of suppression. In the battle of spectacles, day two of the hearings went to the state. In *The Treason Cage,* his book on the proceedings, Anthony Sampson describes an encounter that is in many ways emblematic not only of the Treason Trial but also of the many political trials in South Africa that followed. One day during the lunch break, Sampson was sharing a meal with Professor Z. K. Matthews, one of the most distinguished Africans among the accused. Sampson recalls:

> Two young Afrikaner sportsmen wandered in during the lunch-hour and, seeing the hall full of natives, walked up to one of them who was sitting having lunch with me. "What are these trials about, eh? Who is it they are trying?" one of them asked. "The whole of South Africa is on trial," replied Professor Matthews, looking up darkly from his soup. "You're on trial, we're all on trial. It's ideas that are being tried here, not people."[48]

Matthews responded to the casual Afrikaner observers by telling them they were not innocent bystanders: they too were on trial, sportsmen or no. And he made it clear that the primary defendant in this trial was not people but ideas, a sentiment echoed by defense counsel Vernon Berrangé in his opening address to the court:

> A battle of ideas has indeed been started in our country. A battle in which on one side—the accused will allege—are poised those ideas which seek equal opportunity for, and freedom of thought and expression by, all persons of all races and creeds; and, on the other side, those which deny to all but a few the riches of life, both material and spiritual, which the accused aver should be common to all.[49]

Accusations of communism and treason were central to the government's case. By simply hurling the accusation "communist" at an individual or organization, the state could utilize the powers of the Suppression of Communism Act, passed in 1950, which included, as Christopher Merrett describes:

> The liquidation of unlawful communist organizations; the listing of their office-bearers, members and active supporters, and the forced resignation and/or exclusion of such persons from other organizations, including legislative bodies; a prohibition

on printing, publication and circulation of documents emanating from or reflecting the aims of communist organizations; seizure of documents; proscriptions of meetings; banning of persons from gatherings and from specified areas; and . . . deportation.[50]

The act allowed the state to unleash a torrent of security legislation that curbed civil liberties in every arena. The accused contended that their ideas were not communist but rather were concerned with fundamental issues of human rights, liberty, and representative government. Their approach to the trial was to shift the focus from purported communism to the ideology of apartheid, which institutionalized gross socioeconomic inequities and violations of human rights.

If the Treason Trial was a battle of ideas, a conflict between firing guns and freedom songs, and a duel of spectacles between the courtroom and the political rally, it was also a battle between the domain of the archive and the domain of repertoire. Until 1956, the anti-apartheid struggle was conducted openly with public meetings and a firm commitment to nonviolence. And yet it was largely conducted in the realm of performance, for possessing written documents that the state could confiscate and scrutinize was a liability. In addition, unequal access to education ensured that many of those most acutely impacted by apartheid could not read. So the anti-apartheid struggle was a movement that deployed body and voice as primary instruments of communication. The state, on the other hand, was imposing itself upon its citizenry through escalating degrees of documentation. This burden was nowhere more potently expressed than in the passbook system, which required all non-Europeans to carry identity documents that defined where they could live and work.

But the state's attempts to document (to archive) the supposedly treasonous speeches (the repertoire) of anti-apartheid activists were often woefully inadequate. Early on in the Treason Trial, it became clear that the state's primary evidence of treason hinged upon speeches so poorly transcribed that they were "incomprehensible, incoherent and illiterate."[51] These speeches had been recorded by police who had infiltrated and spied on political rallies. But their methods of transcription were erratic and inept, especially among those who could only write in longhand. Political speeches were improvised performances. As theatre and performance studies scholars well know, performance presents acute methodological challenges, for it is notoriously difficult to record. In the 1950s in South Africa, the police had access primarily to handwritten transcriptions. "During those years it was rare for our speakers to use prepared notes," explains Helen Joseph. "And some of the speeches that were being so mangled and maimed in the Court had been made all of seven years ago—and none less than four. But *we* knew what our leaders used to say; and it wasn't this garbled gibberish, this double-Dutch, this blood-and-thunder nonsense."[52] So painful did the accused find the Crown's gross mangling of their speeches that they sometimes even sent notes of clarification to the front of the courtroom as some detective "fumbled through penciled notes," according to Anthony Sampson.[53]

But the problem of documentation was not the only difficulty these performed speeches presented to the state. Language in South Africa's radically multilingual environment was also a profound issue. At one point in the Treason Trial, the prosecutor produced a witness who read to the court a text he claimed was an accurate transcription of a speech given by a Mr. Press. Lionel Forman writes:

> The detective who was reporting it could not understand English well enough to write down the actual words. But fortunately the speech had been translated into Sesutho for the audience [at the rally]. The detective didn't understand Sesutho either, but the Sesutho had been translated into Zulu. And the detective understood that. But there was no point in him writing the speech down in Zulu because his officers didn't understand Zulu. So he had translated the translation of the translation of the speech into his own English while the speech was still on.[54]

So the spy's transcription of the speech was three generations removed from its original source—as the text went from English to Sesutho to Zulu and back to the detective's "own" version of English, with all the potential for error and inaccuracy compounded with each reiteration. If not for the fact that this witness was called by the state to testify in a case about the most serious of offenses, that of High Treason, for which the accused could potentially be executed, this episode would stand as one of the most comical in South Africa's legal history.

Such absurdities were not uncommon in the early years of the Treason Trial, which, despite its spectacular beginnings, was largely boring. Tedium was relieved by fleeting moments of drama or humor. On more than one occasion, the magistrate had to admonish, "This is not as funny as it seems."[55] But perhaps the Treason Trial's most bizarre convergence (or failed convergence) of archive and repertoire was not a debate about the methodological challenges of transcribing live performance but rather a demonstration and performative reenactment of this very problem. Advocate Berrangé, during his cross-examination of African Secret Police boss John Tabata, contended that the witness was too illiterate to record a speech in English, even if he had an interpreter. Berrangé promised to put Tabata to a test: Tabata said he took his notes while sitting on a motorcycle and so, very well, Berrangé would have a motorcycle brought into court and everyone would be able to see how he fared transcribing under such conditions. "Little wonder then that there was an air of expectancy in the court the next morning," said Lionel Forman. "The proceedings are deadly monotonous and the idea of having a motor-cycle in the witness-box complete with detective perched on it, was one which appealed to everyone."[56] The motorcycle when it came had a sidecar and was too wide to fit through the doorway.[57] Yet the "show" had to go on. Tabata sat on a chair instead and transcribed a speech delivered by advocate Berrangé which was then translated into not just one but two different African languages:

> *Berrangé:* Afrika! Sons and daughters . . .
> *Magistrate:* Tabata seems to be agitated.
> *Berrangé:* I think he is very worried.
> *Magistrate:* I know you think it is simulated.

Berrangé: No, no. Not at all. I'm sure it's genuine.
Tabata: I would like another interpreter.[58]

In this metatheatrical moment of the performed "play" within the trial, the magistrate and advocate Berrangé observe the witness's comportment and discuss whether he is "simulating" (i.e., acting) his emotions of panic or whether these are indeed genuine. Berrangé continued with his recited speech, and this time the accused in their cage also began to play along. The courtroom became a theatre, a performed replication of a political rally. Berrangé said: "Afrika! Sons and daughters of Africa, just as the sun rises in the East, it is sure that through all our vicissitudes we will achieve the aims of the Freedom Charter."[59] Then, as Lionel Forman recalls, "There was a pause for realistic applause, and a cry of '*Afrika! Mayibuye!*' came from the back, until the accused remembered that they were still in court."[60] They were performing the repertoire of resistance. As A. S. Chetty, a former executive member of the Natal Indian Congress explains, such exclamations were essentially one's membership card in the freedom struggle. "The moment you give them [African people] the sign, you're a comrade. You say: '*Afrika!*' and they return it: '*Mayibuye!*' Straight away you're a comrade. Open, come into the house and talk."[61]

At the Treason Trial, this demonstration of a rally was staged into order to reveal the inability of the police to document the crimes they alleged. Yet this moment also created a convergence of the two domains vying for preeminence throughout: the trial and the rally. For a few brief moments, the courtroom became a political rally. It also became a theatre, with the proceedings not just *telling* what had happened but also *showing* through reenactment. The theatre of the Treason Trial involved role-playing: the defense advocate played the role of the accused by delivering one of their political speeches; the accused played the role of spectators, which in South African anti-apartheid rallies was not passive but rather required active vocal interaction; and the policeman played himself. Ironically, the only person who was not "acting," the policeman, was exposed through this dramatization as a fraud. At the end of Berrangé's twelve minute, 533-word speech, Detective Tabata had managed to record 144 words, or 27 percent of the speech.

"One thing stood out as clear as the pimple on the end of Strijdom's nose," Lionel Forman writes. "The Nationalists had bitten off more than they could chew."[62] The high spirits and confidence of the early days of the Treason Trial, however, gave way to boredom and stress as the proceedings dragged on for years and took a toll on the finances and families of the accused. When, after years of preliminary hearings, the actual trial began in August 1958, the venue was moved from Johannesburg to Pretoria, creating further hardship for the accused, who were forced to endure long commutes in addition to hours of tedium sitting in the courtroom. Crowd reduction was certainly the government's chief motivation for changing locales; the new location also made it far more difficult for the rallying masses of supporters to attend the hearings.

That the Treason Trial was no ordinary trial was evident in many ways: the number of the accused, the spectacular nature of their arrest, the wire cage constructed for their confinement in court, the deluge of supporters who thronged the streets outside the courtroom and disrupted the juridical proceedings with songs, and the squadrons of armed police officers who were stationed outside to suppress the rally. But the quasi-juridical nature of the proceedings, the way that the trial existed both inside and outside the law and charted new territory in the nationalist government's devolution into a police state, was perhaps most vividly expressed in the physical venues chosen for these proceedings. The Treason Trial took place in two locations, neither of which was originally built to be a courtroom: first in a converted military hall in Johannesburg and later in the Old Synagogue in Pretoria. The Drill Hall was a "bare barn of a place with a corrugated iron roof," according to Anthony Sampson. It had "an old-fashioned military appearance[,] and a few desultory soldierly activities, such as cleaning of ancient guns, went on in the outhouses."[63] The acoustics were terrible, a problem compounded by the thundering noise from the roof when it rained. Nor was the Old Synagogue in Pretoria particularly well suited to juridical purposes. The first synagogue to be constructed in Pretoria, it was "expropriated" by the government in 1952 after the Jewish population migrated to the suburbs and the building fell into disuse. The government converted it into a special Supreme Court intended to be used "for cases relating to the security situation, the activities of the black opposition movements and socialist/communist alliances."[64] Its "appalling" acoustics aside, the Old Synagogue was designed in a style that did little to mitigate the "the hot and airless Pretoria climate."[65] The building's high narrow galleries, ornate columns, and elaborate moldings contrasted markedly with the Drill Hall's modest functionality and informality, and the transfer of venue coincided with a similar change in tone within the trial.[66] However, the chief purpose for the venue change was to deter the boisterous crowds that assembled outside the court. Pretoria is a remote city that is inconvenient to Johannesburg and certainly to the black townships where many of the accused and their supporters lived.

Although the Drill Hall and the Old Synagogue had been converted from military and religious spaces into judicial spaces, they were still ghosted by their former functions. This ghosting, though probably unanticipated or unintended by the state, provides a revealing perspective on the trial. One of the witnesses in the Treason Trial, M. Mkalipe, brought his Bible into the witness box and to the surprise of the judges read eight verses from the book of Daniel. "The names of Shadrack, Meshack and Abednego rang once more in the Old Synagogue," reflects Helen Joseph. "I looked at the three judges, scarlet-robed, sitting there, where once a rabbi stood alone, perhaps reading these very words to his assembled congregation."[67] Mkalipe was perhaps deliberately invoking the history of the Old Synagogue, a religious space distinct from the Calvinist Dutch Reformed roots of the National Party apartheid regime but nevertheless sharing with it the Judeo-Christian tradition. How can we read the symbolic significance of these venues? The use of nonjudicial spaces for the administration of justice may have been merely a pragmatic choice by the government. Given the poor acoustics of both venues, we can at least surmise that the state intended its political trials to be seen but not heard. However, these venues were nevertheless symbolic of the trial's quasi-judicial status; they inhabited a space that was simultaneously inside and outside the law. The state's expropriations of the Drill Hall and the Old Synagogue expressed a profound transition that was occurring in South Africa: the law of the land was expropriating other areas of civil society, including the military and religion, to fulfill white supremacist ambitions.

The turning point of the Treason Trial came not with its venue change but rather with the Sharpeville massacre in March 1960 and the declaration of a state of emergency. After that, the trial switched course: the accused were incarcerated and were often held in isolation. Escalating repression from the security police prevented defense witnesses from testifying without fear of reprisal, and defense attorneys were afraid to communicate with their clients. In his private correspondence, lead advocate Bram Fischer despaired of the restrictions the state of emergency placed on the ability of the defense to bring witnesses to testify:

> Almost every justification of Congress policy and every attack on government policy would constitute a subversive statement. Hence we could never know that any witness could testify without fear. Nor could any witness testify without subjecting himself and his friends to arrest because of an admission of Congress membership or of participation in Congress activity. . . . Who could ever prove that he had been detained because of something said in court and not some other reason?[68]

In the face of legal obstacles, including obstruction of access to their attorneys, the accused took over their own defense.[69] This development infused the proceedings with moments of excitement and exhilaration, for it enabled the accused to turn the courtroom into a platform for their own ideas. "In many ways, these were the glory days for the accused," recalls Nelson Mandela, "for our own people were on the stand fearlessly enunciating ANC policy."[70] Acting as their own counsel, the accused could be assertive and proactive, not merely passive witnesses who had to wait to be asked a question before they could speak. Mandela says, "Our strategy was simple and defensive in nature: to drag out the case until the State of Emergency was lifted and our lawyers could return. . . . In practice, this strategy became rather comical."[71] Since each of the accused was entitled to conduct his or her own defense, each witness called to the stand would be cross-examined by twenty-seven other defendants, the ones remaining from the original 150 who had been charged. "At that rate," Mandela recalls, "we would be at trial until the millennium."[72]

The toll of the trial's length wore on all the defendants, however, with months, then years spent worrying about families, struggling with finances, and being plagued by uncertainty about what was going on outside prison or what course the trial would take or how much longer it might go on. "It's four years ago today since we were arrested at dawn on this charge of high treason," wrote Helen Joseph in her prison diary. "*Four years—and* we are still sitting here."[73] Then abruptly the trial ended in mass acquittals. What began as grand spectacle and high drama ended suddenly with a fizzle. Many first-hand observers resort to theatrical metaphors when describing the atmosphere and tone of the Treason Trial. "The prologue to the drama which began to unfold with mass arrests at dawn, December 5th 1956, has been spectacular," reported Forman and Sachs. "The vast audience watching the stage responded with boos and catcalls for the producers and directors who expected applause."[74] Anthony Sampson, too, sees the Treason Trial as a stage, one that the whole world was watching:

> The opening of the treason trial hearings in Johannesburg raised the curtain, not only on this most extraordinary trial, but on the whole drama of the African opposition and the emergence of a new Africa beneath the old. The group of African politicians in prison, wobbling between the East and the West, between the black world and the white were likely to play a decisive role, not only in the country, but in the continent.[75]

Yet the great clarity of the drama and the attention it garnered somehow "came adrift."[76] By the time the trial ended, the case had "lost all significance on the political scene," according to Hilda Bernstein. "It was a played out drama bearing little relations to the surroundings in which it was enacted."[77]

Was the show trial over or was it just a first act? As we shall see, the Treason Trial was mainly a prologue to a much longer saga, one that would unfold over two more political trials during an epoch of atrocity. One could argue that this story came to an end only with the elections in 1994 and the beginning of the TRC in 1996. But the Treason Trial set the tone for what followed: the state's use of a judicial space to stage a direct encounter with the anti-apartheid movement, its use of the political trial to vanquish the political rally. These dueling spectacles as well as the battle between the state-controlled domains of the archive and the opposition's repertoires of resistance can be seen in many subsequent political trials and indeed in the proceedings of the TRC.

Incitement Trial

Having failed to make its case in the Treason Trial, the South African government tried a new legal strategy in 1962. The Treason Trial had faltered, among other reasons, because of its large scale and vague charges that alleged no single acts of conspiracy or violence.[78] Two years later, when the government charged Nelson Mandela, it did not make the same mistakes. One person alone was accused, and he was charged on two clear counts of which he was clearly guilty: incitement and leaving the country without a passport. Yet in focusing on one person, the government inadvertently created an icon, for this legal battle also focused the energies, frustrations, dreams, and hopes of a multitude of the oppressed onto the person of Mandela, someone whose extraordinary capacities as a leader were only then being discovered.

Just as the state's legal strategy in the Incitement Trial was far more precise and focused than it had been in the Treason Trial, the opposition's approach to this second trial was far more subtle and particular. For nonwhites in South Africa, close attention to physical behavior could be a matter of life and death, and they habitually watched white bosses to "detect the slightest hint of unease: the brushing of the back of the head with the hand in a moment of bewilderment, the fumbling of papers," as Anthony Sampson explains.[79] Nelson Mandela was a particularly astute observer of behavior. When he first entered the courtroom, he "stared at the magistrate, who was transfixed like a mongoose looking at a snake," said ANC counterintelligence operative Wolfie Kodesh. "It took the magistrate two minutes to get his strength back."[80] Mandela paid close attention to the physical expressions of the prosecutor and judge. He noticed that during the proceedings, the magistrate was "diffident and uneasy" and would not look at him directly. Mandela notes in his memoir:

> The other attorneys also seemed embarrassed, and at that moment, I had something of a revelation. These men were not only uncomfortable because I was a colleague brought low, but because I was an ordinary man being punished for my beliefs. In a way I had never quite comprehended before, I realized the role I could play in the court and the possibilities before me as a defendant. I was the symbol of justice in the court of the oppressor, the representative of the great ideals of freedom, fairness and democracy in a society that dishonored those virtues.[81]

Mandela decided to serve as his own counsel, a decision no doubt informed by his experience serving in this same capacity during the Treason Trial. As a lawyer, he knew how to utilize the mechanisms of the courtroom to his advantage. And he understood, through the subtleties of his oppressors' physical behavior, the role in which he could cast himself, not just in the courtroom but also in the drama playing out in the nation and, indeed, on the global stage. "By representing myself I would enhance the symbolism of my role," Mandela realized. "I would use my trial as a showcase for the ANC's moral opposition to racism."[82] Mandela quite deliberately turned the trial into a showcase, a stage, and a political platform.

Mandela also introduced a new technique to his courtroom behavior: unexpected clothing. He already had a reputation as natty dresser, always "immaculately" turned out in western suits he commissioned from the famed tailor Alfred Kahn (see fig. 2.1).[83] At his Incitement Trial, however, he donned instead a Xhosa leopard-skin kaross, signaling a dramatic departure in his self-presentation (see fig. 2.2). He also wore a thick band of yellow and green beads, the colors of the ANC.[84] He entered the defendant's dock, as is the tradition in South Africa, by climbing stairs from the holding cell below. "As he came up, there was a complete hush," said Wolfie Kodesh. "Even the policemen, I honestly think they went pale, to see this huge black man standing there in his national costume."[85] "The kaross electrified the spectators," Mandela later wrote, well aware that his appearance mesmerized the courtroom.[86] His entrance into the Old Synagogue was ghosted by his previous appearance in this same building just two years before, as an article in *New Age,* the leftist newspaper, reminded readers:

> In Pretoria the last time there was such concentrated excitement outside the Old Synagogue converted to a court was when the treason accused were acquitted after four years—Nelson Mandela among them. . . . At 10.20 as Mandela came into the

Figure 2.1. Nelson Mandela, the snappy dresser, at the Treason Trial in 1958. Courtesy of Jurgen Schadeberg, www.jurgen schadeberg.com.

court the crowd of spectators rose to its feet including even the press gallery. Mandela in leopard skin kaross was an impressive, upright figure and his ringing voice dominated the proceedings as he stated the grounds for a remand of the case.[87]

Anthony Sampson, Mandela's biographer, sees his subject's use of costume in this trial in explicitly theatrical terms: "He was now playing a more flamboyant role, using the magistrates' court as his theater."[88] Mandela further explains his sartorial strategy: "I had chosen traditional dress to emphasize the symbolism that I was a black African walking into a white man's court. The kaross was also a sign of contempt for the niceties of white justice. I well knew the authorities

Figure 2.2. Mandela in traditional kaross in the early 1960s. Photograph by Eli Weinberg. Used by permission of UWC-Robben Island Mayibuye Archives.

would feel threatened by my kaross as so many whites feel threatened by the true culture of Africa."[89] As Mandela returned to his cell, a Colonel Jacobs ordered him to hand over his "blanket."[90] Mandela responded in the language of lawyers, informing Colonel Jacobs that he had no jurisdiction over Mandela's attire and that, if necessary, Mandela was prepared to take the matter all the way to the Supreme Court. After this encounter, Mandela was allowed to wear his kaross— but only in court and not while traveling to and from court, for according to newspaper accounts, it would "incite" other prisoners if they saw the traditional garment.[91]

Every day when Mandela appeared in the Old Synagogue, always wearing his kaross, a crowd of 150–200 African supporters gathered in the well of the court, the segregated area for nonwhites. As Mandela entered the courtroom, his supporters stood as one and raised their fists in the air. Mandela intoned the now-famous call of the struggle, "*Amandla!*" (Power!), which elicited from his supporters in the galley the lower-pitched response, "*Ngawethu!*" ("To the people!").[92] In the years between the Treason and Incitement trials, when the ANC switched its policy on the use of violence, the performed repertoire of the anti-apartheid

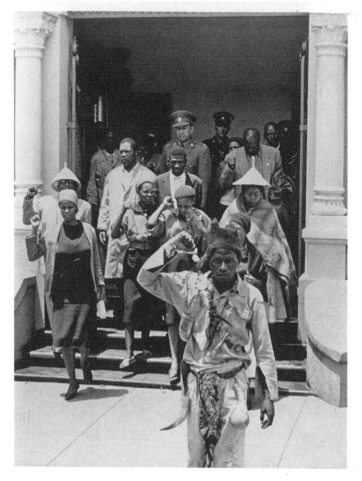

Figure 2.3. The salute among supporters shifted from the thumbs up of the Treason Trial to the more militant fists up during the trials of the 1960s. In the face of severe restrictions on speech, costume became a strategy of communication. Used by permission of UWC-Robben Island Mayibuye Archives.

crowds apparently changed. Whereas the crowds at trials formerly gave a thumbs-up salute, by the time of the Incitement and Rivonia trials they raised their fists in the air (see fig. 2.3). Whereas formerly they had shouted *"Afrika! Mayibuye!"* ("Africa! Come Back!"), they now chanted *"Amandla! Ngawethu!"* ("Power! To the People!").

Mandela was not alone in wearing African costume. On the first day of the proceedings his wife Winnie wore clothing typical of Thembu royalty: a beaded headdress and an ankle-length skirt, which the opposition press described as "regal."[93] In an attempt to legislate the realm of performance, an arena of behavior

Figure 2.4. Protestor outside the court wearing traditional clothing. Notice the Mandela button on her chest, an image that was against the law. Used by permission of UWC-Robben Island Mayibuye Archives.

that as we shall later see the apartheid government seemed impotent to control, the minister of justice served Winnie notice that she would be barred from court if she appeared again wearing "native" dress.[94] Afterward, like a chameleon, Winnie changed her attire each day, often wearing clothing that Nelson had brought back from his travels, including the national dress of Ethiopia, a yellow Indian sari, the black skirt and blouse of the anti-apartheid Women's Federation, or a Dior-style skirt with white cap.[95] The thousands of African supporters who turned out at the Old Synagogue also wore a range of traditional African clothing, as photographs published in local newspapers amply document (see fig. 2.4).[96]

Wearing traditional African clothing was an unusual step for Mandela and for the African National Congress, which was firmly committed to a policy of nonracialism. This strategy originated from the ANC's founding days, when "tribal jealousies" and bitter grievances over the past among various South African ethnic groups were put aside for the larger cause of fighting white domination.[97] Anthony Sampson writes of the Bloemfontein Conference of 1912, at which the ANC was founded:

> It was the first time, not only in South Africa but in the whole continent, that African tribes had dropped their traditional loyalties to form a common nation of black people. It was, in fact, the birth of African nationalism: not in the sense of militancy

Justice in Transition 49

or chauvinism, for the new Congress was obsessed by the need for moderation, white friendships and constitutional methods; but in the sense of a common nationhood of Africans distinguished not by tribes but by race.[98]

By donning traditional clothing, Nelson Mandela and his supporters may have seemed to be putting emphasis on ethnic specificity and departing from the long-standing ANC policy of nonracialism. Winnie Madikizela-Mandela's use of Xhosa clothing, in which she began appearing publicly before the Incitement Trial (as a photograph taken on Afrika Day and printed in the opposition newspaper *New Age* in April 1962 attests), provoked consternation in at least one observer.[99] Paul Mathabe wrote in a letter to *New Age*:

> I think that this tribal dressing is turning the struggle into a Xhosa struggle. To the onlooker and the one who mixes with the crowds, [the] Congress struggle is being relegated to the Xhosa tribe. Now that is defeating the very aim and efforts of the leaders. We have heard remarks made by enemies of the struggle that Mandela was a Xhosa, Sisulu was a Xhosa, Nokwe was a Xhosa, Xuma was a Xhosa, and the predominant tribal dress was Xhosa. . . . Traditional dress and items should be left to the Theatre and stage, the preservers of culture.[100]

In his autobiography Mandela explains that he wore the kaross to impress upon the court the "true culture of Africa," thus stressing a continent-wide sense of authenticity rather than an ethnic particularity such as his Xhosa identity or, more specifically, that of his clan. It is likely that most white observers in the courtroom saw his clothing as representing a nonspecific African "otherness," one that stood in contrast to European identity. Yet Mandela also knew that his kaross would be seen and interpreted by many people who *would* notice its ethnic particularity and that such an emphasis on ethnicity was likely to raise precisely the objections Paul Mathabe voiced. So while Mandela has written that he wore the kaross to show that he was a "black man in a white man's court," it would seem that the clothing was also signifying that he was an *African* man in a European court, an *indigenous* person in an imported forum, and a *Xhosa* man— and royalty at that—forced to operate within a British-derived legal structure.

So what were Mandela and his supporters trying to tell ANC members through this particular use of clothing at the Incitement Trial? Mandela may have been influenced by his recent trip to other African countries where an emphasis on African nativism was central to the anticolonial struggle. Yet I think this is unlikely, as Mandela returned from his travels convinced that "South Africa is different to all the countries of Africa . . . because our population is different, and the whole structure of the country is different. Economically and politically in every way."[101] Mandela's commitment to nonracialism remained as strong as ever. Mandela may have been influenced by the recent popularity of the rival South African opposition party, the Pan Africanist Congress (PAC), which did not share the ANC's policy of nonracialism. Perhaps this was a gambit to try to lure some PAC followers to the ANC. But this also seems unlikely. The most plausible explanation can I think be found on three fronts. First, Mandela's choice of clothing in the courtroom was intended very deliberately to stand in relationship to the rhetorical thrust of his words, especially his speeches during this trial, as I shall explain below. Second, this clothing was consistent with the rhetorical strategies often used by the opposition during the political trials of this era to invert apartheid's reasoning. In this case, the apartheid state made great hay over ethnic differences, using such divisions as a way to divide and conquer the nonwhite population through such policies as separate homelands. Using a "native" costume called the apartheid state's bluff, in a sense. How could it prohibit what it in fact seemed to embrace: so-called natives behaving in native ways?

Finally, this use of traditional clothing was a tactic that allowed both Mandela and his supporters to circumvent stringent press regulations that severely restricted what local newspapers could print about the trial and banned altogether public rallies in Mandela's name. In order to suppress public demonstrations at trials, the government decided just before the start of Mandela's 1962 Incitement Trial to ban all meetings relating to Nelson Mandela and to add his name to a list of 102 persons whose statements could not be published. Minister of Justice B. J. Vorster, using the classically performative phrase "I prohibit," authorized legislation just two days before the commencement of the Incitement Trial that ensured that there would be no publication of Mandela's words in the South African newspapers.[102] As a result, journalists were sometimes awkwardly forced to write "what Mandela said here cannot be reported."[103] A "Free Mandela" campaign mobilized supporters by means of pamphleteering, graffiti paintings on the streets, and silent poster demonstrations outside the Durban City Hall and the Pretoria Union building.[104] Yet this resistance via text was forbidden: members of the Special Branch wrote down the names of those taking part. Likewise there could be no gatherings in Mandela's name, a "gathering" being defined as "two or more people coming together for a common purpose."[105] However, the performative dimensions of the hearing—the songs, fashions, gestures, and actions of Mandela and his supporters could be freely reported, and they were, lavishly, with many pictures. And a crowd gathered wearing traditional dress could not necessarily be labeled a political gathering. They were just "tribes" being their native selves. Supporters of Mandela thus circumvented the restrictions by means of performance. Clothing seems to have been a chief strategy of resistance by Mandela's supporters, but song continued to play an important role. At the close of trial, the throng of supporters left the court singing "Nkosi Sikelel i'Africa," a song that was to become the national anthem of the new democratic South Africa three decades later. And they marched up the street singing "Tshotsholoza Mandela" ("Carry on Mandela") in flagrant disregard of the government's ban on public demonstrations for Mandela.[106]

Mandela's approach to his courtroom appearances during the Incitement Trial succeeded in two ways: visual appearance through costume and verbal impact through the spoken word. By serving as his own counsel, Mandela secured a venue in which to deliver a political speech unimpeded and uninterrupted at an extremely high-profile public gathering—the trial. Mandela gave a lengthy plea of mitigation during the Incitement Trial, an hour-long speech that explained who he was and why he had done what he had done. During the subsequent Rivonia Trial, Mandela chose not to take the witness stand at all but rather to deliver a speech from the dock. Under South African law, a defendant can make such a statement without cross-examination. The testimony carries less legal weight, but Mandela had no intention of fighting the case legally. Instead he manipulated the courtroom, transforming it into platform for communicating with his followers to whom he could not otherwise speak. Mandela followed the strategy of using his trials as "a continuation of the struggle by other means,"[107] and his speeches at the Incitement Trial and the Rivonia Trial implicitly and ingeniously raised a question: Were not these political trials themselves a public gathering in his name?

The text of Mandela's speeches from the Incitement Trial deserves careful analysis, and it is fortunate that such an analysis has been provided by Jacques Derrida.[108] Derrida contends that Mandela used admiration as a force of persuasion. "He becomes admirable for having, with all his force, admired, and for having made a force of his admiration, a combative, untreatable, and irreducible power."[109] In a famous oration that became known as the "Black Man in a White Man's Court" speech, Mandela stated that he admired the principles inaugurated by the Magna Charta, the Universal Declaration of Human Rights, parliamentary democracy, the doctrine of the separation of powers, and the independence of the judiciary. In short, he admired the intellectual, legal, and political principles central to western society, principles and traditions that the South African state in fact claimed to inherit. Using painstakingly careful logic, incisive legal reasoning, and his characteristically measured voice, Mandela cogently demonstrated that the most recent South African constitution, that of 1961, was in fact an inversion, or perversion, of its imported model. "A terrifying dissymmetry," Derrida called it. Mandela told the courtroom he admired the law, was devoted to the law, and was a man of the law—even if he had had to oppose certain specific laws in order to defend the law. "Taking as his witness humanity as a whole," Derrida writes, Mandela addressed himself to the "universal justice above his judges of one day only."[110] Thus Mandela also used inversion: his apparent contempt for the law, he argued, signified his supreme respect for it. In his brilliant analysis of Mandela's speech, Derrida takes no particular notice of Mandela's clothing. However, if we consider the kaross a meaningful rhetorical strategy, one intended to function in tandem with the spoken word, we can see yet another inversion performed by Mandela. His "native" African costume signified a radical otherness before the western law he professed to admire, yet his words—their content, logic, and refined manner of delivery—demonstrated that he was, in fact, a more legitimate heir to the western traditions of the law than were the white judges in their flowing robes who sat before him.

The Rivonia Trial

At the end of the Incitement Trial, Mandela was found guilty and sentenced to five years in jail. However, before he had served his full sentence, he was once again pulled into court, once again in Pretoria. This third trial of

Nelson Mandela was held in the Palace of Justice rather than in a converted judicial outpost like the Drill Hall or the Old Synagogue. Mandela was charged along with eleven others with sabotage in a case known by the name Rivonia, referring to a farm outside of Johannesburg where the arrests had taken place and the alleged sabotage had been planned. The atmosphere at the Rivonia Trial was sober and restrained. The repertoires of resistance available to the accused were far more circumscribed than they had been in any previous trial. The accused were charged with over 200 acts of sabotage "aimed at promoting guerrilla warfare and armed invasion," and this time, unlike in the Treason Trial, they were in fact guilty as charged.[111] The punishment for such crimes was the death penalty, and the very real threat of the gallows cast a pall over the proceedings.

In terms of theatrical genres, the Treason Trial could be characterized as a farce with an enormous cast that lasted too long. The Incitement Trial was a more realistic drama with a single protagonist and a style subtle enough to depict intricacies of expression, gestures, eye contact, clothing, and precise dialogue. The audience came more clearly into view in the Incitement Trial as two halves of the segregated courtroom became the chorus that Mandela addressed. In both trials, there was an acute sense of the audience outside the courtroom: in the Treason Trial, it was the masses standing at the door of the Drill Hall; in the Incitement Trial, it was the growing international attention the trial was garnering in the world at large. The Rivonia Trial represented a progression as global spectatorship became even more intense and the range of performative repertoires available to both spectators and the accused narrowed significantly. If the Treason Trial was a farce and the Incitement Trial a realistic drama, then the Rivonia Trial could perhaps be most closely compared to an ancient tragedy, as even the *Rand Daily Mail* seemed to recognize: "The case has captured the imagination because it seems to tell a classic, ancient story of the struggle of men for freedom and dignity, with overtones of Grecian tragedy in their failure."[112]

At the Rivonia Trial, the crowd was once again a factor. It descended upon the Palace of Justice daily, despite police use of force and intimidation: they demanded passbooks and took surveillance photographs. By 1963 the state seemed to have become more astute in its attempts to control the dramaturgy of the trial. A special dock was constructed to change the physical layout of the courtroom so the accused had to sit with their backs to the audience. The dock had been made with sufficient room that each defendant could be guarded by two private warders, "sitting like footmen in attendance."[113] Mandela's first appearance in court contrasted markedly with the proud robust figure in a royal African kaross last seen at the Incitement Trial. As Mandela entered the courtroom, fellow accused Dennis Goldberg recalls:

> He was in leg irons and handcuffs, wearing sandals, no socks, short trousers, a jacket that looked like a house boy's jacket. Now, you know, to put a man into the dock like that is to create an immediate prejudice. He was usually so elegant, such a snappy dresser, and they set out to humiliate him in his clothes, but he held himself so ramrod straight, so dignified. He had lost an enormous amount of weight in prison.[114]

Yet the black audience sitting in their segregated area of the courtroom was not deterred. "There was a ripple of excitement amongst the public" at the first sight of Mandela.[115] He faced the spectators, raised his clenched fist, and shouted "*Amandla!*" which immediately elicited a chorus of "*Ngawethu.*"[116] The courtroom was packed with officers and security guards and Security Branch policemen, sitting in the benches and guarding every door. They were completely surprised and incapacitated by this verbal outburst from the accused and their supporters. "None of this vast army," advocate Joel Joffe recalls, "was fast enough on their feet to cope with this unexpected demonstration."[117] But shortly thereafter, a new procedure was instituted for the start of each court date. The judge was brought in before the accused, hence putting an end to struggle salutations.[118]

The arena in which the accused might practice their repertoires of resistance was becoming more and more tightly circumscribed. Mandela's primary strategy at the Rivonia Trial was to speak very little until one appointed moment. Unlike at the Treason and Incitement trials, he did not serve as his own counsel. In addition, he refused to give testimony or submit to cross-examination. Instead, he exercised his right to give a speech from the dock, a ploy that enabled him to circumvent the state's draconian and ever-escalating repression of speech. Mandela inaugurated a tradition at South African political trials, as speeches from the dock thereafter became a tactic replicated by many other political prisoners.[119] "The courtroom is often the last forum in which freedom fighters speak out against tyranny and justify their actions not only to the judge but also their fellow citizens and the world at large," says advocate George Bizos, who made a career of defending political prisoners, including the Rivonia accused.[120]

Although a speech from the dock may have been one of Mandela's only means of exercising the repertoire of resistance at this trial, he exploited the possibilities of this speech to their maximum potential. And the impact of his speech was enhanced by the superior acoustics of the Palace of Justice compared with previous trial venues. Also audible was the profound silence of everyone else. "It was amazing to sit through Mandela's speech," recalls advocate Joffe. "There was tremendous silence in the courtroom when he stood and he spoke for a long time, around five hours. He went to the dock ready to die."[121] Mandela had handwritten his speech and conferred with compatriots about its content. His delivery was slow, in a "flat even voice," according to Joffe, which contrasted markedly with the tone prosecutor Percy Yutar usually adopted in the Rivonia proceedings. Yutar is reported to have squeaked, whined, and crackled his way through the Rivonia trial, often resorting to the falsetto registers. Mandela was, in contrast, calm, unwavering, and steady, the antithesis of a hot-headed radical revolutionary. "At no stage did he raise his voice very much, or change from the slow, measured speech with which he had started," says Joffe. "His voice carried clearly across the court. Gradually as he spoke the silence became more and more profound, till it seemed that no one in the court dared move or breathe."[122]

Mandela's statement from the dock is legendary. He spoke for four and one-half hours. The text of the speech is widely available, and legal scholar James Boyd White, among others, has provided incisive analysis of its content.[123] My focus here is rather on the reception of the speech, the audience's silence, especially during the final lines. Mandela concluded by saying the now-famous words: "During my lifetime I have dedicated myself to the struggle of the African people. I have fought against white domination, and I have fought against black domination. I have cherished the ideal of a democratic and free society in which all persons live together in harmony and with equal opportunity."[124] At this moment, Joffe remembers, Mandela paused, a long pause, in which one could "hear a pin drop in the court," and then he looked squarely at the judge as he finished:

> "It is an ideal which I hope to live for and to achieve."
> Then dropping his voice, very low, he added:
> "But if needs be it is an ideal for which I am prepared to die."
> He sat down in a moment of profound silence, the kind of silence that I remember only in climactic moments in the theatre before the applause thunders out. Here in the court there was no applause. He had spoken for five hours and for perhaps thirty seconds there was silence. From the public benches one could hear people release their breath with a deep sigh as the moment of tension passed. Some women in the gallery burst into tears.[125]

Dennis Goldberg describes the moment: "It was terribly moving. Nobody said anything. Even the judge didn't know what to say. I knew it was a moment of history. He emerged then as a great leader."[126] Throughout the political trials of the late 1950s and early 1960s, the opposition leaders and supporters had deployed a tremendous range of repertoires of resistance. Yet this particular speech and the silences in and around this speech proved the most classically theatrical and performative moment of all. Not only was the speech dramatic, it did things, it changed the political landscape profoundly. With this speech, Mandela became a singular personification of the anti-apartheid struggle, even as he physically disappeared from public view for the next twenty-five years.

Mandela's noncompliance with expected protocol and his masterful manipulation of South Africa's legal procedures transformed the courtroom into a media event and, more important, into a trial not of himself or of the ANC but of the racist apartheid government. If, as Mandela argued in the Rivonia case, the trial was a show trial, then the state (and not its so-called saboteurs) was the show. Mandela and his followers contested apartheid and its agents through performance; through performed behaviors, songs, chants, and clothing; and through rhetorically effective speech acts that profoundly affected those who were present in the courtroom and even more profoundly transformed audiences outside the courtroom, who heard reports of the speeches or read clandestinely published pamphlets that reproduced his words. In the townships, people even re-performed his speech by reciting it out loud.[127] Mandela's trial speeches—especially their touchstone phrases such as "black man in a white man's court" from the Incitement Trial and "I am prepared to die" from the Rivonia Trail—reverberated throughout the world and throughout history. His declaration of his willingness to accept the death penalty for the sake of the ideal of a free and democratic society is one of the most famous phrases of the twentieth century. Mandela not only articulated an ideal of a democratic and free society but he actually played a central role in bringing such a society into being. His speeches in these courtrooms were performatives in the Austinian sense.[128] Mandela "did things"—big things—with words. His speeches were extraordinary inasmuch as the words articulated a new constitutional order, one that had yet to come into being.

Conclusion

While the apartheid government demonstrated breathtaking persistence in circumscribing speech, it seemed incapacitated by the challenge of trying to legislate control of song and gesture at political trials. Minister of Justice J. Kruger complained about political trials to Parliament in 1978:

> The accused . . . enter the hall singing and with clenched fists, take up their places in the dock and, standing, turn to the audience, whereupon all of them—accused and audience—then sing inflammatory songs. Brief speeches are also made. . . . When the hearing is adjourned, the accused and the audience all leave the court-room singing, and the entire procedure is repeated with every adjournment and resumption of the trial. The supporters frequently continue their activities outside the court building and in the adjoining streets. To accompany the singing and the clenched-fist salutes, there is dancing, slogans are shouted and posters are displayed for the express purpose of attracting the attention of the Press, film and television photographers.[129]

Kruger's complaint came in the wake of the Stephen Biko inquest and a full fourteen years after Mandela was put in prison for life. As minister of justice, Kruger was one of the most powerful figures in South Africa. His comments reveal not only the impotence of the government to control performed repertoires of resistance but also the extent to which the political trials of the late 1950s and early 1960s set a precedent. Those trials essentially defined the "genre" of the political trial in apartheid South Africa and, in turn, profoundly shaped the type of transitional justice that South Africa embraced as, moving out of apartheid into democracy, it created the Truth and Reconciliation Commission.

While the apartheid regime found songs, gestures, and dance (both in and out of the courtroom) to be uncontrollable, even more striking is how political trials sanctioned revolutionary speeches, the content of which would otherwise have been banned, suppressed, and confiscated. As Oliver Tambo notes, "By 1960 virtually every African leader was muzzled and restricted by Government decree."[130] Yet political trials proved the last outpost of unfettered speech, the final and most potent platform on which Mandela and many freedom fighters who stood trial after him found an opportunity to articulate publicly their objectives and rationale.[131]

If we accept that the TRC inherited the performance genealogy of South African political trials, it is not at all puzzling that on the occasion when TRC chairperson Desmond Tutu publicly presented the truth commission's final report to President Nelson Mandela in 1998, "the two elderly statesmen started to dance—in exultation and celebration."[132] Rhetorician Philippe-Joseph Salazar, noting that this dancing "seemed out of place, out of beat with the dignity of the occasion," speculated that the dance by Mandela and Tutu was a symbolic rebuttal of the "deadly toyi-toyi dance, often performed at mass killings . . . as a tool for gross human rights abuses on the part of the liberation movements themselves."[133] Yet the dance has far greater significance than a rebuttal or inversion of the *toyi-toyi*. Dancing at the formal presentation of the TRC's final report was entirely in keeping with the repertoires of resistance that had been enacted within the courtrooms of South Africa for decades.

At the trials of Nelson Mandela, the inquest of Steve Biko, and countless other political trials in the history of the resistance movement, dance was central to the judicial encounter between the political opposition and the apartheid state. This is why Minister of Justice Jimmy Kruger complained in 1978 that dancing, clenched-fist salutes, and the singing of inflammatory songs had become standard fare at political trials. Song, gesture, and dance were core elements of the repertoire of resistance, both inside and outside courtrooms. While it is true that one dance, the *toyi-toyi*, became quite prominent in the 1980s and its history is connected to black-on-black violence within the townships, Tutu and Mandela's dancing at the presentation of the TRC summary report was about much more than dancing as a prelude to violence in the townships. This celebratory dance at the conclusion of a quasi-judicial proceeding was a continuation of a decades-long tradition of dance in and in front of judicial spaces at political trials. Dance was an enduring accompaniment to trials within the liberation struggle.

The trials of 1956–1964 that I have examined here mark the beginning of a violent militarized epoch of South African history, a period that lasted for over three decades, concluding with the first democratic elections in 1994 and the formation of the Truth and Reconciliation Commission shortly thereafter. These early political trials and the TRC were highly visible public rituals. They each served a legitimizing function for a new nation-state—for the Union of South Africa that was declared in 1961 and for the democracy of South Africa that was voted into power in 1994. During his trials of the 1960s, Mandela acted on the assumption that a compelling performance could overcome and overthrow unjust laws. Though it took many decades, these changes did in fact happen.

That both the Treason Trial and the Truth and Reconciliation Commission coincided with the writing of a new constitution (in 1960 and 1994) is expressive of how deeply transitional both periods were. Constitutions bring a state into being through what Jacques Derrida calls "properly performative" acts, iterations that must "produce (proclaim) what in the form of a constative act it merely claims, declares, assures it is describing."[134] Examining the TRC within the frame of the early political trials illustrates that during times of political transition, constitutions in and of themselves may not be performative enough. During both transitions, a convergence of performance and the law was necessary—performance not just in the sense defined by the speech-act theory of J. L. Austin but rather performance in all of its physical expressiveness, including reenactments, singing, tone of voice, and subtle expressions of physicality. The Truth and Reconciliation Commission and the political trials of 1956–1964 repeatedly—and in all their operations, public hearings, and textual reports—made manifest the values and assumptions of a new political dispensation. The public and juridical events that transpired in the Drill Hall, the Old Synagogue, and the high court and (in the case of the TRC) the quasi-judicial series of events that took place in town halls, churches, and schools throughout the country provided physicalized visible signs of the inward character and identity of a newly constituted state.

"Why was this abortive trial ever staged?" Helen Joseph, one of the accused, asked of the Treason Trial. "Why was it pursued so relentlessly until almost the very end, when the Court itself brought the proceedings to a close? Why were the arrests carried out in such a dramatic, spectacular fashion?"[135] One might ask similar questions of the Truth and Reconciliation Commission: Why was the political transition from apartheid to democracy enacted so publicly on stages, in town halls and churches, in front of live audiences and television cameras? Why were live hearings broadcast so extensively to the citizenry? Why did spectators at the hearings participate so vocally and viscerally?

South Africa's Truth and Reconciliation Commission was unprecedented in many regards: it was the first truth commission in the genre's history of more than thirty years to offer conditional amnesty and the first to embrace public hearings as a defining feature. Within South Africa, the Truth and Reconciliation Commission is often perceived as an import from abroad. Yet the TRC can be productively considered as sharing a genealogy of performance that is as beholden to South African political trials as it is to international transitional justice models.[136] The TRC's performance genealogy can be traced to the Treason, Incitement, and Rivonia trials, during which the South African state tried to enforce the ever-expanding powers of the white minority and justify its increasing erosion of the powers and rights of the African majority. In high-profile political trials, the state met its opposition head on before an audience of witnesses that was both national and international. Anti-apartheid defendants used the courtroom performatively to resist and to offer a counterdiscourse that included the principles of the Freedom Charter, a constitutional speech act that in the mid-1950s could only implement the future perfect tense, a speech act that remained infelicitous for decades to come.[137]

One should be clear: the political trials of 1956–1964 were conducted in courts of law and the TRC was not. Further, it would be misguided to suggest equivalence between a truth commission sponsored by a nonracial and democratically elected government and political show trials promulgated by a racist and authoritarian regime. But if one accepts Mandela's contention that the law of South Africa by which he was tried in the early 1960s was at odds with the Universal Declaration of Human Rights (a document that, interestingly, was admitted by the Crown as part of its evidence against the ANC in the Treason Trial), we can see that these political trials—like the TRC—put the issue of human rights at center stage.[138] The second issue at center stage was the fate of the South African state, which in 1961 had recently departed from the British Commonwealth and had been newly constituted as an independent nation. By putting anti-apartheid leaders in the dock in highly publicized trials, the government inadvertently put South Africa itself on trial in the court of public opinion. British and African newspapers, including Ghana's *Daily Graphic,* discerned clearly that South Africa was on trial at these proceedings.[139] The British *Daily Telegraph* reported that the Rivonia trial was not the end but "rather the beginning of debate on the larger moral issue. It is the law itself that the South African Government has to justify at the bar of the civilized world."[140] South Africa stood at that bar of public opinion for decades, and it was only through the perceived success of the Truth and Reconciliation Commission that the case finally concluded. Final judgment was neither acquittal nor conviction but rather a complex, uneven, often impenetrable report. The unwieldiness of the TRC's final report and its neglected status as a document of the commission suggest that perhaps the report's conclusions and recommendations were not really the "point" of the proceedings. But if the commission's analysis and conclusions were not the point, what was? The answer to that question, I believe, lies in the power of performance itself—in its ability to captivate and persuade an audience; its ephemeral nature enacted very much in the present tense; its agon between opposing sides; its ability to produce empathy and identification as well as terror, pity, and fear among spectators; its human scale, and finally in its ambiguity, simultancity, and layering of meanings.

Just as the TRC bears the imprint of the many truth commissions that preceded it (and of the Nuremburg and Tokyo trials before them), it also inherits a genealogy of performance from important South African political trials. In examining the Treason, Incitement, and Rivonia trials, I have focused on three aspects that I believe have great relevance to our understanding and interpretation of the Truth and Reconciliation Commission: 1) the opposition movement's cultivation of repertoires of resistance and how these became codified and internationally recognizable; 2) moments when the archive and the repertoire explicitly converged and the implications of this convergence for our interpretation of the TRC; and 3) how political trials facilitated a complex process of surrogation, mediating the relationship between particular iconic figures and the masses.[141] While in the Treason Trial 156 people represented the opposition movement, by the time that the Rivonia Trial concluded, one person, Nelson Mandela, had come to stand in for the disenfranchised millions. Over thirty years later, the Truth and Reconciliation Commission attempted to profoundly reconfigure this surrogation though its public hearings. In the TRC, formerly disenfranchised masses (whom Chairperson Tutu called without irony the "little people") would represent themselves as well as the millions of others whose human rights were violated in both "gross" and minor ways.

Activist Joe Slovo has characterized the judicial confrontations of the 1950s and early 1960s as happening on a "gentlemanly" terrain: "There was still a rule of law. You had a fair trial in their courts. Nobody could be kept in isolation. Up to 1963 I know of no incident of any political prisoner being tortured. The whole legal structure which existed lulled us into feeling that we could do much more than we eventually discovered we could."[142] After Sharpeville and Rivonia, everything changed. In the words of George Bizos, "The acquittal of the political leaders at the end of the Treason Trial in 1961 probably marked the end of the administration of justice in accordance with generally accepted procedural safeguards, such as habeas corpus."[143] In 1963, the government imposed a law authorizing 90-day detention without trial, which was later amended to 180 days. Finally, in 1967, with the authorization of Section 6 of the Terrorism Act, the police acquired the right to detain suspects for an indefinite period without any trial at all, thus effectively shutting down the courtroom as a primary stage for the state's enactment of power.

The first reported death in detention was that of Looksmart Solwandle Ngudle, a man in good health at the time of his arrest who was found dead in his cell some forty days later on 5 September 1963. Thereafter, torture became the new staging ground for confrontation between the archive and the repertoire, between the document and the body. Unlike trials, these confrontations took place behind closed doors, with no rules and with virtually no witnesses beyond the police and prison warders and the victims themselves. Along with torture behind closed doors, inquests into the growing number of deaths during detention also replaced trials as a key nodal point, a public site of contestation. Under South African law, an inquest must be held for any unnatural death.[144] The record of Looksmart Ngudle's inquest is chilling, hauntingly evocative of hundreds of stories heard over thirty years later during the proceedings of the Truth and Reconciliation Commission. Mrs. Maria Ngudle testified at the inquest about how she went searching for her son:

> I was shown the prison in Pretoria by some people. I said to the African policeman, "I have come for Looksmart's funeral." The policeman took down my name. He asked me if Looksmart was sentenced to death. I said I did not know. I only knew he was arrested. The policeman said he would go and look. He came back. "We have buried him already because we can't keep a dead person. How can we help you?" I said, "I want his clothes." He said there were none.[145]

The policeman then sent her to another prison where she asked the same questions, and those authorities, in turn, sent her back to the first prison, where she saw the same black policeman, who then sent her upstairs to see a white policeman. Mrs. Ngudle recalled, "I felt they were playing me for the fool. I went home. I could not find out what the cause of death was."[146]

Mrs. Ngudle's story is emblematic of many stories heard later by the TRC: her frantic and frustrating search from place to place, lack of immediate access to legal counsel, forthright demands for the clothes of her dead son, and determined quest to find the cause of death. Also typical was the state's delay in providing information, the hasty burial of the body, the evasion of the police, the delayed and then abruptly scheduled inquest, the coercion of Mrs. Ngudle to sign a statement State Security had crafted, and the sudden banning of the deceased so that even his name could not be published in the newspapers.[147] "Dead Man Banned" was all the Johannesburg evening newspapers could say.[148] Fellow prisoners of the banned person were likewise banned, which meant they could make no public statements or be quoted, so witnesses to the treatment of Ngudle by the police during his detention could not testify in court. Attorneys for the Ngudle family withdrew at the beginning of the inquest because, they said, the banning orders meant that many potential witnesses, including fellow prisoners, could not testify without fear of prosecution.

But at the Ngudle inquest the state had not yet refined either its techniques of torture in isolation (to ensure that there were no witnesses) or the rules of engagement for inquests. At the start of the inquest, Minister of Justice Vorster made a series of rulings he may have come to regret. He determined that a court was a privileged forum, that courts could hear statements by banned persons, and that an inquest proceeding was a court. Therefore, banned persons could testify at an inquest without fear of reprisal. "Suddenly the stillness enveloping the fate of the detained in their cells was broken," recalls Ruth First, an anti-apartheid activist and scholar who was eventually assassinated by a parcel bomb. "The bush telegraph in the jails began to work."[149] Fellow prisoners came forward at Ngudle's inquest, and their tales provided evidence of a widespread pattern of police interrogation by means of torture. Fellow detainee Isaac Tlale testified of his ordeal:

> "I was handcuffed. There were two chairs joined together. I was to sit on those two chairs. I was sitting this way . . ." Tlale indicated how he had sat, with his knees up, his arms wrapped around them. "My hands were handcuffed," he continued, "and in between my knees they inserted a broom handle."[150]

The police inserted the broom handle above his arms and below his knees, so that he was immobilized. They covered his head with a bag and subjected him to electric shocks while they hounded him to make a confession. When more evidence of police torture was heard from other detainees, the state prosecutor finally objected, saying that evidence of the conditions and treatment of other detainees was "irrelevant." The court agreed and declared such evidence inadmissible.[151] The final verdict was that Looksmart Ngudle had committed suicide and that his death was not caused by "any act or omission involving or amounting to an offence on the part of any person."[152] In other words, "no one was to blame," a refrain that families of deceased prisoners and their advocates such as George Bizos were to hear repeatedly for decades to come.[153]

What one sees in the Treason, Incitement, and Rivonia trials is the way law courts became highly theatrical spaces for public acknowledgement of the changes sweeping the country. As the few liberties blacks had were gradually being eroded, including any rights to free speech, the courtrooms became, ironically, spaces that put into the public record the voices, speeches, and perspectives of the opposition. Trials also made visible the direct confrontation between the powerful and the powerless. These were theatres of power. But as the state of emergency went into effect after the Sharpeville massacre, blacks' limited freedoms of speech were ever more tightly circumscribed, even in the courtroom. Protesters who flocked to the courtroom to support Mandela and others could not speak his name, so they resorted to nonverbal means of communication: posters, buttons, costumes, gestures, and song. The opposition's expressive culture was forced into the nonverbal domains of performance.

As the 1960s wore on, the state's methods became more clandestine, calculated to avoid the theatrical and highly public encounters staged by political trials. The number of days the state could detain prisoners without trial kept increasing and the state's methods of oppressing those detained were concealed in prison cells and torture chambers, leaving little documentation except damaged bodies. The primary stage of encounter between the opposition and the state was not in the public space of the trial but in inquests, where the prisoner could no longer speak but where his body could provide testimony through forensic evidence.

Theatricality and performance must be central to our analysis of justice during periods of regime change and political transition. Who would have predicted, for instance, that the Treason Trial, which seemed to be a calculated "attempt to silence and outlaw the ideas held by the accused and the thousands whom they represent," to quote defense advocate Berrangé, would in fact document for the first time the history of the anti-apartheid struggle? "The unwritten history of the struggle for freedom has gone into the record of this trial," Helen Joseph wrote, adding, "It's a macabre university in which we study, facing a capital charge."[154] But then, who would have predicted that in 1996 a marathon state-sponsored public airing of a nation's past atrocities—its systematic killings, tortures, lynchings, and daily violations of human rights committed over three decades—would be expected to lead, of all things, to reconciliation? The paradoxes of justice during times of political transition are indeed many, and these paradoxes are often most vividly perceived when the archive and the repertoire converge.

3. Witnessing and Interpreting Testimony: Live, Present, Public, and Speaking in Many Tongues

> We had come on legal business to consult the accused. But it was clear that they were in no mood for consultation. They were rediscovering, it seemed to us, the joys of speech, not unlike people who had been dumb and had suddenly had the power of speech restored to them. They were miraculously wondering at the joy of it, turning it over on their tongues, feeling the savour of it on their lips; they were drunk with speech, with human communication and contact, with being able to talk, to meet with and touch other people, too involved in all these new sensations, too intoxicated with them to be prepared to consider serious problems of the law.
>
> —Joel Joffe on the Rivonia Trial

> We were told to keep it as brief as possible and only focus on the major points . . . we had to get the facts, but people wanted to tell their story in broad terms.
>
> —Thabiso Mohasoa, TRC statement-taker

The two quotations that launch this chapter contrast experiences of speech in two radically different moments in South African history, moments that are themselves bookends of the TRC's historical mandate. Joel Joffe was speaking of the day the accused in the Rivonia Trial of the early 1960s emerged from their cells to prepare for the upcoming trial. The eleven prisoners—among them Walter Sisulu, Govan Mbeki, Ahmed Kathrada, Dennis Goldberg, and Nelson Mandela—had been held in solitary confinement for months. Imprisonment did not technically deprive them of speech, but isolation deprived them of listeners. The charges against them were grave, the case was complex, and there was much to discuss, far more than could be addressed in the limited time they had. Yet for the prisoners, the privilege of speech and human contact was savored not so much for the restored ability to communicate information as it was for the embodied experience of witnessed speech—their spoken words finally had listeners, recipients who could acknowledge and react.

The Truth and Reconciliation Commission of the 1990s was designed to restore voice, to give people who had often suffered in isolation an opportunity to publicly articulate their experiences through embodied, face-to-face encounters with audiences who listened, heard, and acknowledged. Those who came forward to give statements often wanted to do so in particular ways, with narratives that sometimes meandered or took elaborate, idiosyncratic forms. Yet the commission's procedures for taking statements and for public hearings constrained speech. As statement-taker Thabiso Mohasoa says in the epigraph above, TRC witnesses told their stories in broad terms, yet the commission required testimony to be brief and to the point. Witnesses who were chosen to appear before the HRVC hearings could use their allotted time to speak as they liked, but their speech was constrained by time (generally thirty minutes) as well as by the precedents, tone, and decorum of the hearing format. (For a fuller explanation of the statement-taking process and the types of truth valued by the TRC, see the Afterword to this volume).

In this chapter and the next, I examine how individuals expressed themselves through the Truth and Reconciliation Commission process and how the highly public and mediated nature of the proceedings shaped what kinds of speech and witnessing were possible. The protocols, procedures, and means of publishing the hearings tightly managed both speaking and listening, giving testimony and witnessing, actors and audiences. What do the TRC's modes of performance and transmission tell us about the special form of transitional justice that South Africa brought into being?

The TRC performed a different sort of encounter between the state and its public than did the political trials examined in chapter 2. The trials of the late 1950s and early 1960s staged a confrontation between the genres of political rally and trial, between the embodied repertoires of resistance and the state's escalating repression of all speech. In the years that followed, the role of the trial as a key site of contestation was eclipsed by two other forums: inquests and the torture chamber. Both signify a retreat from public view, a disavowal of witnessing. Frequently, inquests investigated the mysterious deaths of those who had been held in detention. The proceedings generally failed to bring to light the full circumstances and causes of death, concluding too often that no one could be blamed. By the 1980s the state had adopted more clandestine techniques, such as abductions and executions with no preceding arrests, thereby avoiding messy imprisonments and vexing inquests that inevitably arose when prisoners died in detention. Such tactics eliminated—quite literally—the opposition, and also the requirement for public proceedings. Inquests could be too easily transformed into the performative stages of resistance with the chanting and singing that Jimmy Kruger complained about in the wake of the Steve Biko inquest.[1]

The torture chamber, unlike an inquest, was a private, secret space, closed to public view. Adam Ashforth has argued in his study of South Africa's official discourse in the twentieth century that a commission of inquiry is a theatre of power in which a "central 'truth' of state power is ritually played out before a public audience."[2] Ashforth contrasts the "ritualized civility of the commission 'hearing' with that of another theatre of power within modern states—the torturer's chamber." Whereas commissions of inquiry hold out the promise of dialogue based upon reason, the torturer's chamber relies upon silence and fear; it is a secret theatre that is no less potent because of its secrecy. During South Africa's political transition from authoritarian to democratic rule in the 1990s, the Truth and Reconciliation Commission became the newest incarnation of a theatre of power, a forum designed to restore public confidence in all aspects of society, especially the rule of law. When the Truth and Reconciliation Commission made visible the large-scale, mostly hidden abuses of the past—in particular, systematic abduction, torture, and murder—it exposed a secret theatre to public view. The eyes and ears of the nation witnessed as tales of gross violations of human rights were told at hearings and broadcast on television and radio.

While trials and inquests are not usually thought of as being in the same family as torture and commissions of inquiry, they are genealogically linked as theatres of power—albeit of vastly differing types, morality, magnitude, and modes of operation. All of them ostensibly focus on the production of information through processes of investigation. They share an interest in the "accumulation of information."[3] They are epistemological projects, at least nominally. In speaking about Uruguay's legacy of torture and attempts to create mechanisms of political transition, psychoanalyst Marcelo Vignar noted the confluence of widely disparate discourses about knowing:

> This is such a sick little country, all torn and twisted and broken, with so much of the brokenness concentrated around this notion of knowledge, of *knowing*. "You can't possibly know what it was like." "We didn't know, we didn't realise." The torturer's "I know everything about you." The victim's "I don't even know what I said, what I did . . ." The torturer's "Scream all you like . . . no one will ever know."[4]

Despite a shared obsession with knowledge, these various theatres of power diverge profoundly in their degrees of public visibility.

The TRC's decision to have its proceedings transpire in public must be interpreted from this perspective: it sought to make the unknown widely known, the invisible widely seen. Its embrace of publicity broke with all precedent, both within South Africa and internationally. The commission welcomed in addition to live audiences the television cameras and radio microphones that invaded its proceedings and made extraordinary electrical and technical—not to mention ethical—demands on the commission. The TRC gave the media full permission to broadcast without censorship, something that would have been unthinkable in the old South Africa. Through radio and television, mass atrocity became mass media, and this fact fundamentally transformed collective memory to a degree unimaginable had the TRC been publicized only through print media and the publication of its final report.

The commission valued watching, seeing, speaking, testifying, listening, and bearing witness. Those who appeared before the commission gave testimony to ever-expanding layers of audiences, beginning with the language interpreters— the first line of transmission—and extending to the commissioners and lawyers, to the spectators in attendance, and to family members, victims, perpetrators, community members, and journalists, among others. Beyond these audiences, we must consider the much larger anonymous audience tuning in throughout the country on their radios and television sets. For this group of witnesses, the commission was seen and/or heard, experienced not face to face but remotely, from their living rooms and bedrooms, while driving or working. For television audiences, the commission was generally experienced not live but through nightly news items and weekly digests. All of these modes of transmission profoundly shaped the collective experience of the Truth and Reconciliation Commission and the collective memory it produced. Hence it is of great significance to analyze *how* South Africans experienced the commission and how each mode of transmission shaped the message.[5]

In this chapter and next, two crucial intermediary figures command my attention: the simultaneous language interpreters at the hearings and the television journalists who covered these events. Both served as interlocutors, linking the key protagonists—the persons giving testimony before either the Human Rights Violations Committee or the Amnesty Committee—with those receiving that testimony—the audience. The language interpreters were at once protagonists and mediators, actors and audience. They listened intently to the speaker's words, they were the first to reproduce the deponent's speech, and they did so in the first person, thereby assuming the speaker's subject position, the authorial voice. Interpreter Lebohang Mathibela recalls, "You're aware that you are becoming an actor, but you know . . . you didn't even realize that you were acting—you know, you are just looking at the victim as he is speaking and unconsciously you end up throwing up your hands as he throws his, you end up nodding your head when he nods."[6] Mathibela describes his role as interpreter in explicitly theatrical terms, likening his job to that of a stage actor who performs a character with empathy and embodiment.

Like the language interpreters, the television journalists who covered the TRC served as highly charged intermediaries. They too were simultaneously actors and audience. Their role expanded to serving as a chorus, contextualizing the events, explaining the TRC's protocols, isolating key themes, commenting on the action, and directing attention to particular moments. They magnified the commission, transmitting it to remote spectators who were far greater in number than the immediate audience. They also walked a fine line between simply being journalists—that is, reporting on the TRC as "objective" news—and actively *performing* as an extension of the TRC. As I argue in chapter 4, the TRC constituted a media event as defined by Daniel Dayan and Elihu Katz—that is, a historic occasion of state that was televised at it took place and transfixed the nation in the process.[7] Media events, according to Dayan and Katz, are "hailed as *historic*; they strive to mark a new record, to change an old way of doing or thinking, or to mark the passing of an era."[8] The television coverage of the TRC was positioned to do all of these things. Media events involve three primary partners: those who organize the event, the broadcasters who reproduce it, and the audiences, both those who attend in person and those who watch remotely. Broadcasters of media events play a delicate role, providing a bridge between being there and not being there. In fact, televised media events raise the question of whether a definitive "there" exists. Was the center of the TRC event in the hearing rooms or in the living rooms where most South Africans experienced it? Or was the center of testimony not in the present of the hearings but in the past that the testimony at the hearings represented, the events described by survivors, perpetrators, witnesses, and family members? Dayan and Katz note, "We are witnessing the gradual replacement of what could be a theatrical mode of publicness—an actual meeting of performers and public in locations such as parliament houses, churches, convention floors, stadiums—by a new mode of publicness based on the separation of performers and audiences, and on the rhetoric of narrative rather than contact."[9] The TRC's publicness was doubly constructed: it was both a theatrical event—live, embodied, in person—and a media event that separated, both spatially and temporally, the performers from the television's audiences. I propose to look at public performance of the TRC from both angles—the live, in person, and theatrical performance as well as the physically remote, temporally distant, and compressed televised broadcast. Let us begin by looking at the frontline mediators of the live performance of the TRC: the language interpreters. They often sat just a few feet away from the primary protagonist at TRC hearings—the person giving testimony—and their core responsibility was to listen and reproduce the person's words, to carry the witness's testimony from one language to another.

Rough Translation

"If you have seen an interpreting booth, it looks something like a little fish bowl," notes Angela Sobrey, one of the interpreters who served with the TRC. "You're sitting in a one-meter-square cubicle with a door and glass around you. So your audience can see you."[10] These mobile interpreting units—grey edifices with glass windows, a bit reminiscent of the booth in which Adolph Eichmann testified—were a recurring visual motif of the commission (see fig. 3.1). They appeared on television, in photographs, and even in dramatic representations such as the play *Ubu and the Truth Commission*.[11] The booths dramatized, as Theo du Pleissis and Chriss Weigand contend, the right of the victims and those applying for amnesty to follow proceedings in their own language.[12] Although the Promotion of National Unity and Reconciliation Act stipulated that those who appeared before the commission should be able to testify in the language of their choice, their words could be heard in a number of different tongues, as headsets placed throughout the hearing venues broadcast multiple language translations of testimony (see fig. 3.2). Mark Sanders offers a spectator's perspective:

> One is given a headset, puts it on, and turns to the appropriate channel, and can hear the witnesses, and the questioner, speaking in a language not his or her own. Although one hears the echo, in the background, of the witness's actual words, the process of simultaneous translation means a radical dispropriation for each party: the witness speaks in Zulu, yet, as I hear him, he speaks in English. On another channel he might have been speaking Sotho or Afrikaans. Were I to have appeared before the commission, I could have been heard to speak several languages that I do not understand.[13]

Figure 3.1. Inside the interpreter's booth. Courtesy of George Hallett.

Thus the very first line of transmission of testimony was mediated and interpolated—not identical to itself. Interpretation was central to the TRC process. As one observer said, "There would be no truth without the interpreters."[14] Yet the process of interpretation produced particular kinds of truths, and the performed mediation of interpretation has received almost no scholarly attention to date.

Though often referred to by the generic term "translators," linguists who served the TRC were more precisely interpreters. The difference between interpretation and translation is profound, and its significance has been utterly underestimated by nearly everyone concerned with the TRC—including the commission, journalists, and scholars. Too often the TRC treated the process of interpretation as though it were simply mechanical, a pipe that one just opened up and information flowed, in the words of interpreter Wisani Sibuyi.[15] "The interpreter's chief aim is to reproduce the speaker's account as reliably as possible, this reproduction not being a word-for-word translation of the speaker's words, but a transfer of the essential meaning," according to du Plessis and Wiegand.[16] Interpretation thus conveys a reduced truth. It provides a functional rendering of content created within the constraints of an improvised live setting. Translation, in contrast, works with a written transcription of the source language and then carefully parses the best translation from the source to target languages.[17]

The TRC interpreters themselves were troubled by the difference between interpretation and translation. One of them, Luis Nel, has said that he thinks it was fundamentally wrong for the TRC to rely so heavily on transcribed simultaneous

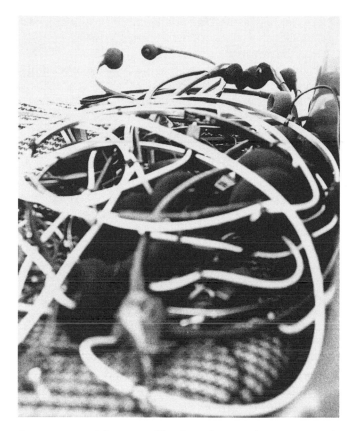

Figure 3.2. Headphones used by the audience to hear interpreted testimony at TRC hearings. Used by permission © Jillian Edelstein.

interpretation. He believes there was "a fundamental misconception of the difference between translation and interpreting. Interpreting is not translation. They are two completely different processes. If you had to record what someone said and then translate that transcription of the recording . . . into English . . . I'm sure a lot less of the essence of what that person was trying to convey with their story would have gone missing. Every individual has his or her own idiom and you can never with one hundred percent surety say what that person is going to say next. That used to throw me to no end."[18]

Interpretation collapses nuance and privileges so-called factual truth over narrative truth, to use the TRC's own terminology (see the Afterword to this volume). The testimony surrounding the case of Fort Calata of the Cradock Four is illustrative in this regard. We now know that Calata was brutally murdered by the police. His murderers pulled out Fort Calata's hair, cut off his fingers, and hacked off his tongue. His wife, Nomonde Calata, testified about this murder during the very first day of HRVC hearings at the TRC. She described what happened when a family friend went to identify the body of her deceased husband. The live simultaneous interpreters at the hearing translated her words as follows: "When he looked at his [Fort Calata's] trousers he realised that the dogs had bitten him severely. He couldn't believe it that the dogs already had their share."[19] A later translation done by Z. Bock, N. Mazwi, S. Metula, and N. Mpolweni-Zantsi at the University of Western Cape using a method that involved transcribing from the source language using videotapes from the TRC and then carefully translating into English renders the passage quite differently: "[When the friend] looked at his [Fort Calata's] trousers he discovered that it looks like he was bitten by the dog. There is nothing that made me feel bad more than knowing the he was also bitten by the dog. That made me feel very bad."[20] In the first interpretation, the perspective of the speaker, Nomonde Calata, is erased altogether. It doesn't tell us, as the second interpretation does, how she felt upon hearing that her deceased husband's body was bitten by dogs. In the second interpretation, the more careful translation, we see that Calata inserts herself, her perspective and emotions, and she interprets which aspects of the news were most significant for her. Through her repetition and commentary, Calata draws the listener's attention not to what the police had done directly—cutting off her husband's hair, tongue, and fingers—but rather to their indirect act of inhumanity—throwing Fort to the dogs. As the pioneering scholars (Bock, Mazwi, Metula, and Mpolweni-Zantsi from the University of Western Cape) who created this second, more careful translation contend, what was often lost in the TRC's interpretation process was emotional content, narrative immediacy, direct speech, and repetition that conveyed significant meaning. If one of the goals of HRVC hearings was to record the truth as the witness saw it, the truth according to that person, then the particularities of speech were quite significant. Mrs. Calata conveyed through her language *her interpretation* of these events, what she found most significant. Yet the simultaneous interpretation process did not favor her perspective but rather flattened it to reproduce only the bare outlines of the story, a rough translation produced in the heat of the moment for functional purposes of conveying basic content.

Interpreters at the TRC were confined in booths and worked in teams of two, each person limited to turns of twenty minutes. The "passive" interpreter would provide support and assistance by taking notes on names and dates, clarifying terms, and translating idiom. Any hearing of the TRC usually provided interpretation into four different languages: English, Afrikaans, the dominant language of the region where the hearing was held, and another language from that region.[21] The method used by the TRC was simultaneous (as opposed to consecutive) interpretation. In this modality, as Kim Wallmach explains,

there is a small delay between the moment the interpreter hears a thought and the moment he or she renders that thought into the target language, because it takes a moment to understand the original message and produce a target-language message. Meanwhile, the speaker goes on to the next thought, so the interpreter must produce the target-language version of the first thought while processing the speaker's second thought, and so on.[22]

Interpretation from one language into the three others was accomplished through something called "relay interpretation." The witness's words were first translated into English and then from English to each of the other three languages represented at that particular hearing via relay. So, for instance, a Xhosa witness would first be translated by the Xhosa-to-English booth and then that English translation would be transmitted to, say, the booths covering English-to-Afrikaans, English-to-Zulu, and English-to-SiSwati.

So English served as the foundational language of interpretation, even though English was not a strong language competency for many of the African interpreters.[23] Interpretations from the booths were broadcast via radio channels to headsets available in the hearing hall for all participants, including witnesses, commissioners, and spectators. There was also a live feed directly to the media. Any errors that crept in—and there were errors, as the interpreters themselves well knew—were amplified and magnified immediately. The whole relay system was a bit like the children's game of telephone in which the players sit in a circle and pass around a whispered message. By the time the starting phrase travels around the circle, it has been mangled, its syntax, vocabulary, and meaning utterly transformed. "I am telling you, we have had nightmares," recalls TRC interpreter Angela Sobrey. Relay, she says, was "where most of the interpretations got lost."[24] Sobrey recalls once being the first voice in the relay team when she suddenly realized she had misunderstood an important word. Her assumptions about that word caused her to misinterpret the entire meaning of what followed. "You'd go off on a certain tangent and then realize two minutes down the line that, 'Shit, I was supposed to be speaking about that!'"[25] In the meantime the error would be magnified as it passed to the other booths, was sent to the headsets strapped on spectators' heads, and, finally, was transmitted to the media and the listening public in the larger world.

Another time, Sobrey was translating the Xhosa phrase "ucele ithuba" and got into some fairly comical troubles. She interpreted the words as "going to ask for cigarettes," and she relayed this meaning to her fellow interpreters. But the live audience of Xhosa speakers began to laugh, and Sobrey's partner in the booth rapidly hit the mute button and barked, "He asked for sexual favors!" "No," Sobrey whispered, "He asked for cigarettes!" "Sexual favors!!" admonished her colleague, hand poised firmly on the button. The phrase is ambiguous, meaning "ask for a chance/opportunity/time," and Sobrey had seen only its literal, surface meaning, whereas the Xhosa audience read a deeper sexual innuendo. All the while, the witness no doubt continued speaking and Sobrey would have rushed to catch up, her mistranslation passing through the relay pipeline, becoming amplified with each iteration.

The TRC's process of interlingual interpreting was thus a highly complex speech act, its difficulty compounded by innumerable factors. One was the unprecedented nature of this sort of interpretation within South Africa. Though the country has long had over twenty-five spoken languages, a legacy of apartheid (especially its devaluing of black culture) was that interpretation was not a recognized, respected profession before 1994. Previously, the courts were the only venues that routinely used interpreters, but until 1998, even these interpreters received little formal training.[26] "The function of interpreting in the courts historically," says Angela Sobrey, "was that interpreters were recruited this way: someone would be walking by and would be asked, 'Hey you, can you speak Afrikaans?' 'Yes, baas.' And they would say, 'Okay. Come, put a jacket on and off you go to court to go and interpret.'"[27] These interpreters were usually accorded enormous esteem within their home communities, for they were seen as having important official jobs in the courts. But within the courts, they were considered low-level functionaries. Sobrey says,

> If you go into some museums and archives of the justice system, [you will see] photographs that were taken of magistrate's courts. You'll see magistrates and prosecutors sitting in chairs in the black cloaks, seated, all white. And the interpreters—grown men—sitting on the ground with their legs crossed. And for African men who are held in such high esteem in their own cultures and communities, this is a very humiliating reversal of roles.[28]

Hospitals are another venue where interpreters were routinely needed. Annelie Lotriet says that "any person who speaks two languages is used as an interpreter. In most instances, nurses, porters, cleaners, etc. are asked to interpret. These are people who have never received any formal training."[29] Historically, African language interpretation in South Africa has been accorded very little respect by whites; the assumption was that anyone with two languages could be an interpreter, that the job took no particular skill.

When the Truth and Reconciliation Commission came into being there was no existing service upon which to draw for language interpretation. Creating a corps of trained interpreters for the commission was an unprecedented and extraordinary step. The "contribution of the Commission to the interpreting industry in South Africa should not be underestimated," acknowledges the TRC's summary report.[30] As du Plessis and Wiegand explain, never before had South Africa seen such extensive and continuous interpretation, never before had so many interpreters been trained (especially from disadvantaged communities), never before had so many African languages been used so consistently in a high-status function, never before had "empowerment through language taken shape in such a manner," and never before had interpreting in South Africa received such continuous media coverage.[31] The result, according to the commission, was "an extensive word harvest, probably even more extensive than that of the Nuremburg trials."[32] By the end of the hearing, the commission estimates, over 57,000 hours of hearings had been interpreted, an estimated 1 billion words, filling roughly 11 million typed pages.[33] Whether this estimate of the voluminous pages of testimony is correct, it is certainly true that "there would be no truth without the interpreters!"[34]

The TRC outsourced interpretation to the Language Facilitation Unit (LFU) of the University of the Free State in Bloemfontein. Within the ridiculously short span of two months, the unit hastily organized the recruitment, selection, and training of a cohort of twenty-four interpreters.[35] Of these, fifteen were employed full-time by the LFU while the remainder worked on a freelance basis. Many interpreters entered the fraught arena of the TRC with no substantial interpretation experience. "The first twenty minutes of every day you'd sit there and basically almost shit yourself because you'd think, 'What the hell is that man going to say next?'" recalls Louis Nel.[36] Inexperience was just one of the challenges the interpreters faced. Regional variations and local dialects within African languages are quite significant, especially in Xhosa, Tswana, Tsonga, and Ndebele. Language in the rural areas could be highly idiomatic, with speakers using variations that were seen as "deeper" or "purer" than usage in cities yet perhaps opaque and inscrutable to an interpreter who had grown up in an urban area. Deponents from the city might combine several different languages and confound interpretation. Du Plessis and Weigand contend that it was a bit "simplistic to think that if one appoints interpreters for all nine African languages they will be capable of interpreting all the varieties of these languages." They commented that "interpreters flounder when moved out of the region familiar to them."[37]

Between languages there were incommensurables. For many technical terms used at the TRC, there was no African language equivalent. With the advent of democracy in South Africa, an appropriate Zulu phrase had to be coined: *ukubusa ngentando yeningi*, which means "to govern with the will or love of the masses." But which Bantu words could convey the calculated inhumanity of apartheid's euphemisms for murder, such as the euphemism "to eliminate"? Simultaneous interpretation requires both listening and speaking at the same time, with the interpreter usually waiting to hear the predicate in a sentence before proceeding. But, as Louis Nel explains, "a very particular problem with the Afrikaans language is they decided to put the damn verb at the end of the sentence."[38] For this verb, the interpreter must wait, and as the pause lengthens, the audience wonders "What's wrong with this interpreter?" The longer the interpreter must wait to interpret the sentence, the greater the chance that information will be lost.

Narrative styles varied dramatically between the two types of hearings. The Human Rights Violations Committee hearings tended to be emotional and strongly narrative, with deponents speaking at length without interruption; the Amnesty Committee hearings were generally formal, laden with arcane vocabulary, and subject to the legal protocols of the courtroom. Yet even the narratives at the HRVC hearings showed great variation in speaking style, level of detail, and tempo. "Somebody that's going to tell their story in Xhosa will be relating something and will go about it in such a roundabout way, because that's the way the language works," explains Angela Sobrey.[39] But often such preambles were untranslatable, for the conventions of the narrative were so culturally specific. "True storytellers can sometimes become a nightmare for the interpreters," said du Plessis and Weigand. "They know no end and go into minute detail."[40]

While the interpreters were supposed to be briefed about each case twenty-four hours in advance, this rarely happened. So interpreters were doing the most difficult type of interpretation—simultaneous interpretation—in the most demanding and complex circumstances imaginable. The language could be quite technical and precise. During his Amnesty Committee hearing, the famed Vlakplaas operative Eugene de Kock reeled off names of guns and ammunition and then interrupted the translators. "He'd sit there and listen, and then he'll say MRPG7, CZ275—what, what, what—eventually he listened in because he seemed to relish the fact that you were getting it wrong," recalls interpreter Abubaakr Peterson.[41] During cross-examinations or question-and-answer periods, there would be multiple speakers from the commission, sometimes over a half-dozen of them—together with deponents, all talking. With so many languages being uttered at once, often at a rapid-fire pace, the interpreters would scramble between buttons and channels, sometimes losing track of which was the lead language in the relay. "I must confess you'd get completely messed up. I didn't know which button I was on anymore," says Louis Nel. On one occasion a spectator pointed out, "Do you know you're interpreting English into English at the moment?"[42]

Such incidents reveal not only the complexity of the interpretation process but also its stressfulness. The booths in which the translators sat for hours were hot and crowded. Interpreter Lebohang Mathibela recalls that the fans in the booths either didn't work or were too loud.[43] That interpreters were required to use the first person in translation presented a host of problems. For instance, African audiences not accustomed to hearing interpretation would often mistake the interpreter for the witness. As Sobrey recalls, "Spectators would look at you with all sorts of expressions, and if you said something that they didn't agree with, they would give you a stern look, and be shaking their heads. Some of them would go the extent of coming to confront you as though *you* were the one testifying. 'Why are you telling lies, my girl? You're lying, that's not what happened!' And you've got to explain, 'No it's actually not me. I'm just saying what he said.' 'But he is lying! Go and tell him too that he's lying! Go and tell the commissioners that he is lying!'"[44]

Interpreters occupied a contradictory position within the commission. They were at once invisible and highly visible. They were "to reproduce the speaker's account as reliably as possible" and in the first person, yet they were supposed to maintain neutrality and emotional distance, even when the witness's demeanor was intensely emotional. Emotional expressiveness was somehow not considered part of the witness's narrative truth.[45] "We had it drummed into us the fact that as interpreters we are merely supposed to be in the background," recalls Sobrey, "we are supposed to be invisible, with an invisible, monotone, low-key voice. And it was even taken to the extreme of us being told, as ladies, that we shouldn't even wear bright colors." No reds, but dull colors; no shouts or lilting tonalities, but rather a monotone; no crying, but neutrality without affect. Be inconspicuous, the interpreters were told.

For black and colored interpreters, emotional neutrality was impossible. "You relate to the victim's pain because you yourself have experienced rejection on the basis of your skin color," says Sobrey. "You can relate to what they are saying."[46] Du Plessis and Wiegand lament the intrusion of empathy:

> The whole of South Africa probably saw how one of the interpreters at a Bloemfontein hearing interpreted with tears literally streaming down her face. It was undoubtedly a touching sight, but raises questions about the interpreter's conduct. Of course, many accounts are moving, despite the fact that one has heard them so often. None the less, the interpreter cannot be dragged into it and has to maintain a professional distance at all times.[47]

Yet the interpreters felt that emotion was an essential part of the truth of testimony and that it should therefore be conveyed through tone of voice. According to Khethiwe Mboweni Marais, "You have to assume that voice, you have to assume that pain of the speaker. The more horrible the stories, the more your voice would distend."[48]

Because the interpreters were not directly employed by the commission, they did not automatically receive the counseling services the commission provided. Chairperson Desmond Tutu, in his preface to the TRC's summary report, notes that "it has been a grueling job of work that has taken a physical, mental and psychological toll. We have borne a heavy burden as we have taken onto ourselves the anguish, the awfulness, and the sheer evil of it all." He singles out the interpreters, who had undergone "the trauma of not just hearing or reading about the atrocities, but have had to speak in the first person as a victim or perpetrator."[49] To underscore his point, Tutu offers two direct quotes from testimony:

> "They undressed me and opened a drawer and shoved my breast into the drawer which they then slammed shut on my nipple!" [and] "I drugged his coffee, then I shot him in the head. Then I burned the body. Whilst we were doing this, watching his body burn, we were enjoying a *braii* on the other side."[50]

Such graphic details were daily fare at the truth commission. "Some of the tales that were told, honestly, in such graphic detail," interpreter Siphithi Mona recalls, "nobody within our society ever stopped to think what effect those details had on the interpreter because the interpreter was the sponge that absorbed all the pain throughout the entire process."[51] Some found comfort in personal support systems: "When we got home we needed someone to embrace us and tell us that things would be fine," says Lebohang Mathibela. Others took out their pent-up emotions on their families: one Tswana interpreter lost his wife and baby when they could no longer endure his violent outbursts.[52] Another interpreter, headed for a hearing, burst into tears on a plane to Johannesburg. "I cannot take this anymore," he announced. "This is unbearable. I don't want to do this kind of job."[53] The play *Truth in Translation,* based upon interviews with TRC interpreters, dramatizes the many ways this constituency coped and endured, including retreating to bars on a regular basis.[54]

Along with all these stressors, the interpreters had to deal with the ongoing legacy of the lack of "parity of esteem" between African languages and Afrikaans or English. Racial tensions developed within the interpreting unit, where full-time interpreters were black (I am including coloreds in this category) and free-lancers were whites.[55] It came to light that there were discrepancies in remuneration between them, with the white freelancers earning four times as much as the black full-timers. The rationale: the white freelancers were supposedly more experienced. The white freelancers were also cast in a supervisory role, told to report back to the LFU if they felt the black interpreters were not behaving properly. Black interpreters lived an itinerant life for the commission for over two years, traveled on an intense schedule, were separated from their families, and engaged in emotionally and physically grueling work for hours on end. They viewed these racialized remuneration discrepancies as a perpetuation of the old order of white supremacy, even under the auspices of the TRC. One of them said: "The people who do the hard job, they do not get the money in every working places. We work harder than the boss who sits in the office. . . . The people on the street, the construction workers, the person who makes it does not get the money. The way the market is structured, if you do the shit job, you do not get anything."[56]

In his book on post-colonialism, Robert Young writes, "Literally, according to its Latin etymology, translation means to carry or to bear across."[57] The TRC interpreters spoke of themselves precisely in such terms, as those who "take the speaker across." Angela Sobrey, Khethiwe Mboweni Marais, and Siphithi Mona talked about the difficulties they encountered, especially when interpreting amnesty hearings. As often as it was drummed into the interpreters' heads that they were to be neutral, the translation of a single Xhosa word could have as many as four versions in English, each with a different connotation.

> *Sobrey:* When it comes down to the crunch, it's your judgment call, you know . . .
> *Mboweni Marais:* Especially if you consider someone is being shortchanged.
> *Sobrey:* It's your call to make, and you decide how you're going to take that speaker across. And I mean this is why it is quite sad that interpreting is not given the recognition that it . . . it . . . it deserves. Because in any case, you make or break the story. You know—the way you decide to bring across that story.
> *Mona:* Either you set him free or you send him to the gallows.[58]

The interpreters were trained to be neutral, but deciding whose idea of "neutral" would be honored, their employer's or their own, was difficult. Their jobs required minute-by-minute choices about words, syntax, tone, emotional expressiveness, and narrative completeness. They had to decide whether to tailor the interpretation to meet the speaker's needs or the listener's needs, whether to favor source or target languages. Each decision had a host of effects, ones that could "make or break" a story and indeed a person's life in the case of amnesty hearings. The very fact that they were interpreters rather than translators made neutrality impossible: they were being asked to provide a reduced truth and functional rendering of content. By what yardstick would they decide what was essential? The interpreters were trained to see emotion and affect as nonessential dimensions of testimony, to produce interpretations that filtered out affect. And yet emotional truth was often central to the witnesses' perception of value. Interpreters *performed* testimony in their glass booths; in their bodies; in the cadence and tone of their voices; in their choices of words, grammar, syntax, and style; and in other choices that they were forced to make. Their repetitions always involved revision, and those revisions should command much more of our analytic attention.

What is the significance of this information, ultimately? Yes, the interpreters had a difficult, even impossible job. Yes, they suffered from employment discrimination and the psychological trauma of having to narrate atrocities at first hand. Some were haunted for years afterward by nightmares about rape. One was so affected by testimony he could no longer eat red meat. But ultimately, what is the relevance of these details to the so-called narrative truth that the TRC was supposed to have brought into being? Many observers have said that the most profound of the TRC's aims was accomplished not through the summary report, the commission's findings, or its amnesty decisions but rather through the public hearings. For instance, Constitutional Court judge Albie Sachs, one of the architects of the truth commission, praises the TRC's summary report: "It's written in a very lively way. It's spirited. It's not a boring summing up for the board of activities for the last year. It probes. It asks questions. It illustrates with examples. It's philosophical. And very well structured, and I think quite a literate document." However, during our interview he qualified his encomium, observing that neither the report nor the commission's findings or decisions was really the point of the TRC:

> It wasn't about findings. It was about the acting out of a story of revelation, discovery, and human interaction. And at times the interactions were extremely painful. At times they were pretty stiff. At times they were disappointing. But there was that sense of something, real, special, and dramatic happening all the time. . . . It's seeing the people, the faces, hearing the voices, it's the tears, the actual tone of voice, the body language that's so recognizable—what people can identify with—that makes such an impact. It's not the actual report. It's not the statement of culpability or responsibility, significant though those things are.[59]

Thus, it is the live testimony that Sachs sees as the most significant feature of the TRC, the way that hearings acted out a "story of revelation, discovery, and human interaction." Interpretation—specifically, language interpretation—was inextricably bound up with the acting out of that story.

The testimonies included in the TRC's online database of transcripts are interpretations, not translations. The difference is significant. Scholarly interpretations that use (or misuse) these transcripts are yet another extension of the TRC's relay interpretation, promulgating whatever distortions, omissions, and transformations of testimony occurred on the spot during the hearings in the hot and crowded translator's booths. Imagine what might happen to cultural studies of South Africa and the truth commission if we took seriously what Luis Nel, one of the TRC's language interpreters, says about these transcripts: "Something went awry. . . . It's something that the TRC did fundamentally wrong: transcribing an interpreted version of what someone said."[60] I am not advocating for a narrowly positivist recovery of "fact" or the "real truth," as if what witnesses actually said in their own languages is the only relevant shade of truth for a scholar or historian to examine. TRC testimony has been subjected to many interpreters, from the language interpreters to the commissioners to the authors of the TRC report to the journalists who covered the hearing and finally to the authors of the many books written after the TRC took place. All of these instances of interpretation produce their own truths, each with its own validity; each can tell us much about South African cultural history. I argue, however, that there is a wealth of knowledge in this testimony that not only has been ignored but actually has never been *heard* or received. Hearing and receiving the fullness of this testimony is part of continuing the performance of the Truth and Reconciliation Commission, part of serving as witness, as receiver of the evidence the commission placed in the public record. As this chapter's opening epigraph about the Rivonia accused made clear, the significance of acquiring speech for those who have long suffered violations of human rights in silence and isolation is more than gaining the opportunity to convey information. It is the human connection when one's speech is received, when people actually listen—and listen fully—to what one says.

"To Speak to People Who Will Listen to Me"

However flawed the TRC transcripts may be, they are useful resources that (astonishingly) scholars rarely examine. Most writers on the TRC tend to use sound bites of testimony taken from Antjie Krog's memoir *Country of My Skull* if they use testimony at all. This reliance on a single secondary source persists despite the fact that *Country of My Skull* is, by Krog's admission, a "quilt," a highly personal account that presents her truth as she was trying to achieve it. In her book, Krog seeks to give words to moments of the commission that exceeded words, moments that seemed beyond articulation. The way that embodiment that is intensely emotionally expressive comes to stand in for the actual content of what people said is a paradigmatic phenomenon within TRC literature. One moment from the public hearings that stands out as singularly iconic is the testimony of Nomonde Calata, wife of murdered activist Fort Calata, who appeared before the commission during its first sessions of public hearings. Deputy chairperson Alex Boraine recalls:

> In the middle of her evidence she broke down and the primeval and spontaneous wail from the depths of her soul was carried live on the radio and television, not only throughout South Africa but also to many parts of the world. It was that cry from the soul that transformed the hearings from a litany of suffering and pain to an even deeper level. It caught up in a single howl all the darkness and horror of the apartheid years. It was as if she enshrined in the throwing back of her body and letting out the cry the collective horror of the thousands of people who had been trapped in racism and oppression for so long. . . . Nomonde Calata's sorrowful cry was played

over and over . . . on the SABC. Many people told me afterwards that they found it unbearable and switched off the radio.[61]

Commissioner Wendy Orr recounts that Calata's wail "shook the very foundations of the hall. She flung her head back in desolation. I cannot forget that cry."[62] Tutu calls the wail the "defining sound of the TRC," and he writes about how he adjourned the commission at that moment, only to resume minutes later by leading everyone present in a rendition of "Senzeni Na?" a hymn that asks over and over in its simple refrain "What have we done?"[63] A recording of Calata's cry occurs near the beginning of the SABC audio documentary of the commission, a production on six CDs called *South Africa's Human Spirit*, the narrator of which claims that the cry "ushers in" the truth commission.[64] Philip Miller's cantata on the commission, called *REwind* (the subject of chapter 5), includes an aria based on Calata's cry.[65] Antjie Krog includes in *Country of My Skull* an extensive passage on Calata's testimony, a passage that both reproduces Calata's testimony and sets it within a larger frame: a fabricated conversation between Krog and "my friend Professor Kondlo, the Xhosa intellectual from Grahamstown."[66] Kondlo says, "For me, this crying is the beginning of the Truth Commission— the signature tune, the definitive moment, the ultimate sound of what the process is about. She was wearing this vivid orange red dress, and she threw herself backward and that sound . . . that sound . . . it will haunt me for ever and ever."[67] He adds in the next paragraph, "So maybe this is what the commission is all about—finding words for that cry of Nomonde Calata." The quintessence of testimony from the TRC has come to be represented (not just by Krog but by a whole host of interpreters) as something beyond language, as something that cannot be known or that requires other people, even if they are invented academics like Kondlo, to "give words." In July 2007 I visited Nomonde Calata in her home in the farming center of Cradock in the Eastern Cape. When I asked how she felt about her cry becoming an iconic moment of the commission, one broadcast again and again on television and discussed endlessly by pundits, she answered, "If only the people who are bringing this thing each and every time up would feel as I felt that day, they wouldn't have done it."[68] Calata went to the commission longing to "speak to people who will listen to me." Her emotions had long been pent up and unexpressed. "That is why I screamed—because I wanted the pain to come out. I was tired of keeping it inside me because even the time when my husband died, people would not allow me to cry because I was expecting a baby, so they were thinking that my crying would affect the baby. So I never had enough time to cry." Her desire in coming before the commission was simultaneously to express her emotions *and* to speak to people who would listen to her. When I asked her, "How do you feel when that cry is used over and over again?" Calata confessed, "I feel sad. I feel sad. Because I still feel that I'm still crying. I do feel sad. I don't watch [the rebroadcast on television] actually. When it comes out . . . I just get up and walk away." Despite all the attention her case received, she has never received psychological counseling. Thus, while the moment of expressed grief at the commission made her feel "a little bit better," the effect was fleeting. "What came out of me, it's still there, and I have no one to talk to at home." What Calata continues to need are not words for her grief but someone to listen to what she has to say.

The commission's touted role as a healer that bestowed the "talking cure" has been criticized by many.[69] Rather than focus on that controversy, I instead invoke the reception of the cry of Nomonde Calata to underscore how this moment of emotional expressiveness came to stand in for the testimony and suffering of some 2,000 people who appeared before the commission. A prelinguistic expression of grief seems to have mattered far more than the actual words people said. I contend that the obligation of those who witness such testimony—whether they are commissioners, spectators, or journalists or the legion of academics busy spilling ink about the commission a decade later—is not to "give words" to the grief of those who testified but to listen to the words that survivors such as Cynthia Ngewu, Nomonde Calata, and many others actually gave to their own experiences. And in listening, we should do so in a way that honors the completeness, specificity, and integrity of those words as they were spoken. There are 2,000 testimonies available online, and I estimate that less than 20 percent of these cases have been cited or analyzed in the secondary literature on the TRC.

The Telephone Effect

To "carry across" the words of the speakers at the TRC was not solely the task of language interpreters and journalists. It is also what scholars of the TRC do when we write books like the one before you and what artists like Philip Miller do in creating works based on the TRC, like the *REwind* cantata discussed in chapter 5. The process of interpretation is full of ambiguity, nuance, and minute decisions that can profoundly shape outcomes. While there is no one right way to interpret, for interpretation is by definition a divergence from some supposedly empirical knowledge called "fact," some interpretations do better than others in observing the integrity and specificity of testimony.

In contrast to the swelling academic literature on the TRC, which is remarkably lacking in quotations from testimony, Antjie Krog's popular nonacademic book *Country of My Skull* does make use of testimony, and it does so liberally.[70] The book reproduces much of what appears to be verbatim transcriptions of TRC hearings. For any testimony not given in English or Afrikaans, Krog relies on the TRC's simultaneous translations and transcriptions into English. She then edits this testimony heavily, although she presents it in her text as though it were literal. Quotations often appear in chapters without editorial context, ellipses that would indicate modifications, or bibliographic citations that would say when or where a given hearing happened or how one might access the full transcript. When one compares passages of *Country of My Skull* with the TRC's transcriptions from the HRVC hearings, it is clear that an editorial hand was hard at work. That hand happens to belong to an author who is also one of South Africa's most acclaimed poets. Moonlighting from her career as a prolific poet who writes both in Afrikaans and English, Krog covered the TRC hearings for two years as a radio journalist with the SABC. Her account of the commission was one of the first to be published, and *Country of My Skull* remains one of the most distinctive and effective in terms of its rich use and reproduction of testimony.

Yet Krog's editorial interventions have not sat well with everyone. For instance, Yazir Henry, who testified before the TRC, took great issue with how his testimony was "appropriated, interpreted, retold and sold," especially by Krog, who featured a portion of his testimony in her chapter entitled "The Narrative of Betrayal Has to Be Reinvented Every Time."[71] The excerpt is printed with no introduction by Krog, no comment about how the text has been edited.[72] Henry's English-language testimony as transcribed by the commission comprises 6,131 words, whereas the portion published in *Country of My Skull* is just over 1,500 words, thus representing less than 25 percent of Henry's testimony. Henry's narrative is in fact one of betrayal—his betrayal of a comrade, Anton Fransch, who subsequently died at the hands of the police. The narrative is reinvented by Krog, but her agency in that reinvention is erased.

Interpretation is always an intervention based upon selection, omission, imposition, distortion, and aesthetic embellishment. The principles I wish to highlight here are those of interpretive selection. By her own admission, Krog did not structure her editorial inventions according to any academic methodology and did not implement standards of ethical journalism. She describes the book as "my own, highly personalized version of the experiences of the TRC. *Country of My Skull* is NOT a journalistic or factual report of the Truth Commission."[73] As previously mentioned, Krog calls her book a "quilt" that patches together personal, South African, and international perspectives.[74] She also says that *Country* should be read not as pure documentary but as "creative non-fiction," a text that freely and creatively transgresses the boundaries between fact and fiction. Such license is, as they say, poetic, and Krog, if anyone, is entitled to it. However, one must note the inadequacy of this approach from the point of view of academic method which Krog never intended her work to follow—in light of the fact that subsequent scholarship on the TRC has often ignored Krog's admissions and erroneously cited testimony in her text as though it *were* verbatim transcription from the hearings. For instance, Ashleigh Harris presents a critique of Krog's book that is precisely about the dangers of Krog's trope of "quilting," the way her method flattens out and universalizes particular voices of testimony while muddying distinctions between genres and disguising the seams, sutures, and scars of her quilting process. Yet instead of consulting the TRC transcripts, Harris quotes victim testimonies from Krog's book as though they were actually what victims said. When invoking the often-cited claim of Lucas Sikwepere that his sight was restored or Cynthia Ngewu's lament that the police who killed the Guguletu Seven left not even one witness alive, Harris quotes and analyzes Krog's text as though it is a primary source.[75] Similarly, Laura Moss offers a trenchant critique of *Country of My Skull,* noting how frequently the book is misread as documentary. But she, too, erroneously treats the testimony in Krog's book as "direct testimony" from victims, family members, and amnesty seekers when it is indirect testimony, reported speech that has been heavily edited.[76] And Dirk

Klopper, in his scholarship on Winnie Madikizela-Mandela's testimony before the TRC, uses excerpted TRC testimony drawn from either *Country of My Skull* or from Max du Preez's televised news program *TRC Special Report* as though these sources are primary evidence from the commission itself.[77]

I agree with Klopper that the burning question about the TRC is not what it achieved or failed to achieve but rather "how it is read." However, I wish this *how* included readings of actual testimony as coherent and meaningful speech acts that have integrity.[78] In retellings, certain narrative threads become dominant while others are obscured entirely. This process is amply illustrated by the various renderings that have emerged of the famous testimony of the mothers of the Guguletu Seven, which was heard on 23 April 1996 in Cape Town. I propose to treat this case, which is frequently referred to in the TRC's secondary literature, as a kind of scholarly version of the relay interpretation performed by linguists in the TRC translation booths. If we take the time to listen a bit more carefully to what the bereaved mothers said and how they said it, what insights into this case, into the subjectivity and perspective of witnesses, and into the TRC's staging of encounter between witness and community does it reveal? To address this question, I will compare the complete English-language translation and transcription of testimony from the hearing (which is available online) with excerpts that have been reproduced in several accounts of the TRC. I will also compare a verbatim translation with the TRC's English-language transcript that resulted from simultaneous interpretation. Finally, I will examine how the emphasis and lacunae of testimony change when we are attentive to the visual, kinetic, and tonal dimensions of testimony.[79]

At the hearing under discussion, mothers of four of the deceased seven activists from Guguletu appeared before the committee. In the chapter of *Country of My Skull* entitled "Then Burst the Mighty Heart," Antjie Krog reproduces, apparently verbatim and without commentary, the testimonies of Cynthia Ngewu, Eunice Miya, and Ms. Konile.[80] However, her version of the mothers' words is highly compressed and edited. Krog shapes the testimony in particular ways, ways that suit the narrative thrust of both the chapter and the book. Upon comparing Krog's extractions with a more complete account of the women's testimony, one sees how Krog manipulated victim testimony and which shades of truth were projected to a wider audience and which were filtered out.

Krog presents Cynthia Ngewu's testimony, for example, as primarily about the discovery of her son's death. Unresolved questions about this event continue to haunt her. In Krog's telling, Ngewu begins her testimony by describing how on the day of the murder some "comrades" arrived to inform her there had been a shooting. Ngewu visited the police station and then the mortuary looking for her son. She found his body, made a report, and then went home and watched the news, only to witness a video of the shooting's aftermath. She saw an image of her son's dead body being pulled by a rope as police tried to determine whether the body had a grenade. Ngewu turned off the television. At the TRC hearing she says, "During that time, when all this happened, I was too weak."[81] Ngewu talks briefly of the time after the death and the funeral. Her testimony, as narrated by

Krog, ends plaintively with a series of questions: "When I am just alone, I am thinking to myself... was there no survivor out of all these killings? And why did the boers kill everyone? Couldn't they just warn them, or even shoot them in their legs just to save their lives? Didn't these boers have any feelings at all? Why did they just kill everyone? Not leaving even one to give witness. Now nobody knows the real, real story."[82]

Krog's version of Ngewu's testimony highlights victimhood and grief, the bursting of the "mighty heart." Her excerpt represents only about 20 percent of what Ngewu said before the TRC on 23 April 1996. If we consider the totality of Ngewu's testimony—together with the visual evidence provided by video footage—a very different image of both of Ngewu and the truth commission emerges. Cynthia Ngewu is a formidable woman with broad shoulders, thick arms, and a steely facial expression. On the day of the hearing, she wore over her red floral dress a white jacket. Glasses and a crisp white head scarf that jutted out around her neck made her resemble a matron in church. Her testimony was stern and forthright, faltering at only at a few moments.

In her full testimony, Cynthia Ngewu describes how the police repeatedly antagonized her household in the days and weeks after her son's death. The Boers "kept on coming" to her house, standing outside and inside. A policeman named Officer Barnard was rude, laughed at the family, and taunted them by asking where their son was. "We didn't answer him," says Mrs. Ngewu. A week before the funeral, she received orders from the magistrate that the family was to bury Christopher right away and not wait until other family members arrived from the rural areas.[83] "We refused," said Ngewu, and she engaged a lawyer to help her win this battle. "We ended up burying them [the Guguletu Seven] at the time that we wanted." One morning after the funeral, the police arrived at the Ngewu house at 6:30 AM and said they wanted to take Ngewu to make a statement. She replied, "What statement when you have killed my son? I don't know what statement to give you. I wasn't there when you killed my son. You are the ones who killed my son. You are the ones to make the statement." The drama of this encounter builds as Mrs. Ngewu narrates, "Oh! I got ready! My house all of a sudden was full of detectives.... I saw that there were police at the backyard with guns. I asked them, 'What are you doing here?' They didn't tell me anything. I said, 'Are you here to shoot me? Now you have already shot my son, now you want to shoot me.'" She saw five or six police vans parked in front of her house. "Get out of my yard," she commanded. "You have already killed my son. Now you want to kill me."[84] Her rebuke made them all retreat, and they left to go sit in their vehicles. The police waited there as they tried to persuade her come down to the station for questioning.

The story that Cynthia Ngewu told at the TRC hearing was about much more than Christopher Piet, her son, the official "victim" of gross violations of human rights, whose death authorized her appearance in front of the Truth and Reconciliation Commission. Her story was about much more than the broken heart in the title of Krog's chapter. In her testimony Ngewu wove the story of Christopher's death into a larger narrative of violations of human rights that were not in themselves severe enough to warrant a hearing in front of the commission: agents of the state invaded her home without a warrant. They tried to deprive her of her right to bury her son when and how she wished. Mrs. Ngewu's agency and will in the face of these repeated insults and abuses by the state is the focus of the tale *as she has structured it*. An unarmed woman rails against an entire fleet of armed policeman and, amazingly, she forces them to leave her house and go sit in their cars until *she* is ready to comply with their demands. Yes, Ngewu, like many of the women who appeared before the TRC, was ostensibly testifying about what happened to a man in her life, but the way she structured her story makes it also very much about her. She is the chief protagonist of this tale, something worth considering in light of the dismay many have felt about the reluctance of South African women to testify about their direct experiences of gross violations of human rights before the commission.[85]

Eventually Mrs. Ngewu did get in the car that day, and she did go to the station and submit to police interrogation. So her agency and ability to resist the state was finite. She did not prevail at the two inquests into the Guguletu Seven case. These inquests happened in a place far from Mrs. Ngewu's home and in a language she did not understand (Afrikaans). The inquests determined that "nobody can be blamed" for the death of the Guguletu Seven, echoing a refrain that resistance lawyer George Bizos heard often.[86] But then the police amended their statement and told Mrs. Ngewu that 'no one was to be blamed because it is only the children who were offenders.'" Her narrative concludes, "Now nobody knows—knows the real-real story." TRC deputy chairperson Alex Boraine then states, "And that is one of the reasons why you are here." Emphatically Ngewu replies, "That's precisely why I am here."[87] Cynthia Ngewu defies the stereotypical description of TRC victims. She is hardly a "voiceless" little person lurking in the shadows.[88] When we consider the totality of Mrs. Ngewu's testimony together with her physical embodiment, she appears not as a plaintive victim but as a strong, confident, highly vocal advocate for her family. Whether her home is being invaded at dawn by armed police or she is being asked questions by commissioners at public TRC hearings and inquests, Cynthia Ngewu represents herself as a decisive person, someone with clarity of purpose, confidence, and, indeed, a degree of agency that seems to far surpass her social position.

When the hearing starts, Mrs. Ngewu, the first of the Guguletu women to speak, is a bit remote, her body still, her face unexpressive. Yet right from the beginning her focus is straightforward, her cadence even. Ngewu's testimony becomes increasingly animated physically, but these movements are a "slow burn" rather than a widely gesticulating eruption. At three moments during Mrs. Ngewu's testimony the rhythm of her speech breaks and the depth of emotions and grief that undergird her words becomes visible. One is the moment when she describes witnessing on television her son's dead body being pulled by a rope and she actually mimes the police pulling the rope. She looks up at the ceiling, clearly working to maintain her composure. Yet the momentum of her tale propels her; she doesn't give in. Ngewu has come to tell a story not just about the discovery of her son's body but also about her encounters with the police and authorities afterward. Her narrative rolls on, gaining speed and intensity, punctuated with gestures from her left hand. As she leads listeners through her discovery of her son's death, her identification of the body at the mortuary, her experience of police harassment about the funeral date, and the demands of the police that she give a statement, Ngewu is authoritative and bold. "We ended up burying them at the time *we* wanted to," she tells the commission. She is a confident storyteller producing through direct quotations dialogue from the scenes she narrates. The second emotionally delicate moment of the testimony, the point at which Ngewu's forward momentum breaks, is when she tells how a female police officer invading her house asks why she always keeps a lit candle on her mantel. Though Ngewu relates unflinchingly how she stood down an entire armed police force, she is most affected when narrating this small detail, an incidental conversation. "There's this candle that has been burning all this time. What is it about?" asks the officer. At this moment in the TRC hearing, one sees the enormous restraint Mrs. Ngewu has been exerting throughout. Her grief lies underground, deep and vast.

Ngewu also tells of her experience attending the inquest for her son's death. The English transcript of the TRC's simultaneous interpretation reads as follows:

As the trial went on, just at the end—towards the end of it, these boers said to me, if you want, you can also come to the place where these people were shot, the crime scene. But I forgot to tell you this before, but this—this sight we want to—we want to—we want to do this again, just to show you again how everything happened.

We said we cannot show—we cannot see that drama again. We can—we cannot re-life [*sic*] this whole experience. Now we were told that nobody can be blamed about this, it's only our children who had—who were the offenders. Thank you.[89]

Yet a more complete translation of Ngewu's Xhosa-language testimony reads quite differently:

While we were still waiting as the trial went on end, these *Boers* said, if you too want us to take you to the scene where these children were shot we invite you. Even on my statement I forgot to include this part. They would even dramatize [the actions described in] my statement, some playing as policemen, and the others played the role of the victims (our children). They will show us how the children were standing and how they died. We as the mothers of those children said that we couldn't go and watch that drama they are telling us about. We then sat and they told us no one was to be blamed because it is only the children who were offenders. Thank you.[90]

The police offer in the first version is muddied and vague, whereas in the second we begin to see just how precise and elaborate is their offer to restage a murder, a murder we now know (and the mothers strongly suspected at the time) that the police had actually committed. The translation gives a vivid sense of the dynamics between the mothers and the police. The offer by the police to restage the murder scene in such detail is haunted by evidence that the original murder itself was staged.[91] As Mrs. Ngewu narrates this last part of the tale, she again loses composure and says her final words gulping, struggling to articulate through her emotions. She concludes her uninterrupted testimony at that point, after having spoken for sixteen minutes, covering in that time an epic tale with many twists and turns. Yet all the while her rage and determination are as palpable as her grief.

Near the end of the hearing, the mothers of the Guguletu Seven were asked what they hoped to achieve by coming before the commission and how they would respond if they could confront the people who injured their sons. Mrs. Konile's reply expresses disorientation:

> I wouldn't be able to talk to them, it is their fault that now I am in this misery, now I wouldn't know what to do them—to do with them. I wouldn't know, I would never be able to say what—I can never tell them what to do, I've just given up everything, I don't know. I don't know anything. I will be just—be grateful if I can just get anything, but I personally cannot do anything.[92]

Konile's reply is fragmentary, a series of incomplete sentences, a cascade of negatives softened with conditional "woulds." When asked by Commissioner Pumla Gobodo-Madikizela, a psychologist, how she feels now that she has vented to the commission, she replies: "No nothing is better about the whole thing. I don't know. I cannot tell you how I feel."[93] This response is not the cathartic narrative of testimonial healing that the TRC hoped to achieve.

Cynthia Ngewu's reply to the same question is quite different in tone and style, and yet she too defies the TRC's mandate and mission. In lawyerlike fashion, Ngewu enumerates what she hopes to achieve through her appearance before the commission:

> I personally feel what the Commission can do for me is that these people should be brought to justice. The whole nation must see these people and they must say why they shot our children. They must account for the death of our children. Why would they drag my son? Was he a dog? Were their hands better than mine? Better than my son's? Were their hands so clean that they couldn't even touch my son? Why did they have to drag him? Barnard would come in and out of my house and he would be telling me that "Your dog, Christopher, is dead."[94]

First and foremost, Cynthia Ngewu wants justice and public accountability. She abhors the antagonistic behavior of police: they pulled her son's dead body with a rope (at one of the inquests police claimed they feared the body was rigged with explosives), they casually invaded Ngewu's home, and they taunted her by calling her dead son a "dog." Cynthia Ngewu expresses her desire for retribution and economic reparation to the TRC:

> I was pregnant for nine months with my child. . . . After my child was killed they got promotions and they got more money. They were put in high positions, but today— Barnard also died like a dog. . . . When I heard that, I said ["]the way . . . my son died, will be the way all these people will die too.["][95]

She notes that the other officers are still alive and living well today, many having received promotions and monetary rewards for having killed her son. Yet today she is poor, living in misery, and she finds it very difficult to feed and educate her son's children. Her husband was destroyed by this whole traumatic ordeal. Now, Ngewu says:

> I am the only one. I am the mother and father in that house. It is this boer's fault. . . . My request is that these boers must be put in front of us—in front of this Commission so that everybody here can see them. We want them to be put here so that the people can see.

> They are living with their families happily, our families are incomplete now, we are still crying—we still have this big lump in our throats. If—if they can be put here in front of us maybe that lump can go away.[96]

Ngewu systematically enumerates five objectives she wishes to achieve: justice, national and public exposure of the perpetrators, retribution ("may they die as my son died"), economic reparations, and healing for herself and her family. The Truth and Reconciliation Commission was established to accomplish healing and national exposure of perpetrators. It was also supposed to help provide economic reparations (which in the end were quite disappointing). However, the TRC was not equipped to mete out criminal or civil justice, Cynthia Ngewu's first priority. Nor was the TRC framed as a mechanism of retribution. So one sees in the complete testimony of Ngewu a narrative that prioritizes justice, accountability, retribution, Ngewu's strength, resistance, and agency as well as her forthright assertion of her demands of the commission, even if those demands ran counter to the commission's mandate.

At the hearing, Deputy Chairperson Alex Boraine asked Mrs. Ngewu what she thought had happened to her son; now, when she looks back on it, how does she think he died? "What is your feeling about what actually took place?" The TRC interpreter gave her answer as follows:

> I think what happened is that even when I am just alone I am thinking to myself I was just thinking was there any survivor out of all these—out of all these killings and why did these boers kill everyone? Could they just warn them, or even kill—or even shoot them on their legs to save their lives.

> Didn't these boers have any feelings at all, why did they just kill everyone, absolutely everyone. Not to leave one to give witness. Now nobody knows—knows the real-real story.[97]

The passage is plaintive and mournful. Ngewu laments the lack of survivors and the thoroughness of the Boers' killing. She wonders about the humanity of the killers—didn't they have feelings? Most of all she laments the lack of a story, a true story, an accurate story about what happened. Yet the translated version of this same passage reads quite differently:

> I thought to myself, had my child survived, they would have been the ones to give evidence; that is what I thought about these Boers. Why did they kill all of them? Why didn't they warn them and shoot them on their legs so that they can survive? Didn't these boers have feelings? They killed all of them so that no one could give evidence about why they were shot. Nobody knows the truth of this story.[98]

Rather than a lament, as characterized by Antjie Krog's version of her tale, Ngewu's testimony is insistent and demanding. Cynthia Ngewu knows why the Boers killed all of the Guguletu Seven: not so much out of cruelty—though there was surely that—but rather so there would be no witness, no one to give evidence. The truth would not be known. "Nobody knows the truth of this story."

An often-cited passage from this day of testimony is that of Mrs. Eunice Miya. She speaks of having learned of her son's death by watching the news on television with her family. The TRC's interpretation of her testimony reads:

> One of the children was shown on TV who had a gun on his chest. He was facing upwards and there was a gun on his chest and now we could see another one and the second one only to find that it's my son Jabulani.

> We were arguing myself and my daughter, she said it's him, I said no it can't be him, I just saw him this morning, it can't be him. I can—I can still remember what he wore this morning. He had navy pants and green jacket and a warm—and a warm woolen hat. I prayed I said oh! no Lord, I wish—I wish this news can just rewind. Why is it just him, why were the others not shown, why is it just him.[99]

This passage has been used quite famously in Philip Miller's cantata *REwind*, the title of which is derived from this passage of testimony. For Miller, Eunice Miya's testimony contained a rich metaphor of rewinding an analog tape. Miya, he believed, wanted the news about her son to rewind, to not have happened, so that her son would not have died. And yet a careful translation of her Xhosa testimony conveys a far more literal meaning for that word "rewind":

> A child appeared with a gun on his chest and another one appeared and he was my son, Jabulani. So we started to argue with my daughter. She said mama it is not Jabu and I said it is him because I know what he was wearing this morning when he accompanied me to the station. (She is crying louder). I told her that he was wearing a navy blue pant and a green jacket and a warm woolen hat. I prayed and said "God, as we are arguing about this child I wish this news could be rewinded and show his picture only." It really happened; he appeared alone on the screen.[100]

While Eunice Miya certainly would wish more than anything that the killing of her son had not happened, her use of the term "rewind" was not metaphoric. She wanted the news to be rewound so she could study the image. She wanted to positively identify her son, Jabulani, as being among the deceased. The literalness of her need at this moment spoke more eloquently of her situation than the metaphoric renderings that have been imposed, relayed, and amplified by the multiple processes of interpretation: from Miya's Xhosa to the interpreter's booth, from the English interpretation made in the booth to Antjie Krog's book, from Krog's distilled and edited version of the English interpretation of Miya's words to Philip Miller's libretto for *REwind*. These refractions of meaning are also interesting and revealing. The misunderstandings tell us something about truths and realities other than the one Eunice Miya was trying to convey. But the fundamental issue is that we have not really heard and understood what Eunice Miya said. The TRC's "rainbow of truths" seems to have been created by a prism when what we may really need is a corrective lens.

Conclusion

The significance, importance, and power of language and the interpretive process at the TRC hearings have been grossly underestimated. The secondary literature on the TRC and the TRC's own processes have been overwhelmingly dominated by quantitative analysis. What is needed is much more scholarship that *is qualitative* in nature, humanistic research rather than social science. I agree with Mark Sanders that the truth commission "revealed more than expected," but I would add that scholars' expectations for the commission have often been so narrow that the full significance of commission's revelations have yet to be appreciated, acknowledged, or indeed even perceived. Transcripts should be studied for what they tell us not just about gross violations of human rights but also about demands for revenge, articulations of grief, the trials of daily life under apartheid, and, finally, about the simultaneous and conflicted urges to both remember and forget, all of which are evident in the words of testimony.[101]

The testimonies from public hearings—so far one of the few primary documents from the TRC archive that is readily accessible to the public—demand analysis that is attentive, among other things, to the coherence and totality of particular testimonies. Far too often testimonies, when they are used at all, are analyzed in fragments: the scholar excerpts a potent sound bite to prove a point rather than letting the interpretive points arise from a thorough and complete analysis of a particular testimony or set of testimonies. A second priority should be to illuminate the ways that embodiment—such as intonation, gesture, cadence, and eye contact—forms a crucial part of narrative/personal truth in public testimony. Third, the HRVC record needs to be examined much more thoroughly, with scholars actually reading testimony rather than relying on secondary sources and reading testimonies that have not received wide attention. The same few testimonies have received an inordinate amount of media and scholarly scrutiny, becoming essentially iconic, while the majority of 2,000 public testimonies before the Human Rights Violation Committee have received no qualitative analysis whatsoever. We have heard so often of Nomonde Calata's cry ("the signature tune, the definitive moment, the ultimate sound of what the process is about"); of Joyce Mtimkulu holding in her hand the hair of her son who died by poisoning; of Jeffrey Benzien demonstrating before the commission his wet-bag torture technique; of Dirk Coetzee's affectless description of the *braai* (barbeque) of dead torture victims and his feigned contrition ("Remorse, I can assure you, a lot, a hell of a lot"); of Lucas Sikwepere, blinded by a policeman's bullet, saying that testifying before the commission had given him back his sight; of Winnie Madikizela-Mandela's long-withheld and vague admission that "things" with her Mandela United Football Club "went horribly wrong."[102] But who knows about Geoffrey Yalolo, who was so transformed by months of torture at the hands of the police that when fellow prisoners showed him his reflection in a mirror, he didn't recognize himself? ("Have you seen you?" his comrades asked).[103] Or about Elsie Jantjie, who testified by asking over and over: "Who is guilty? Who is guilty? Who is guilty? Who is guilty?"[104] Or about Sisana Mary Maphalane describing life in a war zone, "People did go to work. . . . We managed to go through these bullets you know, going to work between bullets."[105] Or about the man who came before the commission to speak lovingly of his friend, Alfred Khumalo, only for the interpreters to gradually realize that this friend whom he held in his arms, polished, and slept with was actually his AK-47.[106] Or, finally, about the heartbreaking story of Nomusa Shando, an Inkatha Freedom Party supporter who witnessed the execution of her entire family ("On the 20th, in other words, Bethwell, Mfiki, Linda, Zipporah, Primrose and Thulile, those are the only people who died on the 20th, and Masiki as well. Mfiki was the last one to die").[107]

I am calling for a radical revision of the scholarship done on the TRC: scholarship that honors the complexity of the interpretive process; scholarship that looks for truths embedded in testimony that run counter to the commission's mandate; interpretations that shelve the interminable assessment of the commission's virtues or faults; books and articles that actually quote testimony and quote widely the hundreds of testimonies that have heretofore received no attention beyond their initial hearing; analysis that considers the publicly available TRC archive to be worthy of rigorous study; research that examines the performative, embodied, linguistically embedded nature of testimony; interpretations that accord those who gave testimony dignity by bothering to read what people said—as well as how they said it—in their own languages. This chapter is a methodological intervention aimed at demonstrating what qualitative, humanistic, language-based, and performance-based approaches to the TRC archive can reveal about the gradations of meaning, empirical richness, and historical potential of the testimonies given at public hearings. The premise of this work is quite simple yet also profound: what people said before the commission *matters,* and it matters enough that scholars should actually read and study this testimony closely and with integrity.

4. Eyes and Ears of the Nation: Television and the Implicated Witness

The televising of public occasions must meet the challenge not only of representing the event, but of offering the viewer a functional equivalent of the festive experience. By superimposing its own performance on the performance as organized, by displaying its reactions to the reaction of the spectators, by proposing to compensate viewers for the direct participation of which they are deprived, television becomes the primary performer in the enactment of public ceremonies. Such performances by television must not be considered mere "alterations" or "additions" to the original. Rather, they should be perceived as qualitative transformations of the very nature of public events.

—Daniel Dayan and Elihu Katz

Liveness is ideological . . . it is rooted in an unexamined belief that live confrontation can somehow give rise to the truth in ways that recorded representations cannot.

—Philip Auslander

The TRC's embrace of public display placed enormous stock in being present and face to face. The liveness of the hearings, the physical presence of victims and perpetrators in one room before a crowd of witnesses, the ability of audiences to see the faces and experience testimony in real time, to hear the rhythms, phrasings, and intonations of speech—all these elements seemed to carry a truth effect capable of inspiring in some an innate confidence that what was transpiring was somehow real and genuine. Constitutional Court justice Albie Sachs has said that more significant than the truth commission's findings was the fact that the story played out in public.[1] Even if the content of testimony was not perceived by spectators to be absolutely truthful (indeed, many testimonies, especially those by perpetrators, were seen as outright lies), the crowds assembled served not only as witness but also as judges of the proceedings. Having the TRC transpire in public *implicated* that audience, it drew them in as active witnesses, participants, and performers. Audiences could evaluate for themselves how particular words came out of particular mouths, could ask and consider what complexities and shades of other truths might be submerged in a facial tic, an averted eye, or an unfinished phrase. "See for yourself," the TRC public hearings seemed to imply.

By witnessing the TRC hearings, audiences became entwined with the commission. They became involved in the stories told before commission and implicated by the consequences of those stories. The implicated witness is a concept I explore throughout this chapter, for I argue that the commission performed one of its core values, *ubuntu,* by folding together the teller and receiver of the narratives the commission presented. There are two levels of witnessing here: the one who provides testimony and the one who bears witness to that testimony. The truth commission bound these two constituencies together. The personalization of testimony at the TRC and its embodiment before an audience gave a sense of reality to a cascade of narratives that were *hard to believe.* These stories were fantastic in their gruesomeness, in the elaborate webs of intrigue, corruption, and depravity they revealed. Yet hearing the stories in the first person by direct witnesses gave some sense of individuation and humanity, drawing attention to the fact that the deeds being narrated were done by *people* to other *people.* According to Albie Sachs, the most distinctive aspect of the hearings was that they provided

> a sense of reality, a sense of real personalization—not through actors playing the parts of the different personae, but through seeing this person who had been tortured, victimized—somebody who could be living next door to you in certain communities, through seeing the sergeant, the colonel, the police officers dressed up in their suits, their tight, often stiff body language. But the voices were our voices. The tears were our tears. The emotion—it was the emotion of everybody. And it had a register and resonance that you certainly don't get in court trials, which are very formalized and stylized—so this had a much more open quality. The stories just went on and on. They came pouring out without the interruptions that you get with witnesses [in a court of law].[2]

Embedded in the TRC's investment in embodiment and emotional expressiveness were some of the ideological underpinnings Philip Auslander has identified as being central to the notion of "liveness": namely, the unexamined belief that live confrontation "can somehow give rise to the truth in ways that recorded representations cannot."[3] The TRC benefited from this common assumption, but it also suffered from it. Confidence in the veracity of liveness has a flip side, a Janus face known as "antitheatrical prejudice." This bias assumes that what transpires before an audience, especially on a stage, is inherently false and artificial.[4] The live and performative elements of the TRC triggered these twin and vacillating prejudices: on one hand, the unexamined confidence in the truthfulness of the live encounter; on the other, the inherent suspicion that acts done on stage for show are false—not something you want in a "truth" commission.

If the TRC was in fact putting on a show, then who was the intended audience? For whom were stories at public TRC hearings told? For commissioners? Desmond Tutu? Politicians? Judges? Local communities where the TRC presided as it moved around the country? Those who gave testimony before the commission ostensibly did so for the commissioners: it was they who would make findings, determine amnesty cases, decide who would be counted a victim of gross violations of human rights and thus be eligible to receive whatever reparations the government might decide to dole out. But the audience for the TRC was far greater than the commissioners. They, I argue, were surrogates, standing in for a larger audience, one more central to the TRC's mission: the nation at large. The spatial arrangements at TRC hearings made visually manifest the layers of audiences and their relative importance. At the first HRVC hearings, for instance, the commissioners were arrayed on stage before the audience while the witness sat at the front of the house, back to the audience, facing the commissioners. This spatial arrangement changed fairly quickly in the TRC process, for organizers felt it did not accurately symbolize what the commission was about. The new format placed witnesses on the stage adjacent to the commissioners, both seated at tables angled slightly toward each other. The arrangement enabled both the commissioners and the witness to face outward toward the house, making clear who the real audience was for the TRC and for the testimony given before the commission.

Some witnesses looked at the commissioners as they talked. Others cast their gaze to the audience in the hall. Still others turned their focus downward, facing no one at all, avoiding eye contact, perhaps from shame or shyness, perhaps because avoidance was the only way to maintain composure while narrating ghastly traumatic events. Some commissioners chose yet another focal point: they looked directly at the television camera trained on them when they spoke. By doing so, they privileged a third audience that was not present at the hearing. They spoke to the nation at large.

The TRC's shift from addressing immediate spectators to reaching an audience assembled remotely via the media represents a dramatic intervention in the TRC process, one that raises some profound questions: Where did the boundaries of the "real" TRC event end and televised representation or documentation begin? Was television merely a record of the "real" event of the TRC—the live hearings—or was television an extension of the commission, a performative iteration in its own right? The truth commission was certainly a media event as Daniel Dayan and Elihu Katz define the term. It was a ceremonial event of historic significance that transfixed a nation, and with the introduction of television into the proceedings, it moved "off the ground and 'into the air.'"[5] This aspect of the truth commission has been entirely unexamined, and yet it is tremendously important. We must examine how television created its audience, invited spectators to interact with the screen and with the unfolding stories of the commission, isolated key moments, sustained interest, and shaped particular narratives that gained currency and prominence over the many others it could not cover. Yet at its core, what is most significant about television is not how it functioned as a document but how it became a surrogate for the commission.

Dayan and Katz have said of media events:

What we offer you, says television, is not just an unobstructed view of "there," but a wholly different experience that is available only to those who are *not* there. Making full use of the powers of spectacle, television presents its viewers with new, modern modes of participation in lieu of the old. Instead of a pale equivalent of the ceremonial experience, it offers the uniquely televisual "experience of not being there." As a matter of fact, says television, there may not be any "there" at all.[6]

Like the live TRC hearings, television provided audiences the experience of seeing the faces and hearing the words, having an experience that was visual and sonic. In these ways television contrasted markedly with the publication of a summary document, the textual means by which all truth commissions prior to South Africa's had been publicized. Television created an experience of the commission that was at once immediate and remote: immediate because one could see more faces more closely than would ever be possible if attending the event live; immediate because viewers saw images from multiple perspectives that no one person at the live hearing would have experienced; remote because television coverage removed that important element of human presence, the live, face-to-face encounter; and remote because unlike the actual hearings, which moved to specific locations to hear testimony about events that had happened in that area, television removed geographic specificity. You could sit in Gauteng and listen to testimony from Duduza or Victoria West or Kimberly. Television was also temporally distant, for its coverage did not take place in real time: continuous live coverage was suspended after the first week of hearings due to cost.

It is impossible to determine how many people viewed the commission on television (South Africa does not have precise audience measurement tools). However, we do know that far more people watched on television and listened on radio than ever attended the TRC in person or read the commission's summary report. Many believe that the very nature of this mode of transmission had a profound impact on the national collective experience of the commission and hence on collective memory. Three leading authors of the summary report—Janet Cherry, John Daniel, and Madeline Fullard—admit that broadcasting the story of a single victim on television "had more impact upon national consciousness than any number of volumes of the report."[7] Even when people chose not to watch the TRC on television, that decision constituted a deliberate way of interacting with the commission. In the words of Albie Sachs, "Even those who switched off the set when the truth commission came on were involved, they were taking a stand. They weren't ignoring it."[8]

If we consider televised coverage of extraordinary national events such as the TRC not as mere representations but rather as qualitative transformations of the very nature of the event, as Dayan and Katz argue, then the entire analysis and appraisal of South Africa's Truth and Reconciliation Commission must shift gears. Far too much of the secondary literature has focused on critiquing the TRC's summary report. If so few have read it, how much does the document really matter? Because most people in South Africa experienced the truth commission via broadcast media, that mediated transmission constituted their experience of the commission. In many ways, broadcast coverage *was* the commission for this larger general audience.

This chapter focuses on one television representation of the commission, *TRC Special Report,* an 87-episode current affairs program televised by the South

African Broadcasting Corporation (SABC) and produced by the famous rene-gade Afrikaner journalist Max du Preez.[9] The first program aired on 21 April 1996 and weekly installments continued through 29 March 1998, a duration that generally coincided with that of the public proceedings of the Human Rights Violations Committee and Amnesty Committee hearings. One reason *TRC Special Report* is significant and should command our analytic attention is because it provides an exemplary document of the commission and of the way the com-mission was experienced by millions of South African. When one watches the entire series in sequence, one gets a strong impression of the TRC as an unfold-ing *process* rather than as a static iteration of "findings." *TRC Special Report* ar-guably did more than any other manifestation of the commission to enlist public participation in that process. Yet ultimately I believe that *TRC Special Report* was more than a representation: it was a performative iteration of the commission. Through television's ability to manipulate time, to direct the spectator's focus, to capture details through the use of close-ups, to intercut footage from multiple locations and time periods, and to show statements being made and spectators reacting, television not only conveyed and reported on the commission, it *per-formed* it.

Scholar Annelies Verdoolaege has made the most extensive analysis of *TRC Special Report* to date, but her work examines just thirty-four of eighty-seven episodes, or roughly 39 percent of the series.[10] The analysis I provide here is based upon a comprehensive viewing of the complete series in chronological or-der as well as multiple viewings of particular episodes.[11] The questions I ask in-clude: How did *TRC Special Report* shape the TRC experience for audiences? How did the cinematic and structural conventions of the program create, posi-tion, and anticipate its audience(s) and, by extension, the experience of public witnessing of and participation in the TRC as a national ceremony? How did *TRC Special Report* use narrative? What kinds of storytelling did the program engage in? How did the program negotiate the uncomfortable alliance between the critical distance mandated by journalism and the active promulgation of the TRC as a public event?

In the way of all media events, the program walked a fine line between jour-nalism and participation, between reporting the event and actively propagating it.[12] An episode shown in May 1997 ended by telling viewers that if they were considering applying for amnesty, "here are the phone numbers. Please don't write to *Special Report*. We are a completely independent agency. We just report on the commission."[13] Anxious though the producers were to create a distinction between *TRC Special Report* and the truth commission, the conflation of the two in the perception of the public was unavoidable. *TRC Special Report* performed an act of surrogation, functioning as a secondary shadow commission that, simi-lar to the TRC, took statements, conducted investigations, aired confessions (in-cluding confessions *not* heard before the TRC), made findings, and even made retractions bordering on apology. The show compensated viewers for being de-prived of direct participation by giving them, as its motto claimed, the "stories behind the stories." The substitute it offered for being there was being in multiple theres across space and time: the producers wove together "then," as seen in archival footage, with the "now" of the TRC hearings and interviews conducted in local communities. In order to provide the context and explanatory narratives that were so often missing at the public hearings, *TRC Special Report* intercut testimony being given at the truth commission, which had the potency of embodiment, with disembodied voiceovers. The rigorously edited programs mixed the formality of TRC testimony, which was given in public spaces, with the intimacy of interviews with the same witnesses in their living rooms or at the gravesites where loved ones had been buried or at the places where loved ones had been tortured and killed. While *TRC Special Report* struggled to maintain critical distance from the TRC, a perspective it needed for journalistic credibility, the program's status was inevitably liminal and conflicted. Was it a document of the commission or a critical reaction to it? Was it a surrogate for the commission and the witnesses or a surrogate for the public? Was this the feature article or the review? Television was both a representation of the commission and a central actor in its unfolding drama. Such conflicts were not unique to television: all participants in the TRC process, including television and radio audiences, faced such quandaries. To be a witness, they learned, is also to be a participant. There is no place outside the event. To witness is to be implicated, as television enacted and made manifest.

Being There versus Not Being There

In order to illustrate how *TRC Special Report* performed the stories of the TRC, I focus on several iterations of a story about a woman named Maki Skosana. Skosana was the first victim of the series of so-called necklacing murders that arose in the violent latter days of the apartheid regime. In the 1980s, the ANC adopted a strategy of making the state ungovernable, and the state in turn drew upon its most violent, underhanded, and insidious techniques in a desperate attempt to maintain white power. The practice of necklacing, or covering a victim with a gasoline-doused tire and setting it alight, claimed more than 979 lives between 1984 and 1992.[14] While it is true that within narrow parameters of analysis necklacing was black-on-black violence, it is also true that agents of the apartheid state fanned and even ignited the flames of township violence that led to such incidents as necklacings. This brutal form of lynching, which some people in the townships inflicted on suspected police informers, captured national and international attention during the 1980s and early 1990s as gruesome images of these murders were broadcast in South Africa and internationally. Some South Africans pointed to necklacing as an example of the bankruptcy of the apartheid legal system, which provided such limited protections for those in black townships that they were forced to form their own people's courts and mechanisms for punishment. Others—namely the white apartheid state—interpreted necklacing as evidence of the primitivism of blacks and their inability to govern themselves.

Maki Skosana's sister, Evelina Puleng Moloko, testified before the Human Rights Violations Committee on 2 February 1997. Her testimony begins abruptly:

> It was on the 20th of July 1985, but I would first like to start where the whole issue started because there were certain rumours that they wanted to kill Maki and they also stated the reason as to why they wanted to kill her. There were rumours that they wanted to kill her because she caused the death of certain youths who died due to being blown up by hand grenades. Now, those youths who were allegedly killed by hand grenades were three and the whole three died next to my place.[15]

A story of high drama: three people dead, hand grenades, rumors of death threats—all in the first two sentences. Like many stories of trauma, the text embodies the very disorientation it represents. "It was on the 20th of July," Moloko begins, but she doesn't say what "it" is. "They" wanted to kill Maki, and yet "they" is an orphan pronoun with no antecedent. This is a story of action: three people killed by hand grenades. And yet the first sentence obscures agency with the passive voice: "there were certain rumours."

The TRC commissioners were prepared to receive such decontextualized stories because they were briefed prior to hearings by staff researchers who summarized the background and context of particular cases and concisely described patterns of violence in the region. But the press was not always privy to this information. So their burden was to discover a context—some context, any context—in which to place a story (and rapidly!) if it was to appear in newspapers, on radio programs, or on television shows within days or even hours of the hearing. In the TRC's summary report, Skosana's case receives a few short sentences:

> Was "necklaced" and her body mutilated by named perpetrators on 20 July 1985 in Duduza, Nigel, Tvl, after the funeral of four youth activists. She was accused of being a police informer.[16]

Skosana's story is also briefly covered in Antjie Krog's *Country of My Skull*. Krog highlights her role as narrator:

> I can talk about nothing but the Truth Commission. Yet I don't talk about it at all. Until the day in Queenstown. It is bitterly cold. Coated, scarved, we listen to one necklacing experience after another—grim stories, a relentless procession of faces in a monotonous rhythm.[17]

A footnote explains necklacings and says that the truth commission has heard allegations that Skosana's necklacing was instigated by "third-force elements," meaning covert government operatives working to fan the flames of unrest within the townships. In Krog's coverage of necklacing, we learn much about Krog's psychological state as narrator but very little about the individuals who were killed or the circumstances that led to these murders. Only a footnote provides a brief exposition and details.

In contrast with the TRC report's decontextualized and highly compressed summary of Skosana's case and Krog's self-absorbed reportage, the coverage on *TRC Special Report* was extensive, spanning four episodes.[18] Taken together, these four segments convey a tremendous amount of information about Skosana as a person, about necklacing as a practice of vigilante violence in the townships in the 1980s, and about the role of government-sponsored "third-force" activities in encouraging and publicizing necklacing. *TRC Special Report* connects neck-lacing to Vlakplaas, which deliberately sought to create strife and suspicion in the townships. According to the program, Vlakplaas had planted booby-trapped hand grenades among activists, the same type of grenades mentioned in Molo-ko's testimony above. We also learn the sequence of events within the commu-nity that led to Skosana's killing as well as new information about her death that came as a result of amnesty hearings.

I focus on the Maki Skosana case to give some sense of the storytelling *TRC Special Report* deployed, of the way the program's producers provided complexity, and of how successive coverage of particular cases over time managed to convey factual and analytic detail as well as sophisticated explanatory frames. The pic-ture that emerges from these four segments—which together total less than twenty minutes—reveals an intricate web of specific individuals, larger state forces, and systematic oppressions that led to Skosana's death. Truth emerges gradually as a process, unfolding over time. The process is dialogic, with multiple perspectives that ultimately remain unresolved; truth appears in the program as neither singu-lar nor closed. We see the web of connections between key actors in the TRC epic drama. One woman's death is eventually linked to a chain of command that reached the highest levels of government: former brigadier Jack Cronje, Police Commissioner Johan van der Merwe, General Johan Coetzee, and even President P. W. Botha. These men did not target Maki Skosana, but they did authorize an *askari,* a black informer named Joe Mamasela, to set a trap that led to her death. Mamasela posed as an ANC activist; he recruited and incited young men to attack the homes of policemen and councilors. He equipped a group of young comrades, who were also Skosana's friends, with hand grenades that were rigged to explode as soon as the pins were removed. It was Maki Skosana's unfortunate fate to be a minor pawn in this elaborate plot. When the rage over these murders mounted, she—unlike Mamasela, Cronje, van der Merwe, Coetzee, or Botha—was at the wrong place at the wrong time: on the ground in the townships, facing a swirling tide of frustration and becoming the scapegoat for growing rage.

One sees in the four *TRC Special Report* segments on this case some uncanny juxtapositions of past and present: Desmond Tutu makes an appearance in archi-val footage, wearing the purple robes he wore throughout the TRC hearings. The footage shows Tutu heroically intervening to save a man from being necklaced during the funeral of one of the activists killed by the booby-trapped hand gre-nades. Maki Skosana was murdered at the second of the funerals held for the activists. Had Tutu attended this funeral, might Maki be alive today? Were the TRC hearings over which Desmond Tutu presided as chairperson a substitute intervention, a place where he saved Skosana's reputation even though her life had been lost?

TRC Special Report defies many assumptions about television reportage of the TRC that critics have voiced, including their general assumption that television simplified and decontextualized TRC stories.[19] In fact, the eighty-seven episodes of *TRC Special Report* provide far more background on specific cases than does any other iteration of the TRC, including the live public hearings themselves. The story of Skosana as covered by *TRC Special Report* is both micro and macro in scope, covering both the individual level of the event and its connection to larger national patterns and to state forces and structures. In four segments totaling twenty minutes, *TRC Special Report* conveys more details, facts, and context than the live hearings, the TRC's summary report, or indeed any other representation of the commission to date.

The first segment on Maki Skosana aired on 23 June 1996, very early in the TRC process; this was only the seventh episode of *TRC Special Report*.[20] The segment focuses on the practice of murder via necklace, which the TRC glossary defines as "a car tyre filled with petrol used mainly by United Democratic Front supporters to burn political opponents, especially those regarded as collaborators and police informers."[21] The program's executive producer Max du Preez edited this segment, and his voice can be heard over grainy footage of a vigilante murder of an unidentified victim taking place in a township. Du Preez tells us that between 1984 and 1987 at least 350 people died with a tire around their necks. The program then shows footage of TRC testimony given by Benedict Marenene, the son of a man who died by necklacing. After this story, the segment returns to grisly grainy archival footage of a densely packed crowd kicking and pounding bricks into the charred remains of a body blackened by fire. The disembodied voice of du Preez asks, "What was it about our people or our history that made this ghastly practice possible and so popular?"

Sandila Dikeni, a poet and journalist, is selected to give an answer. He theorizes necklacing within a succession of political acts, starting with boycotting Bantu-education schools because of their inferior quality, then writing a protest poem, then using a hand grenade or petrol bomb against the police. The process accelerates to the point where a young militant activist targets and kills a person. Dikeni identifies two key elements in the potency of necklacing: first, it gave the powerless a feeling of supreme power over another human being; and second, the images of this form of murder were widely circulated on television. While people far removed from the violence can easily see the role these images played in state propaganda justifying the brute force of apartheid, those mired in poverty and violence in the townships saw these images in the media differently, as expressing their power, even when the conditions of poverty and injustice surrounding them overwhelmingly reinforced their powerlessness. Dikeni also places the perpetrators of necklacing within a context of anti-apartheid activism, claiming they were on the "edges," the "foot soldiers," not really part of the intellectual articulation of resistance. Intercut with the Dikeni interview are more horrific images of necklacing. Du Preez's eventual naming of Maki Skosana indicates that the images we've been seeing are of her murder, images that have historical significance not only because Skosana suffered the first known instance of necklacing in South Africa but also because the murder was immediately broadcast in South Africa and throughout the world. Thus, like the Guguletu

Seven case, the case of Skosana represents an intricate interweaving of television itself as a key performer. The fact that the state (in the form of SABC television cameras) happened to be present at this first necklacing in South Africa subsequently raised questions about the covert role of government in this heinous vigilante act, which the apartheid state represented as "black-on-black" violence and grotesque evidence that blacks are not capable of civilized behavior, much less leadership of the country. In this *TRC Special Report* episode, Dikeni says that just after Skosana's murder he was outspoken in condemning it, even though he was pressured from within the anti-apartheid movement to avoid speaking publicly about necklacing. At that time, Dikeni says, "nobody in the movement wanted to condone necklacing, but nobody wanted to condemn it either."[22] Dikeni then makes an explicit, race-based comparison of those who committed gross violations of human rights. The perpetrators of necklacings, he predicts, will be "humble" enough to come forward to "confess" before Bishop Tutu, but the members of the South African Defence Force, who also perpetrated gruesome murders, will be much less likely to do so.

TRC Special Report anchored the sensational images of necklacing inside a larger historical and structural analysis. By doing so, the program was signaling a dramatic departure from past journalistic practices, when the SABC news carried stories of necklacing without such context. This first episode (lasting a brief seven minutes) presents Maki Skosana's story as paradigmatic of the larger story of necklacing as a type of gross violation of human rights, and the segment's aural and visual registers provide dense and conflicting information. On the one hand we see sensational and grisly images, scenes that ten years earlier had been widely shown on television as propaganda for the apartheid state. But these are underscored with a sophisticated analysis that touches upon larger structural issues of oppression as well as on the state's use of the media for its own purposes and the anti-apartheid struggle's reluctance to assertively halt such gruesome practices. The very airing on the "new" SABC of archival footage shot by the "old," apartheid-era SABC in a new critical context performed transformation, as often happened on *TRC Special Report,* transformation of civil society, of public discourse, of the role of journalism in the old and new state. In this way *TRC Special Report* served, like the TRC, as a historic bridge between the past and present.

The second *TRC Special Report* episode to cover Maki Skosana's case aired many months later, on 9 February 1997, shortly after the HRVC hearing at which her sister testified. The episode again linked Skosana's case to a larger issue by showing two back-to-back segments contrasting the death of Maki Skosana, who was killed by vigilantes in the township, with that of Mary-Anne Serrano, a white woman killed by a limpet mine planted by Umkhonto we Sizwe operatives in a Wimpy restaurant. In both cases, the alleged perpetrators were black and the program presented the victims as innocent.[23] The structuring of this episode conveys a particular editorial point that *TRC Special Report* wanted to make: both whites and blacks were innocent victims in the country's violent past.

TRC Special Report identifies Skosana's murder as the first necklacing seen on television, and it says that even those responsible for her murder now confess that she was not a police informer. It includes a portion of testimony given by Evelina Moloko before the TRC as well as footage of one of the commission panelists, Tom Manthata, listening to and then responding verbally to Moloko's testimony.[24] Manthata says that Maki Skosana has emerged as a hero and that those who in the hall and elsewhere have heard Moloko's testimony (including, we can infer, those who watch this episode of *TRC Special Report*) are witnesses to Maki's noble spirit. He asks the audience to stand and observe a moment of silence, and during that moment the camera pans to the audience in a small, cramped venue. Cutaways to the audience, both long pans and close-ups, were a common feature of *TRC Special Report,* far more common than images of the commissioners listening to testimony. Cinematically, the program constructed the spectators in the hall (not the commissioners) as the audience, the true receivers of testimony. By extension, the program positioned spectators attending the live hearings as surrogates for us, those watching at home.

This segment on the Skosana case concludes with du Preez in the studio, wearing the Nehru-collared shirt that became a sartorial signature for him during the two-year course of this series. Du Preez addresses the camera, stating that the myth of necklacing is that "this was an example of African brutality. The truth as we now know is that this repulsive form of killing was first started by white Rhodesian security forces in the 1970s and then brought to South Africa by the Security Police."[25] Here, Du Preez performs the role for which he is famous in South Africa, especially from his days with the newspaper *Vrye Weekblad* under apartheid: the tough, hard-nosed investigative journalist making unprecedented revelations about corruption and depravity. (After this episode aired, the Flame Lily Foundation, an association of former Rhodesians, filed a complaint with the Broadcasting Complaint Commission of South Africa stating that du Preez's claims about Rhodesian forces were not substantiated. The commission upheld the complaint and du Preez was forced to read a statement to this effect on his program four months later, which he then followed with his rebuttal.)[26]

TRC Special Report constructed itself as a venue that revealed truths, including truths the TRC was *not* producing. The very first episode told of how the families of a group of missing men known as the Pebco Three had gone before the commission seeking answers but had gotten none.[27] Du Preez says, "Tonight we *will* give the Pebco families some answers," meaning that *TRC Special Report* would satisfy the quest for truth when the commission did not.[28] Thus, the program functioned in some ways as a shadow TRC, an alternate venue seeking truth about atrocities from the past. That Max du Preez had to recant, to some extent, the program's claims about the origins of necklacing also performed its version of "reconciliation." This moment in the program demonstrated that in telling its versions of the truth, *TRC Special Report* and Max du Preez were still accountable—to the state and the public, and even, though du Preez complained bitterly about this, to representatives of the army and police of the former Rhodesia, both of which had a long and proven history of brutality. The program could tell its truths, but it was accountable and could even be forced to flirt with apology. At such moments, *TRC Special Report*'s ambiguous role as witness, performer, and surrogate of the truth commission was most apparent.

Going Public

The broadcast of TRC hearings via television and radio was an exceptional media event in South African history.[29] Two contrasting episodes, thirty-three years apart, reveal a radically changed climate for broadcast journalism. At the Rivonia Trial, the state courted the national and international press. Prosecutor Percy Yutar reputedly had a "passion for publicity," as was evident from his frequent interviews with the press and circulation among journalists of advance copies of the Rivonia indictment as well as printed copies of his opening address, "all beautifully bound and tied up in green tape."[30] But Yutar's appetite for publicity brought the courtroom to a point beyond which Judge Quartus de Wet was not willing to venture. During Yutar's opening address, defense counsel Bram Fischer noticed a strange intrusion in the courtroom. He abruptly stood up, as fellow counsel Joel Joffe recalls:

> He pointed at a small black microphone which had grown up overnight on the desk in front of Dr. Yutar. It hadn't been there before, but while we had been waiting for the case to start we had noticed some technicians of the South African Broadcasting Corporation tinkering around and doing tests on this microphone. It appeared to us that someone had decided to broadcast the prosecution's opening address. This may be normal in some countries, but broadcasting any part of a court case was utterly unknown in South Africa. It had never happened at any time in history.[31]

Resistance to cameras and microphones in courtrooms was and is quite typical internationally. But South Africa's apprehensions about mass media went beyond typical. In a state run by a minority that was rabidly trying to preserve unequal distribution of wealth and power at the expense of a poor, disenfranchised majority, broadcasting was widely recognized for its ideological potency.[32] The National Party therefore tightly controlled broadcast journalism for decades. Few radio stations existed in South Africa at the time of the Rivonia Trial, and efforts to introduce television into the country were blocked until 1976, when TV1 began broadcasting a tentative five hours per day.[33] Yet if we jump ahead to 1996—just two decades later, when the public hearings of the TRC commenced—we see a state-sponsored theatre of power that was literally overrun by broadcast journalists, not just from South Africa but also from around the world. Antjie Krog led the radio team that covered the TRC for SABC radio. In her memoir, she provides a journalist's perspective on competition among broadcasters:

> The first sign of the International Journalist in your midst is the subtle fragrance. Male or female, overseas journalists can obviously afford perfumery that you won't find on

the shelves at Pick 'n Pay. The second sign is the equipment. Microphones like cruise missiles on launching pads appear in front of interviewees, and you have to find space next to them for your humble little SABC mike. They are equipped with recorders that produce fully edited sound bites and reports at the push of a button, computers they can carry in their inside pockets, and cell phones no bigger than lipsticks.[34]

Joffee and Krog's stories share an image of a tentative SABC microphone. But whereas Percy Yutar felt an inchoate impulse to broadcast the drama of the Rivonia courtroom, it was not until thirty-three years later that the South African state could embrace mass media transmission of its judicial (or quasi-judicial) theatres of power.

That the South African Parliament chose to allow the TRC to be so widely broadcast was an extraordinary decision, especially when one considers that just a few years prior to the commission any statements made by Archbishop Desmond Tutu were edited out of SABC news coverage. As Evita Bezuidenhout (aka the comedian Pieter-Dirk Uys) recalls, in the "old days" one never saw Tutu for more than twenty seconds on television, and when he appeared all you could hear was the word "sanctions."[35]

The revolutionary nature of the broadcast coverage of the TRC was perceived globally, since most truth commissions in the world prior to South Africa's had transpired not only off camera but also behind closed doors.[36] Justice Albie Sachs says that when the truth commission was being considered, he opposed public hearings:

> I just couldn't imagine that the people who came to be called perpetrators would come up with the truth if they had to do so in public. And I felt that we would get far more information and material if it were done behind closed doors. They could really own up to what they had done.[37]

However, various civil society groups in South Africa that opposed any version of a truth commission (they contended it would violate the principles of accountability central to the rule of law) agreed to a compromise solution: the TRC proceedings could go on if hearings took place in public.

In the early 1990s, the Standing Committee of Parliament that had debated the legislation authorizing the TRC decided initially that the operations of the proposed truth commission, especially its amnesty hearings, should transpire behind closed doors. The so-called blanket secrecy clause provoked clamorous debate among nongovernmental organizations (NGOs), some of which lobbied, ultimately successfully, to have this clause removed from the legislation.[38] These groups argued, first, that victims of human rights abuse were entitled to learn who ordered and perpetrated such deeds. Second, they contended that a truth commission would be instrumental in creating a new institutional culture based on transparency. According to Graeme Simpson and Paul van Zyl of the Centre for the Study of Violence and Reconciliation (an NGO), to create the new dispensation, the "best of disinfectants" was needed: public scrutiny.[39] They asserted, "In the absence of full disclosure and public knowledge of past human rights

Figure 4.1. The media scrambles to capture Jeffrey Benzien's reenactment of the wet bag torture technique. Courtesy of George Hallett.

abuses, the inherited institutions of the new government may well retain unchallenged their organizational culture of clandestine, unaccountable and covert activity."[40] The TRC was not just charged with conducting investigations into past incidents of gross violations of human rights, it was also charged with being *seen* to conduct these investigations. In the end, it was seen doing this on television.

What were the implications of the TRC's decision to allow an invasion of microphones at its hearings, to welcome the looming television cameras numbering at the most popular hearings nearly a half-dozen, and to tolerate great swarms of photographers, their telephoto lenses protruding a half-meter out in front of their faces?[41] (See figs. 4.1 and 4.2.) In a country that for fifty years had severely curtailed freedom of speech, how did this level of media access to a state-sponsored commission even *happen*? In answering these questions, it is useful to parse with greater precision the different levels of audiovisual media involvement in the commission, from still photography to radio and television broadcasting. The TRC's attitude toward still photographers was conflicted and never fully resolved. Eventually they were allowed to scoot forward during the hearings, snap witnesses being sworn in, and then dash back to their places for the duration of testimony. At the Mandela United Football Club hearing (popularly known as the "Winnie" hearings), a flock of photographers scurried around like long-billed sandpipers alternately chasing and fleeing the ocean tide.[42] Meanwhile television cameras faced intense opposition from the Amnesty Committee, which "raised vociferous objections to the presence of TV cameras in hear-

Figure 4.2. Photographers outside "Winnie" TRC hearing. Courtesy of George Hallett.

ings," according to Commissioner Wendy Orr. "The Amnesty Committee took the stance that their proceedings should be equated with those of a court of law—no television cameras in court, therefore no television cameras in Amnesty [Committee] hearings."[43] In the TRC's summary report, the Amnesty Committee explains its concerns about television coverage of hearings: it might discourage people from applying for amnesty or giving testimony or counsel might exploit the media for advantage. The TRC prevailed in the end, and the Amnesty Committee agreed (albeit reluctantly) to allow television cameras. Afterward, even the Amnesty Committee admitted that the media played a "constructive and important role" in covering the hearings: "The role of the media in communicating the essence of the amnesty process and involving the public in the proceedings cannot be underestimated," noted the committee report. "It must be said that the process was considerably enriched by this contribution."[44]

Broadcast coverage of the TRC took several forms. First, the SABC covered the TRC through regular news bulletins delivered on television and by its twenty-three radio stations.[45] Second, live hearings were broadcast via continuous coverage on television during the first week of hearings and thereafter exclusively via Radio 2000, an SABC-owned outlet.[46] Live broadcast was costly and the SABC had difficulty sustaining it. Continuous radio transmission had to be suspended just five months into the TRC process and resumed eight months later only when the Norwegian government provided a subsidy.[47] A third broadcast category was digests that were offered on both radio and television. Various radio stations carried weekly summaries and in-depth current affairs programs in all languages, mostly on Friday evenings.[48] The television current affairs program that more than a million South Africans watched was Max du Preez's *TRC Special Report*. The program aired nearly every Sunday evening from April 1996 to March 1998.

One can plausibly argue that most South Africans experienced the commission through radio. The TRC's director of media communications, John Allen, confirms that the "conventional wisdom is that radio reached the highest numbers of people, followed by television and print newspapers."[49] In support of this view, the TRC's final report indicates that its Media Department targeted radio as the "most effective communication medium for its proceedings to the widest number of people."[50] The geographic distribution of radio in South Africa exceeds all other media, especially in rural areas, and radio transcends barriers of language, literacy, and technology. At the time of the TRC, the multilingual SABC radio stations reached 3.3 million Zulu-speaking listeners and 1.6 million Xhosa-speakers, 1.5 million SeSotho-speakers, 1 million SeTswana-speakers, 700,000 Afrikaans-speakers, 450,000 English-speakers, and 116,000 Venda-speakers.[51]

So the first thing to note about media coverage of the TRC is that it was largely an *aural* media event for most South Africans. This was a commission experienced sonically, heard through transistor radios on the streets, blaring over sound systems in cars and taxi vans. People listened as they drove, as they worked, and as they shopped or did laundry, for unlike television, radio forgivingly allows people to continue with the activities of their lives even as they listen to broadcasts.[52] Even commissioners experienced the TRC via radio. Wendy Orr recalls listening to testimony of Chief Mangosuthu Buthelezi as she drove around the town of Paarl looking for briefers for an upcoming hearing.[53] Gillian Slovo, daughter of anti-apartheid activists Ruth First and Joe Slovo, recalls people at the time of the hearings reporting how they drove around with the radio on while listening to the SABC broadcast of the TRC. They were "so affected by what they heard that they had to stop their cars and vomit," says Slovo.[54] Unfortunately, apparently no studies were done at the time of the commission about the extent, nature, and scope of radio coverage, nor do there appear to be archival records that would sustain a retrospective analysis of multistation and multilingual radio coverage of the TRC.

However a very rich and complete archive exists of the television coverage of the TRC in the form of the weekly digest *TRC Special Report*. While television may have reached fewer people than radio did, its impact was much more experientially rich, bringing visuality, embodiment, archival footage, location shots, and a whole range of techniques of communication not available through radio. "Without a doubt," writes Wendy Orr, "the TV images which appeared during the Commission's lifespan were compelling and conveyed the magnitude of our work with an impact which neither print nor radio could achieve."[55] Even the TRC's report acknowledged television's role in promulgating its proceedings: "The images relayed to the nation through television news bulletins and the SABC-TV weekly programme 'TRC Special Report' were probably the single most important factor in achieving a high public profile for the Commission."[56]

The first episode of *TRC Special Report* begins with an extraordinary SABC exclusive interview of black *askari* (informer) and Vlakplaas operative Joe Mamasela, who confesses to his involvement in state-sponsored murders and executions of numerous activists. Images from this interview, which was shot at such close range that Mamasela's face can sometimes be seen only in partial view, permeate later *TRC Special Report* episodes. Mamasela made disclosures that either broke open or complicated many cases that subsequently came before Human Rights Violations Committee and Amnesty Committee hearings.[57] The Mamasela confession on *TRC Special Report* is yet another example of the program's serving as a surrogate commission, a place where perpetrators could confess instead of at the commission if they so wished.

This first episode also contained footage of an incident that became an icon of the truth commission: Nomonde Calata in a bright red sweater tipping back in her seat and letting forth an unabashed cry from the heart.[58] Episode after episode featured "silver-haired elders and impassioned young lions" speaking their truths before microphones.[59] Johannes Roos, when talking of how his family was obliterated when they drove over an ANC-planted land mine, asked the commission: "Do you know how it feels to bury the brain of your own son, eight years old? How does one become a human being again after such an experience?"[60] Viewers also witnessed the advocate George Bizos obliterate Clive Derby-Lewis using his notoriously grueling cross-examination style during Derby-Lewis's amnesty hearing for commissioning the murder of ANC leader Chris Hani.[61] The images of Ernest Malgas being carried upstairs in his wheelchair on his way to give testimony or of Joyce Mtimkulu displaying the hair of her son, who had been poisoned with thallium, were seared into public memory, remembered and reinvoked long afterward.[62] *TRC Special Report* was to some degree responsible for the creation of iconic moments, for it returned repeatedly to certain images throughout the life of the program. A particularly illuminating example of this practice was a retrospective digest of the commission that aired on 29 June 1997.[63]

Television's dynamic combination of aural and visual registers made it a potent medium for promulgating the commission, as did its ability to convey personalities, characters, emotions, conflict, exposition, and story—in short, the very elements of TRC hearings that made them dramatic. Recalling his years as executive producer of *TRC Special Report*, Max du Preez notes, "I had this strong perception that the cameras were seen as the ear of the nation," a statement that oddly conflates cameras with hearing. "The ear, not the eye?" I asked during our interview, to which he responded, "The ear and the eye."[64] Through the cameras, witnesses could be both seen and heard. Those who gave testimony used the cameras to imagine particular audiences. According to du Preez, witnesses often told him that they knew they were speaking to the "whole nation" through his cameras. Simultaneously, they were also speaking to very specific imagined audiences. Perpetrators, for instance, "addressed their peers and their families through the cameras," according to du Preez.[65]

For those who testified at the HRVC hearings, the cameras may have been more about what the speakers received from them than what they conveyed to a particular audience. Victims had of course often told their stories, but they had told them to family members, furtively, in private. If they told their stories to the police or to other public entities, they were often not believed. But in the public TRC hearings, they could speak openly, freely, and uninterrupted for thirty minutes, and they were speaking not just to family or community members or to a small group of government officials but to the entire nation. As they gave their stories to the camera, *the camera gave them recognition*. As du Preez explains, under apartheid these stories

> couldn't be told publicly because of fear. You don't stir up more [trouble] if you're already in trouble. And the government made them out to be liars, or said, "You deserved it [whatever bad thing happened] because you are an enemy of the state." And for the first time now they could come again and tell the story, but not only to their closest friends, but to everybody. And that was justice. That was recognition—because of the cameras.[66]

Those who came before the TRC seemed to be aware of the cameras and their potency for communicating to a larger world. "Even traditional people from deep rural areas who have never seen a television camera before knew" what the camera was and what it meant, says du Preez. But he is quick to add that witnesses before the TRC did not act as politicians, who often search for and look directly into the camera to establish the feeling of eye contact with the viewer. "You never saw that," says du Preez, "never once."[67]

The cameras were witnesses. They gave recognition to victims while at the same time reproducing the images and sounds of the commission to larger audiences, imagined as both an anonymous entity (the "nation") and as specific individuals implicated in the story being told. The cameras helped shape, create, and define the commission's audience. Sometimes the camera and the editors of *TRC Special Report* suggested that the primary audience for a testimony was a particular spectator at that very hearing—perhaps Winnie Madikizela-Mandela in her diamond-studded and darkly tinted designer glasses sitting impassively next to her attorney at the Mandela United Football Club hearings or the widow of Chris Hani listening to flimsy evasions by her husband's killers during their amnesty hearing. Sometimes the audience was the media itself, as when energetic photographers and camera operators were seen outside venues of high-profile hearings muscling and elbowing each other like rugby players. Sometimes *TRC Special Report* chose footage that showed direct interchanges between a witness and a commissioner or between a witness and an advocate or judge. On such occasions, the cinematography implied that the primary drama of the commission was between these individuals, not necessarily between the witness and "us." But these were exceptional moments rather than the rule.

Interestingly, *TRC Special Report* rarely showed commissioners listening to testimony. Chairperson Desmond Tutu was seen very infrequently on the program, a notable difference between *TRC Special Report* and Antjie Krog's *Country of My Skull*, which features Tutu as a key protagonist in the TRC story. In Krog's book, Tutu is master of ceremonies, orchestrating the whole commission process, on stage and off. And if one reads testimony from Human Rights Violations Committee and Amnesty Committee hearings, a strong impression is created that the drama of the hearings was in the exchanges and dialogues between the witnesses, the commissioners, the judges, and/or the advocates. But on *TRC Special Report*, the deponents were central, and the program intercut their images with shots of "ordinary" people who had come to listen in the hall, individuals who by extension represented us, the television audience.

Through this method of editing, *TRC Special Report* portrayed TRC hearings as a storytelling experience aimed primarily at the live (and by extension, television) audience rather than the commissioners who were ostensibly the intended recipients of these speech acts at the actual hearings. In this regard, *TRC Special Report*'s tone, style, and mode of address *implicated* its television audience as though they were part of the commission. Spectators had an intimate connection to these stories now. Victims who gave testimony before the TRC did so for a purpose. They wanted something to happen—perhaps they wanted reparations or revelations of more information or even public acknowledgement of their story. Testimony was a two-way street. The way *TRC Special Report* intercut victim appearances with general audience reactions implicitly shifted the burden of response from being exclusively the response of the commission to include the response of the pubic as well, those "ordinary people" who sat in the TRC halls, listened on headphones, and sometimes wept or gesticulated in response to testimony. These spectators at the live event were surrogates for the television audience. Through hearing these stories, spectators became entwined in the stories and their consequences. They were implicated in the sense that they became involved in a crime via close connection, the close connection of the closeup.

Victims came before the commission to say what they had heard and seen. Through the media event of the TRC, especially via television, the country was called upon to witness their testimony. Television demonstrated the implications of witnessing by itself serving as exemplary witness: when the cameras "saw," they soon turned around and *testified* by broadcasting the story, transmitting it to others. Like a chorus in an ancient Greek play, television was witness, narrator, and commentator on the action, giving editorial opinions and interpretations, shaping our experience and guiding our focus. Occasionally television even intervened in the action.

The Stories behind *TRC Special Report*

The SABC faced several problems in deciding how to cover the Truth and Reconciliation Commission. Here was a type of commission—a truth commission—that had never been experienced in South Africa. In addition, no truth commission had ever been seen on television. So there was no precedent for how the TRC should be covered on television. Compounding this problem was the fact that just a few years earlier the SABC had been "apartheid's loudest mouthpiece" but now, in the new political dispensation, it was scrambling to define and enact a radically transformed mission with a new staff.[68]

Among the influx of new journalists was Max du Preez, who joined SABC in 1994 as a television anchor and documentary producer. Previously du Preez had been a print journalist, first as a political correspondent for South Africa's *Financial Mail* and *Sunday Times* and after 1987 as a founding editor in chief of the first and only anti-apartheid Afrikaans-language newspaper, *Vrye Weekblad*. This renegade publication specialized in investigative journalism, and it published the first exposés on the subjects that were later to become central to the Truth and Reconciliation Commission: stories of death squads, assassinations, and systematic torture perpetrated by the police and the South African Defence Force. *Vrye Weekblad* survived for seven years until it was closed down just prior to South Africa's democratic elections, at which time du Preez moved into broadcast journalism with the SABC.

A month before the TRC began, du Preez went to his supervisors at the SABC and asked, "Are you just going to cover this in a news bulletin?"[69] While du Preez clearly anticipated the tremendous potential of the TRC as a television news story, the SABC did not seem to share his perception or enthusiasm. At the last moment, the SABC decided to launch an in-depth current affairs program on the TRC, and they approached a visiting Australian journalist to produce it. But he was hesitant, sensing perhaps that this was a bigger commitment than he was prepared to take on. So he sought assistance from du Preez, who refused, saying, "This is not a story for foreigners. This is a story for *us* to tell. And we don't need foreign intervention. We didn't need foreign intervention to make peace in '94, and we really don't need foreigners to tell our stories for us."[70]

Who du Preez meant by "us" is worth some examination. His statement is redolent with pride about South Africa's new democracy. But his patriotism is also ghosted by identity politics of another sort: Du Preez is an Afrikaner, hardly an uncomplicated identity in the old or new South Africa. The complexity of his identity is further complicated by his reputation as a rebellious liberal traitor to his intensely nationalistic "tribe." Considering the history of racial polarization among South African journalists (especially in the white liberal press) that came to light during special TRC hearings focused on the media as well as the differences in how black and white journalists covered the TRC, one could well imagine a scenario in which black, colored, or Indian South African journalists might say to a white Afrikaner journalist like du Preez, "We don't need *you* to tell our stories for us."[71]

Interestingly, two of the primary broadcast journalists the SABC chose to convey the TRC to the nation via television and radio were Max du Preez and Antjie Krog, both Afrikaners. The perception and reception of their identities by the public is worth further consideration. Evita Bezuidenhout (the ditzy, middle-aged Afrikaner persona created by satirist and playwright Pieter Dirk-Uys) commented in a review of *TRC Special Report* how important it was that "we are hearing stories of TRC through the voice of an Afrikaner."[72] Evita's "we" is never specifically defined, but it raises the question of audience. What was the real and imagined audience for *TRC Special Report*? It seems that the majority viewership of *TRC Special Report* was black, and indeed, many, including producer Jacques

Pauw, believed that few whites were watching the program.[73] Though whites were statistically a marginal segment of *TRC Special Report's* audience, du Preez saw white audiences, especially conservatives, as an essential constituency. His knowledge of them, his anticipation of their biases against the truth commission and the questions and skepticisms they had about the TRC process all informed how he designed, shaped, edited, and paced the program. Du Preez was intensely conscious of the power of his role as someone who could enlist a sense of ownership in the TRC among whites, especially Afrikaners. Commissioner Denzil Potgieter acknowledged that the TRC was largely dependent upon the media to "communicate its message" to the nation. For him the media was "the only way of involving the nation in healing and reconciliation."[74] For du Preez, engaging conservative whites in the TRC process was an overarching agenda that drove editorial decisions. Having worked previously with an Afrikaans newspaper, du Preez knew how delicate a balance had to be struck in order to lure whites to watch *TRC Special Report* once and then entice them to tune in again next week. "If we wanted to make an impression on the white community, we had to be very sensitive about how we portrayed this," he said. Whites, broadly speaking, may have believed that apartheid was "not good," says du Preez, but they "didn't think it was so fundamentally evil."[75] When one compares apartheid to other oppressive regimes, such as Chile under Pinochet, the number of government-sponsored deaths in South Africa between 1948 and 1990 appears relatively modest. So for the benefit of a conservative white constituency, *TRC Special Report* created special segments showing apartheid as a larger, systemic force of evil, with documentary features on topics such as pass laws, forced removals, residential segregation, the hostel system, and Bantu education.[76] According to du Preez, these segments were specifically created to educate the program's white viewership about the systematic macroprocesses of apartheid, the ways that the system itself was a crime against humanity.

Two points are particularly worthy of note here. First, these special features on the context of apartheid, which depicted how its tentacles reached insidiously into so many aspects of daily life, demonstrate that *TRC Special Report* was by no means the ahistorical, decontextualized reporting of which mass media coverage of the TRC is often accused. Second, these special features on pass laws, the hostel system, and forced removals represent a significant departure from the rhetorical construction of the TRC. In interpreting its brief (which was about gross violations of human rights and more specifically "bodily integrity rights"), the commission tended to focus on individuals and their actions rather than on larger systemic violations of human rights enacted through the apparatus of the apartheid state.[77] A narrowness of scope and a limited interpretation of its mandate are chief conceptual criticisms leveled against the TRC. The commission usually operated on an individual level: individuals could apply for amnesty or apply for consideration as victims of gross violations of human rights. Working from individual statements, the TRC staff frantically coded, entered data into computers, analyzed, corroborated, researched, and eventually produced charts and graphs demonstrating patterns of violence and made official findings. In fulfilling its parliamentary mandate to produce "as complete a picture as possible" and highlight "systematic patterns of abuse," the TRC, according to critics such as Mahmood Mamdani, considered policies of apartheid to be a kind of background context for the commission's work, while only specific actions—violations of bodily integrity rights—perpetrated by specific individuals could be deemed violations of human rights about which the commission would make findings.[78] Mamdani argues that the "big picture" that the commission obscured was apartheid itself and its systematic crimes against humanity perpetrated by forced removals, pass laws, coerced labor, a racialized/ethnicized legal structure, and the like.[79]

While the commission found these topics to be outside its scope, *TRC Special Report* did not. The special documentary segments on the many aspects of apartheid were rebroadcast multiple times during the life of the series, rhetorically suggesting to viewers that individual cases heard before the TRC must be seen within this larger context of systematic crimes. *TRC Special Report's* iteration of the commission may have compensated for what some have seen as a profound inadequacy of the official TRC process. Far more people experienced the commission by watching *TRC Special Report* than by direct participation in the commission either through attending hearings or reading the summary report, and this large constituency was led by the program to see violations of human rights not as atomized individual acts but rather as part and parcel of systemic violence perpetrated by the state, a whole apparatus premised, in fact, on acts of atrocity.

Among the audiences *TRC Special Report* anticipated when it was constructing and pacing its shows was a very particular small group: former security police, soldiers, policemen, the military establishment and the families of these groups. Du Preez wanted this group to watch the show and through it to become engaged in the TRC process. A primary strategy by which du Preez lured them was through revelations: naming names, identifying perpetrators. According to du Preez, watching *TRC Special Report* became for this group about revelations:

> Who is going to be named next? So we would space it. We would have a number of revelations. We would sort of not break all of them at once, because there was this thing of [viewers saying], "We have to watch on Sunday night because there is a possibility that I'll get named, and I have to see it." Or "Which of my mates will be on camera?" You know, that kind of thing. So that was part of the theatre for us. We thought we made theatre.[80]

Here du Preez posits revelations as the primary action of the theatre that his show made. He suggests that his goal was to transform this particular constituency from audience, from mere passive spectators, into protagonists, into the faces that would appear before the commission in future weeks. One sees in this moment the dynamic process of witnessing, the implications of witnessing—you may see and hear something that will then cause you to *do* something. Watching the TRC on television may change your life.

It is not accurate to say that *TRC Special Report* uncritically reproduced a message of the TRC. Clearly the program envisioned a role for itself in educating people about the commission. Hence it created and repeatedly rebroadcast episodes that simply explained the processes of the Human Rights Violations and Amnesty committees. *TRC Special Report* also saw its role as enlisting the country's participation in the process; it especially saw its role as targeting whites. But this goal is not necessarily the same as "uncritically promoting the objective of the TRC," as Annelies Verdoolaege contends.[81] Indeed, if we consider the program a media event, we can see that broadcasting national ceremonial and historic events such as the TRC always clouds the division between witnessing and transmitting the action. As Dayan and Katz contend,

> Giving media-event status to a proposed event implies a belief in mystery. . . .
> Attendance cannot be neutral and uncommitted. Television here is not simply an observer or a producer. Its presence reactivates an ancient function: the act of attending, of "being there," and of being an eventual propagator, a subsequent medium. Those present at early Christian events were used as such "media." They were called "witnesses," or, in Greek, "martyrs."[82]

The conflation here of media, witness, and martyr is significant. If television can find no neutral place outside an event such as the TRC, is the same true for all spectators?

Given the complexity of the roles *TRC Special Report* had to perform, one might assume that the program had a long lead time to plan installments and a generous budget. *TRC Special Report* had neither. It commenced in 1996 at a breakneck pace, with only a week of preparation before hearings began. The initial hectic working conditions never abated for two years. "We work seven days a week almost every week," du Preez told the Johannesburg *Mail & Guardian*. The program became known as one that was "slim on resources but big on ideas."[83] In order to produce a one-hour weekly program like *TRC Special Report*, the British Broadcasting Corporation (BBC) would have required between twenty-five and forty staff, according to a BBC producer who served as consultant to the hearings. However, *TRC Special Report* operated with only five to seven staff, working on a streamlined budget of 4,000 rand (US$880 in 1997) per day.[84] Its largest production staff was assembled for high-profile cases like the "Winnie hearings," when the demand for footage from foreign news services could sustain as many as five cameras. But usually *TRC Special Report* was shot with only two camera operators: one trained on the witnesses and commissioners and another focused on the audience.[85] The editing was done live by the producer of each segment, who sat behind the monitors, directed the cameras, and used a rudimentary switcher to cut together different camera angles.[86] Because the Human Rights Violation and Amnesty committees occasionally had simultaneous hearings in different parts of the country, sometimes multiple *TRC Special Report* teams worked at different locations during the week. On Friday nights all staff would fly back to Johannesburg to transcribe, edit, and assemble the final program, which ran on Sunday evenings for thirty to sixty minutes.[87]

Soon after the TRC began its hearings, *TRC Special Report* was established as a primary means for getting a compact summary of the week's events. In his memoir of serving as deputy chairperson of the commission, Alex Boraine paid tribute to the program, commending du Preez and his crew "for the sensitive and professional way" they covered each week's proceedings.[88] Du Preez himself claims, "Everybody knew that this is where the story is going to be told. Not the 30-second bits on the news bulletins. . . . People knew that this story will unfold on Sunday afternoons, or Sunday evenings. There's going to be a good hour and the main stories will be there. And the nation was listening."[89] In its first year, *TRC Special Report* achieved an estimated viewership of 1.2 million people weekly.[90] The program eventually topped television ratings across all channels, surpassing even the obsessively watched soap opera *The Bold and the Beautiful*.[91] For its quality, *TRC Special Report* garnered critical acclaim: a Pringle Award and the 1996 Award for Outstanding Journalism from the Foreign Correspondents' Association of South Africa.

While there has been relatively little scholarship on the media coverage of the TRC, the little analysis that exists raises several points of criticism about television and *TRC Special Report*. Some critics assert that television tended to focus on individual protagonists, heroes, and villains at the expense of larger processes and context. However, *TRC Special Report* was an exception to this claim. With an event like the truth commission, one might expect television to focus on what it does best: conveying the words spoken live by witnesses at hearings, with all of their affective, rhetorical, and authenticating powers. Print media, on the other hand, is less able to convey the power of live testimony and would generally be expected to focus more on background and context. However, *TRC Special Report* achieved the tasks of both television and print, and in the end, it provided far more context than testimony. Based on my viewing of all eighty-seven *TRC Special Report* episodes, I estimate that in a story lasting seven minutes, only a minute or less of testimony from the TRC was used. The reasons for this ratio are many: for one, the testimony given at hearings was densely compressed and often lacked the exposition and context needed to make the story clear to viewers, a point made evident by the testimony of Maki Skosana's sister analyzed above.

The few scholars that have begun to analyze broadcast coverage of the TRC agree that the TRC made for "excellent television."[92] Hearings brought forth emotional, graphic, riveting stories about real people—old and young, rich and poor, black and white. But many observers believe that the impact of television came at the expense of complexity, sophistication, and rational analysis. Several assumptions have been made about mass-media coverage of the TRC. First, critics charged that the commission's televisuality encouraged simplistic renderings of individual "characters" or "protagonists." For instance, some accused the media of creating a stark dichotomy between perpetrators as villains and victims as heroes. Others say that the media tended to be racially polarizing, focusing on victims who were generally black and perpetrators who were generally white. What is astonishing about this accusation is how little it grapples with the demographics of perpetrators. Of the 7,115 people who applied for amnesty, only 293 were agents of the apartheid state; the overwhelming majority was allied with the ANC—a constituency that was largely nonwhite. If the media did, in fact, focus on white perpetrators, they would have had to ignore the vast majority of amnesty cases and in all likelihood would have had difficulty cobbling together a coherent story about the amnesty hearings during the many weeks of the commission.[93]

Another criticism is that the media gave undue attention to images of reconciliation instead of to other responses to past and present conflict, such as lack of forgiveness, bitterness, and calls for justice or retribution.[94] Allegedly, the media provided very little coverage of the category or concept of "survivor," so the agency of those labeled "victim" by the TRC disempowered them through skewed reporting. Edward Bird and Zurida Garda contend that "media reports would quote extensively from a survivor's testimony, especially evidence of their suffering, but fail to report on the survivor's life afterward or on their demands and requests from the commission."[95] Bird and Garda are referring here to the ways that those who appeared before the commission often came with specific and explicit demands, such as asking for health insurance, bursaries for surviving children, or memorials. Or sometimes very pointedly they asked for very specific information about past crimes or even retribution. These sorts of assertive behaviors by those who appeared before the commission, according to Bird and Garda, received inadequate coverage in the media.

A second theme of the criticism charges that television and photography amplified and promulgated the TRC as a "trauma spectacle."[96] Some scholars believe that television succumbed to sensationalism by favoring emotional, character-driven, and uncomplicated messages.[97] The intensity of feeling constituted its own evidence, authenticating details through graphic detail and strong emotions rather than through objective empirical analysis of data.[98] A third common criticism is that the media was partisan, pushing agendas both overtly and covertly by choosing which stories to cover or by adopting the core assumptions of the commission without challenging them. *TRC Special Report*, in particular, has been singled out for "uncritically promoting the objective of the TRC," although this is also a criticism leveled at the media more generally.[99] Others perceive bias in the media's failure to make a moral distinction between those who struggled "against a criminal regime and those who enforced it."[100]

Finally, television is accused of failing to provide adequate coverage of contexts and causes of oppression and violence, especially underlying structural inequities and injustices. Critics say television favors moral and ahistorical "human" issues that can be readily conveyed through character and conventional narrative. Deborah Posel contends that "if the more scientific fact-finding pursuit commands a careful attention to the details of particular cases, the television hearings tended to extract more general, universal truths about experience, truths about suffering and victimization, remorse and reconciliation, which undergirded the TRC's moral performance."[101] Ron Krabill, who shares Posel's view, argues that mass media is "pulled toward the exceptional individual and the dramatic story. Our eye is drawn to the face of the hero or villain, the protagonist of history. The televisual medium makes it difficult to get beyond the mass media cult of personality into structural issues."[102] In other words, we might say that television works well with an Aristotelian model of storytelling—narratives with defined characters; clear beginnings, middles, and ends; and crisis, resolution, and an emotional catharsis—all in the service of some large theme of "universal" significance. We might also say that television coverage of the TRC was perhaps *not* well suited to Marxist or materialist narrative techniques (as one can see in the theatrical work of the Bertolt Brecht): that is, stories that lead audiences to resist catharsis, to think beyond individual heroism and villainy and to focus instead on macroprocesses and political structures that have ultimately put particular characters in untenable situations and that should therefore be changed.[103]

Many of these criticisms of *TRC Special Report* simply do not hold up to scrutiny. While such criticism may apply to ordinary television coverage of a media event, *TRC Special Report* was no ordinary program. For instance, it was not produced by journalists experienced in television. Most *TRC Special Report* journalists came from print journalism, and they brought to their work attributes and skills that were distinctive.

In selecting his team of producers, du Preez chose reporters for their knowledge of the "struggle": he chose those with strong backgrounds in the alternative press:

> Only two of us had any television experience. The rest came from radio and print. And most of them went into that first hearing not knowing television as a medium at all. Because we had to . . . you know we couldn't take the old SABC people. They were part of the problem. So we had to get people with the right kind of political background. So I had to get all my friends who were sort of struggle journalists, and they were not in television, and Anneliese [Burgess] was in radio, Jann Turner was in mostly print.[104]

The stories of the TRC put incredible demands on all journalists but especially those working in an unfamiliar medium. Yet while the *TRC Special Report* journalists may have struggled technically—or even aesthetically—to understand the unique properties of storytelling through moving images, they excelled at knowing the content: they knew what story needed to be told. And not just the story that unfolded before the commission but also the story behind the story. Du Preez claims that "eighty percent of what came before the truth commission was familiar to us."[105]

In selecting a context, the producer could potentially go in many directions. The background might be expositional about one case or it might place the case within a regional or historical profile or in a pattern of types of violence such as covert action or soft targets. It might contrast one type of victim with another type of victim or one political party with another. Sometimes segments of an episode were freestanding stories, each focused on a single case. For other programs, *TRC Special Report* sutured together a number of cases with a common theme, such as death squads, death in detention, cross-border raids into places such as Swaziland and Botswana, exhumations and reburials, abuses in ANC training camps, or state conscription of white soldiers.

Many potential contexts existed for any story the commission heard. Contrary to conventional criticisms about mass-media coverage of the TRC, *TRC Special Report* never gave a story without a context. And the contexts it provided were almost never ahistorical universal themes such as forgiveness. If general themes like the "nature of evil" or "what is reconciliation?" were covered—and they sometimes were—the features on them were usually separated from footage of testimony, illuminated through interviews with a range of pundits rather than connected to any particular TRC story.

As a document of the commission, *TRC Special Report* is thus exceptional for the variety and richness of the contexts it provided for TRC stories and, indeed, for its ability to tell a story and tell it well. Unlike the TRC's report, which is notable for its social-science methods favoring quantitative data and an impersonal writing style, *TRC Special Report* focused on stories and storytelling. It can be read as a representation or iteration of the commission that in fact embraced most fully a genuine sense of narrative—and remember, so-called narrative truth was one of the TRC's primary objectives. Du Preez specifically selected producers for his team that he thought were good storytellers. The program he envisioned departed markedly from standard current-affairs programs. "We didn't do a straight sort of news report," he says. "We told stories. We used our crude documentary skills to tell stories. So whenever we had an incident that we had to report on, we did a beginning and a context and bit of overlay and . . . you tell the story."[106] The TRC's summary report could not afford to tell stories on an individual level with any kind of nuance, precision, or aesthetic sophistication. The report was about making findings, so only fragments of individual testimonies were quoted as illustrations or colorful details. Despite the fact that "narrative truth" was one of the four definitions of truth the commission was designed to value, its final report seemed largely devoid of the art of narrative.[107]

Given the skills of its producers, it is no surprise that *TRC Special Report* offered a unique combination of television and print journalism. Episodes focused both on individuals (the program's journalists interviewed victims and visited locations of killings or torture, and bystanders and experts gave additional perspectives) and on the larger level of patterns and emerging themes among multiple stories. To a far greater extent than in the TRC's final report, *TRC Special Report* managed to honor the integrity of particular stories while at the same time attending to larger contexts.

When one compares *TRC Special Report* to the memoirs that have been penned by TRC commissioners, staff, and journalists, it also stands out as an extraordinary archival record of the commission. *TRC Special Report* is a contemporaneous document, unfolding in "real time" during the life of the commission rather than composed in retrospect.[108] Furthermore, it is a multiauthored work; each episode includes several segments produced by different journalists. While du Preez served as executive producer, his team of journalists varied over the twenty-three months of the series, generally including between five and seven people who were racially, ethnically, and linguistically diverse.[109] While *TRC Special Report* was at times implicitly and often explicitly editorial—it unquestionably had agendas—the program was overtly focused on conveying stories from the commission. Unlike Antjie Krog's *Country of My Skull,* which is also a dense summary of multiple TRC stories, *TRC Special Report* gives almost no indication of the psychological trauma or angst of conscience experienced by those who narrated the story (the journalists), which is not to say that working on the program did not take a significant toll on them.[110] "The stress just creeps up on you," said veteran *TRC Special Report* producer Gail Reagon.[111] The first team of producers collapsed entirely and had to be replaced. "Many were too shocked by the intensity of the first testimonies and the burden of two more years covering the truth commission loomed too large."[112]

Despite the personal difficulties and hardships of covering the TRC and producing a weekly current-affairs television program, the *TRC Special Report* journalists remained focused on "the stories behind the stories," the program's motto that was often repeated in introductory and closing remarks.[113] Many *TRC Special Report* segments used surprisingly little TRC footage but rather supplemented a featured story from the commission with context, exposition, location shots, and direct interviews with witnesses in which they were asked to narrate again, directly for the camera, what they had previously told the commission. This instruction allowed for a different style and mode of address, as witnesses looked directly at the camera rather than at the panel of commissioners. Direct interviews were also made more intimate through location, for they were frequently conducted in people's homes amid their familiar possessions and family members or at a site that was relevant to their story. In addition, *TRC Special Report* interviewed a range of people who were related to the story but did not testify before the commission, including witnesses, family members, perpetrators, police officers, and so forth. Some episodes used archival footage from the old SABC, which provided in this new context an implicit contrast between what passed as the "truth" on television in the old and new South Africas. As du Preez explains:

> We find it really helpful to play in the old SABC's television news bulletins on the event in question at the beginning of the report. It gives some of the visual elements to the story as it happened, but more importantly, we give viewers a good idea of how racist, propagandist and untruthful the old SABC—and thus the regime and the public they served—were. That is part of the story of our past.[114]

TRC Special Report thus played a rehabilitative role for the media by re-airing old footage in a new editorial context. In giving the "stories behind the stories," the program forced audiences to reflect on how they had heard these very same stories before, on which information was included and which was suppressed during the old regime.

But beyond *TRC Special Report*'s exemplary status as a record of the commission, as an archive of how the commission unfolded in real time over many weeks or as a documentary about the cases heard before the TRC, its real significance was not as a record but as a performer and implicated witness. *TRC Special*

Report was a primary performer of the commission, transmitting, promulgating, enacting, translating, and interpreting the process for the general public. Just as the language interpreters studied in the previous chapters were positioned as a primary means of transmission, so too were the television journalists. Without them, there may still have been a commission, but it would not have been the truth commission in South Africa as it came to be known nationally and internationally: a media event of enormous proportions in which the country was, like it or not, engaged. Television saturated the event and brought it into people's homes.

Conclusion

The choice of the commissioners to embrace cameras and microphones at hearings meant that the public experienced the TRC not as a text but as an embodied expression in which visual and aural signification were as important as words. Television was a particularly potent and unrivaled medium for conveying registers of signification present in the body, such as intonation, pauses, facial expression, cadence, and gesture—or simply for conveying the authenticating presence of a real person. *TRC Special Report* also spotlit the TRC as a *process* rather than as the static product of a report that summarized findings. According to many experts, it was the TRC's novel, imaginative, unprecedented, and highly visible process that was its most significant contribution to transitional justice, both internationally and to the transitional process in South Africa.[115] *TRC Special Report* documented that process as it unfolded from week to week and month to month, and the entire collection of episodes provided not just a view of the process of the TRC but, more important, the process as many South Africans experienced it.

Many of the criticisms leveled against television coverage of the TRC simply do not hold up when one studies the entirety of the series *TRC Special Report*. While there were moments of emotion, the show rarely presented a story, even a highly emotional one, without a context, demonstrating how one case could be linked to larger themes, structures, and chains of command. The program gave far more context than the TRC hearings did, for testimony in hearings often began in medias res. Hearings were just one stage in an ongoing conversation between the witnesses and the commission, a relationship often begun weeks earlier, when the person had spoken to a statement-taker or a perpetrator had applied for amnesty. So the dramaturgy of the hearings often assumed that participants knew a great deal of exposition. Commissioners, of course, usually knew the background of individual cases, for a staff existed whose primary job was to brief them. Live audiences also often knew a great deal of background, since the hearing they were attending usually arose from their own community. However, with the exception of extremely high-profile cases, the larger television audience often did not have a clue. *TRC Special Report* embraced the challenge of giving them a clue. Exposition was a defining and primary mission of the program.

It provided far more context than did the TRC's summary report, which boiled down findings on HRVC cases to just a few sentences, and—astonishingly—did not print its findings in Amnesty Committee cases anywhere.[116] Finally, the series defined its mission in ways that may have more fully grappled with the larger context of apartheid as a *system*. Throughout the nearly-two-year life of *TRC Special Report* the program provided regular segments on forced removals in places like District Six and Sophiatown, pass laws and the insidious way they criminalized nearly all blacks who were required to carry them, townships such as Alexandria, coerced labor in mines, and living conditions in hostels. While *TRC Special Report* did have an agenda, that agenda was its own and it was not necessary consonant with that of the commission. Frequently du Preez used his editorial latitude as program anchor to make direct demands on or issue criticisms of the commission.

The process of the commission was volatile, a disruptive combination of passionate emotions and dispassionate legal argument, of poor people speaking of atrocity and of formerly powerful perpetrators smugly admitting what they had done and sometimes receiving amnesty for their confessions. The volatility of content provokes volatile reactions, some of them hastily dismissive. And on a certain level, people are still uncomfortable with those microphones springing up in a court of law or in any venue that even resembles a court. There is a fundamental anxiety about the media as mediator, as an entity that inherently reshapes stories, that never tells them for the first time but rather repeats them, often with a difference. This, too, is a fundamental anxiety that springs from the process of witnessing: to witness is to see, to witness is to tell, to witness is to be implicated. And that is never comfortable.

5. Dragons in the Living Room: Truth and Reconciliation in Repertoire, 2006

My deepest sadness is that by and large, the South African white community has yet to acknowledge the incredible generosity that has come from the black community. I would say the white political leaders should tell their supporters: "You don't know how damn lucky you are."

—Desmond Tutu, 2006

Should there not be some acknowledgement of the Afrikaner's historically unparalleled deed of expiation in terms of which they sacrificed centuries of struggle for self-determination as a people to help create a new and non-racial South Africa? Should white South Africans not also enjoy some recognition as co-creators of the new South Africa?

—F. W. De Klerk, 2006

The future is certain; it is the past that is unpredictable.

—Evita Bezuidenhout, aka Pieter-Dirk Uys, 2006

In 1994, prior to the beginning of the Truth and Reconciliation Commission, the Institute for Democracy in South Africa organized an international conference with human rights and transitional justice experts from such places as Argentina, Chile, Bulgaria, and Germany. They came together to discuss with South Africans how best to plan and envision a truth commission for the country. The conference title, "Justice in Transition: Dealing with the Past," signified the importance of history to the restorative justice process in which South Africa was about to engage.[1] Somehow in order to accomplish justice during a time of political transition, one had to "deal" with history, a site of unresolved trauma.

"Dealing" suggests a transaction, an agreement, a pact, an exchange, a buying and selling, or a distribution, as in "dealing the cards." Twelve years after this generative conference and eight years after the TRC presented its summary report, the past in South Africa still requires "dealing" in the present continuous tense. As Evita Bezuidenhout (the persona created by comedian Pieter-Dirk Uys) has said of South Africa in the epigraph above, "The future is certain; it is the past that is unpredictable." The past refuses to conform to grand narratives and explanatory frames. It bursts at the seams of the macronarratives promulgated in the TRC's summary report. All history is, of course, irrepressible, and exceeds the bounds of the historian's text. And yet in the case of the TRC, the failures of its historiography are actually failures to fulfill the law: the commission had a legal mandate to "determine the causes, nature and extent of gross violations of human rights" between 1960 and 1994 and "to establish the truth in relation to past events as well as the motives for and circumstances in which gross violations of human rights have occurred."[2] Historians do not usually conduct their research via legislative mandate.

If the TRC's brief was in part to produce a history, what kind of history did people imagine the commission would write? Former president of South Africa F. W. de Klerk believed the purpose of the TRC was to bring together all communities and political parties of South Africa to try to "hammer out a common version of our past." According to him, "The commissioners should have been locked in a room until they emerged with a version of our history with which all of us could associate."[3] While de Klerk yearned for a stable and unified history, Archbishop Desmond Tutu predicted in his preface to the TRC's final report that the past would never comply: "The past, it has been said, is another country. The way its stories are told and the way they are heard change as the years go by. The spotlight gyrates, exposing old lies and illuminating new truths. As a fuller picture emerges, a new piece of the jigsaw puzzle of our past settles into place."[4] Tutu's metaphors are mixed and dynamic: the past is a puzzle being assembled, a foreign country where they "do things differently," the focus of a gyrating spotlight, a story told and retold, and a story continuously heard anew. Sounding uncharacteristically postmodern, Tutu even seems to suggest that history may be as much about old lies as new truths.

For governments undergoing political transition from authoritarian rule, the impetus to close the door on the past is extremely strong, says Tina Rosenberg: "Most governments have made the political call that to leave the past alone is the best way to avoid upsetting a delicate process of transition or to avoid a return to past dictatorships. The attitude is that there is a dragon living on the patio and we had better not provoke it."[5] Yet even at the 1994 TRC planning conference, Mary Burton, who later became a commissioner, knew that for South Africa, the monster was not outside. "In our case," she said, "the dragons will be right inside the living room with other wild creatures."[6] These dragons are the subject of this chapter: How are they getting on with the other tenants of the household—wild or domesticated—in a "new" South Africa that is no longer quite so new?

The year 2006 marked the tenth anniversary of the first hearings of the Truth and Reconciliation Commission, an occasion that prompted many to reflect upon the achievements and limitations of this grand experiment in transitional justice. When the TRC began in 1996, stories from its public hearings dominated the news. Audiences tuned in by the millions to hear daily radio broadcasts, and every Sunday they watched Max du Preez's award-winning television digest *TRC Special Report*.[7] Yet as euphoria over the country's political transition waned and the commission's ambitious promises were either unfulfilled or underachieved, public ambivalence grew. Some of those who testified before the commission in

1996 as "victims of apartheid" were calling themselves "victims of the TRC" three years later.[8] By the commission's tenth anniversary, most victims who had appeared before it were not living in peace, according to former commissioner Yasmin Sooka, but rather "in the twilight zone, never being allowed to forget their pain and not being able to heal or put closure to their memories."[9]

Despite its optimistic promises, the TRC actually had no economic capacity to alleviate the suffering of victims: the commission could only *recommend* to the government what form and amount reparations should take. In an excellent overview of the TRC's reparations program, Christopher Colvin states that "victims have still not benefited from full and binding elaboration of what reparations would mean for them."[10] Reparation payments came too little and too late, in the opinion of many: the final amount the ANC government chose to allocate, which was far less than the TRC recommended, was a one-time payment of 30,000 rand (US$3,900 in 2003) paid to each victim four years after the Rehabilitation and Reparations Committee submitted its recommendations. While the TRC had only recommending power for reparations, it nevertheless enjoyed full power to grant amnesty, which it did for 849 applicants. The TRC also had authority and indeed a mandate to "make its findings known" by producing a report that would "establish the truth" in relation to past events as well the motives and circumstances that led to those events.[11] Unfortunately, due to the high cost and limited distribution of the TRC's final report—which advocate Howard Varney calls "one of the least read reports of its kind in the world"—very few South Africans have ever even learned what the commission found out.[12] Furthermore, the TRC's archives, which were intended to be open to all, have been locked away. The owner of the collection, the Department of Justice, guards access jealously and in a Kafkaesque manner. An estimated 95 percent of the TRC's archival holdings are presently inaccessible to researchers or even to the victims and perpetrators whose stories are documented therein.

How does one understand South Africa's current ambivalence and suppression of information about a process that was intended to promote transparency, democracy, and respect for human rights? What does the TRC mean to contemporary South Africa? Loved and loathed, revered and reviled, the TRC continues to simmer in public life. Despite deep ambivalence, truth and reconciliation remain very much alive in the country's "repertoire," to use Diana Taylor's concept of embodied memory.[13] Many years after the TRC concluded, the TRC still provokes regular headlines, disruptions, denials, appraisals, accusations, lawsuits, "infinitely naïve" acts of forgiveness, and dramatic gestures of atonement.[14] For instance, in 2006 the apartheid-era minister of police spontaneously walked into the office of a man he had tried to kill and literally washed his victim's feet. The mother of a woman murdered in the apartheid-era Heidelberg Tavern massacre refused to cooperate with the National Prosecuting Authority when it tried to bring the case to trial. The mother had so thoroughly reconciled with the perpetrator that together they had founded a foundation for peace.[15] When the ruthless former president P. W. Botha, the "great crocodile," died in 2006, the black-dominated ANC South African government ordered flags flown at half mast and offered to provide a state funeral. Botha, who had presided over some of the worst years of racial oppression from 1978 to 1989, had refused to appear before the TRC. Yet when he died, the ANC government refrained from the finger-wagging for which Botha himself was so famous.

I read such public acts and behaviors as part of the TRC's repertoire, how "people participate in the production and reproduction of knowledge by 'being there,' being part of the transmission."[16] This chapter examines key stories related to the TRC that made news headlines in 2006 for what they reveal about the commission's repertoire. I then anchor the question of the TRC's legacy in an analysis of a new artistic work called *REwind: A Cantata for Voice, Tape, and Testimony* (2006), an adaptation of TRC testimony composed by Philip Miller, which I interpret as a "living memorial of reconstruction."[17] Using what is arguably the most vital musical instrument of South Africa—the human voice—*REwind* replays and incorporates the actual words of victims and perpetrators who testified before the TRC. Through the cantata, their voices were once again heard—and, as before, in front of live audiences and against a background of suppressed memories and locked archives.

The Prosaic Rooms of Our Later Understanding

Desmond Tutu anticipated even before the TRC that if South Africa as a country "got it right" in terms of peace, reconciliation, and a successful transition to democracy, it would become "the paradigm for the rest of the world."[18] With so many races, religions, languages, ethnicities, and cultures, with a history of intense violence and long-standing socioeconomic stratification, South Africa is a "microcosm of the world," said Tutu. If truth and reconciliation could make it there, couldn't they make it anywhere? The South African Truth and Reconciliation Commission currently enjoys celebrity status internationally as a harbinger of the potential for reconciliation. "I am amazed at how much interest the world had in our process," said Nomfundo Walaza, the former director of the Cape Town Trauma Center.[19] Former commissioners and staff as well as journalists who covered the TRC are frequently invited to speak to audiences around the world who are overwhelmingly enamored with the "miracle" of South Africa and the TRC's perceived role as midwife to that miracle. Many countries consider the TRC to be a model for how to facilitate transition from authoritarian rule to democracy. In places like Columbia and Syria, Desmond Tutu said, it is as if South Africa's former commissioners hold some kind of "magic wand."[20]

Yet within South Africa, those associated with the commission often encounter ambivalence, hostility, or just plain ignorance about the TRC. "There doesn't seem to be an appreciation that we did something that will be recorded in history as a major human achievement," remarked journalist Max du Preez.[21] In South Africa today, he said, "it is politically correct to be cynical about the TRC, whether you are white or black, on the left or the right."[22] Despite or perhaps because of the TRC's politically incorrect status, the loyal few—the former commissioners and staff members and the journalists and academics who have written about the commission—mounted in 2006 not just one but three conferences to honor the TRC's tenth anniversary.[23] Prior to the first of these conferences, Charles Villa-Vicencio, the former director of research for the TRC, expressed a common sentiment when he said that the TRC is "often more readily lauded elsewhere in the world than at home."[24]

What accounts for this discrepancy between the national and international perception of the TRC? Perhaps the answer to that question lies in Brian Raftopoulos's paradoxical assessment that the TRC was "both a major achievement and a distinctive evasion."[25] Somehow its achievements are more apparent abroad, while its evasions are all too glaringly obvious at home. According to Raftopoulos, a list of its "evasions" might include genuine accountability for perpetrators *and* beneficiaries, retributive and economic justice, the construction of appropriate memorials, and proper reparations to victims. According to the *Pretoria News,* when one looks at the status of the TRC's primary stakeholders today, one sees that

> most perpetrators who shunned the amnesty process still walk free. Beneficiaries and the privileged in our society are yet to make personal and collective amends, while those wounded South Africans who brought their stories to the TRC are still waiting for appropriate remedies, be it counseling, truth recovery or material assistance.[26]

The absence of prosecutions of perpetrators who were either denied or never applied for amnesty means that such people enjoy today a de facto blanket amnesty. This situation undermines the entire premise of the TRC. The threat of prosecution was the stick that gave force and motivation to the TRC's carrot of conditional amnesty. The failure to prosecute apartheid-era crimes at the conclusion of the TRC corrupts all forms of justice, both retributive and restorative.

Furthermore, the large numbers of the white community who merely stood by and benefited economically from apartheid but who did not themselves commit gross violations of human rights—a constituency that, as Mahmood Mamdani has long pointed out, the commission never addressed—has little incentive to reflect deeply upon the source of the privileges they still enjoy today.[27] "White South Africans continue to live a privileged life unperturbed by the fragile moral basis of their accumulated wealth and privilege," said Salaudin Majnoon in the *Mail & Guardian.*[28] While some might argue that these lives are in fact "perturbed" by the prevalence of crime in South Africa, others would say that random incidents of redistribution of wealth will not ultimately mitigate the potentially explosive implications of still-pervasive socioeconomic inequities. "If the gap between the rich and the poor is not narrowed dramatically, we can kiss reconciliation goodbye," warned Desmond Tutu in 2006.[29] He, like many others, sees economic injustice as a "powder keg" upon which the future of South Africa rests. Whatever progress toward reconciliation the TRC accomplished will surely be undone if gross socioeconomic inequities are not rectified. (This prediction was borne out in May 2008, as we shall see.)

Yet leveling the economic playing field was a task far beyond the scope, resources, and mandate of the Truth and Reconciliation Commission. Its duty, as articulated in its enabling legislation, was to investigate and report on certain types of gross violations of human rights: murder, torture, abduction, and severe ill treatment. Perhaps the TRC's interpretation of its mandate was too narrow, and former commissioners have acknowledged as much. "We were timid in our formulation of the terms of reference of the TRC," reflected former vice-chancellor of the University of Cape Town Mamphela Ramphele at a conference in 2006. "Leaving out crimes committed in socio-economic terms in our country was a grave mistake."[30] However, as the alleged "evasions" of the TRC pile up, one cannot help wondering whether the TRC is being held responsible for failures of the state. The TRC was, after all, an ad hoc government *commission* that worked within extremely limited time, material, human, and legal constraints. "The credibility of the TRC was probably never going to be in the hands of the TRC," said Charles Villa-Vicencio. "It had to do with what government and business and civil society did in response in taking the TRC's work forward."[31] The TRC was a messenger, and it delivered its message: an ample and detailed report. Very few of its messages have been heeded by government or civil society. And the TRC has suffered the archetypal fate of the messenger: "shot" in the arena of public opinion, at least among some sectors within South Africa.

Despite widespread ambivalence about the TRC, the commission remains an abiding presence in contemporary life, as is evident by its recurrent appearance in the news. The year 2006 began with Nonceba Zokwe commemorating the eighteenth anniversary of her son's death by finally restoring and rebuilding his room. Riddled with broken glass, bullet holes, and a gaping crevice from a grenade, the room was preserved faithfully by Ms. Zokwe from the time when her son, political activist Stembele Zokwe, was killed there in 1988. In an act of improvised community memorial, she decided to use the room as a "heritage site" to focus attention on the death of her son. She resolved not to change anything until Stembele's killers were brought to justice. In late 2005, they finally were: two former apartheid-era security policemen were sentenced for twenty years each for the murder of Stembele Zokwe.[32] Ms. Zokwe's improvised site of heritage and memorial could finally, after eighteen years, be reconstructed.

Zokwe's case was the first prosecution of those perpetrators denied amnesty by the TRC, and it appeared that many more such prosecutions might follow. Early in 2006 the National Prosecuting Authority (NPA) unveiled a new policy on prosecutions of apartheid-era human rights offenders. Coming a full seven years after the conclusion of the TRC, the policy was so late that many asked, "Why the lengthy delay in bringing unrepentant transgressors to book?"[33] TRC chairperson Desmond Tutu had often publicly lamented that the failure to hold apartheid perpetrators to account was undermining the rule of law. "We are allowing impunity," he said.[34] While the National Prosecuting Authority rationalized its delay by speaking about the need for "broad consultation," many forgave its tardiness, grateful that the new policy offered hope that justice might finally be done. Yet there were the predictable detractors to the NPA policy: those who claimed that the spirit of reconciliation in the country would be replaced by a spirit of retribution or those who argued that prosecution would rekindle the strife and intense contestation that they claimed the TRC had produced. One editorial stated: "While we don't wish to bury our heads in the sand and pretend all was well in the past, we do ask what purpose is served by bringing all this up again now? Atrocities and gross violations of human rights were committed on both sides. As part of the settlement there was an element of agreement to move on. . . . Blaming old foes won't solve today's woes."[35] Some questioned why the initial cases the NPA announced did not include more ANC (as opposed to Inkatha) perpetrators or more black instead of white perpetrators (i.e., why wasn't Winnie Madikizela-Mandela among the cases identified for trial?).[36]

Yet the resistance to the NPA policy that eventually gathered the most force was from an unexpected source: the very constituents who would seem most invested in seeing that such prosecutions take place. A group of civil-society organizations that included the two biggest NGOs that represent apartheid victims, the International Bar Association, prominent international human rights lawyers such South African constitutional court judge Richard Goldstone, and former TRC commissioners such as Yasmin Sooka all formally objected to the new policy.[37] One letter of appeal addressed to President Thabo Mbeki said: "While aiming to combat impunity, the guidelines may actually provide a de facto amnesty for perpetrators and undermine the rule of law."[38] Most alarming to these critics was the broad discretionary power the new policy granted the director of public prosecutions, power that "effectively replicates the truth-for-amnesty procedure under the former TRC."[39] Amnesty under the TRC was to be a one-time opportunity, not something that could be renegotiated later based upon the discretionary powers of the director of prosecutions. Former commissioner Yasmin Sooka took issue with the director's powers to decide which cases would be prosecuted and to take into account factors such as the degree of cooperation the alleged offender had offered, the personal circumstances of the alleged offender, and the nature of the offense in question. Sooka asked, "Since when has [ill health] been a criterion to consider whether or not to prosecute. . . . Why should the offender's ideology be a factor for consideration as to whether to prosecute or not? This sets a very dangerous precedent."[40] Thus, while the NPA announcement about impending prosecutions initially appeared to fulfill the threat of eventual prosecution that was a foundational premise of the TRC, the policy, when carefully scrutinized, actually appeared to offer back-door amnesty for apartheid-era offenders.

When the NPA targeted particular unresolved cases from the TRC, its announcement produced some unexpected results. One case that was identified for trial concerned victim Frank Chikane, the former secretary-general of the South African Council of Churches and the present director general of the South African presidency. In the 1980s, Chikane was nearly killed when his clothes were laced with poison. The perpetrators were never identified and did not seek amnesty before the TRC, but Chikane was determined to get to the truth: "I wrote to everybody I thought would have an idea of what happened," he said.[41] One Saturday in August 2006, former police minister Adriaan Vlok arrived at Chikane's office and handed him a Bible saying, "I have sinned against the Lord and against you, please forgive me." According to Chikane, Vlok then "picked up a glass of water, opened his bag, pulled out a bowl, put the water in the bowl, took out a towel, and said, 'You must allow me to do this,' and washed my feet in my office."[42] Vlok's dramatic and performed act of atonement—his symbolic cleansing of a past act of poisoning, his *doing* of an apology rather than merely saying he was sorry—produced a firestorm of controversy. His former deputy Leon Wessels, who is now a South African human rights commissioner, was "extremely happy" with Vlok's apology, and the African Christian Democratic Party's Rev. Kenneth Meshoe thought Vlok a "real man of courage" to show such "guts and humility" to ask for forgiveness.[43] Even President Thabo Mbeki praised Vlok. In his online ANC weekly newsletter, Mbeki said that to hear that a 69-year-old Afrikaner was washing "the feet of a black man he grew up knowing belonged to a sub-human species" forces us to ask "whether we are indeed listening to and hearing one another."[44] However, Shirley Gunn, a woman imprisoned with her child when Vlok falsely accused her of bombing Khotso House, saw his act as "provocative and insensitive." She said, "He can't just wash Frank Chikane's feet and think that is the end of it. . . . He needs to apologise to his victims directly."[45] According to the former director of the TRC's Investigative Unit, advocate Dumisa Ntsebeza, the act was an "empty" gesture. However, for the former South African president F.W. de Klerk, Vlok's foot-washing was sincere and the fact that his apology was "widely rejected" was a pity.[46]

Other commentators spoke about what Vlok did *not* do. "Rather than going around washing people's feet and going to church," said political scientist John Daniel, who had been a senior TRC researcher, "what we really want is information." He suggested that if Vlok was serious about coming clean, he should sit down and write a comprehensive document that says "This is what I know."[47] Journalist Max du Preez, while acknowledging the great significance of such a highly symbolic act within the context of a largely conservative Christian country, also wanted a greater ratio of truth to sensational gestures of reconciliation: "Mr. Vlok, doesn't your Bible also say that if you really are repentant, you will confess your sins? Or do you believe the Bible had a kind of blanket amnesty in mind—you don't have to be specific, you can just say 'I've sinned' and all will be forgiven? Isn't your God curious about the details?"[48] Du Preez and Daniels prioritize the production of information, thereby reiterating the values articulated by the TRC, which privileged full disclosure over expression of contrition. Many observers couldn't help speculate about the relation between Vlok's sudden and well-broadcast act of remorse and the NPA's previous announcement that Chikane's case was targeted for prosecution. Was this just a cheap sensational pitch for leniency? Chikane himself was able to compartmentalize his response: on the one hand, as a Christian minister, he received Vlok's gesture as "genuine, honest and extraordinary." But as a citizen, he also stressed that foot-washing would not stop the wheels of justice. Of those responsible for his poisoning, Chikane said: "I can't stop them from being prosecuted—the law must take its course. That project is still on, it's not going away, it can't go away. The fact that I can't mention the names of these people tells you that it can't go away."[49]

Vlok's public act of atonement suggests that while the dragons in the living room may have failed to "hammer out" a common history via the TRC, they did seem by 2006 to be slightly more *friendly* dragons: they went around carrying bowls and towels and washing people's feet. Vlok's performed gesture is remarkable and, one suspects, somehow deeply indebted to the TRC, both through its overt performance and embodiment of reconciliation and its inherent opacity of meaning. Viewed as an expression of the TRC's repertoire, Vlok's foot-washing apology exceeds the TRC's brief, on the one hand, for perpetrators were not required to express remorse in order to receive amnesty. They only had to tell the truth, to give full disclosure, and to prove that their acts were politically motivated and proportionate. However, the TRC was nevertheless shadowed by an overtly Christian discourse of forgiveness and atonement, one reinforced most explicitly by its chairperson, Desmond Tutu, and deputy chairperson, Alex Boraine, both of whom were ministers. When presiding over public hearings, they would frequently use the concluding moments of a victim's testimony to deliver a brief homily that placed the witness's particular narrative in a larger discourse, one that thoroughly enmeshed the "truth and reconciliation" of the TRC's mandate with Christian-based values of forgiveness and atonement.[50] Would this extraordinary encounter between Chikane and Vlok have taken this particular form had there been no TRC, a commission led by an archbishop in purple ecclesiastical robes who preached forgiveness? Would Vlok have chosen such a performative form for his apology had the TRC transpired, as other commissions had, behind closed doors—if there had been no televised public expressions of grief or radio broadcasts of primordial cries of mourning or images of Winnie Madikizela-Mandela hugging the mother of a child her Mandela United Football Club had murdered or widely circulated video footage of a torturer's demonstration of his wet-bag torture techniques? The spotlight gyrates, as Tutu predicted it would, exposing old lies and illuminating new truths. Though our perspective on the past may change, the past is not going away: "It can't go away," as Frank Chikane has said.

Another case of unfinished business from the TRC that the NPA targeted for prosecution was the case of the Heidelberg Tavern bombing incident of 1993. This massacre, perpetrated by the Azanian People's Liberation Army, had been ordered by Letlapa Mphahlele, who freely admits that he launched the attack. He also "defiantly refused" to request amnesty from the TRC.[51] In subsequent years, Mphahlele became not only the president of the Pan Africanist Congress but also an internationally known advocate for peace. At a book launch for his biography *Child of This Soil* in 2002, he was confronted by Ginn Fourie, the mother of Lyndi Fourie, a 23-year-old white woman killed in the Heidelberg bombing. Ms. Fourie describes how Mphahlele "came straight from the podium to where I was sitting, and he said 'I'll do anything if you'll meet with me this week.' In that moment I saw remorse in his eyes and body language. It would have been so much easier if he'd been a monster with horns and a tail."[52] An act of reconciliation enabled by body language and eye contact eventually resulted in Mphahlele and Fourie creating together the Lyndi Fourie Foundation, an organization dedicated to reconciliation. Once sees in this incident the centrality and salience of the embodied face-to-face encounter as a central feature of the repertoire of reconciliation that the TRC fostered in South Africa life.

When the National Prosecuting Authority announced its new policy on prosecution of apartheid-era crimes in 2006, the Heidelberg Tavern bombing incident was among the cases targeted for prosecution. The NPA approached Ginn Fourie about assisting with the investigation of Mphahlele. Fourie, who was reluctant, asked what would happen if she did not cooperate. The NPA threatened to subpoena. She then told the NPA she would trust Mphahlele with her life, "which is not something I could say about you [the NPA]."[53] The NPA responded by calling Fourie "infinitely naïve."[54] So the National Prosecuting Authority, while trying to move forward with post-TRC prosecutions so that perpetrators would no longer enjoy impunity, found its work inhibited by perpetrators and victims who were so reconciled that they refused to cooperate with prosecutions. If the goal of the TRC was to facilitate reconciliation, the Heidelberg Tavern story is perhaps evidence of its success. But if the goal of the TRC was also to restore public faith in the legitimacy of government structures (such as the National Prosecuting Authority), the Mphahlele-Fourie story suggests that that goal has yet to be attained.[55]

In January 2006, the *Sunday Independent* noted that as the government was preparing to celebrate the tenth anniversary of the Truth and Reconciliation Commission, "two pending clashes show just how wide the gulf between civil society and the government over the commission's legacy has grown."[56] One of these cases was the constitutional challenge to the NPA's policy on prosecution of apartheid-era crimes. Another was a lawsuit filed in the United States by South African victims' rights groups using an obscure U.S. federal law from 1789. The Alien Tort Claims Act allows non-Americans to bring lawsuits against U.S. individuals and companies for violations of human rights that took place outside the United States. Lawyers representing thousands of apartheid victims filed suit in 2002 against multinational corporations and banks—such as Barclays, BP, Hewlett-Packard, Coca-Cola, Ford, and Shell Oil—accusing them of having abetted and economically benefited from apartheid. The Alien Tort Claims lawsuit, which was heard on appeal in 2006, represents a unique angle on retributive justice, for it tackles the structural and economic factors that underwrote the apartheid state instead of scapegoating particular individuals such as prominent leaders or their henchmen.[57]

Within the field of international human rights and transitional justice, there is widespread agreement that in the aftermath of crimes against humanity—and apartheid is included among such crimes—there is a duty to prosecute.[58] Prosecutions are crucial to honoring the victims and restoring the rule of law. But in the case of apartheid, who should be prosecuted? The Alien Tort Claims suit brought against multinational corporations on behalf of South African victims of apartheid presents one model. Another model advocated by human rights leader Aryeh Neier targets individuals, especially the most senior officials, "those with the highest level of responsibility for the most outrageous crimes." He said,

"When German border guards are convicted while Erich Honecker is allowed to go free, an appearance of unfairness is created. It is more important to prosecute the Honeckers than the border guards, but I would not let the guards go unchallenged either."[59] José Zalaquett, who shares Neier's position, makes a distinction between "exemplary prosecutions and scapegoats."[60]

If the principle of exemplary prosecutions is applied to South Africa, top on the list of likely defendants would be P. W. Botha, leader of South Africa from 1978 to 1989. A dictator, a symbol and defender of apartheid, and a confirmed racist, Botha might well have been prosecuted for his "total strategy," which elevated the powers of the police and military over those of Parliament and the cabinet and authorized covert and often murderous operations to be planned in secret. Though Botha could well have been a prime target for prosecution, post-apartheid South Africa did not choose to take him to court, other than for his failure to respond to a subpoena from the TRC. Yasmin Sooka, former TRC commissioner and executive director of the Human Rights Program in Pretoria, believes this was a mistake. Botha "should have stood trial. Can you imagine the generosity that allowed him to live out his life peacefully still enjoying the benefit of state resources?"[61] Instead, the infamous leader who promulgated but could not follow his own credo of "adapt or die," finally did the latter, passing away in a seaside resort town on the coast of Western Cape in November 2006. He seems to have taken with him important cabinet minutes that were found to be missing from the National Archives and Records Service of South Africa.[62] The director of the South African History Archive (SAHA), Piers Pigou, vows to chase after the incriminating evidence: "The last chapter on P. W. Botha and his complicity in gross human rights violations has not yet been heard. Basically the search for evidence of his complicity continues."[63] Pigou is determined that even if Botha escaped a court of justice, he will nevertheless be tried in the court of history once the incriminating paper trail is found and made public. Given the primary role that SAHA has played in the recovery of documents about apartheid-era crimes, there is reason to be hopeful. SAHA has a proven track record in this regard: when thirty-four boxes of sensitive material from the TRC on topics such as chemical and biological warfare went missing at the ministry of justice, SAHA brought legal action and successfully won an out-of-court settlement to get the records transferred to the National Archives.[64] SAHA scored another major victory in 2006 via the Promotion of Access to Information Act when a Pretoria high court ordered that documentary filmmaker David Forbes be granted access to the TRC archival holdings relating to the case of the Cradock Four.[65] This seems to be one of the first known cases where someone has gained access to the 95 percent of the TRC archive that is presently locked away.

Some secrets of apartheid's past were, in all likelihood, forever buried with P. W. Botha. Yet while Botha was interred, other secrets from the apartheid past were being unearthed. Even as "mourners converged on the small town of George . . . for the funeral of apartheid-era leader P. W. Botha—respected and hated in equal measure for his authoritarianism," the Argentine Forensic Anthropology Team was busy elsewhere in South Africa exhuming skeletons of those killed in apartheid violence and buried in unmarked graves.[66] Beginning in 2005 and continuing through 2007, the Argentinean team has been applying their extraordinary skills in tracking hidden remains in South Africa. Their world-renowned expertise in forensic recovery was acquired through their search for the remains of disappeared persons during Argentina's Dirty War. The first South African exhumations by this team happened in March 2005, when the body of an Umkhonto we Sizwe (MK) freedom fighter named, appropriately, "Justice" was unearthed:

> An almost eerie silence settles over the crowd huddled by the two open graves at Thandukukhanya, a rundown cemetery in the remote town of Piet Retief. They watch hopefully as a team of forensic anthropologists from Argentina sifts through muddy unmarked graves to find the skeletons of two MK combatants buried there as unidentified paupers more than 20 years ago. As the team unearths the remains and brings them to the surface, the quiet is broken by the weeping from relief—as much as sadness—of the families and comrades.[67]

Exhumations of missing persons fulfilled a recommendation of the TRC's final report, which urged that unsolved cases from the commission, its most significant piece of unfinished business, be solved. The TRC saw exhumations as part of "symbolic reparations," along with tombstones, memorials, and the renaming of streets.[68] When the TRC presented the codicil to its final report in 2003, President Thabo Mbeki decided that 477 cases of missing freedom fighters should be resolved. The National Prosecuting Authority assumed the task of exhumations in the wake of the TRC, whether or not this work explicitly led to prosecutions. The most important thing, said NPA spokesperson Makhosini Nkosi, was "not necessarily prosecutions, but to solve the cases."[69] As with the Truth and Reconciliation Commission, the production of knowledge was again privileged over the administration of justice.

Milan Kundera has said famously that "the struggle of humanity against power is the struggle of memory against forgetting."[70] In South Africa today, which impulse is prevailing? How are South Africans "dealing" with the gradually uncensored past in the wake of the TRC? They are doing so actively, in the present continuous tense, and with deep ambivalence. The bodies of missing and assassinated Umkhonto we Sizwe soldiers are being recovered even as the bodies of legendary apartheid leaders are being laid to rest. Important evidence documenting the chain of command for apartheid-era atrocities goes missing even as the TRC's archival records—so paradoxically inaccessible—are now slowly and by court order being made public. Considering that P. W. Botha was seen by many to be a preeminent pariah and symbol of oppression, the public reaction to his death in 2006 was remarkable not only for the ANC's magnanimous gestures of mourning but perhaps more significantly for the public's muted response.[71] Jan Hofmeyer, senior researcher at the Institute for Justice and Reconciliation, said that the general lack of interest in Botha's death was an "indication that South Africans have moved on. . . . People are already passed the stage of retribution.

They don't want to dwell on the past because it doesn't contribute to the improvement of the quality of their lives."[72]

So have the dragons finally left not only the house but the neighborhood as well? Can the tenants finally get on with their lives without fear that a menacing past might suddenly erupt in the "unpredictable" ways that Evita Bezuidenhout foretold in the epigraph that leads this chapter? Tutu's prediction of a powder keg later proved quite prescient: in May of 2008, South Africa erupted into a conflagration of xenophobic violence unlike anything the country has seen since the end of apartheid. From Cape Town to Mpumalanga, Gauteng to Durban, "foreigners" (meaning fellow Africans from Zimbabwe, Malawi, Botswana, Somali—indeed, from all over the continent) were assaulted by angry mobs, robbed of their possessions, stabbed, and burned alive. In the span of two short weeks, forty-two people were killed and over 25,000 people displaced, many of whom sought refuge in police stations or left South Africa altogether. This eruption of xenophobic violence casts a pall on South Africa's global image and tarnishes the often-rosy image the world has held of the TRC. Has South Africa indeed passed the "stage of retribution," as Hofmeyer contends? Has South Africa *really* "moved on"? Is the recent violence symptomatic only of present socioeconomic discrepancies between rich and poor, which are indeed profound? Or is this violence a "restored behavior" of apartheid, a replication of apartheid's "repertoire" of inhumanity honed over so many decades but reenacted now with a slight adjustment in the cast of characters?

I have thus far addressed such questions by surveying major 2006 news items related to the TRC and its legacy. However, these stories are admittedly anecdotal, and in a country with limited literacy and eleven official languages, English-language print media provides a skewed perspective on public sentiment. Fortunately two significant recent studies have attempted a quantitative analysis of South African public attitudes and opinions about issues such as race relations, human security, historical confrontation, dialogue, political culture, and cross-cutting political partnerships as well as attitudes toward the TRC. These surveys, which were conducted by the Institute for Justice and Reconciliation and by professor of government James L. Gibson, use research techniques that take into account the country's diversity, especially in terms of factors such as race, culture, language, and place of residence (urban versus rural).[73] Since 2003, the institute has conducted an annual survey-based study, *The South African Reconciliation Barometer* (SARB). Of the 3,500 South Africans interviewed in 2006, 80.6 percent agreed with the statement: "I want to forget about the past and get on with my life."[74] The *Barometer* also confirmed a high degree of segregation among groups (including whites, blacks, Indians, and coloreds); 56 percent of respondents said that they "never interact informally" with people from other population groups, either at their home or in the homes of friends.[75] Only a third of respondents expressed a perceived need for greater communication among groups, and when asked what stands in the way of greater interaction among South Africans, 40 percent of the respondents said that they "do not trust people of other racial groups."[76]

On a more optimistic note, the *Barometer* found widespread agreement among all respondents of all races that apartheid was indeed a crime against humanity (87.7 percent concur with this view) and high levels of approval for the idea of a united South African nation (76.2 percent).[77]

According to the *Barometer*, whites have historically been the most reluctant population group to see apartheid as a crime against humanity and to embrace the idea of a united South Africa, so this most recent survey provides tangible evidence that attitudes of whites seem to be gradually coming in line with those of the majority. White exceptionalism was also a notable feature of a quantitative survey conducted by James L. Gibson about attitudes toward the TRC.[78] Gibson notes that the impression one gets about public opinion of the TRC based upon print media and the secondary literature is that "complaints and condemnations of the truth and reconciliation process seem to far outnumber laudatory assessments."[79] Yet his empirical research of public opinion reveals the opposite. Conducted in 2000–2001 with a representative sample of 3,727 South Africans and an overall response rate of 87 percent, the survey found that "vast racial differences exist in how people evaluate the TRC, with the extremes being defined by blacks and whites. For instance, while roughly three-quarters of black South Africans approve of the work of the commission, only slightly more than one-third of whites are so inclined."[80] These quantitative studies indicate that the general South African population (as opposed to those who participated directly in the TRC) is indeed ambivalent about reconciliation, race relations, and the legacy of the commission. But there is actually far less ambivalence about the TRC than secondary literature and media coverage might lead one to think. If one expected the commission to definitively unearth truth and produce reconciliation, then the TRC was, of course, a disappointment. But perhaps for the nonwhite majority that looks favorably on the TRC, the work of the commission was not perceived as a terminal destination but rather as a catalyst, part of a larger ongoing process. The conclusions of the 66 percent of whites Gibson surveyed who discredit the commission might conveniently rationalize an acceptance of the status quo: if the commission's findings and its implications do not need to be respected, no change in their behavior is required. For beneficiaries of apartheid, such a position would certainly be self-interested.

The prominence of the TRC in the news during 2006 indicates that no matter what people think about commission, people are still thinking about it. The commission's embodied repertoire remains very much alive, as is evident in prosecutions and refusals to prosecute, ablutions of atonement and ridiculed acts of forgiveness, anniversary commemorations and public statements of the desire to forget the past and "move on," the opening of the TRC archives in 2006 (however briefly), and the continued exhumations of the long-buried disappeared. The repertoire of the TRC can also be seen in the artistic sphere, with films and plays appearing in recent years that engage with the legacy of the truth commission via the realm of the aesthetic. For instance, in 2005–2006 several films about the TRC were launched, including *In My Country* (Sony Pictures Classics 2005; dir. John Boorman), a Hollywood adaptation of Antjie Krog's influential memoir

Country of My Skull; a film adaptation of Gillian Slovo's novel *Red Dust* (HBO 2006; dir. Tim Hooper), an amalgamation of a number of TRC stories told through the point of view of a young white lawyer who returns from exile to serve as counsel for an amnesty hearing; and the locally made and locally cast South African film *Forgiveness* (California Newsreel 2004; dir. Ian Gabriel). The proliferation of films about the commission as well as a new play about the TRC translators entitled *Truth in Translation* (2006) raise the question of the role of the aesthetic sphere and the TRC.[81] In this last segment, I turn to the realm of art to examine its potential role in memorial and commemoration and how the performing arts in particular participate in the continuation of the repertoire of truth and reconciliation in contemporary South African life.

Sound Memory, Living Memorials

At a meeting to discuss a memorial project in Cape Town, constitutional court justice Albie Sachs questioned whether physical monuments are truly effective vehicles for remembering. "The liveliest, the most important memorial is not out there; it is in our heads, conveyed through words and images, songs, and gestures."[82] Since the inception of the TRC, Sachs has advocated for the concept of "living memorials of reconstruction," of which the District Six Museum in Cape Town is a prime example.[83] Called "a hybrid space of research, representation and pedagogy" by historian Ciraaj Rassool, the District Six Museum is located in and commemorates the neighborhood where between the 1970s and 1990s more than 60,000 nonwhite residents were evicted from a once-thriving community.[84] The museum memorializes and acknowledges the trauma of forced removals. But it does much more than that: it is an ongoing community-based history project aimed at restoring "the corporal integrity of District Six" by documenting and promulgating a history that was long suppressed and dispersed, by facilitating debate over the highly fraught issues that are a legacy of forced removals, and by playing a leading role in efforts to restore the community via land claims.[85]

South Africa is home to several other sites that one could call "living memorials," of which Robben Island is a preeminent example. Here former inmates directly narrate their experiences as political prisoners for the successive waves of pilgrims and international tourists who arrive daily on the island.[86] Less well known but no less significant is the Constitutional Court in Johannesburg, the place where the new constitution is literally *performed,* enacted, brought into being each day. It is located on the site of the Old Fort Prison, where so many political prisoners were held in solitary confinement and detained without trial during the old regime.[87] The building sits on one of the highest points of the Witwatersrand, and while standing on the old rampart a few years ago, Mark Gevisser noted how the location was poised between two worlds, with the Old Fort falling down on one side and the new court being erected on the other: "We were suspended between the past and the future, the past derelict and misunderstood and the future still very much under construction—a utopian dream of what we might be able to achieve in this country but is nowhere near being built yet. This society is still very much in transition and the values of the Constitution remain an ideal rather than something that has been realized."[88] The Constitutional Court is truly a living memorial of reconstruction: alive with judges, lawyers, plaintiffs, and defendants who are daily—through each hearing and decision—legislating respect for human rights on the reconstructed site where formerly these same rights were routinely violated.

Metaphors can shape expectations and outcomes, and it is worth reflecting on the assumptions embedded in particular metaphors about the TRC's relationship with the nation, with political transition, and with the past. In the commission's statements about itself as well as in the vast secondary literature on the TRC, one typically sees phrases like "dealing with the past," "coming to terms" with the past, or the "healing of a nation."[89] Michael Ignatieff has asked provocatively what baggage the phrase "coming to terms" might carry: "Do nations, like individuals, have psyches? Can a nation's past make a people ill as we know repressed memories sometimes can make individuals ill?"[90] The TRC promoted the metaphor of a journey. Banners and posters throughout the halls where the public hearings took place bore the phrase "Truth: The Road to Reconciliation." Suggesting one road—truth—and one destination—reconciliation, this metaphor posited reconciliation as closure, a fixed point, a terminus, a telos, or, as Meg Samuelson has said, "the end of the journey of the unraveling story of the past."[91] An alternate model proposed by Albie Sachs has advocated that rather than a "Truth and Reconciliation Commission," what South Africa needed was a "Commission of Truth and *Repair*."[92] I find this metaphor of "repair" provocative and useful, especially in a post-TRC context. Repair is a continuous process, at once practical and immediate. If the nation, like a house, is to be habitably maintained, repairs will be ongoing and never ending. Repairs can also proliferate: some repairs may spur renovations, some renovations may necessitate excavations, and excavations may unearth long-buried knowledge from the past that the inhabitants may decide to rebury—perhaps in secret or perhaps in a different place or perhaps with a commemorative placard saying "never again." The metaphor of repair does not delimit a particular number of people, unlike the "coming to terms" metaphor which, as Michael Ignatieff argues, imposes on that nation the character of an individual psyche: "We do vest our nations with consciences, identities and memories as if they were individuals. But if it is problematic to vest an individual with a single identity, it is even more so in the case of a nation."[93] And this is especially true in South Africa, the paradigmatic rainbow nation of diversity.

If we accept the hypotheses that what South Africa needs in the wake of the TRC are living memorials instead of static and inanimate ones and memorials that engage in a process of repair and reconstruction instead of arriving at destinations of commemoration, what might such memorials look like? Perhaps they might not "look" at all but rather resonate, as did *REwind: A Cantata for Voice, Tape, and Testimony,* a new musical work by composer Philip Miller that premiered in 2006 in honor of the tenth anniversary of the start of the TRC (fig. 5.1). Composer Miller is known for his television and film scores, especially his col-

Figure 5.1. *REwind* performed at The Market Theatre, Johannesburg, in 2008. The image behind the soloists is a film of a letter impregnated with dye that slowly bleeds ink when submerged in water. The projection (designed by Gerhard Marx) accompanies a song that uses the TRC testimony of Anglican priest Father Michael Lapsley, who lost both his hands due to a parcel bomb. Photograph by John Hodgkiss, courtesy of Key Films in association with The Market Theatre, 2008.

laborations with internationally acclaimed visual artist William Kentridge. The impetus for *REwind* came from poet and journalist Antjie Krog, who was so moved by Miller's score for the film *Forgiveness* that she encouraged him to consider writing an independent composition on the TRC. Krog "felt that there were not enough artistic projects being made in South Africa that related to the Truth and Reconciliation Commission," according to Miller.[94] She had heard about *The Human Rights Cantata* that had been written in Chile and wondered if Miller might consider using the cantata form.[95]

A cantata is essentially "a piece of music that works with voice and orchestra," says Miller. "Over the years it has become something that lends itself to working with poetry or epic history, and obviously its most important resonance is its voice."[96] The cantata form is particularly appropriate for the TRC material in many regards. First, South Africa is a country of rich choral traditions. "Often people say, 'Oh the drum is the African instrument,'" says Miller. "It's not. In South Africa, it's the voice. The voice is the first instrument."[97] Second, song was central to the resistance struggle, as is documented so compellingly in the film *Amandla! A Revolution in Four-Part Harmony* (2002; ATO Pictures/Kwela Productions dir. Lee Hirsch). Through singing, people could connect across barriers of language or even barriers of incarceration: singing could penetrate the isolation of solitary confinement. Singing provided for many in the struggle an emotional solace and an affirmation of humanity even in the face of relentlessly dehumanizing conditions. Furthermore, song was used strategically to mobilize and organize people at mass protests. Finally, in the post-apartheid era, South African love of song has manifested in a near-fanatical interest in opera—especially among blacks—as is evident in the popularity of the Cape Town Opera and the theatre troupe Dimpho di Kopane (recently reconstituted as Isango Portobello Productions). Recently, Isango Portobello Productions has adapted operas such as *Carmen*; its critically acclaimed *U-Carmen eKhayelitsha* is set in the bustling township of Khayelitsha, outside Cape Town.[98]

However, Miller's interest in voice extends beyond singing: the TRC gave *voice* to the formerly disenfranchised. Through hearings, people "for the first time, could use their voices again," says Miller, and "what we hear are people telling their stories—terrible, horrific; sometimes depraved, sometimes perpetrators with their own devastating evil."[99] While much has been said about the "narrative truths" of the TRC and the importance of storytelling to its human rights agenda,[100] Miller's work highlights something beyond narrative: the aural qualities of testimony, the texture of sound, the grain of the voice.[101] *REwind* had its world premiere in Cape Town on 16 December 2006 (directed by Janice Honeyman) during the annual holiday known as the Day of Reconciliation. Subsequently it has been performed in 2007 in Brooklyn, New York, at the Celebrate Brooklyn! festival and at Williams College in Williamstown, Massachusetts, that same year. Most recently it was performed at The Market Theatre in Johannesburg, South Africa, in April 2008. At times subtitled a musical work for "voice, tape, and testimony," *REwind* includes a choir, vocal soloists, and a string ensemble as well as archival audio recordings from the TRC public testimony—the words spoken by victims, perpetrators, and their translators and the nonverbal expressions of sighs, inhalations, gasps, and wails of grief. Miller calls such sounds the "creative seed" of the cantata.[102] To describe *REwind* as weaving spoken word with music, says Miller, does not do it justice, for the music actually *originates* with the recorded voices and their timbre and emotional intensity:

> Something about hearing the testimony as live voice working with sound makes it even more intense to hear the inflections and nuances of the people who testified—often, I might add, mediated by translators, because in South Africa there are over eleven official languages and we will hear the emotion in the translator's voice—or not. But even when you don't, there's very interesting complexities of emotions coming through because you have several voices telling the story.[103]

Thus "voice" in the cantata signifies the metaphorical and symbolic significance of how the TRC gave repressed voices a hearing within an official state-sanctioned forum; the content of what was communicated verbally in those testimonies; and the sonic texture and complex registers of emotional expression within those human voices—their vocal (as opposed to verbal) signification. As Julia Walker argues, vocal expression "can create, augment and/or reverse the presumed meaning of words by using pronunciation, tone coloration, and inflectional variation to speak to an emotional as well as conceptual register of 'meaning.'"[104] Miller's use of the sonic record of the public hearings of the TRC reanimates aspects of communication that tend not to survive what Roland Barthes calls the "trap of scription," the moment when speech is "embalmed" as text.[105]

The potency of vocal signification at TRC hearings is further intensified when one considers the added layer of translation. Those who attended live hearings could listen to testimony via headsets as the words of witnesses and commissioners were translated into South Africa's eleven official languages. Television and radio broadcasts often foregrounded the interpreter's voice—with its own tones, colorations, accent, and gender—which was layered on top of the voice of the witness. One might argue that translation at the TRC highlighted almost in a Brechtian manner the whole issue of mediation. When victims' voices were eclipsed by the voices of interpreters, I was reminded of the layers of mediation not only of interpretation but perhaps also of the whole process by which the commission selected which victims would get a public hearing and which would not. Yet the voices of victims were so potent that for many auditors they signified the unmediated and authentic voice of "truth." "There is perhaps an ease of empathy, a suspension of critical judgment, in listening and watching," says anthropologist Fiona Ross of TRC public testimony.[106] Likewise, one TRC staff member who was responsible for listening to recordings spoke of the empathic engagement she experienced through sound: "When I listen to the people crying at the hearing on tape, I cry with them, but it remains in my head. It is tearing me apart. . . . I wonder if this will ever go away."[107] The experience of hearing the voices of the formerly oppressed and disenfranchised is especially compelling in Africa. In the field of African history, the oral source has been a primary means for substantiating that Africa, contrary to Hegel's prejudices, actually *had* a history.[108] As Luise White, Stephan F. Miescher, and David William Cohen contend, "The African 'voice'—cradled, massaged, liberated, and authenticated within the expert approaches of the African historian—comes to represent . . . truth while it bolsters scholarly claims to objectivity."[109] For those within African studies for whom African voices hold an "essential authority and power to represent Africa and its past across all the complexities of racism, colonialism, and suppression,"[110] South Africa's Truth and Reconciliation Commission was a field day: 22,000 "ordinary" people telling their stories and placing them in the public record.[111]

In focusing on the aural archive of the commission, *REwind* evokes the medium by which most South Africans experienced the TRC: radio. South Africa is a country with limited literacy, multiple languages, and a nonwhite majority that is often still living in settlements where electricity and televisions may not be readily available. In such a context, radio coverage of the TRC reached farther than any other medium, especially into the rural areas.[112] Radio also literally covered more of the TRC than did television or newspapers, as we saw in Chapter 4.

Radio's influence on the creation of *REwind* is quite direct: when Antjie Krog encouraged Miller to consider writing the cantata, she lent him cassette tapes from her years of reporting on the commission. Like Krog's coverage of the TRC, Miller's creative process favored the potent sound bite over extended narrative.[113] "REwind," the title song of Miller's cantata, begins with the sound of a woman crying. A very brief segment of recorded testimony is rewound and replayed, again and again, as if a CD has skipped. The rewinding produces a high-pitched screech like a train braking, a sound that when sustained over time warbles unstably. This sound is layered over the woman's cry. Gradually, a women's choir accompanies—they sing two tones, alternating between major and minor keys, and a string ensemble gently plucks the same notes. The testimony is that of Eunice Miya, one of the mothers of the Guguletu Seven, a well-publicized window case from the TRC. Miya, like many who appeared at the Human Rights Violations Committee hearings, was overcome with emotion and cried during her testimony. Miller uses a brief clip of that crying sound as a generative basis for his composition. He explains, "I found a musical equivalent of that crying sound, which became a musical motif which I could then work and build up an entire song based upon the gasping sound of Eunice Miya."[114]

In her testimony, Miya narrates how she first learned of the death of her son via a television news report. When she saw the body of her deceased son Jabulani on the television, she told the TRC that she wished the news could just "rewind." Miller was struck by the metaphor of rewinding. While writing the cantata, Miller constantly listened to testimonies, literally rewinding and fast-forwarding on analog cassette tapes. "So there was the literalness of what I was doing, the physical process of rewinding and fast forwarding the testimonies." Miller explains:

> And then of course there was the more metaphorical meaning to the idea of going back and retelling testimonies, rewinding your memory, your thoughts. Then [there was] this question of what it means to go back and record things. What is the purpose of that? Is it cathartic or is it a way of . . . retraumatizing? . . . Was I sort of opening up things that should in fact be kept closed? Should those testimonies just stay in the archives? Later I went to those archives and realized—it struck me—how those tapes were just sitting there in boxes, piles and piles of boxes of tapes and videocassettes. And in actual fact they shouldn't just be closed up in a room, in an archive. . . . We should be listening to those voices in other ways, whether it is through texts or the way I am doing it with sound. And suddenly I got the courage to take this on.[115]

At its core, *REwind: A Cantata for Voice, Tape, and Testimony* is about the dilemma of memory for a nation with a traumatic past, with dragons on the patio and in the living room—a country that while it wishes to acknowledge the past, honor those who suffered, and ensure that past atrocities happen "never again" is nevertheless completely immersed in inventing a new, democratic, and prosperous future in which dwelling on the past may be of limited use. Miller's composition gives musical expression to the pull of memory and the push of forgetting. Woven into the ebb and flow of the piece is an antiphonal structure that expresses contradictory forces as they collide dynamically, remaining ultimately unresolved. The *New York Times* identified Miller's "conversational vocal lines, stormy choruses and chugging rhythms" as expressing "lessons absorbed" from the likes of composers Philip

Glass and John Adams. But South African journalists heard in *REwind*'s aesthetic and conceptual resonances a "peculiarly South African identity."[116]

REwind is a fitting living memorial to the TRC on many levels. As did the commission, the cantata juxtaposes personal stories of trauma with monumental themes, connecting the individual with the national, connecting personal memory with collective memory. Particular testimonies invite the listener to enter through quotidian detail and situation. One particularly moving song entitled "Mrs. Plaatjie" (sung in the Williamstown and Johannesburg productions by the famous mezzo-soprano Sibongile Khumalo) evokes the image of a boy home from school making a peanut-butter sandwich in the kitchen as his mother looks on.[117] But as with life under apartheid, the quotidian veers off into unexpected horror: the boy's life is interrupted by violence—a random and fatal gunshot. Through their sequential compilation in the cantata, sound bites of testimony become part of a larger experience of epic proportions: the founding of a nation, the anguish of human suffering and death, narrated deeds of unspeakable evil, the mysteries of atonement and forgiveness, and the tenacity of the will to survive. The TRC posited that its public hearings "constituted the core of the commission's work," a place to give victims voice and acknowledged their suffering.[118] Like the commission's hearings, the cantata uses live, performed, embodied communication as its primary means of communication. As with the TRC, *REwind* is a grand production with many performers and a complex score. But also like the commission's hearings, the cantata is ultimately fleeting, ephemeral, leaving no trace in the venues where it is performed. Both *REwind* and the TRC hearings exploited the aural dimensions of communication, with the potency of sound resonating not just in the cognitive but also the affective registers of communication beyond verbal signification.

While *REwind* shares many key features of the TRC's public hearings, Miller departs dramatically from the commission in his methodology. The TRC's mandate was to give as complete a picture as possible of the past violations of human rights and to make findings about the contexts, causes, and patterns of human rights violations. In light of this brief, the commission privileged quantitative social science methods over humanistic ones and produced a lengthy report that tried to meet the expectation of completeness.[119] Miller's approach was entirely opposite. Working intuitively and randomly, he listened to testimony for what he calls "shards," fragments that he found evocative or compelling. Miller said, "I set my own creative boundaries" in terms of "what I choose to use, and what I don't choose to use."[120] Sifting through tapes, Miller selected segments that were for him emblematic or poetic or expressive of certain themes he wished to address. He used fragments that were disconnected from context but nevertheless resonant with specific and precise detail. A press release for the cantata called these "poignant representations of an emotive institution."[121] Miller made no claims to completeness, nor does the cantata attempt to tell coherent narratives. I asked him whether he wished to produce different kinds of truths or a different kind of completeness than did the TRC. Does he see his approach as being antithetical to that of the commission inasmuch as he is producing a deliberately incomplete picture? For Miller, *REwind* is "not about finishing, or completing, or giving anyone an idea of the enormity of the testimonies and . . . what was said."[122] He is also quick to point out the fallacy of the TRC's claims to completeness, for the commissioners had their "own criteria in terms of who could come and give testimony and what was considered a human rights violation. They set the parameters anyway. So this notion that there is one huge set of testimony out there that would kind of represent all the atrocities is a fiction, isn't it?" The selectivity of the TRC has been noted by many others, most prominently Mahmood Mamdani.[123] Likewise, the Khulumani Support Group, the major NGO in South Africa that represents victims, estimates that 110,000 individuals—five times the number of testimonies recorded by the TRC—were in fact victims of human rights violations during the period under investigation by the TRC.[124]

Yet artistic license did not grant Miller full freedom to choose any material. Early in his process, he found that he could not ignore an issue that had persistently vexed the commission: representativity. How well does a particular choice to include one person's testimony reflect the breadth and diversity of the human rights violations suffered nationally or locally? Hugh Lewin, a former member of the TRC's Human Rights Violations Committee, tells how difficult it was to choose which 10 percent of the statements taken in any community would be selected for a TRC hearing:

> You've got a submission of about 150, say 200, statements which have been solicited . . . by the statement takers in the area. They come in and they sit there, and you go through them. How do you then choose the 10 or 12 who are going to appear on that particular day from that particular place? This is our brief. Cover everywhere. Go throughout the country. So how do you choose?[125]

Should the committee choose the well-known political activist who died in the struggle or the story of the domestic worker killed by a random police bullet in township violence? How many blacks, how many whites, how many coloreds, and how many Indians should be given an opportunity to speak? What is the balance of men versus women or those who were themselves victims versus those testifying on behalf of others or the religious diversity among those who testified? What about party affiliation? Was the political landscape appropriately represented in the lineup for a particular day? Or how about historical representation in terms of coverage of the 34-year historical period the TRC was mandated to investigate? For those who worked behind the scenes at the commission, such questions were, in Lewin's words, "the most difficult and painful" aspect of the TRC process. These were daily, persistent, and emotionally fraught questions for which there were no "right" answers.[126]

In selecting material for the cantata Miller was, of course, not tied to an act of Parliament, nor was he making a nonfiction documentary. He was rather making a work of art, and he was doing so in a society that now enshrines freedom of speech in its constitution. However Miller could not disregard questions of representation. About halfway through his compositional process, he realized that he had selected testimonies only of victims who were black. "Even though I wasn't trying to tell the *whole* story," said Miller, "I still had to be careful not to skew it completely through my selection."[127] The TRC hearings were, in fact, not neatly divided along racial lines, though this is a common misperception of the commission outside South Africa. The story of the commission, as with the story of South Africa, is far more complex. Many of those seeking amnesty were black and a significant number of victims were white. So to project through the cantata a simplistic racial polarity would be highly problematic.

Cognizant of the bias represented by his initial selection of material, Miller began looking for testimony by white victims. But this was difficult. He didn't want to emphasize color too much, for he was concerned about implying a hierarchy of tragedies and human rights abuses. "Is there a value you can ascribe to the color of a person suffering?" he asked rhetorically during our interview.[128] The testimony he ultimately selected was that of Bishop Retief, who had been the head of the St. James Church in Cape Town when it was attacked by the armed wing of the Pan Africanist Congress. In 1993, gunmen burst into a Sunday church service and opened fire with machine guns, killing eleven people and injuring fifty-six, most of whom were white. An interlude in the cantata uses the archival recording of Retief's testimony that conveys fragmentary memories of that fateful day: Retief describes getting off a plane, being informed of the attack, and the flashing lights of the police cars as well as his shock: "I could not actually believe what I was hearing." The next song, an aria titled "No Greater Than," uses not an archival recording but rather the words of Retief's testimony as libretto: "We recognized that our sorrow and tragedy was no greater than anyone else's. . . . We had a one-off experience, but the stories that have unfolded here are stories of years and years of being traumatized by violence. So we recognize that there's nothing special or exceptional about what we went through at that time."[129] Here is a TRC story that is about white victims. The libretto says that "our" suffering— that of the congregants—was "no greater" than anyone else's who came before the commission; that this suffering has created within the congregation greater empathy with others throughout the country; and finally, that theirs was a "one-off experience" of violence whereas for so many who testified before the TRC, violence was routine and long-standing. The phrase "one-off experience" is sung lightly in high-pitched, succinct notes in a punctuated staccato rhythm, but the phrase "years and years" is repeated twelve times in rapid succession. So while there may not be a value one can ascribe to the color of a person suffering, the song does present a comparison of duration, contrasting staccato "one-offs" with sustained "years and years."

We know that several of Miller's key artistic decisions were prompted by race, but how do audiences actually *perceive* race when experiencing *REwind*? Race is, after all, not something that registers aurally to the degree that it does visually. Nothing in the libretto reveals that the victims described by Retief were white. Nor did the program at the cantata's premiere clarify race: it merely lists "St. James Church Massacre" next to Retief's name. The song "No Greater Than," which uses which Retief's words as the libretto, was sung by a tenor soloist at the December

2006 premiere of the cantata who happened to be white. But from its very beginning, the cantata establishes a performance convention whereby the identity of the singers and that of the witnesses they represent are disconnected. For instance, in the song "Who's Laughing," the black baritone Fikile Mvinjelwa sings the words of the white Afrikaans former president P. W. Botha. Likewise, in the song "Edward Juqu," we hear the archival recording of Edward Juqu's testimony, which is interpreted by a woman, hence providing a disruption of gender and for some listeners, a momentary confusion. Who is speaking? Is the woman's voice speaking in English actually representing Juqu, who can be heard, muffled in the background, speaking Xhosa? Or is the female voice someone else, perhaps a TRC commissioner? So throughout the cantata, *REwind* demands that audiences become accustomed to a kind of Brechtian disconnect between performer and "character." Race and gender are destabilized, and visual, aural, and textual clues do not clarify identity, at least with any certainty. So in fact the only way an audience member would recognize the racial significance of Miller's choice of Retief would be if that person read the program and already knew the story of the St. James massacre as being a black armed assault on a white church. For many South Africans, this massacre was a touchstone episode of violence in the chaotic years prior to the elections, so it is likely that many who read the program would have "gotten it." But such comprehension is not likely to be sustained over time, say ten years from now, as memories of apartheid-era atrocities fade. Nor is such comprehension likely for non–South African audiences who are unfamiliar with the TRC material.

"Hamba Kahle—The Bag" is another song in the cantata that is highly dependent upon prior knowledge. The piece begins with a now-infamous recording of the torturer Jeffrey Benzien giving a dispassionate description of his "wet-bag" technique, how he suffocated those he interrogated to the brink of death. For South African audiences, Benzien's testimony is iconic, even nine years after it was aired at the TRC, for it was and continues to be widely circulated as a paradigmatic moment of the commission. Miller juxtaposes Benzien's testimony with a well-known ANC struggle song, "Hamba Kahle." "Carry on, spear of the nation," says the song, which was a kind of anthem of the military wing of the ANC, Umkhonto we Sizwe. It was typically sung as comrades went off for training in exile or into the line of duty or when comrades died, sung as a funeral dirge. A white tenor named Arthur Swan sang "Hamba Kahle," a deliberate casting choice by Miller. He felt that with a black soloist, the piece too easily collapsed into a simple racial dichotomy, whereas with a white soloist, the piece became much more complex. For black South African audiences and for some whites, particularly those who had been involved in the struggle, "Hamba Kahle" would be immediately recognized. By putting these two things together—Benzien and "Hamba Kahle"—and adding in the unexpected dimension of a white soloist, Miller musically poses a number of questions: "What is the soloist now? Is he the spirit of the struggle, which was interracial? The spear of the nation? But he's a white man singing—is he somehow the voice of Benzien, that he knows the struggle will go on, despite his torturing?"[130] To layer in even greater complexity, Miller added in a black soprano who sang high, ethereal, and haunting notes as well as a deeply resonant all-male choir.[131] With all but one voice being male, "Hamba Kahle—The Bag" has an overt gendered dimension, which is especially poignant considering the gendered dynamics of the TRC: of the 7,128 perpetrators who applied for amnesty, 99 percent were male.[132] The majority of those who testified before the Human Rights Violations Committee were women, but they usually testified on behalf of others, such as husbands or sons who died in apartheid-era violence.[133] Someone listening to this song who is familiar with the TRC might also reflect on an ironic link between Benzien and "Hamba Kahle": a state torturer and the armed wing of the ANC represent antithetical positions, yet they nevertheless share one thing in common—professed patriotism.

This sort of dynamic overlay, the ironic juxtaposition, the familiar iconic motif cast in an unfamiliar register produces tremendous complexity and in many ways is a defining feature of the cantata, which almost seems to orchestrate elements that otherwise exist as a cacophony of contending and opposed positions. The song that achieves the most climactic collision of such discourses is "Who's Laughing," based upon a press interview with P. W. Botha in his home after he refused to obey a subpoena to go before the TRC. The song begins with baritone Fikile Mvinjelwa chanting "U Left, U Right, Nyamazan(e)!" He calls out to the chorus, "Come Guerilla!" and they respond by singing the chant and stamping on the ground, from left to right foot, doing the *toyi-toyi*, a militaristic dance of foot-stomping and spontaneous chanting that was an integral part of protest culture of the late apartheid era. Midway through the piece, Mvinjelwa switches his character. He moves upstage behind a podium and starts to impersonate the former Botha, with wagging finger and wide eyes. The audience hears a recording of Botha as he says, "I'm a believer, and I'm blessed by my creator," a phrase echoed by Mvinjelwa as he sings and impersonates Botha. The recording continues with Botha's voice saying that apartheid is "an Afrikaans word that can be easily replaced by a proper, positive term: good neighborliness," a statement that of course echoes the infamous words of Hendrik Verwoerd, apartheid's architect, from some five decades earlier. Someone at the press conference laughed when Botha said this preposterous statement about "good neighborliness." The Great Crocodile Botha then asked suspiciously, "Who's laughing? Who's laughing?" Mvinjelwa repeats the phrase, impersonating Botha, and as he does so, Botha's rhetoric collides head on with the restless, insistent, militaristic *toyi-toyi* from the choir. The two discourses, each with their own patriotism and violence, run right into each other. The result is raucous as the chorus chants: "Haha ha hahaha, Ha hahahahaha," even as Botha through the recording and through the soloist Mvinjelwa asks suspiciously, menacingly, shaking his finger in the air: "Who's laughing? Who is laughing?" The music reaches its crescendo, drawing the audience into a vortex of ironic laughing. The humor of this moment, perhaps the lightest in *REwind*, is nevertheless haunted by the menace of Botha's wagging finger and the fury that lies behind the *toyi-toyi*'s physical agitation. The *toyi-toyi* was a potent weapon in the struggle, and like all potent weapons, it was hard to control. This chant mobilized massive demonstrations by which tens of thousands of people moved through the streets in defiance and protest, demanding their rights. But this chant was also an ugly prelude to vigilante murders of blacks by blacks in the townships of those suspected of being informers, or *impimpis*.

REwind reflects and refracts a complicated history. Yet the piece will resonate quite differently with listeners depending upon what each person brings to it. Such vicissitudes of reception raise the question of who is the intended audience for this cantata. According to Miller, *REwind* is, on one level, for anyone "who is interested in retelling stories and memories of personal history," whether that person is from Chile, the United States, Germany, or wherever.[134] It is for audiences interested in transitional justice and also for those who may be interested in choral music, classical music, or new compositions. For a general arts-going international audience, *REwind* is likely to be rewarding, even if it is experienced on a purely aesthetic level. Musically the work is multidimensional with stirring melodies, deeply haunting solos, and dynamic orchestration.

Miller acknowledges the value of the work for international audiences and notes the irony that he is far more able to obtain funding outside South Africa than within it. But his first priority is to reach a South African audience: "And when I say a South African audience, I mean an audience that is both white and black. This isn't about color. It's just about . . . everyone who is committed to being in the country, being South African," says Miller, for them "to think about what happened."[135] Miller feels that contemporary South Africa is not really dealing with the legacy of the TRC, that people are shutting themselves off from the past and burying history in the archives. His views are certainly consistent with the analysis of contemporary attitudes toward the past and the TRC provided in the first half of this chapter. Miller hopes *REwind* will be a catalyst for raising questions such as Does the act of retelling enable us to reconcile?[136] Is telling cathartic? What does it mean to listen? What does it mean to acknowledge what has been said? The cantata sets out a series of musical questions, narratives and counternarratives, and dissonant juxtapositions. Neat four-part harmonies from familiar Christian hymns become disrupted, dissonant, and asymmetrical in his work, which might prompt South African audiences to think about what the promotion of "national unity" in the TRC's enabling legislation might actually mean.[137] Does unity mean unison or does it allow for multiple autonomous melodic lines? Does unity mean harmony or can it also accommodate dissonance? Miller is interested in revealing the complexity of the TRC process, the "shades of culpability, shades of responsibility."[138] For him, *REwind* is about lack of resolution, musically and metaphorically, as well as about our desire to hear resolution. Essentially, "*REwind* is a question," Miller says. And yet the cantata's central question—whether to rewind at all—is one that Miller has already answered for himself: he believes it *is* important to remember and reflect, to rewind and learn from what happened in the past. "We have to keep this stuff alive," says Miller, so the TRC testimonies don't only end up in "libraries and dusty archives, whether it's sound or written word. In fact, this is part of public memory, sound memory."[139]

The intended audience for the cantata is thus South Africans of all races as well as citizens of the world. But who has been its actual audience thus far? As of this writing, *REwind* has had three public performances, the first of which was a lecture demonstration at the Spier wine estate in the Western Cape in March 2006. Spier gave commissioning seed money for the creation of the cantata. In contemporary South Africa, according to Miller, Spier is the only arts trust that has been "investing money in the arts in any relevant way" in terms of developing new work.[140] The audience for the lecture demonstration was entirely white. The second public appearance of *REwind* was in America, a "work-in-progress" presentation in September 2006 co-presented by Williams College and the Massachusetts Museum of Contemporary Art.[141] The composer, the director, four vocal soloists, and a string quartet were brought from South Africa, and at the performance they were accompanied by the Williams College Concert Choir. The audience for this rural New England performance was what one might expect in terms of diversity (or lack thereof).

The third performance, the world premiere of *REwind*, took place on a most auspicious day—16 December 2006, South Africa's National Day of Reconciliation—and in a most auspicious location—St. George's Cathedral in Cape Town. The cathedral had been for years a place of safety for demonstrators during the anti-apartheid struggle, and it was also the pulpit from which Desmond Tutu, chairperson of the TRC, served as archbishop of the Anglican Church of Southern Africa. The audience for the world premiere of *REwind* included the victims and families of those whose testimony was used in the cantata as well as leaders who had served on or were instrumental in creating the TRC, such as Archbishop Tutu, Pumla Gobodo-Madikizela, Glenda Wildschut, Dullah Omar, and Albie Sachs. But the general audience, described by this production's director Janice Honeyman as "old lefties and their mothers," was predominately white.[142] Reflecting afterward, Miller asked, "Is this a case of preaching to the converted?"[143] Albie Sachs, who attended both the dress rehearsal and the premiere performance, believed that "the main audience for this piece should be those South Africans who have experienced what the piece represents. They will understand the modulations of the music, the familiar songs in an unfamiliar setting, with an operatic arrangement and singers. They will get the complexity and subtlety."[144] Sachs volunteered that the next performance should be at his place, the Constitutional Court in Johannesburg. And while symbolically and logistically this would be a site more conducive to reaching the sort of audience Sachs described, who would produce it? Who in South Africa would have both the financial capacity and the will to hire an entire choir, soloists, a string ensemble, a musical director, and all the technical equipment necessary to present and promote a musical work of this magnitude and on this subject? A second South African production was finally mounted at The Market Theatre in Johannesburg in 2008 with assistance from European funding sources for an extremely short run of five days.

As the cantata has gestated over two years, it has grown considerably in technical complexity. Projections created by designer and director Gerhard Marx have added a compelling visual component to the cantata while at the same time enhancing its legibility and accessibility. Marx incorporated transcriptions and translations of testimony into the visual aesthetic of the piece with well-chosen sentence fragments that scroll on a screen. Without projected text, much of the cantata's verbal content would be inaccessible, both because of language barriers and the muddied quality of the original TRC recordings that are incorporated into the music. This text is intermeshed with visual animations Marx created, which are projected onto a scrim between the soloists and the eighty-person choir (see fig. 5.1). These are often quite beautiful, containing dense and potent images that slowly morph: a leather easy chair that disintegrates, a montage of house exteriors, an image of a letter that seems to be impregnated with dye and submerged in water and appears to smolder and bleed as we hear testimony about a parcel bomb. These images add dense layers of visual metaphor to the cantata's textured musical score. However, these new visual components of the cantata also add considerably to the cost and technical complexity of producing the show. The composer's original dream of having the cantata tour nationally to sites where the TRC appeared is now quite impossible, at least if Marx's visual component is retained. One could argue that the aesthetic and artistic ambition of the work is at odds with the composer's political commitment to serving a multiracial South African audience.

There are two big obstacles to *REwind* reaching a wider, more diverse audience in South Africa: the state of arts funding in South Africa and the ambivalence of potential funders and producers about the truth commission material. The lead producer for the premiere of *REwind,* Spier, has a constituency that tends to be wealthy enough to own private cars. Most performances in the Spier Arts Summer Season, of which the cantata was a part, are held in open air venues at the Spier wine estate in the lush rolling hills of wine country outside Stellenbosch, a place that is also home of the De Zalze Winelands Golf Estate, the Camelot Spa Group, the Cheetah Outreach (popularly known as "Cheetah Park"), and the exotically themed Moyo restaurant where people dine in Bedouin tents and gazebos as elaborately costumed and painted live performers entertain by playing drums and *mbiras,* telling African fables, "and so much more!"[145] Performances at the Spier wine estate are physically inaccessible to those, say, who live in the sprawling townships that line the N1 highway that leads to Spier from downtown Cape Town. After a *REwind* lecture demonstration at Spier in March 2006 attracted an exclusively white audience, Miller agitated to move the premiere to a more accessible venue. He chose St. George's Cathedral because of its central location in downtown Cape Town and its symbolic and historical significance. But marketing for the premiere was extremely limited. Spier is fully capable of producing slickly designed brochures and posters, such as the clever multicolored and richly illustrated ticket packet that was the 2006 Spier Arts Summer Season brochure. Yet for some reason *REwind* was the only event out of eighteen advertised in this brochure that had no accompanying photo. In the days leading up to the cantata's premiere, I saw almost no signs and posters promoting the cantata on the streets of Cape Town. I found only one notice in the newspaper, and the only advance feature article was in the Afrikaans press.[146]

At the premiere, the families of victims were in attendance, which was very significant. They were there because their attendance was organized by the composer and by filmmaker Liza Key (who has made a documentary on the cantata), not by the producers. Spier did not seem to have prioritized audience diversity, nor did it seem to embrace—or perhaps even perceive—the potential of this event as a living memorial, as something that could continue the repertoire of the TRC by bringing together communities that have been and continue to be segregated. Logistically and financially bringing together diverse communities can be quite difficult. The challenge of this should not be underestimated, but neither should the simplicity of potential solutions: Malcolm Purkey, artistic director of The Market Theatre in Johannesburg, suggested that the easiest way to diversify the audience would be to give complementary tickets to every member of the choir, most of whom were black. Given that the dress rehearsal for the cantata, which was a ticketed event, was only filled to about 40 percent capacity, such a strategy would not have incurred any negative financial impact. But of course, the goal of diversifying, of building community, of reaching across barriers of segregation and bringing together people across racial and class divisions would need to be a priority for the producers for such creative solutions to be found.

So what is the future of *REwind*? Will it be able to reach a wide and racially and economically diverse South African audience? The artist's dream is to take the cantata to every town throughout the country where the TRC held hearings. Given the scale of the production, the challenging nature of the music (which requires trained musicians), and the state of funding for the arts in South Africa, this dream is not likely to be realized. The U.S. premiere of the work took place in July 2007 in Prospect Park, Brooklyn, as part of the Celebrate Brooklyn! festival and was subsequently presented a second time at Williams College in late September (one year after a workshop version had been presented in conjunction with the Massachusetts Museum of Contemporary Art). Both events were produced by an American, Rachel Chanoff, who has been able to raise far more funds for *REwind* in the United States than Miller and his team could raise in South Africa. Such is the case for many South African artists, who find far more financial support abroad than at home. South Africa has a very "unhealthy public arts funding program," says Miller. "Like in most countries, the arts are very low down on the agenda in terms of funding—education, health, all that other stuff comes first."[147] Those basic human needs are so monumental and multiple in South Africa, given the socioeconomic legacy of apartheid and the ravages of the AIDS epidemic, that there is almost nothing left for the arts. In addition to these usual problems of arts funding, *REwind* has the added obstacle of the cantata's content. Gcisakazi Mdlulwa, who has been helping Miller raise funds, says that potential corporate sponsors find *REwind* to be a piece of work that is too overtly political. They say, "Oh, this is a downer. This is a downer. TRC? Truth and Reconciliation Commission? Atrocities of apartheid? It's a downer. We don't want to fund this."[148] The other avenue for funding is through government agencies. But "last year [2006] the Department of Arts and Culture ran out of budget very quickly earlier in the year," said Miller, "and they weren't able to fund this."[149] In South Africa at the moment, funders—both private and government—are interested in underwriting work that promotes cultural heritage and lost heritage. "African Renaissance, our history as great peoples from Africa from millions of years. All of that stuff is far more fashionable," says Miller.[150] The TRC is definitely not fashionable. "The fact is that in some ways we just don't want to know about this thing in South Africa—and that includes funding a project like this. It's a really ambivalent state."

So as a living memorial of reconstruction, REwind has one great liability when compared to physical memorials and monuments: it is completely contingent upon the consistent interest of funders. Without willing sponsors to underwrite performances, the cantata does not exist. Of course museums and statues also require funding. But once raised, the work physically exists, it occupies space and mass. The cantata, in contrast, is a time-based art form, and money must be raised for each iteration of the work. The cantata will be released in later 2009 as a commercial recording, distributed via CD. But the live enactment of REwind is so much more than a recorded performance on a CD. Performances have the capacity to bring people together into common space across lines of past and present segregation. Performance provides the opportunity for audiences to hear, to acknowledge, to witness in person the words of those who gave testimony. And to receive TRC testimony through the medium of music—which so potently registers emotions, transcends language, and mitigates the often-repellant nature of horrific stories of atrocity by refracting them through the realm of the aesthetic—can foster and cultivate collective memory in unique and complicated ways.

However, if REwind is a living memorial of reconstruction, it would be a mistake to focus exclusively on product—that is, on fully realized public performances—as the only expression of memorial's acts of reconstruction. For as with the District Six Museum, *process,* the making of the work, how it engages its communities and constituencies, is as important as *product,* the mounting of a particular exhibit or a performance. So we must ask whether and how the making of the cantata—writing, researching, rehearsing, directing, producing, and attempting to reproduce (even if those attempts are unsuccessful)—are part of the repertoire of truth and reconciliation in South Africa, how "people participate in the production and reproduction of knowledge by 'being there,' being part of the transmission."[151] The point of entry for such a question is through the victims. How has the REwind cantata engaged them? Haunted by Theodor Adorno's dictum that "to write poetry after Auschwitz is barbaric," artists working on projects like REwind must navigate an ethical minefield, especially in relation to those who suffered gross violations of human rights.[152] One person who testified before the TRC, Yazir Henry, took great exception to the way Antjie Krog used his words in her book *Country of My Skull,* which is a hybrid genre, part fiction, part nonfiction.[153] Of such artistic adaptations, Henry has said:

Not only do I question the intentions of writers such as Antjie Krog; I assert that their work has, in various ways and with serious personal consequences to myself, impacted negatively upon my life. Serious thought needs to be given to the ethics of appropriating testimony for poetic license, media freedom, academic commentary and discourse analysis. Arguing these lines and "It's on the public record" are too easy positions to take since they do not address the rights of self-authorship and the intention of the speaker, the reclamation of one's voice and one's agency.[154]

Artists who enter the quagmire of ethical issues that Henry describes must ask, as Loren Kruger asks, "Do [we] have a right to represent [victims]? How can [we] do justice to the truth by being both theatrically compelling and ethically persuasive?"[155] The whole question of ownership of stories from the TRC, tales that were told at enormous personal cost, makes aesthetic adaptation of the testimony highly fraught, especially so when the words are performed and embodied. Critic Mark Sanders has argued persuasively in *Complicities: The Intellectual and Apartheid* that speaking on behalf of another does not always mean appropriating that person's voice; in certain circumstances, it plays a crucial role of advocacy.[156] Yet the issues are so fraught that artists have been quite hesitant to tackle the TRC material. While there have been a number of theatrical adaptations of TRC material over the years, including the well-known play *Ubu and the Truth Commission,* there have been far fewer adaptations than one might expect given the inherently theatrical nature of the TRC.[157] Theatre artists have tended to represent TRC testimony obliquely, using, for instance, voiceover or puppets or by having the actual victims appear on stage, as they did in *The Story I Am About to Tell,* which included actors and non-actors who had testified at the TRC.[158] The most recent theatrical adaptation of TRC material, a play called *Truth in Translation* (2006), takes as its unique point of entry the lives of TRC interpreters, so the characters are one step removed from the victims.[159] Yet again this is a choice by artists to sidestep direct representation of victims in performance.

How did Philip Miller deal with these ethical issues when he composed the *REwind* cantata? When the work received its first public airing at the lecture demonstration at Spier in March 2006, these ethical questions exploded, completely dominating the discussion of the work with extreme views on both sides. Miller recalls that people asked:

Did I have the right to use [this testimony]? Would I need the permission of the people whose testimony I used? Should I then make them part of the process? Should I in fact not speak to them at all? Some said that I didn't need in any way to ask them for permission, that I was free to do what I wished because this was part of our public domain and that this is something we should celebrate—these are the voices of everybody and in no way should I treat [the project as] needing some form of legal/ethical/moral permission. . . . Questions of ethics also arose about whether permission was needed from the victims and the perpetrators, or just the victims. And then there was a very interesting person [who] said, "You know you can't use one set of rules for the victims and another set for the perpetrators." And if I was going to get permission from Mrs. Miya, I would also need to get permission from P. W. Botha.[160]

So immediately upon the first exposure of the work, Miller was deluged, caught in a political and ethical maelstrom. People were angry—furious even, with "very, very strong feelings."[161] However, in light of the racially polarized reactions to the TRC that James L. Gibson documented in his quantitative survey, it is notable that the audience at this lecture demonstration was completely white. One of the few black persons present at the event was a soloist, contralto Anne Masina, whose family had actually testified before the TRC about her father, Elias, who died in a bomb blast in Pretoria in 1988 and was named as a victim in the TRC's final report.[162] Masina apparently did not speak at the lecture demonstration, but afterward she told a reporter that she did not think the cantata should "shy away from the recorded testimony."[163] She also told Miller, "I don't know what these white people are on about. It's completely mystifying. *Of course* the testimony must be used. *Of course* those voices must be heard. And I cannot understand why people should take offense to that."[164] So at this particular event—this enactment of the TRC's repertoire in 2006—an all-white audience was completely polarized, deadlocked in a debate about the ethics of using TRC testimony. Meanwhile one of the few nonwhite persons present, someone who actually lost her father to apartheid-era violence, told a reporter and the composer that she saw no reason why TRC testimony should not be used in projects like the cantata. As Peter Storey, who was instrumental in creating the commission, has said, white liberals are historically very keen to speak on behalf of the "victim."[165] But in the new South Africa, as in the old South Africa, it seems the victims may still not be central players in determining if and how their stories should be reproduced. While the members of the white audience at the Spier lecture demonstration apparently had many views and opinions about the cantata and its future, that audience apparently was not particularly exercised about the complete lack of racial diversity in their discussion.

The lecture demonstration, which happened before Miller was very far along in the composition, threw him into a tailspin: "I just remember taking in all these things and finding this whole thing SO complicated, Catherine, that from the time that thing finished, I thought I don't know WHAT to do. I froze of fear afterwards. I completely froze with fear after that Spier lecture demonstration. I just thought, I can't do this. WHY am I doing this? Why am *I* taking this on? . . . That was a crisis for me."[166] After an initial period of paralysis, Miller changed gears for a while and stopped using the testimony altogether, favoring instead material that was clearly and unequivocally in the public domain. He started experimenting with found texts, such as a quote about atonement from the Old Testament, Leviticus 5:7, which he heard at a bar mitzvah for a son's friend. This text became the inspiration for a song in the cantata called "Offering of the Birds." He also mined South African vernacular and choral music traditions such as the Christian hymn "Liza lis'idinga Lakho," which translates as "Confession of Our Sins Makes Us Whole." Miller describes this hymn as "completely integral to the South African choral music scene," dating back to mission schools of the seventeenth and eighteenth centuries.[167] The hymn was also sometimes sung at TRC public hearings.[168] "Liza lis'idinga Lakho," which appears three times in the cantata, is sung the first time by the full choir in a traditional manner, with its beautiful, simple melody resonating in robust four-part harmony. But later in the cantata, near the very end, the hymn reappears as a trio, and, shifting into a minor key, the soloists sing musical phrases sometimes in unison but more often independently. There are moments of hesitation and dissonance and ultimately a lack of resolution. The result is a kind of unraveling that allows moments of darkness within the overall brightness of the melody. "Instead of being a resolved major four-part harmony hymn," Miller explains, "it becomes something that is more open, that allows people to think about what it meant to go through a process like the TRC hearings where people were talking about such incredible moments of evil, and then incredible moments of confession and forgiveness, darkness and light."[169]

In addition to hymns and biblical texts, Miller began experimenting with African struggle songs by collaborating with Mduduzi Mofokeng on the libretto and on arrangement. Together they searched for musical expressions for the 1980s that would be iconic, that would readily signify the protests from that period. "Mofokeng immediately began singing," Miller recalls. "He did a chant. It was the *toyi-toyi* chant, and he was doing it in my living room and doing it with the movements, and I was blown away by that, and loved that energy. I said, 'Ja, let's start writing a piece of music together.'"[170] The result was "Who's Laughing" as well as the piece "Siyaya" that opens the cantata, the lyrics of which are from a mass protest: "*Siyaya iPitoli,* We are marching, We are going forward to Pretoria."

Miller's shift away from TRC testimony and the ethical quagmire surrounding the use of those testimonies re-catalyzed his creative process. After he regained momentum with his composition, he once again returned to the question of ethics. How should he proceed? Though his mentor for the project, Antjie Krog, counseled that he had no need whatsoever to consult with the victims or ask their permission, Miller sought his own counsel:

> Literally I just said, "What would I do if I was a parent, who had testified at the TRC, who had broken down and cried, and my voice recording and my voice crying—because of the love and the loss and all that—was used by someone else in a piece of art. How would I feel?" And I thought, "I would like to know beforehand that that would be the use of my voice. I would like to be given the option of saying it's okay or it's not okay." Once I thought that, then, I thought, okay, that's the way I have to treat this. Therefore I knew I couldn't ignore the people whose words I was using. I literally placed myself in their position. It's a very humanistic approach in which I asked, "How would I want to be treated if I was in that position?" And then I knew what I had to do, which was to tell them what I was doing and say that if they didn't want it, they had an opportunity to say no.[171]

In addition to imagining himself in a different subject position, Miller also drew upon well-honed protocols of copyright within the music world, where sampling of material is routine. Composers who wish to use a fragment from someone else's material must both give credit and often pay a fee for use. As Miller says, "The basic principle is that other people's work, creative work, has to be accounted for if you are going to use it."[172] Miller used this copyright principle in addition to his own ethical compass. Though testimony was not a creative composition in the same sense that a song is, the words from the TRC nevertheless were for Miller a "creative seed," a core inspiration for the cantata. So in addition to obtaining permission from victims and perpetrators whose testimony he used, Miller decided that he also needed to give each person whose testimony he used an honorarium for his use of their material. Compared to the TRC's reparation settlement to victims, the amount of this honorarium was certainly commensurate and respectable.[173] Miller contacted each person via a formal letter. Despite the great tirade of objections that Miller heard at the TRC lecture demonstration, not one perpetrator or victim whom he approached about including their words in the cantata declined permission. Perpetrator Jeffrey Benzien said he was not interested in the project, and P. W. Botha died before Miller could establish contact. But all of the others responded positively. Miller says that when Lucas Sikwepere heard that the cantata was being written, he called him and said, "It's so wonderful that you're doing this. I so want you to do this. I'm so excited that my words are going to be heard."[174] Upon hearing a recording of the cantata, he said, "This is great. The words of the songs are really food to the soul."[175] When Mrs. Eunice Miya was asked about how she felt prior to attending the world premiere of REwind, she said, "The event we are going to this weekend will give us good memories about Jabulani. It will make the children proud of him. I think this is very good."[176] When a recording of the music was played for Mrs. Plaatjie in her home, she said, "The music makes me happy. I feel special."[177] Mrs. Juqu said that hearing her husband's voice in the cantata is "a great thing to me," but she lamented that because he had passed away, they would not be able to attend the premier together. "We would cry together if he was still alive," she said.[178] It seems that those whose voices were used in REwind: A Cantata agreed with Anne Masina: "*Of course*, the testimony must be used. *Of course* those voices must be heard."[179] The question is: Are audiences prepared to listen?

Conclusion

The world premiere of *REwind: A Cantata for Voice, Tape, and Testimony* happened on 16 December, a new holiday that democratic South Africa inaugurated in 1995, a National Day of Reconciliation intended "to affirm our solemn constitutional compact to live together on the basis of equality and mutual respect."[180] But as with many acts of commemoration, this one involved mutation and surrogation. Joseph Roach has written provocatively of surrogation that it is a way that memory, performance, and substitution work interactively as a culture reproduces and recreates itself. "Displaced transmission," he writes, "constitutes the adaptation of historical practices to changing conditions, in which popular behaviors are resituated in new locales." Loss, departure, or the demise of an old political order create absences, voids, cavities into which survivors often "attempt to fit satisfactory alternatives."[181] The result is contradictory, complex, and selective, necessitating both the expressions of remembering and public enactments of forgetting. South Africa's National Day of Reconciliation is a prime example of displaced transmission. During the apartheid regime, December 16th was at first called Dingaan's Day; then, after the National Party was elected to power in 1948, the day became the Day of the Covenant; and then, in the 1980s, it was renamed again the Day of the Vow.[182] All these appellations marked the Battle of Blood River in 1838 when, as Rayda Becker says, "the Voortrekkers, the Boer colonists who had left the Cape Colony for the Transvaal, vowed that if they won the battle against the Zulus they would build a church and keep the anniversary a holy day."[183] December 16th was a foundational icon for Afrikaner identity, fueling an emergent white supremacist discourse as well as a repressive ethnic nationalism based upon the narrative of the Great Trek. On 16 December 1913 the Nasionale Vroune Monument (National Women's Monument) was inaugurated, commemorating the death of thousands of Afrikaans women and children in British concentration camps during the Anglo Boer War. This plinth and obelisk with relief panels is a memorial to unresolved atrocities from the past, a case of "white on white" violence that is a key to understanding much of twentieth-century South African history. One hundred years after the Battle of Blood River, on 16 December 1938, the foundational stone of the massive Voortrekker monument in Pretoria was laid as an enormous crowd gathered for a historical reenactment of the Great Trek from Cape Town, the trek that the Boers were on when they encountered the Zulus at Blood River. When the monument was completed eleven years later, its unveiling on 16 December 1949 occasioned once again a highly theatrical and performative event attended by thousands dressed in historical Voortrekker costume.[184] Annie E. Coombes describes the monument as "some misplaced Bakelite radio, ostentatiously positioned in the sight line of the Union Buildings, which were originally built as the symbol of South Africa's domination status within the British Empire."[185] She sees the monument as having had a "monstrous legibility—inescapable even to those who never visited the site."[186]

From the narrative of the Great Trek as the story of the migration of Dutch-speaking farmers in the Eastern Cape who were disenchanted with British rule over mountains in wagons to the battle with Zulus at the Blood River and finally to the sufferings of Afrikaans women and children in British concentration camps during the Anglo Boer War—the holiday of December 16th has long been associated with a traumatic and unresolved past. Ciraj Rassool, Leslie Witz, and Gary Minkley assert that "heritage is never more repressive than when it claims to recover a national past."[187] So we must scrutinize the renaming of 16 December in 1995 as the National Day of Reconciliation in the "new" South Africa for displaced transmission and for the way the holiday both remembers and forgets.

When Nelson Mandela first inaugurated the new holiday, he did not directly substitute one heroic narrative for another. He did not, for instance, offer a direct counternarrative of nationalist founding by saying, as he could have, that 16 December 1961 was the day when the African National Congress finally departed from its decades-old policy of nonviolence and embraced armed resistance with the formation of Umkhonto we Sizwe, the Spear of the Nation.[188] Nor did Mandela directly refer to the significance of 16 December within Afrikaner nationalism. He said rather that the new government chose this particular day as the National Day of Reconciliation "precisely because the past had made December 16 a living symbol of bitter division. Valour was measured by the number of enemies killed and the quantity of blood that swelled the rivers and flowed in the streets. Today we no longer vow our mutual destruction but solemnly acknowledge our inter-dependence as free and equal citizens of our common Motherland."[189] Thus, only through the mention of "blood," "vows," and "bitter division" did Mandela obliquely refer to the holiday's prior pedigree.

He also articulated in this speech conflicting attitudes toward the past: on the one hand he said that the people of South Africa have made a "decisive and irreversible break with the past" and that "we shall free ourselves from the burden of yester-year; not to return there." But on the other hand he also said that reconciliation "does not mean forgetting or trying to bury the pain of conflict."[190] So Mandela was simultaneously advocating a break with a past, declaring it a "no go" zone but at the same time saying we must neither forget nor bury it. This highly contradictory attitude toward the past uttered within the span of Mandela's brief speech echoes the contradictory impulses in Chairperson Desmond Tutu's preface to the Truth and Reconciliation Commission's summary report. He describes the past by offering a cascade of mixed metaphors: "The past, it has been said, is another country. The way its stories are told and the way they are heard change as the years go by. The spotlight gyrates, exposing old lies and illuminating new truths. As a fuller picture emerges, a new piece of the jigsaw puzzle of our past settles into place."[191] But Tutu then concludes his preface with an image of the past that is much more closed: "Having looked the beast of the past in the eye, having asked and received forgiveness and having made amends, let us shut the door on the past."[192] Is this beast of the past the dragon in the living room? Tutu advocates closing the door in its face. But is it not possible the beast will knock once again or perhaps enter elsewhere uninvited?

Of the many news stories carried during the tenth anniversary of the TRC, one was about a woman who had experienced a gross violation of her human rights who, it seems, did not testify before the TRC. Although Lindelwa Ngxamngxa was not politically involved during the apartheid years, she lived in an ANC-dominated township. One day, while she was watching television, a man "came into her living room and shot her repeatedly in the chest, arms and head."[193] She was left paralyzed from the chest down and still lives today, ambulating in her wheelchair in the same neighborhood where the man who shot her also still resides. Even though she reported her assailant to the police, the case was dropped. Ngxamngxa suspects that this was because the assault was in fact orchestrated by the police who supported the Inkatha Freedom Party, the ANC's rival. She spoke of what it was like to encounter regularly the man who paralyzed her: "When he comes, I have to hide because he knows I have identified him. If I am still alive, it's a problem for him."[194] So for Ngxamngxa, it is not possible to look the beast of the past in the eye and shut the door.

The new paradigm in South Africa is rife with unsettled accounts from the past, only a fraction of which received some kind of airing through the TRC. The lack of resolution for so many past atrocities means that the social landscape is unstable and highly volatile. Some believe it is necessary to hear and acknowledge stories from the past, such as those documented by commission. Yet others are wary and skeptical, such as Yazir Henry and Shirley Gunn, who both appeared before the TRC as victims. They are concerned that new iterations and appropriations of such stories will yet again fail to benefit the victims.[195] And then there are the opinions of those who may not have supported apartheid but who nevertheless benefited from it, the sort of audience that gathered at the Spier lecture demonstration of REwind. Impulses to close the door on the past are countered by those who advocate the importance of keeping memory alive: those who say the past "can't go away," those who say that "blaming old foes won't solve today's woes," and those who are "curious about the details."

Creative writer Njabulo Ndebele, former vice-chancellor of the University of Cape Town, describes the climate of South African public culture in the aftermath of apartheid as a "humanizing space of immense complexity." In the aftermath of dismantled binary oppositions from the old days—between black and white, between apartheid and resistance—South African public culture today is

infused with risk-taking, trust and suspicion, intrigue, transparency and obfuscation, real and imaginary boundaries, negotiation and imposition, honesty and dishonesty, concealment and discovery, alignments and realignments, shifting identities, the pains and horrors of lapses, loyalties and betrayals, idealism, greed, courage, doubts and certitudes, redeeming truths and insights leading to optimism and progress and the excitement of infinite possibility.[196]

During the tenth-anniversary year of the TRC in 2006, stories from the commission were heard anew. Different meanings emerge with the passage of time. As Tutu says of the past, "The way its stories are told and they way they are heard change as the years go by."[197] The TRC churned up a great mass of information, most of which was undigested even by the commission and certainly by the general public. And it does seem that certain constituencies in South Africa have lost their appetite. "The TRC? Truth and Reconciliation Commission? Atrocities of apartheid? It's a downer. . . . We don't like to . . . want to hear this stuff."[198] But even with the forces of forgetting so actively repressing a history of atrocity, the past is far too insistent to be ignored. The history recorded by the TRC is very much alive in contemporary society. There is still a generation that can say, as Holocaust survivors could, "I saw it" and "I could not believe what my eyes have seen."[199] For survivors, there is an imperative to acknowledge and document what they have experienced.

The inability of the TRC to provide reparations was its greatest shortcoming.[200] Yet reparations are far more than monetary compensation. "A major contribution to reparation is the act of recognition," says Marjorie Jobson, the acting director of Khulumani, a major NGO that represents victims. "Repairing damage is not just narrowly handing out financial packages, but it is doing things in more collaborative ways, putting victims at the centre of what we do."[201] In this spirit, the acknowledgement of victims through REwind sets one example of how memorial projects can honor victims, give them agency to accept or reject use of their words, and involve them in the process. But with subsequent Days of Reconciliation and with future anniversaries that commemorate the TRC, there will come a turning point in South African history when collective memory will no longer be so informed by living witnesses of the apartheid past. For such audiences, even the notion of "rewinding" an analog tape will be remote—if sounds such as the rewinding tape are even recognizable at all for a thoroughly digital generation. The thousands of cassette tapes of the TRC testimony that sit now at the National Archives, the content of which has been translated and transcribed in only the most cursory and unsatisfactory way, will degenerate with time, perhaps becoming inaccessible before being converted into another format or before some diligent listener will be "curious enough about the details" to really listen and then perhaps translate and transform their narrative truths into other mediums. "The usual aim of any nation's monuments," James E. Young argues, "is not solely to displace memory or to remake it in one's image: it is also to invite the collaboration of the community in acts of remembrance."[202] REwind not only invites collaboration, it depends upon it: the performance will only exist if audiences and funders call it into being by sponsoring it and attending its performances. What other sorts of rituals, performances, and representations might animate stories from the TRC, either in aural or textual form, in the future? Using this material in other contexts—whether in books or works of art—can be an ethical minefield.[203] But if they are not used at all, if the tapes of the public TRC hearings are allowed to deteriorate beyond repair in the archive without people listening to, studying, analyzing, translating, and promulgating them through books, recordings, artistic and nonfiction representations, what are the ethics of that? The unresolved history that those tapes represent is not going away. "It can't go away," in the words of Frank Chikane. What Miller's REwind cantata suggests is the potential and potency of the TRC's performative archive and repertoire to process shards from the past in ways that are productive, complex, and relevant to the present. As Anthea Buys said in the Mail & Guardian, REwind constantly reminds us that "the sheer enormity of the suffering caused under apartheid could never be adequately soothed by any artwork, piece of writing and perhaps not even by . . . the TRC hearings."[204] Perhaps the greatest misunderstanding about the TRC was that in its mandated promise to provide a "complete picture" of past abuses, audiences were led to expect closure. Yet what was evident at every turn in the TRC process was the impossibility of this goal. Performative iterations during the live hearings, through televised coverage, and through artworks like REwind that have followed in the TRC's wake reveal a key argument of this book: that while South Africa's Truth and Reconciliation Commission was designed to contain and make manageable the effects of atrocity, the magnitude of that atrocity constantly exceeded the commission's bounds and the domain of performance was called upon to cope with this excess.

Conclusion

Testimonies are not monologues; they cannot take place in solitude. The witnesses are talking to *somebody*: to somebody they have been waiting for [for] a long time.

—Shoshana Felman and Dori Laub

Paradoxical and unresolved tensions riddled South Africa's TRC process: between the desire to remember and the impulse in transitional societies to forget the past and move on, between the impossibility of forgetting and the need to forget, between the desire for justice and the impossibility of achieving justice for atrocities perpetrated on a massive scale. These are among the core paradoxes that brought transitional justice into being in the first place in the wake of the Nuremburg and Eichmann trials. South Africa's version of the truth commission format seemed to promise resolution: truth was described on the TRC's posters as "the road to reconciliation," and some people imagined reconciliation as a destination, a terminus, a goal. No wonder there was a crisis of expectations in the wake of the TRC. Yet it becomes very evident when one studies the performed dimensions of the commission's public hearings that the impossibility of closure does not negate the value of these hearings. When seen as a live, affective, kinetic, sonic, and visual event that relied upon interpretation by linguists, the media, and audiences in order to reach a larger South African public, the TRC as a performance had unique potency that its written record does not capture. Its performed dimensions were at once indelibly seared into public memory and highly ephemeral. They were forums for restoring humanity *by means of* the human— that is, through human-centered encounters, through spoken, physical testimony before an audience of witnesses. One sees the power of performance to express both the magnitude of the TRC's ambitions and the inevitability of its failure to achieve closure. Yet a failure to achieve closure does not mean the TRC was a failure. A careful and nuanced analysis of the public enactment of the TRC shows that state transition can be validly and meaningfully experienced as an ongoing process with many stages.

The TRC enacted state transition on a number of fronts. Media coverage of the commission, for instance, directly performed a rehabilitation of the South African Broadcasting Corporation as old SABC archival footage was rebroadcast in new contexts, reframed with TRC testimony that forced audiences to question how the old truths that had been promulgated in the past related to the new truths being broadcast under a democratic regime. Transition was likewise performed by the TRC's creation of a large organizational apparatus for interpreting African languages. Such interpretation services had never before existed in South Africa on this scale for languages other than English and Afrikaans. While the actual working conditions of black interpreters at the TRC often ran counter to the "parity of esteem" that South Africa's Constitution promises all language groups, the very fact that a public event of such national prominence was *trying* to deliver interpretation services in all eleven languages performed a new state, participated in bringing that new state into being.

In all facets of the TRC public hearings, the epistemic gulf between the old and the new was manifest, even if the road between those positions was obscure. The TRC as performance suggests the potential for such forums as truth commissions to dramatize the complexity of the present's relationship with the past in places that have experienced mass state-sponsored violations of human rights. Through the incongruities of multiple interpretations aired in performance, the pictures that emerged of the past at the TRC were partial amalgamations, fragments, mixed genres with multiple genealogies. The unexpected disruptions and improvised violations of protocol in public hearings complicated and complemented the findings published in the TRC's summary report. The untidiness and volatility of the live event stood in stark contrast with the order that report tried to achieve. In the end, the report was not the point. It was read by very few people. But many, many people attended hearings, followed articles on the TRC in newspapers, listened to hearings on the radio, and watched Max du Preez's weekly TRC news digest on television. These were more than representations of the commission; on a fundamental level they were extensions of the commission, part of a chain of interlocutors who made the commission publicly known and, more important, publicly experienced.

This highlights a fundamental feature of South Africa's commission: to give testimony meant, inherently, to *be* interpreted. My quest in this book has not been to assert one authentic and singular interpretation but rather to posit that a precise excavation of the many layers of meaning that the public hearings brought forth tells us much about the TRC, about South Africa, about transitional justice, and about the complexities of meaning the commission made manifest. I believe if we take these layers of signification into account, the TRC process was far more multifaceted than the secondary literature on the commission would indicate. The dissonance, gaps, and fissures between interpretations are central to the story of the TRC as a performed enactment of transition. Like the relay interpretation system used by the TRC, each re-presentation was a stage in a process. Just as testimony went from Zulu to English, from English to Xhosa, and from Xhosa to Afrikaans, so too has testimony from the TRC been told and retold, with changes of meaning happening along the way. Mrs. Eunice Miya told the TRC that she wished that the news program where she learned of her son Jabulani's death could "rewind." Her meaning of "rewind" was not the same as composer Philip Miller's interpretation of her words in his cantata ten years later. But both renderings tell us something significant about desire, whether Mrs. Miya's desire to rewind the news so that she can definitively identify her son or a composer's interrogation of his country's conflicted relationship with its past and of a truth commission process meant to interrogate and repair that past. With each instantiation of TRC material, certain meanings are repeated, distorted, and/or abandoned even as new valences are acquired. These sorts of ambiguities of meaning are vexing for positivists and empiricists, for sure, which may be why some of the most sophisticated renderings of the TRC have come not from historians or social scientists but rather from artists. Projects such as *Ubu and the Truth Commission, Truth in Translation,* and the *REwind* cantata have engaged the truth commission's archive in a far more sustained and nuanced way than have academics. Why is it that artists rather than ethnographers are convening symposiums of the former TRC language interpreters? Why is it that artists rather than historians are spending hours and days watching unedited video footage of TRC hearings held at the National Archives? Like language interpreters and journalists, artists form yet another layer of interpretation in the TRC process, serving as key interlocutors between the archival memory of the commission and public memory of the event in the present. Artists are able to accommodate the contradictions, opacities, and ambiguities unearthed by the truth commission without needing to reduce this content to tidy evaluative summaries or recommendations for policy.

Do truth commissions better serve the didactic objectives that so bedeviled the Nuremberg and Eichmann trials? Do they more successfully and humanely grant victims voice and agency, record past atrocities, and promulgate collective memory? These are important questions, and in order to answer them one needs empirically rich studies of particular commissions that show how they have operated in specific national and geographic contexts, how they have engaged their publics and to what end. This book is one such study, and it happens to be about a paradigmatic and particularly influential truth commission that has come to define the "industry" of transitional justice. Since South Africa's TRC, many other countries have mounted similar commissions, including Guatemala, Nigeria, Sierra Leone, Ghana, Timor-Leste, Peru, Morocco, and Liberia.¹ An important project that I hope will follow in the wake of my book is a comparative analysis of the role of performance within these recent commissions.

South Africa's truth commission was distinctive, among other reasons, for its embrace of embodiment, storytelling, emotional expressiveness, media spectacle, and public participation—in short, its prioritization of performance. While I do think that this feature of the South African TRC's was instrumental to whatever successes the commission achieved, my point is not necessarily to advocate for performance. Rather I want to assert that in order to understand what this particular instance of transitional justice did, we must examine the extent to which the commission was experienced by South Africans not as text but as performance, not as findings but as process. We must also consider the particular ways the TRC used performance: for instance, that it was site specific, touring the country in specific towns and cities where stories from those locations were its focus; that it was attentive to the multilinguistic character of the country; that it was a media-saturated performance and (fortunately) benefited from particularly astute television journalism; that its hearings were highly dependent upon the personality and performance skills of key actors such as the charismatic and irrepressible Desmond Tutu; and that it did not require amnesty applicants to convey or "perform" even a hint of contrition or remorse.

But most important, we must consider that the TRC's public hearings required the presence of an audience and thereby implicated that audience as both participant and witnesses. South Africa's truth commission conveyed its findings through a voluminous text, but it conveyed its *process* through embodiment, the grain of the voice, the cadence of spoken language, the potency of emotional expressiveness. Performance provided a necessary corrective to the often-narrow epistemologies that governed the TRC's statement-taking protocols, investigative and corroborative processes, and findings. A narrow positivism prevailed in the investigative, research, and publication phases of the TRC. But in the public hearings, other ways of knowing were made available and accessible. Performance gave audiences the experience of witnessed speech. These narratives were often horrific tales of atrocity, yet they were told by human beings in a face-to-face encounter with other human beings. Performed witnessing was at the center of the TRC's public enactment, and this aspect of its performance expressed the very essence of *ubuntu*—the African philosophy that animates the core of South Africa's TRC. The humanity of the victims and perpetrators who appeared before the TRC was affirmed by the presence of other human beings who were in the hall or listening in on radios or watching on their television sets from home. This experience of national witnessing implicated everyone who experienced it, and it may even implicate you, reader, for this text is part of the ongoing relay interpretation process that the commission began. This book has made you a secondary witness.

Afterword: What "Truth" Meant to the TRC

One of the challenges of writing this book is that my audience includes some readers who know a great deal about the South African Truth and Reconciliation Commission and some readers who may know very little about this commission. For readers coming to this topic for the first time, a fundamental question that must be answered is what exactly the TRC meant by "truth." This is a subject that has attracted a great deal of critical writing. I provide in this afterword a summary of some of the key issues and a guide to the relevant bibliography.

While South Africa's Truth and Reconciliation Commission had an Orwellian-sounding title, the commission parsed its quest for "truth" less ominously as a search for multiple truths. In what Deborah Posel and Richard A. Wilson have called the TRC's "rainbow of truths," there were four hues: factual/forensic, personal/narrative, social/"dialogue," and healing/restorative.[1] This typology, which has been criticized as "wobbly," coexisted without any clear protocols for how the four different types of truth were to interact.[2] Within the operations of the commission, this situation often led to what Lars Buur has called a clash of "memory genres": one genre focused on calendar time, police reports, medical journals, and other types of formal discourse while another was composed of memory environments, sounds, scars, enacted sayings, gestures, and ritualized behavior.[3] The need to value the narrative truths of victims was often cut short by the need to gather cold facts, hard data, and quantifiable information—that is, factual/forensic truth that could be efficiently coded and entered into a massive database. Even at the level of statement-taking, struggles erupted between regimes of truth. Statement-takers were forced to focus on the "cold facts" while deponents wanted to tell their stories in their own ways. Some deponents even refused to sign their statements because they felt that important information had been left out.[4]

While the truth commission in theory valued four types of truth—factual/forensic, personal/narrative, social, and healing/restorative—this typology is a bit misleading. Scholars generally agree that there were "only two main paradigms of truth under which all others congregated," as Richard Wilson has said.[5] These were the forensic/factual truth and the personal/narrative variety. Behind the scenes, the commission favored factual/forensic truth above all else. Information collected by the commission, however imperfectly it was gathered, was subjected to extensive statistical analysis in the commission's summary report. But personal/narrative truth was seen as somehow self-evident, a truth effect that conferred the appearance of authenticity and veracity while simultaneously defying, thwarting, or simply seeming unworthy of sustained, thoughtful, and systematic qualitative analysis. I do not fault the TRC for its emphasis, for I believe the conditions under which it came into being and operated left little room for the sort of humanistic approach I am advocating. However, I believe that the personal narratives brought forth in the human rights violations hearings of the TRC deserve a far more careful, nuanced, and extensive analysis than they have generally received.[6]

What exactly did the commission mean by personal and narrative truth?[7] First, the commission set a premium on storytelling—hence the prominence of the word "narrative" in the TRC's deliberations. As the summary report makes clear, narrative for the commission was synonymous with storytelling:

> By telling their stories, both victims and perpetrators gave meaning to the multi-layered experiences of the South African story. . . . In the [South] African context, where value continues to be attached to oral tradition, the process of story telling was particularly important. . . . The stories told to the Commission were not presented as arguments or claims in a court of law. Rather, they provided unique insights into the pain of South Africa's past, often touching the hearts of all that heard them.[8]

But narrative also was also a way that the commission connected individual stories to a larger collective narrative. While the TRC sutured together information from multiple statements to create a macronarrative of larger patterns of violence, personal/narrative truth spoke to the discrete, the particular, and the individual. The TRC's personal/narrative truth was subjective and valued subjectivity as a valid form of knowing and knowledge. While the TRC did check facts and verify statements, by the time a case was chosen to receive a public hearing the testimony had become a performative act with its own veracity. Testimony was the truth as the deponent saw, remembered, or experienced it. Personal/narrative truth was conveyed through physicalization as well as the conventions of orality so central to African cultures. The ideal medium of personal/narrative truth for the TRC was a live encounter between the person giving testimony and multiple secondary witnesses. Thus this type of truth demands, implicitly, an audience. And finally, the commission operated on the assumption that narrative/personal truth held tremendous powers, including the ability to recover memory—either for the person giving testimony, who may have had to suppress such painful memories in order to survive, or for the nation, which suffered from decades-long, state-promulgated amnesia. Personal/narrative truth captured individual perceptions, stories, myths, and experiences, especially from those who had been largely ignored or were voiceless in official discourse.[9] Whereas the TRC's notion of factual/forensic truth demanded a positivist approach—one that sought to combat a past record of lies and half-truths with "hard," authenticated, accurate, and comprehensive data, or "cold facts"—it treated personal/narrative truth as innately expressive of complexity, multiple layers of experience, and emotional density and a way of conveying the dignity of the individual giving testimony.

The TRC's embrace of factual/forensic truth is best expressed through precisely the sort of tables, graphs, and statistical analyses that dominate the TRC's summary report. These data visualizations show, for instance, which regions had the most abductions or deaths in detention, which time periods saw the greatest incidence of certain types of deaths or methods of torture, and which political parties carried out the greatest number of certain types of violations. However, personal/narrative truth was best expressed in the live hearings, especially of the Human Rights Violations Committee. As Deputy Chairperson Alex Boraine notes: "To listen to one man relate how his wife and baby were cruelly murdered is much more powerful and moving than statistics which describe a massacre involving many victims. The conflict of the past is no longer a question of numbers and incidents; the human face has shown itself, and the horror of murder and torture is painfully real."[10] Boraine's statement sets out a series of contrasts: hearing versus reading, the individual versus the multitude, horror conveyed through a human face versus through numbers. Personal/narrative truth is spoken, heard, and seen—not read. In short, it is performed.

The stories told at public hearings were often perceived as unmediated, so directly did they transport the listener to some kind of authentic, undeniable truth. Yet the process of giving testimony was in fact highly mediated. Mediation began with the initial statement-taking process, which gathered roughly 22,000 statements. Of these, less than 10 percent of cases were selected for public hearings. But what of the 20,000 remaining victims who had given statements? Were their narrative truths recorded? If so, how? And were they ever analyzed? Designated statement-takers, who worked in all nine provinces of South Africa, numbered 40 persons in 1996 and grew to 400 in 1997; many were hired from NGOs and community groups.[11] While the statement-taking procedure initially allowed deponents ample room for shaping their narratives as they saw fit, the commission soon realized that the nature and scope of the information was so great that it had an information crisis. The solution was to systematize the statement-taking process so that information could be easily coded and input into a database. After all, the commission's mandate set a premium on making findings about particular cases (was someone a victim and therefore entitled to reparations?) and tracing larger patterns of violence and gross violations of human rights. Thus, the backstage operations of the TRC overwhelmingly privileged factual/forensic truth that was evidenced, as we shall see, in a controlled vocabulary and statement-taking protocol that reduced complex human experience to boxes and formulaic questionnaires.[12]

In his address to the National Assembly when the Promotion of National Unity and Reconciliation Bill was debated, Minister of Justice Dullah Omar asserted that "individual truth" was "important to establish the dignity of victims and their relatives." However, Dullah continued, the commission's quest for "global truth" had other aims: "The global truth is necessary to see whether it is possible to establish a pattern of violations and why they occurred. This will enable the commission to make recommendations on steps to be taken in an endeavor to ensure that no similar violations occur in future."[13] Thus, the commission invested enormous energy into creating the quantitative analysis of patterns of violence, a macroproject that had been constructed rhetorically as instrumental in realizing the commission's "never again" mandate.

Researchers involved in the TRC process say that the narrative section of the statement-taking protocol was initially open-ended, often producing as many as fifteen to twenty pages of transcribed text.[14] This "narrative" portion was transcribed only in English. While the TRC valued South Africa's multilingual constitutional mandate by providing trained language interpreters for public hearings, it did not do so for the statement-taking portion of its activities. Statement-takers had two jobs: they had to translate as well as record information, and they rarely read the resulting English text out loud or gave it to the statement-giver to verify.[15] Even so, the information gathered through early statement-taking methods proved too unwieldy, too inconsistent, and too complex to be processed in an efficient quantitative manner, and this problem necessitated the adoption of an information management system.[16] The commission began using a large-scale human rights database called Infocomm that had been developed by the American Association for the Advancement of Science so that it could fulfill its mandate to provide a "complete picture" of the nature and extent of human rights abuses.

Gradually the narrative section of statement-taking was eroded, replaced by a "series of questions to be answered and boxes to be ticked."[17] Richard Wilson, who conducted extensive ethnographic research on the commission, writes of the new form, "Complexity was lost, and one member of the Research Unit I interviewed likened it to a vehicle registration license, and then an information manager present less charitably revised that to 'maybe more like a dog registration license.'"[18] Even as the protocol changed, growing through various versions from eight to twenty pages, the space assigned to recording victims' "narrative truth" shrank from six pages to one and a half and at one point disappeared altogether. Thus, while the public perception of the commission (which was largely shaped by the hearings) was that it upheld the importance of narrative/personal truth, the commission's actual practices behind closed doors were largely positivist and favored factual/forensic truth.

The disparity between the quantitative social science methodologies that predominated in the statement-taking process and the qualitative methods that were operative—or were at least suggested and invoked—in the TRC's human rights violation public hearings is worth noting. The statements victims gave away from the glare of television lights required interpretation in order for the TRC to "make sense" of the testimony. Yet the personal/narrative truth told before the public HRVC hearings seemed to be beyond interpretation. This testimony was highly, even mysteriously efficacious. Researchers who helped craft the final report—Janet Cherry, John Daniel, and Madeleine Fullard—concur with Alex Boraine that the testimony of a single victim broadcast on television had far more impact than any number of volumes of the summary report they wrote: "The enduring memory of the Commission will be the images of pain, grief and regret conveyed relentlessly, week after week, month after month, to a public that generally remained spellbound by what it was witnessing."[19] The Human Rights Violations Committee hearings were, in the words of Desmond Tutu, the "public face of the commission."[20] That public face featured real individuals narrating their stories, speaking their truths. Their revelations were perceived to be authentic, meaningful, and transformative for listeners. According to Commissioner Mary Burton, the impact of telling stories to the South African public was "incalculable": even if someone witnessing public testimony questioned the truthfulness of the stories, "you couldn't deny the actual experience of the people who were talking."[21] On the other hand, Commissioner Wendy Orr writes that "it seems clear that most white people tried very hard to dismiss the testimony of the approximately two thousand victims of human rights as being over emotional, half true or even lies and propaganda. But when the amnesty applicants— most of them white—started giving evidence, whites could no longer ignore the true horror of our past. Why would they lie about their own crimes?"[22] It was this contrapuntal structure—first, victims were seen and heard while telling their stories, then perpetrators corroborated the atrocities (in testimony also seen, heard, and embodied)—that produced in listeners belief in the veracity of what was being said. Thus, having the body (habeas corpus) had a persuasive potency in convincing people of the testimony's veracity.

Commissioner Yasmin Sooka concurs: "I think if the commission had one single most important contribution to make[,] it dealt with the denial of the past, and it could never have done that without the public nature of the hearings."[23] Though she acknowledges that people saw a "very minute" number of hearings on television, the potency of the imagery was immense. "Suddenly you weren't reading it in the newspapers: it was live, real people who were speaking about what happened to them." For Sooka, a significant part of the process was that when the victims spoke, some observers still said, No these things didn't happen. "But when they publicly saw white Afrikans men saying, 'Well actually we did it, and it's worse than you think it was,' then suddenly that discourse changed to, 'We didn't know that these things were happening.'"[24]

The words spoken by witnesses in the first person and in whatever language they wished formed the quintessential genre through which the TRC's valuation of personal/narrative truth was made manifest. So potent was this form of truth-telling that it seems to have required little analysis by the commission in order for the public—constituted either as those attending live hearings or as the nation witnessing via media—to make sense of the testimony. Truths spoken and heard from the mouths of victims were, apparently, self-evident truths. This obvious point may well be the reason that actual verbatim testimony gets short shrift in the TRC's summary report. In all seven tomes of this project, victims' actual testimony constitutes an astonishingly small fraction of the text. This was a self-conscious decision by the commission, as the report makes clear. In his preface to the first volume, Desmond Tutu writes, "Everyone involved in producing this report would have loved to have had the time to capture the many nuances and unspoken truths encapsulated in the evidence that came before us.

This, however, is a task which others must take up and pursue."[25] Later in the report, the commission defers the task of interpreting the richness of individual accounts to some nebulous future date:

> It is impossible to capture the detail and complexity of all of this in a report. The transcripts of the hearings, individual statements, a mountain of press clippings and video material are all part of an invaluable record which the Commission handed over to the National Archives for public access. This record will form a part of the national memory for generations yet to come. In this report, the Commission has tried, through a range of detailed "window cases" and selections from the testimonies of many victims, to capture some part of the richness of the individual accounts heard before it.[26]

So has this task been taken up by others? By what process will the archives be transformed into "national memory," especially for those too young to have experienced the TRC live? It is perhaps symptomatic of the extent to which the growing secondary literature on the TRC focuses myopically on assessing whether the commission was "good" or "bad," "worthy" or "foolish" that one finds remarkably few studies that analyze testimony in any detail. How will the complexity of this national memory become known by the larger public and those "generations yet to come" if it is not read, analyzed, represented, and circulated in forums that move beyond assessments of the commission?

Fiona Ross is one of the few scholars to have subjected the TRC's narrative/ personal to sustained analysis and close reading. In a chapter of her book *Bearing Witness,* Ross analyzes testimonies for the ways speakers used narrative forms and tropes that arose from Southern African oral traditions.[27] She also tries to be attentive to disruptions of language through pause, gesture, and silence and to what these nonverbal elements might signify. Ross's approach addresses both the content and form of testimony as well as the performative aspects lost in transcription.[28] Ross's work is only a beginning: though many of the testimonies she examines were originally given in African languages, she works only with the English translations and transcriptions provided by the commission. As chapter 3 of this work recounts, these transcriptions of simultaneous interpretation were often highly problematic and lost much information and nuance, distorted facts, and even made outright mistakes in interpretation.

Indeed, few studies have gone beyond the official, if error-ridden, transcriptions to analyze the original language of testimony. Both the TRC's mission statement and South Africa's Constitution nominally value the state's eleven official languages, nine of which are Bantu languages (belonging to a large group of mostly tonal languages spoken by seventy million Africans). But all testimony that ended up online on the TRC's Web site was recorded in English or Afrikaans, the official languages of the old apartheid state. Interpreters available at public hearings translated testimony into any of the official languages, but these interpreters were hastily trained and were given no orienting information on particular cases. Often the resulting interpretation was cursory—perhaps sufficient only for purposes of the hearing itself, so that those in attendance could understand each other. Recordings of the simultaneous English-language interpretations were then transcribed by the TRC and subsequently posted online as the official record of hearing. Yet much was lost in the process. If the TRC is to fulfill its mandate both to value narrative/personal truth and to honor the multilingual promise of the Constitution of South Africa, new translations must be undertaken.[29] Since the commission has now disbanded, this project, if it is to happen, is likely to be conducted by researchers with appropriate language skills or with the will and financial capacity to hire translators. Whether or not one agrees with the TRC's ostensible valuation of narrative/personal truth, using testimony—rather than vaguely excerpted sound bites—and getting more accurate translations is, quite simply, good scholarship. Narrative truth may be more subjective than forensic truth, but it is truth all the same, requiring and deserving of rigor of method and sustained analysis.

Notes

Preface and Acknowledgments

The first epigraph is from Yazir Henry, "Reconciling Reconciliation: A Personal and Public Journey of Testifying Before the South African Truth and Reconciliation Commission," in *Political Transition: Politics and Cultures*, ed. Paul Gready (Sterling, Va.: Pluto Press, 2003), 269. The second is from Denis Hirson, *White Scars: On Reading and Rites of Passage* (Auckland Park, South Africa: Jacana Media, 2006), 47.

1. Susan Sontag, *Against Interpretation* (New York: Farrar, Straus & Giroux, 1966), 126.
2. Jody Enders, *Rhetoric and the Origins of Medieval Drama* (Ithaca, N.Y.: Cornell University Press, 1992), 2.
3. Louis Bickford, "Transitional Justice," in *The Encyclopedia of Genocide and Crimes Against Humanity*, ed. Dinah L. Shelton (Farmington Hills, Mich.: Macmillan Reference, 2004), 1045–1047.
4. Hannah Arendt, *Eichmann in Jerusalem: A Report on the Banality of Evil* (New York: Penguin Books, 1963).
5. For performance studies research on these subjects, see Branislav Jakovljevic, "From Mastermind to Body Artist: Political Performances of Slobodan Milosevic," *TDR: The Drama Review* 52, no. 1 (2008): 51–74; Diana Taylor, *Disappearing Acts: Spectacles of Gender and Nationalism in Argentina's "Dirty War"* (Durham, N.C.: Duke University Press, 1997); Ananda Breed, "Performing the Nation: Theatre in Post-Genocide Rwanda," *TDR: The Drama Review* 52, no. 1 (2008): 33–50; Ananda Breed, "Performing *Gacaca* in Rwanda: Local Culture for Justice and Reconciliation," in *Conflicts and Tensions*, ed. Helmut K. Anheier and Yudhishthir Raj Isar (Los Angeles: Sage, 2007), 306–312; and Shanee Stepakoff, "Telling and Showing: Witnesses Represent Sierra Leone's War Atrocities in Court and Onstage," *TDR: The Drama Review* 52, no. 1 (2008): 17–31.
6. Eric Hobsbawm, *The Invention of Tradition* (Cambridge: Cambridge University Press, 1992).
7. Keith Breckenridge, "From Hubris to Chaos: The Makings of the Bewysburo and the End of Documentary Government," paper presented at the Wits Institute for Social and Economic Research, University of Witwatersrand, 20 May 2002.
8. Ibid., 23. A revised form of this paper was later published as Keith Breckenridge, "Verwoerd's Bureau of Proof: Total Information in the Making of Apartheid," *History Workshop Journal* 59 (2005): 83–108.
9. Ambrose Reeves, *Shooting at Sharpeville* (London: Victor Gollancz, 1960), 29.
10. Athol Fugard, John Kani, and Winston Ntshona, *Sizwe Bansi Is Dead*, in *Statements: Sizwe Bansi Is Dead, The Island, Statements After an Arrest under the*

Immorality Act/3 Plays (1974; New York: Theatre Communications Group, 1986), 43.

11.   Within the field of performance studies, the discipline from which this book arises, such a concept is known as "performativity." See J. L. Austin, *How to Do Things with Words,* 2nd ed. (Cambridge, Mass.: Harvard University Press, 1975).

12.   Pricilla Hayner, *Unspeakable Truths: Confronting State Terror and Atrocity* (New York: Routledge, 2001), 1, 4.

13.   On the significance of oral sources in Africa, see Luise White, Stephan F. Miescher, and David William Cohen, eds., *African Words, African Voices: Critical Practices in Oral History* (Bloomington: Indiana University Press, 2001).

14.   David William Cohen and E. S. Atieno Odhiambo, *The Risks of Knowledge: Investigations into the Death of the Hon. Minister John Robert Ouko in Kenya, 1990* (Athens: Ohio University Press, 2004), 19.

15.   See, for instance, *Nunca Más: The Report of the Argentine National Commission on the Disappeared* (New York: Farrar Straus Giroux in association with Index on Censorship, 1986).

16.   Edith Hall, *The Theatrical Cast of Athens: Interactions between Ancient Greek Drama and Society* (New York: Oxford University Press, 2006), 6.

17.   Walter Benjamin, "Berlin Chronicle," in *Reflections: Essays, Aphorisms, Autobiographical Writings,* ed. Peter Dementz (New York: Harcourt Brace Jovanovich, 1978), 25–26.

18.   Christopher J. Colvin, "Overview of the Reparations Program in South Africa," in *The Handbook of Reparations,* ed. Pablo de Greiff (New York: Oxford University Press, 2006), 176.

19.   The bibliography on South Africa's TRC is extensive. For an overview, see Olayiwola Abegunrin, "Truth and Reconciliation," *African Studies Review* 45, no. 3 (2002): 31–34; and Richard Dale, "The Politics of the Rainbow Nation: Truth, Legitimacy, and Memory in South Africa," *African Studies Review* 45, no. 3 (2002): 39–44. Key secondary sources include Kader Asmal, Louise Asmal, and Ronald Suresh Roberts, *Reconciliation through Truth: A Reckoning of Apartheid's Criminal Governance* (Cape Town: David Philip Publishers in association with Mayibue Books, University of the Western Cape, 1996); Wilmot Godfrey James and Linda van de Vijver, eds., *After the TRC: Reflections on Truth and Reconciliation in South Africa* (Athens: Ohio University Press, 2001); Deborah Posel and Graeme Simpson, eds., *Commissioning the Past: Understanding South Africa's Truth and Reconciliation Commission* (Johannesburg: Witwatersrand University Press, 2002); Fiona C. Ross, *Bearing Witness: Women and the Truth and Reconciliation Commission in South Africa* (Sterling, Va.: Pluto Press, 2003); Mark Sanders, *Ambiguities of Witnessing: Law and Literature in the Time of a Truth Commission* (Palo Alto, Calif.: Stanford University Press, 2007); Charles Villa-Vicencio and Wilhelm Verwoerd, *Looking Back, Reaching Forward: Reflections on the Truth and Reconciliation Commission of South Africa* (New York: St. Martin's Press, 2000); Charles Villa-Vicencio and Erik Doxtader, *The Provocations of Amnesty: Memory, Justice, and Impunity* (Trenton, N.J.: Africa World Press, 2003); Richard Wilson, *The Politics of Truth and Reconciliation in South Africa: Legitimizing the Post-Apartheid State* (Cambridge: Cambridge University Press, 2001).

20.   TRC, *Truth and Reconciliation Commission of South Africa Report,* 5 vols. (London: MacMillan, 1999), 1:55.

21. TRC, *Truth and Reconciliation Commission of South Africa Report,* 5:113. See also Alex Boraine, *A Country Unmasked: Inside South Africa's Truth and Reconciliation Commission* (New York: Oxford University Press, 2000), 63; Deborah Posel, "The TRC Report: What Kind of History? What Kind of Truth?" in *Commissioning the Past: Understanding South Africa's Truth and Reconciliation Commission,* ed. Deborah Posel and Graeme Simpson (Johannesburg: Witwatersrand University Press, 2002), 151–154.

22. Wilson, *The Politics of Truth and Reconciliation,* 225.

23. See Lars Buur, "Monumental Historical Memory: Managing Truth in the Everyday Work of the South African Truth and Reconciliation Commission," in *Commissioning the Past: Understanding South Africa's Truth and Reconciliation Commission,* ed. Deborah Posel and Graeme Simpson (Johannesburg: Witwatersrand University Press, 2002), 66–93.

24. Richard Schechner, *Between Theatre and Anthropology* (Philadelphia: University of Pennsylvania Press, 1985), 36.

25. Erving Goffman, *The Presentation of Self in Everyday Life* (Garden City, N.Y.: Doubleday, 1959).

26. Jonas Barish, *The Antitheatrical Prejudice* (Berkeley: University of California Press, 1981).

27. Diana Taylor, *The Archive and the Repertoire: Performing Cultural Memory in the Americas* (Durham, N.C.: Duke University Press, 2003).

28. On the concept of performance genealogies, see Joseph R. Roach, *Cities of the Dead: Circum-Atlantic Performance* (New York: Columbia University Press, 1996).

29. Cohen and Odhiambo, *The Risks of Knowledge.*

30. Piers Pigou, "There Are More Truths to Be Uncovered before We Can Achieve Reconciliation," *Sunday Independent* (Johannesburg), 23 April, 2006, 9.

31. If South Africa had engaged in a full criminal and civil prosecution for past atrocities, the courts would have been completely overwhelmed for years. The TRC provided a different model of justice. It gave incentives for individuals to come forward and bring to public light information that had been hidden, specifically information about disappearances, torture, and murders. The underlying concept was one of "restorative justice" rather than retributive justice. The TRC produced information that gave victims of gross violations of human rights the possibility of finding out what had really happened to them or their loved ones. This production of information was deemed to be preferable to the administration of justice through prosecution, judgment, and retribution through incarceration or civil damages.

32. The Cradock Four—Matthew Goniwe, Sicelo Mhlauli, Sparrow Mkhonto, and Fort Calata—were killed in June 1985 by security police. Their bodies were mutilated and burned. This high-profile case received much attention at the TRC.

33. Nomonde Calata, interview with Liza Key and the author, Cradock, 2 July 2007; Kate Allen, interview with the author, Johannesburg, 9 September 2005.

34. Ibid.

35. Ibid.

36. Kitty Calavita, "Engaged Research, 'Goose Bumps' and the Role of the Public Intellectual," *Law & Society Review* 36, no. 1 (2002): 13.

37. Ibid., 12.

38. Liz McGregor and Sarah Nuttal, ed., *At Risk: Writing on and over the Edge of*

South Africa (Jeppestown, South Africa: Jonathan Ball, 2007); Jonathan Ball, "Stories That 'Engage with South Africa's Rough Public Space'—*At Risk* Launched," 29 August 2007, available at jonathanball.book.co.za/blog/2007/08/29 (accessed 12 June 2008).

39.   Calavita, "Engaged Research," 11.

40.   Malcolm Purkey, interview with the author, Johannesburg, 10 September 2005.

41.   See Paul Gready, ed., *Political Transition: Politics and Cultures* (Sterling, Va.: Pluto Press, 2003).

42.   Sanders, *Ambiguities of Witnessing*, 12.

1. Spectacles of Legality

The first epigraph is from George Bizos, interview with the author, Johannesburg, 25 July 2006. The second is from Lawrence Douglas, *The Memory of Judgment: Making Law and History in the Trials of the Holocaust* (New Haven, Conn.: Yale University Press, 2001), 41.

1.   Deborah Posel, "Truth? The View from South Africa's Truth and Reconciliation Commission," in *Keywords: Truth,* by Ali Benmakhalouf, Ganesh Devy, Yang Guorong, Bertrand Ogilvie, Douglas Patterson, and Deborah Posel (New York: Other Press, 2004), 1–25; Shoshana Felman, *The Juridical Unconscious: Trials and Traumas in the Twentieth Century* (Cambridge: Harvard University Press, 2002), 106–130.

2.   Hannah Arendt, *Eichmann in Jerusalem: A Report on the Banality of Evil* (New York: Penguin Books, 1963).

3.   Ibid., 4. See also Douglas, *The Memory of Judgment,* 98. It is not uncommon for transitional justice to be enacted in theatrical spaces. While the title of the Commission to Clarify Past Human Rights Violations and Acts of Violence That Have Caused the Guatemalan People to Suffer would have been a challenge to market as theatre, the emotional presentation of its final report took place in the National Theater in Guatemala City before an audience of thousands. See Pricilla Hayner, *Unspeakable Truths: Confronting State Terror and Atrocity* (New York: Routledge, 2001), 48.

4.   Arendt, *Eichmann in Jerusalem,* 6.

5.   Ibid., 9.

6.   Ibid., 6.

7.   Ibid., 8.

8.   Ibid., 294.

9.   Ibid., 267.

10.   See Douglas, *The Memory of Judgment,* 6–64.

11.   Stephen Landsman, "Those Who Remember the Past May Not Be Condemned to Repeat It," *Michigan Law Review* 100, no. 6 (2002): 1571.

12.   Louis Bickford, "Transitional Justice," in *The Encyclopedia of Genocide and Crimes Against Humanity,* ed. Dinah L. Shelton (Farmington Hills, Mich.: Macmillan Reference, 2004), 1045–47.

13.   Landsman, "Those Who Remember," 1571.

14.   Arendt, *Eichmann in Jerusalem,* 253.

15.   Marie-Bénédicte Dembour and Emily Haslam, "Silencing Hearings? Victim-

Witnesses at War Crimes Trials," *European Journal of International Law* 15, no. 1 (2004): 151–177.

16. Martha Minow, *Between Vengeance and Forgiveness: Facing History after Genocide and Mass Violence* (Boston: Beacon Press, 1998), 47.

17. Mark Osiel, *Mass Atrocity, Collective Memory, and the Law* (New Brunswick: Transaction Publishers, 1997), 59.

18. This is not to say that performance and the law are incompatible. Indeed, if we understand the term "performance" to describe the full range of behaviors analyzed by Erving Goffman, then most human activity is on some level a "performance"—including everything that people do in courtrooms. See Erving Goffman, *The Presentation of Self in Everyday Life* (Garden City, N.Y.: Doubleday, 1959). The distinction I wish to make here is between "performance" and "theatre," the latter suggesting an overt embrace of theatricality, which many critics see as problematic when combined with the administration of justice. For an introduction to the ways that "performance" is defined and used within the field of performance studies, see Marvin Carlson, *Performance: A Critical Introduction* (New York: Routledge, 2003); D. Soyini Madison and Judith Hamera, eds., *The SAGE Handbook of Performance Studies* (Thousand Oaks: SAGE Publications, 2006); and Richard Schechner, *Performance Studies: An Introduction* (New York: Routledge, 2002). On the term "theatricality," see Tracy C. Davis and Thomas Postlewait, eds., *Theatricality* (New York: Cambridge University Press, 2003).

19. See Dembour and Haslam, "Silencing Hearings?" 151–177. See also Peter Brooks and Paul Gerwitz, eds., *Law's Stories: Narrative and Rhetoric in the Law* (New Haven, Conn.: Yale University Press, 1996).

20. Felman, *The Juridical Unconscious,* esp. 5–6. See also Judith Lewis Herman, *Trauma and Recovery: The Aftermath of Violence—From Domestic Abuse to Political Terror* (New York: Basic Books, 1997); Shoshana Felman and Dori Laub, eds., *Testimony: Crises of Witnessing in Literature, Psychoanalysis, and History* (New York: Routledge, 1991).

21. For a moving depiction of the potentially offensive way that victims are positioned and treated in the International Criminal Tribunal for the former Yugoslavia, see Dembour and Haslam, "Silencing Hearings?" 151–177.

22. For an overview of transitional justice, see Neil J. Kritz, ed., *Transitional Justice: How Emerging Democracies Reckon with Former Regimes,* 3 vols. (Washington, D.C.: United States Institute of Peace Press, 1995).

23. Landsman, "Those Who Remember," 1589.

24. Hayner, *Unspeakable Truths,* 40–45, 305–336. Ambivalence about the outcomes of the TRC is evident in such works as Christopher James Colvin, "Performing the Signs of Injury: Critical Perspectives on Traumatic Storytelling after Apartheid" (Ph.D. diss., University of Virginia, 2004); Brandon Hamber, Traggy Maepa, Tlhoki Mofokeng, and Hugo van der Merwe, *Survivors' Perceptions of the Truth and Reconciliation Commission and Suggestions for the Final Report* (Centre for the Study of Violence and Reconciliation and The Khulumani Support Group, 1998), available at http://www.csvr.org.za/wits/papers/papkhul.htm (accessed 25 May 2009); and Terry Bell in collaboration with Dumisa Buhle Ntsebeza, *Unfinished Business: South Africa, Apartheid and Truth* (Cape Town: RedWorks, 2001). Yet the most extensive empirical survey conducted on the reception of the TRC in South Africa suggests that the process is viewed by the majority of

South Africans—and especially by nonwhites—as having succeeded in achieving its goals. See James L. Gibson, *Overcoming Apartheid: Can Truth Reconcile a Divided Nation?* (New York: Russell Sage Foundation, 2004); and James L. Gibson, "The Truth about Truth and Reconciliation in South Africa," *International Political Science Review* 26, no. 4 (2005): 341–361. For more about Gibson's survey work about the TRC, see chapter 5.

25. An excellent treatment of South Africa's transitional period is Allister Haddon Sparks, *Tomorrow Is Another Country: The Inside Story of South Africa's Road to Change* (Chicago: University of Chicago Press, 1996).

26. In authorizing the Truth and Reconciliation Commission to grant amnesty, South Africa's Promotion of National Unity and Reconciliation Act drew upon principles composed by Carl Norgaard, former president of the European Commission of Human Rights. The Norgaard principles state that the following factors must be taken into consideration when determining whether an act had a political objective: 1) the motive of the person who committed the act, omission, or offense; 2) the context of the act; 3) the legal and factual nature of the act as well as the gravity of the act; 4) the object or objective of the act; 5) whether the act was executed in response to an order or on behalf of or with the approval of a political organization or the state; and 6) the relationship between the act and the political objective pursued, in particular the directness and proximity of the relationship and the proportionality of the act to the objective pursued. For more on the parameters of amnesty, see Richard Lyster, "Amnesty: The Burden of Victims," in *Looking Back, Reaching Forward: Reflections on the Truth and Reconciliation Commission of South Africa*, ed. Charles Villa-Vicencio and Wilhelm Verwoerd (London: Zed Books, 2000), 188–189.

27. On the notion of performance genealogies, see Joseph R. Roach, *Cities of the Dead: Circum-Atlantic Performance* (New York: Columbia University Press, 1996).

28. See Hayner, *Unspeakable Truths,* 40–45. Hayner writes: "The South African Truth and Reconciliation Commission succeeded in bringing this subject to the center of international attention, especially through its public hearings of both victims and perpetrators outlining horrific details of past crimes. Although quite a few of such truth commissions existed prior to the South African body, most did not hold hearings in public, and none of the others included such a compelling (if also ethically problematic) offer of individualized amnesty, which succeeded in enticing many South African wrongdoers to confess their crimes in front of television cameras" (5).

29. Alex Boraine, *A Country Unmasked: Inside South Africa's Truth and Reconciliation Commission* (New York: Oxford University Press, 2000), 89.

30. The bases upon which cases were chosen for public hearings will be discussed later in this chapter.

31. Wendy Orr, interview with the author, Johannesburg, 24 July 2006.

32. See Christopher Merrett, *A Culture of Censorship: Secrecy and Intellectual Repression in South Africa* (Macon, Ga.: Mercer University Press, 1995).

33. TRC, *Truth and Reconciliation Commission of South Africa Report,* vols. 1–5 (London: MacMillan Reference Ltd., 1999); vols. 6–7 (Cape Town: Juta, 2002).

34. Quoted in TRC, *Truth and Reconciliation Commission of South Africa Report,* 1:56–57.

35. "Argentina: The National Commission on Disappeared Persons (CONADEP),"

part of "Strategic Decisions in the Design of Truth Commissions," available at http://www.truthcommission.org/commission.php?cid=0&case_x=0&lang=en (accessed 25 May 2009); and *Nunca Más: The Report of the Argentine National Commission on the Disappeared* (New York: Farrar Straus Giroux in association with Index on Censorship, 1986).

36. Diana Taylor, *Disappearing Acts: Spectacles of Gender and Nationalism in Argentina's "Dirty War"* (Durham, N.C.: Duke University Press, 1997), 12.

37. On the report, see Deborah Posel, "The TRC Report: What Kind of History? What Kind of Truth?" in *Commissioning the Past: Understanding South Africa's Truth and Reconciliation Commission,* ed. Deborah Posel and Graeme Simpson (Johannesburg: Witwatersrand University Press, 2002), 147; Posel, "Truth?" 16; Piers Pigou, "There Are More Truths to Be Uncovered before We Can Achieve Reconciliation," *Sunday Independent* (Johannesburg), 23 April 2006, 9.

38. Pigou, "There Are More Truths," 9.

39. Although the TRC was a media event of the century both nationally and internationally, there has been astonishingly little scholarship on this aspect of the commission. Exceptions are Edward Bird and Zureida Garda, "Reporting the Truth Commission: Analysis of Media Coverage of the Truth and Reconciliation Commission of South Africa," *Gazette* 59, nos. 4–5 (1997): 331–342; Ron Krabill, "Symbiosis: Mass Media and the Truth and Reconciliation Commission of South Africa," *Media, Culture & Society* 23 (2001): 567–585; Annelies Verdoolaege, "Media Representations of the South African Truth and Reconciliation Commission and Their Commitment to Reconciliation," *Journal of African Cultural Studies* 17, no. 2 (2005): 181–199.

40. Charles Villa-Vicencio, "On the Limitations of Academic History: The Quest for Truth Demands Both More and Less," in *After the TRC: Reflections on Truth and Reconciliation in South Africa,* ed. Wilmot James and Linda van de Vijver (2000; repr., Athens: Ohio University Press, 2001), 24.

41. Janet Cherry, John Daniel, and Madeleine Fullard, "Researching the 'Truth': A View from inside the Truth and Reconciliation Commission," in *Commissioning the Past: Understanding South Africa's Truth and Reconciliation Commission,* ed. Deborah Posel and Graeme Simpson (Johannesburg: Witwatersrand University Press, 2002), 34–35.

42. Krabill, "Symbiosis," 568.

43. Desmond Tutu, *No Future without Forgiveness,* 1st ed. (New York: Doubleday, 1999), 120.

44. Yasmin Sooka, interview with the author, Pretoria, 26 July 2006.

45. Ibid.

46. Wendy Orr, *From Biko to Basson: Wendy Orr's Search for the Soul of South Africa as a Commissioner of the TRC* (Saxonwold, South Africa: Contra Press, 2000), 51–52.

47. Sooka, interview with the author.

48. Mary Burton, interview with the author, Cape Town, 4 August 2006.

49. Ibid.

50. Mahlubi "Chief" Mabizela, interview with the author, Pretoria, 25 July 2006.

51. Sooka, interview with the author.

52. "Promotion of National Unity and Reconciliation Act, Act no. 34, 1995," *Government Gazette,* 26 July 1995, 16579. Available online at www.doj.gov.za/trc/legal/act9534.htm (accessed 17 March 2009).

53.   Sooka, interview with the author.

54.   Ibid.

55.   The cartoon, which was originally published in *The Natal Witness*, is reproduced in Wilhelm Verwoerd and Mahlubi Mabizela, *Truths Drawn in Jest: Commentary on the TRC through Cartoons* (Cape Town: David Philip Publishers, 2000), 54.

56.   Mary Strine, Beverly Long, and Mary Francis Hopkins, "Research in Interpretation and Performance Studies: Trends, Issues, Priorities," in *Speech Communication: Essays to Commemorate the Seventy-Fifth Anniversary of the Speech Communication Association*, ed. Gerald Phillips and Julia Wood (Carbondale: Southern Illinois University Press, 1990), 181–204.

57.   See Kay McCormick and Mary Bock, "Negotiating the Public/Personal Interface: An Analysis of Testimonies on Human Rights Violations," n.d., unpublished paper in author's possession.

58.   Julia A. Walker, "Why Performance? Why Now? Textuality and the Rearticulation of Human Presence," *The Yale Journal of Criticism* 16, no. 1 (2003): 149.

59.   Mark Gevisser, "Setting the Stage for a Journey into SA's Heart of Darkness," *Sunday Independent* (Johannesburg), 10 August 1997, 4.

60.   Bizos, interview with the author.

61.   Ibid.

62.   Belinda Bozzoli, "Public Ritual and Private Transition: The Truth Commission in Alexandra Township, South Africa 1996," *African Studies Quarterly* 57, no. 2 (1998): 167–129.

63.   J. L. Austin, *How to Do Things with Words*, 2nd ed. (Cambridge, Mass.: Harvard University Press, 1975).

64.   I use the word "victim" following the TRC's own terminology. But this language was controversial, as the TRC's summary report explains: "From the outset, the commissioners expressed some discomfort with the use of the word 'victim'. Although the term is commonly enough used when talking about those who suffered under apartheid, it may also be seen to imply a negativity or passivity. Victims are acted upon rather than acting, suffering rather than surviving. The term might therefore be seen as insulting to those who consider that they have survived apartheid or emerged victorious. Unlike the word 'victim', the word 'survivor' has a positive connotation, implying an ability to overcome adversity and even to be strengthened by it. This does not, of course, mean that many (if not all) survivors were not still experiencing the effects of the trauma they had suffered. It also does not mean that all survived. There were, indeed, many who did not survive and on whose behalf others approached the Commission. . . . For the sake of consistency, the Commission ultimately decided, in keeping with the language of the Act [the authorizing legislation of the TRC], to use the word 'victim'. In doing so, however, it acknowledged that many described as victims might be better described and, indeed, might prefer to be described as 'survivors'." See TRC, *Truth and Reconciliation Commission of South Africa Report*, 1:59.

65.   Sooka, interview with the author.

66.   Tim Kelsall, "Truth, Lies, Ritual: Preliminary Reflections on the Truth and Reconciliation Commission in Sierra Leone," *Human Rights Quarterly* 27 (2005): 361–391.

67. Pumla Gobodo-Madikizela, *A Human Being Died That Night: A South African Story of Forgiveness* (Boston: Houghton Mifflin, 2003), 131.

68. Bozzoli, "Public Ritual and Private Transition," 169.

69. Victor Turner, *The Anthropology of Performance* (New York: PAJ Books, 1986), 74–75.

70. Pumla Gobodo-Madikizela, "Prefatory Remarks, and Response to *Long Night's Journey into Day*," paper presented at the Brandeis Initiative in Intercommunal Coexistence, 27 March 2001.

71. Boraine, *A Country Unmasked,* 99.

72. For the ways that performance studies traces the connection between theatre and ritual, see Richard Schechner, *Between Theatre and Anthropology* (Philadelphia: University of Pennsylvania Press, 1985).

73. *Long Night's Journey into Day: South Africa's Search for Truth and Reconciliation* (2000, California Newsreel; dir. Frances Reid and Deborah Hoffmann). Transcript available at www.newsreel.org/transcripts/longnight.htm (accessed 20 April 2005).

74. Krog, *Country of My Skull,* 78.

75. The TRC's Web site is not as helpful as it could be about providing access to transcripts of testimony and interpretations of testimony. However, once the correct path is followed, over 2,000 transcripts are easily accessible. To access the transcript of this speech by Tutu, go to the main page of the TRC's Web site (www.doj.gov.za/trc). Click on the link labeled "Read More about the TRC and it's [sic] Committees" in the lower right corner of the page; this takes you to the main page for accessing transcripts. Click on "Transcripts" under "Human Rights Violations Committee," then "East London," then "Day 1" in the section labeled "2. Port Elizabeth—21–23 May 1996." The quote is halfway down the page. Emphasis added.

76. Ibid. Note that the transcriptions available on the TRC's web site are mostly in English. Transcriptions were created hastily at the time of the commission, and the fullness of the testimony of speakers who switched between languages, as Tutu habitually did, often was not transcribed. This was due to the nature of the translation and transcription process, which had difficulty coping with speakers who switched languages within their testimony. See Z. Bock, N. Mazwi, S. Metula, and N. Mpolweni-Zantsi, "An Analysis of What Has Been 'Lost' in the Interpretation and Transcription Process of Selected TRC Testimonies," *Stellenbosch Papers in Linguistics PLUS* 33 (2006): 1–26. The quotation listed here is my transcription of Tutu's speech, based upon my viewing of unedited video footage held at the South African National Archives Repository Service. The speech was given on Day 1 of the East London/Port Elizabeth HRVC hearings, 21 May 1996. The version of this speech transcribed on the TRC Web site does not reflect Tutu's switching between English and Xhosa, and some of the English passages are not transcribed at all on the Web site.

77. Thomas Postlewait and Tracy C. Davis, "Theatricality: An Introduction," in *Theatricality,* ed. Tracy C. Davis and Thomas Postlewait (New York: Cambridge University Press, 2003), 4.

78. SAPA (South African Press Association), "TRC Is a Circus Led by a Clown and Should Be Shut Down: IFP," 22 May 1997, available at http://www.doj.gov.za/trc/media/1997/9705/s970522e.htm (accessed 15 September 2006).

79. "PW Botha to Be Prosecuted," *Mail & Guardian Online* (Johannesburg), 7 January 1998 (accessed 1 November 2006).

80. Elaine Scarry, *The Body in Pain: The Making and Unmaking of the World* (New York: Oxford University Press, 1985), 29.

81. The Guguletu Seven were Zabonke John Konile, Godfrey Jabulani Miya, Zanisile Zenith Mjobo, Mandla Simon Mxinwa, Christopher Piet, Zola Alfred Swelani, and Themba Mlifi Zanisile.

82. For an excellent video documentary on this case, see *The Guguletu Seven* (2001, Ring Records; dir. Lindy Wilson). The lead investigator in the case has written a memoir about his experiences; see Zenzile Khoisan, *Jakaranda Time: An Investigator's View of South Africa's Truth and Reconciliation Commission* (Cape Town: Garib Communications, 2001). The Guguletu Seven are also featured in *Long Night's Journey into Day: South Africa's Search for Truth and Reconciliation* (2000, California Newsreel; dir. Frances Reid and Deborah Hoffmann); transcript available at www.newsreel.org/transcripts/longnight.htm (accessed 20 April 2005).

83. Cynthia Ngewu testified on the first day of testimony on the case of the Guguletu Seven. From the "Read More about the TRC and it's [sic] Committees" link on the main page of the TRC Web site (www.doj.gov.za/trc), follow these links: "Transcripts" under "Human Rights Violations Committee," then "Cape Town," then "Christopher Piet—killing," in the 23 April 1996 portion of the section labeled "1 Heideveld 22–25 April 1996" (accessed 25 April 2005).

84. For more on this case, see Mark Sanders, "Renegotiating Responsibility after Apartheid: Listening to Perpetrator Testimony," *Journal of Gender, Social Policy & the Law* 10, no. 3 (2002): 587–595.

85. For close analysis of this testimony using new translations from the Xhosa, see chapter 3.

86. For the transcript of Mrs. Konile's testimony, follow the "Read More about the TRC and it's [sic] Committees" link on the main page of the TRC Web site (www.doj.gov.za/trc), then follow these links: "Transcripts" under "Human Rights Violations Committee," then "Cape Town," then "Christopher Piet—killing" in the section entitled "Day 2—23 April 1996" (accessed 25 May 2009).

87. Khoisan, *Jakaranda Time*, 73.

88. Partly through these video images, counsel for the murdered men's mothers finally proved that the police had planted evidence at the crime scene; see Wilson, *The Guguletu Seven*.

89. According to Eunice Miya, one of Christopher Piet's sisters threw the shoe. See Eunice Miya, interview with filmmaker Liza Key and the author, 14 December 2006, Guguletu, Cape Town, translated by Gcisakazi Mdlulwa.

90. Joseph Aranes and John Yeld, "Top Cops Storm Out of Hearing into Guguletu 7," *Cape Argus,* 28 November 1996 (accessed 4 November 2004).

91. From the "Read More about the TRC and it's [sic] Committees" link on the main page of the TRC Web site (www.doj.gov.za/trc), follow these links: "Transcripts" under "Human Rights Violations Committee," then "Cape Town," then "Day 3: Introduction and Showing of Video," in the section labeled "10. Guguletu 7—Pollsmoor 26–28 November 1996," (accessed 29 June 2005).

92. Ibid.; emphasis added.

93. Ibid.

94. Douglas, *The Memory of Judgment*, 29.

95. Ibid., 145–149.
96. Black Sash was an organization formed by mostly privileged white women in 1955. Throughout the subsequent years until the end of apartheid in 1994, the organization was active in staging overt resistance to apartheid policies such as pass laws and providing aid to families adversely affected by these policies.
97. Though Gobodo-Madikizela was not technically a commissioner, she was a member of the Human Rights Violations Committee and was an enduring presence at public hearings, especially human rights violation hearings in Cape Town.
98. The Bisho massacre happened in 1992 in Bisho in the Ciskei, a so-called independent homeland of apartheid South Africa, when the Ciskei Defence Force killed twenty-eight members of African National Congress and one soldier.
99. See *TRC Special Report*, 24 November 1996.
100. Ibid.
101. John Allen, *Rabble-Rouser for Peace: The Authorized Biography of Desmond Tutu* (New York: Free Press, 2006).
102. "*Ubuntu*" means "humaneness" and was a key principle of the TRC, expressed metaphorically in the phrase "*Umuntu ngumuntu ngabantu*," which means "People are people through other people." See TRC, *Truth and Reconciliation Commission of South Africa Report*, 127.
103. Krog, *Country of My Skull*, 338.
104. Orr, *From Biko to Basson*, 30.
105. On the underlying structures required for successful musical improvisation, see Paul Berliner, *Thinking in Jazz: The Infinite Art of Improvisation* (Chicago: University of Chicago Press, 1994).
106. Richard A Wilson, "Reconciliation and Revenge in Post-Apartheid South Africa: Rethinking Legal Pluralism and Human Rights," *Current Anthropology* 41, no. 1 (2000): 80.
107. Annelies Verdoolaege, "Managing Reconciliation at the Human Rights Violations Hearings of the South African TRC," *Journal of Human Rights* 5 (2005): 61.
108. Posel, "Truth?" 17.
109. Bird and Garda, "Reporting the Truth Commission," 331–342.
110. Posel, "Truth?" 17–18.
111. Posel contends that the TRC summary report is a "disconnected compilation of discrete chunks of information, with little effort at a synthetic unified analysis." Ibid., 19. Three individuals who were coauthors of the report responded to Posel's critique by contextualizing the report's weaknesses, noting the limitations of the commission's time and resources, but also by asserting that a truth commission report is a new genre, a new type of text, and thus it demands new critical standards for evaluating its unusual combination of history, law, psychology, and philosophy. See Cherry, Daniel, and Fullard, "Researching the 'Truth': A View from inside the Truth and Reconciliation Commission," 17–36.
112. The status of the TRC archive is fraught and contested, as is described throughout this book. While the majority of the TRC archive is de facto inaccessible to researchers, my point here is that the video and audio portions of the TRC archive *are* fully accessible and vast. Yet this rich resource is grossly underutilized. The only study to date that has made extensive use of this video collection

is Anne Fleckstein, "Performing Truth: Performative Aspekte der öffentlichen Anhörungen der Wahrheitskommission in Südafrika" (M.A. thesis, Humboldt University of Berlin, 2006).

113. David William Cohen and E. S. Atieno Odhiambo, *The Risks of Knowledge: Investigations into the Death of the Hon. Minister John Robert Ouko in Kenya, 1990* (Athens: Ohio University Press 2004), 19.

2. Justice in Transition

The first epigraph is from Michel Leiris, "Apartheid," in *For Nelson Mandela,* ed. Jacques Derrida and Mustapha Tlili (New York: Seaver Books, Henry Holt, 1987), 71. The second is from Hélène Cixous, "The Parting of the Cake," in *For Nelson Mandela,* ed. Jacques Derrida and Mustapha Tlili (New York: Seaver Books, Henry Holt, 1987), 213.

1. See, for instance, Leslie and Neville Rubin, *This Is Apartheid* (London: Christian Action, 1966). This pamphlet defines apartheid solely through a litany of extracts from apartheid legislation.
2. The 1962 trial of Nelson Mandela is often confused with the earlier Treason Trial and also with the later Rivonia Trial, I suspect in part because the 1962 trial has no comparably recognizable name. Hence I have given it one: the "Incitement Trial," indicating the chief charge against Mandela on this occasion.
3. Otto Kirchheimer, *Political Justice: The Use of Legal Procedure for Political Ends* (Princeton, N.J.: Princeton University Press, 1961), vii.
4. Philippe-Joseph Salazar has argued that dissident rhetoric in apartheid South Africa was confined to three sites for codified and public expression: universities; judicial commissions and high courts at the trials of so-called terrorists; and churches, especially via homilies delivered at funerals. Philippe-Joseph Salazar, *An African Athens: Rhetoric and the Shaping of Democracy in South Africa* (Mahwah, N.J.: Lawrence Erlbaum Associates, 2002), 8.
5. Diana Taylor, *The Archive and the Repertoire: Performing Cultural Memory in the Americas* (Durham, N.C.: Duke University Press, 2003), 19.
6. Ibid., 20.
7. Ibid., 25.
8. Thomas G. Karis, "The South African Treason Trial," *Political Science Quarterly* 76, no. 2 (1961): 21.
9. Helen Joseph, *If This Be Treason* (London: Andre Deutsch, 1963), 37.
10. See, for instance, Peggy Phelan, *Unmarked: The Politics of Performance* (New York: Routledge, 1993), 146–148; Taylor, *The Archive and the Repertoire*; and Philip Auslander, *Liveness* (New York: Routledge, 1999).
11. Joseph R. Roach, *Cities of the Dead: Circum-Atlantic Performance* (New York: Columbia University Press, 1996), 25.
12. Ibid., 26.
13. "Exit Sighing," *Time,* 24 March 1961, available at www.time.com (accessed 21 July 2008).
14. Christopher Merrett, *A Culture of Censorship: Secrecy and Intellectual Repression in South Africa* (Macon, Ga.: Mercer University Press, 1995), 21.
15. In his influential history of South Africa, Leonard Thompson includes two chapters on the apartheid era that together span the period 1948 to 1989. See

Leonard Thompson, *A History of South Africa*, 3rd ed. (New Haven, Conn.: Yale University Press, 2000), 187–264.

16. Jacques Derrida, "The Laws of Reflection: Nelson Mandela, in Admiration," in *For Nelson Mandela*, ed. Jacques Derrida and Mustapha Tlili (New York: Seaver Books, Henry Holt and Co., 1987), 18.

17. Thompson, *A History of South Africa*, 211.

18. Albie Sachs, foreword to Ruth First, *117 Days* (New York: Monthly Review Press, 1989), 11. For an overview of the early apartheid period, see Thompson, *A History of South Africa*, 187–220; Leslie Rubin, *This Is Apartheid* (London: Victor Gollancz, 1960); and Philip Bonner, Peter Delius, and Deborah Posel, eds., *Apartheid's Genesis, 1935–1962* (Johannesburg: Ravan Press and Witwatersrand University Press, 1993). Deborah Posel argues that between 1959 and 1961 apartheid "shifted gear into a discrete second phase" that should not be simply seen as a continuation and extension of what came before it. See Deborah Posel, *The Making of Apartheid, 1948–1961* (New York: Oxford University Press, 1991), 227–255, quote on 227.

19. Akil Kokayi Khalfani and Tukufu Zuberi, "Racial Classification and the Modern Census in South Africa, 1911–1966," *Race & Society*, 14, no. 2 (2001): 166.

20. Paul Sauer quoted in Karis, "The South African Treason Trial," 236.

21. Anthony Sampson, *The Treason Cage: The Opposition on Trial in South Africa* (London: Heinemann, 1958), 41–52.

22. TRC, *Truth and Reconciliation Commission of South Africa Report*, vol. 1 (London: MacMillan, 1999), 55.

23. Nelson Mandela, *Nelson Mandela: An Illustrated Autobiography* (Boston: Little, Brown and Co., 1996), 46.

24. Hilda Bernstein, *The World That Was Ours: The Story of the Rivonia Trial* (London: SAWriters, 1989), 20.

25. L. J. Blom-Cooper, "The South African Treason Trial: R. v. Adams and Others," *International and Comparative Law Quarterly* 8, no. 1 (1959): 59.

26. Lionel Forman and E. S. Sachs, *The South African Treason Trial* (New York: Monthly Review Press, 1958), 11.

27. Ibid., 19.

28. The term *kwela* is derived from the Zulu for "get up," though in township slang it also referred to the police vans, the *kwela-kwela*. See "South African Music: Kwela," at http://www.southafrica.info/about/arts/922564.htm (accessed 4 April 2009).

29. Forman and Sachs, *The South African Treason Trial*, 22.

30. Ibid.

31. Sampson, *The Treason Cage*, 203.

32. Nelson Mandela, *Long Walk to Freedom: The Autobiography of Nelson Mandela* (Boston: Little, Brown and Co., 1994), 201.

33. Sampson, *The Treason Cage*, 5.

34. Quote from the jazz pianist Abdullah Ibrahim in the documentary film *Amandla! A Revolution in Four-Part Harmony* (2002, ATO Pictures/Kwela Productions; dir. Lee Hirsch).

35. Joseph, *If This Be Treason*, 91.

36. Hilda Watts quoted in ibid., 26.

37. See Mandela, *Long Walk to Freedom*, 202; and Jeremy Cronin, "Death Row," in Jeremy Cronin, *Inside* (Johannesburg: Ravan Press, 1983), 26–31. Ruth First,

who was detained for 117 days, said, "Those held in prison pending political trials or during the 1960 State of Emergency and the days of the 1961 Mandela strike, had emerged from a spell of community jail life with morale marvelously unimpaired. Every new stretch of prison for a group of political prisoners gave birth to a new batch of freedom songs." See First, *117 Days*, 140.

38. "Mandela Wins Week's Adjournment," *Cape Times*, 15 October 1962, 3. I am grateful to research assistant Bianca Murillo for her painstaking work in locating this and many other articles on the political trials of 1956–1964 in South African newspapers.

39. Joel Joffe, *The Rivonia Story* (Cape Town: Mayibuye Books, University of Western Cape, 1995), 205.

40. Forman and Sachs, *The South African Treason Trial*, 34.

41. Ibid.

42. Raymond Suttner was a political prisoner from 1975 to 1983, imprisoned for his activities with the ANC. He is now a professor at the University of South Africa. Jeremy Cronin was also imprisoned during the apartheid era for his political activities with the South African Community Party. He is a well-known poet and presently serves as a Deputy Minister of Parliament in South Africa.

43. Raymond Suttner and Jeremy Cronin, eds., *30 Years of the Freedom Charter* (Braamfontein: Ravan Press, 1986), 86.

44. Forman and Sachs, *The South African Treason Trial*, 49.

45. Ibid. See Sampson, *The Treason Cage*, 11. For news service film coverage of this disruption, see *Hearst Telenews*, issue 9, tape 256, which shows images of demonstrators disrupting the treason trial in Johannesburg on 24 December 1956. Footage located at the UCLA Film & Television Archive, Los Angeles, California.

46. Anthony Sampson, *Mandela: The Authorized Biography* (New York: Alfred A. Knopf, 1999), 12.

47. Sampson, *The Treason Cage*, 13–14; Forman and Sachs, *The South African Treason Trial*, 51–53; Blom-Cooper, "The South African Treason Trial," 60.

48. Sampson, *The Treason Cage*, 28.

49. Vernon Berrangé quoted in Joseph, *If This Be Treason*, 16.

50. Merrett, *A Culture of Censorship*, 22.

51. Forman and Sachs, *The South African Treason Trial*, 88.

52. Joseph, *If This Be Treason*, 38.

53. Sampson, *The Treason Cage*, 30.

54. Forman and Sachs, *The South African Treason Trial*, 88.

55. Sampson, *Mandela: The Authorized Biography*, 27.

56. Forman and Sachs, *The South African Treason Trial*, 123.

57. Sampson, *The Treason Cage*, 24.

58. Forman and Sachs, *The South African Treason Trial*, 126.

59. Ibid.

60. Sampson, *The Treason Cage*, 24.

61. A. S. Chetty quoted in Suttner and Cronin, *30 Years of the Freedom Charter*, 48.

62. Forman and Sachs, *The South African Treason Trial*, 20. J. G. Strijdom was South Africa's prime minister from 1954 to 1958.

63. Sampson, *The Treason Cage*, 10.

64. Quoted from "Pretoria, South Africa," available at http://www.edwardvictor.com/pretoria_main.htm (accessed 24 October 2006). George Bizos confirmed

this history of the Old Synagogue in an interview with the author, Johannesburg, 25 July 2006.

65.   Hilda Bernstein, "No. 46—Steve Biko," available at http://www.sahistory.org.za/pages/library-resources/online%20books/biko-no46/vi-inquest.htm (accessed 4 April 2009).

66.   Joseph, *If This Be Treason*, 25.

67.   Ibid., 103. After the Treason Trial, the Old Synagogue was also the site of the Mandela Incitement Trial of 1962 and the inquest into the death of Steven Biko in 1977.

68.   Bram Fisher to Rev. Canon L. John Collins, 2 May 1960, Treason Trial Documents, I3/S/726, Mayibuye Archives, Historical Papers Archives, University of Western Cape–Robben Island.

69.   Mandela described in *Long Walk to Freedom* how "consultations between the accused and our lawyers [became] virtually impossible. Our lawyers, who were based in Johannesburg, had trouble seeing us in prison and were unable to prepare our case. They would often drive up and be informed that we were not available. Even when we were able to see them, consultations were harassed and cut short." Mandela, *Long Walk to Freedom*, 246. Because of the state's obstruction of contact between the accused and their attorneys and the risks that anyone faced who testified on behalf of the accused under the State of Emergency, the accused decided to have their attorneys withdraw from the case and conducted their own defense.

70.   Mandela, *Long Walk to Freedom*, 253.

71.   Ibid., 247.

72.   Ibid.

73.   The quote is from Helen Joseph's diary entry for 5 December 1960. Joseph, *If This Be Treason*, 133.

74.   Forman and Sachs, *The South African Treason Trial*, 201.

75.   Sampson, *The Treason Cage*, 6.

76.   Joseph, *If This Be Treason*, 17.

77.   Bernstein, *The World That Was Ours*, 20.

78.   Karis, "The South African Treason Trial," 234.

79.   Sampson, *The Treason Cage*, 30.

80.   Sampson, *Mandela: The Authorized Biography*, 171.

81.   Mandela, *Long Walk to Freedom*, 317.

82.   Ibid.

83.   Two of Mandela's biographers note his reputation as an impeccable dresser; see Sampson, *Mandela: The Authorized Biography*; and Martin Meredith, *Nelson Mandela: A Biography* (New York: St. Martin's Press, 1997), 106.

84.   "Mandela Wins Adjournment," *The Cape Times*, 15 October 1962, 3. Mandela describes the skin he was wearing this day as a Xhosa leopard-skin kaross. However, Winnie Mandela's biographer says Nelson was dressed in a lion skin, "the traditional garb of a chief, which had been a gift from the paramount chief." See Anne Marie du Preez Bezdrob, *Winnie Mandela: A Life* (Cape Town: Zebra Press, 2003), 108.

85.   Wolfie Kodesh, interview with John Carlin, available at www.pbs.org/wgbh/pages/frontline/shows/mandela/interviews/kodesh.html (accessed 26 October 2006).

86.   Mandela, *Long Walk to Freedom*, 324.

87.   "Bombs, Protests as Mandela Trial Opens," *New Age* (Cape Town), 18 October 1962, 3.

88.   Sampson, *Mandela: The Authorized Biography*, 173.

89.   Mandela, *Long Walk to Freedom*, 325.

90.   Colonel Jacobs used the word "blanket." Mandela wrote "The colonel never again tried to take my 'blanket,' but the authorities would permit me to wear it only in court, not on my way to or from court for fear it would 'incite' other prisoners." Ibid.

91.   Ibid.

92.   "I Am Guilty of No Offence," *New Age* (Cape Town), 1 November 1962, 6.

93.   Mandela, *Long Walk to Freedom*, 324. See also "Bombs, Protests as Mandela Trial Opens," *New Age* (Cape Town), 18 October 1962, 3.

94.   Bezdrob, *Winnie Mandela: A Life*, 108.

95.   "I Am Guilty of No Offence," *New Age*, 1 November 1962, 6.

96.   See in particular "'I Have Nothing to Regret,'" *New Age*, 15 November 1962, 4–5. This is an extensive article with photographs.

97.   See Sampson, *The Treason Cage*, 45.

98.   Ibid., 47–48.

99.   "Mrs. Mandela on Afrika Day," *New Age* (Cape Town), 26 April 1962, 3.

100.   Paul Mathabe, "Tribal Dress," *New Age* (Cape Town), 1 November 1962, 2.

101.   These words are Wolfie Kodesh's paraphrase of Mandela in Wolfie Kodesh, interview with John Carlin.

102.   "Vorster Bans All Mandela Meetings for Two Days; Trial Switched to Pretoria," *The Star*(Johannesburg), 13 October 1962. See also "Mandela on the List," *The Star* (Johannesburg), 12 October 1962, 1.

103.   "Verwoerd's Secretary Speaks at Mandela Trial," *The Star* (Johannesburg), 22 October 1962, 3.

104.   "Release Nelson Mandela!" *New Age* (Cape Town), 16 August 1962, 1; and "Mandela Slogans in Jo'burg," *New Age* (Cape Town), 16 August 1962, 1.

105.   Bernstein, *The World That Was Ours*, 2.

106.   Nelson Mandela, *We Accuse: The Trial of Nelson Mandela* (London: African National Congress, 1962), 36.

107.   Mandela, *Long Walk to Freedom*, 360.

108.   For the text of the speech, see Nelson Mandela, "Black Man in a White Man's Court," in *No Easy Walk to Freedom*, ed. Ato Quayson (New York: Penguin Books, 2002), 105–142. For an important reading of this speech, see Derrida, "The Laws of Reflection," 13–42.

109.   Derrida, "The Laws of Reflection," 15.

110.   Ibid., 27.

111.   Tom Lodge, *Mandela: A Critical Life* (New York: Oxford University Press, 2006), 108.

112.   Quoted in Bernstein, *The World That Was Ours*, 240.

113.   Joffe, *The Rivonia Story*, 37.

114.   Dennis Goldberg quoted in Mac Maharaj and Ahmed Kathrada, eds., *Mandela: The Authorized Portrait* (Kansas City: Andrews McMeel Publishing, 2006), 116.

115.   Joffe, *The Rivonia Story*, 37.

116.   Ibid.

117.   Ibid.

118.   Ibid., 58.
119.   For a moving compilation of these statements, see Mary Benson, ed., *The Sun Will Rise: Statements from the Dock by Southern African Political Prisoners,* rev. and exp. ed. (1974; London: International Defence and Aid Fund for Southern Africa, 1981).
120.   George Bizos, "Reflection on the Past," *Sunday Times* (Johannesburg), 11 May 2003.
121.   Joel Joffe quoted in Maharaj and Kathrada, *Mandela: The Authorized Portrait,* 121.
122.   Joffe, *The Rivonia Story,* 131.
123.   See Mandela, *No Easy Walk to Freedom,* 105–142; James Boyd White, *Acts of Hope: Creating Authority in Literature, Law, and Politics* (Chicago: University of Chicago Press, 1994), 275–294.
124.   For a complete transcript of this speech, see chapter 15, "The Rivonia Trial," in Mandela, *No Easy Walk to Freedom,* 143–170.
125.   Joffe, *The Rivonia Story,* 133.
126.   Recording of interview reproduced in "The Underground Movement," part 2 of the five-part series *Mandela: An Audio History,* an audio documentary by Joe Richman and Sue Johnson, available at http://www.npr.org/templates/story/story.php?storyId=1851882 (accessed 17 March 2009). This series originally broadcast on National Public Radio in the United States in 2004.
127.   Bernstein, *The World That Was Ours,* 198.
128.   J. L. Austin, *How to Do Things with Words,* 2nd ed. (Cambridge, Mass.: Harvard University Press, 1975).
129.   Entry for 12 May 1978, in Parliament of South Africa, *Debates [of the House of Assembly of the First Parliament of the Republic of South Africa]* (Cape Town: Parliament of South Africa, 1978), 6846.
130.   Mandela, *No Easy Walk to Freedom,* xxv.
131.   Benson, ed., *The Sun Will Rise.*
132.   Salazar, *An African Athens,* 76.
133.   Ibid., 85–86.
134.   Derrida, "The Laws of Reflection," 18.
135.   Joseph, *If This Be Treason,* 14.
136.   This genealogy also includes a history of commissions of inquiry within South Africa, of which there have been over a thousand. For an analysis of key South African commissions from 1903 to 1981, see Adam Ashforth, *The Politics of Official Discourse in Twentieth-Century South Africa* (New York: Oxford University Press, 1990), especially 15n5. The TRC acknowledged this legacy by printing in its report a list of South African commissions of inquiry from 1960 to 1995; see TRC, *Truth and Reconciliation Commission of South Africa Report,* 1:498–510. On the history of truth commissions internationally, see Pricilla Hayner, *Unspeakable Truths: Confronting State Terror and Atrocity* (New York: Routledge, 2001).
137.   Suttner and Cronin, *30 Years of the Freedom Charter.* "Infelicitous" here refers to the work of speech act theorist J. L. Austin, who proposed that performative speech acts are those in which one *does* something by *saying* something, such as when one says "I do" during a wedding ceremony. Such speech acts are, in Austin's terminology, either felicitous (successful) or infelicitous (unsuccessful). If one said "I do" during the wedding ceremony and was actually already married

to someone else, this would be an infelicitous speech act. See J. L. Austin, *How to Do Things with Words,* 2nd ed. (Cambridge: Harvard University Press, 1975).

138. Nelson Mandela, "'Black Man in a White Court': Nelson Mandela's First Court Statement, 1962," available at www.anc.org.za/ancdocs/history/mandela/1960s/nm6210.html (accessed 17 March 2009). On the evidence presented by prosecution at the Treason Trial, see Sampson, *The Treason Cage,* 21.

139. "South Africa on Trial," *Daily Graphic* (Accra), 24 October 1962, 5.

140. Quoted in Bernstein, *The World That Was Ours,* 239.

141. On the idea of surrogation, see Roach, *Cities of the Dead,* 2–3.

142. Joe Slovo quoted in Thomas G. Karis and Gail M. Gerhardt, eds., *Nadir and Resurgence, 1964–1969,* vol. 5 of *From Protest to Challenge: A Documentary History of African Politics in South Africa, 1882–1990* (Stanford, Calif.: Hoover Institution Press, 1997), 24.

143. George Bizos, *No One to Blame? In Pursuit of Justice in South Africa* (Cape Town: David Philip Publishers; Bellville: Mayibuye Books, 1998), 3.

144. Ibid., 4. Bizos wrote that "between 1963 and 1990s, 73 detainees are known to have died in detention," the youngest of whom was 16 and the oldest 63 years of age (6). His book details his own experience serving as advocate for many of these cases.

145. Mrs. Maria Ngudle quoted in First, *117 Days,* 84.

146. Ibid., 85.

147. In South Africa, banning was "an administrative action by which publications, organizations, or assemblies could be outlawed and suppressed and individual persons could be placed under severe restrictions of their freedom of travel, association, and speech. Banning was an important tool in the South African government's suppression of those opposed to its policy of apartheid." "Banning: South African Law," *Encyclopædia Britannica Online,* available at www.britannica.com/EBchecked/topic/52092/banning (accessed 4 April 2009).

148. First, *117 Days,* 86.

149. Ibid., 86–87.

150. Isaac Tlale quoted in Bizos, *No One to Blame,* 12.

151. First, *117 Days,* 95.

152. Ibid., 96.

153. Bizos, *No One to Blame,* 13.

154. Joseph, *If This Be Treason,* 131.

3. Witnessing and Interpreting Testimony

The first epigraph is from Joel Joffe, *The Rivonia Story* (Cape Town: Mayibuye Books, University of Western Cape, 1995), 23. The second is from Richard Wilson, *The Politics of Truth and Reconciliation in South Africa: Legitimizing the Post-Apartheid State* (Cambridge: Cambridge University Press, 2001), 44.

1. See chapter 2.

2. Adam Ashforth, *The Politics of Official Discourse in Twentieth-Century South Africa* (New York: Oxford University Press, 1990), 7, 59. For a similar comparison between the private, hidden nature of torture and the public testimonies

about and even demonstrations of torture enabled by the TRC, see Rory Bester, "Trauma and Truth," in *Experiments with Truth: Transitional Justice and the Processes of Truth and Reconciliation*, ed. Okwui Enwezor, Carlos Basaualdo, Ute Meta Bauer, Susanne Ghez, Sarat Maharaj, Mark Nash, and Octavio Zaya (Ostfildern-Ruit, Germany: Hatje Cantz Publishers, 2002), 155–173.

3. Ashforth, *The Politics of Official Discourse in Twentieth-Century South Africa*, 7.

4. Marcelo Vignar quoted in Lawrence Weschler, "Uruguay," in *Dealing with the Past: Truth and Reconciliation in South Africa*, ed. Alex Boraine, Janet Levy, and Ronel Scheffer, 2nd ed. (Cape Town: Institute for Democracy in South Africa, 1997), 43.

5. The brief bibliography on the relationship between the TRC and the South African media includes Anthea Garman, "Media Creation: How the TRC and the Media Have Impacted on Each Other," *Track Two* 6, no. 304 (December 1997); Tanya Goodman, "Setting the Stage for a 'New' South Africa: A Cultural Approach to the Truth and Reconciliation Commission" (Ph.D. diss., Yale University, 2004); Zubeida Jaffer and Karin Cronjé, *Cameras, Microphones and Pens* (Cape Town: Institute for Justice and Reconciliation, 2004); and Annelies Verdoolaege, "Media Representations of the South African Truth and Reconciliation Commission and Their Commitment to Reconciliation," *Journal of African Cultural Studies* 17, no. 2 (2005): 188–199.

6. Antjie Krog, *Country of My Skull: Guilt, Sorrow, and the Limits of Forgiveness in the New South Africa* (1998; New York: Three Rivers Press, 1999), 290.

7. Daniel Dayan and Elihu Katz, *Media Events: The Live Broadcasting of History* (Cambridge: Cambridge University Press, 1992).

8. Ibid., 12.

9. Ibid., 118.

10. Angela Sobrey, interview with the author, Johannesburg, 26 July 2006.

11. Translators have also been the subject of a recent theatre production entitled *Truth in Translation*, produced by the Colonnades Theatre lab, directed by Michael Lessac. For more about the play, see www.truthintranslation.org.

12. Theo du Plessis and Chriss Wiegand, "Interpreting at the Hearings of the Truth and Reconciliation Commission: April 1996 to February 1997," in *Language Facilitation and Development in Southern Africa*, ed. Alex Kruger, Kim Wallmach, and Marion Boers (Pretoria: South African Translators' Institute, 1998), 30.

13. Mark Sanders, *Ambiguities of Witnessing: Law and Literature in the Time of a Truth Commission* (Palo Alto, Calif.: Stanford University Press, 2007), 18–19.

14. Du Plessis and Wiegand, "Interpreting at the Hearings," 30.

15. Wisani Sibuyi used this metaphor at the TRC interpreters' retreat sponsored by the Colonnades Theatre Lab/*Truth in Translation* Project, March 2003. Director Michael Lessac and his production team generously shared the transcript of the retreat with me.

16. Du Plessis and Wiegand, "Interpreting at the Hearings," 30.

17. Taking the issue of interpretation versus translation seriously in my own research was no easy task. It took me many months to find raw video and/or audio recordings of hearings. The SABC seemed initially to be the only source, and when they finally managed to return my messages, they quoted an astronomical

fee (US$50 per hour of tape, and they had thousands of hours of footage with no index or finding aids). Finally I learned that I could procure these unedited recordings from the National Archives. Although this audiovisual material is the only part of the National Archives' TRC collection in the public domain, the archive unfortunately has no audiovisual equipment on site for accessing and copying tapes. Thus, materials must be outsourced to yet another government agency for duplication, with a great number of documents, deposits, and paperwork required in the interim. After I finally procured the recordings, I had to find qualified individuals first to carefully transcribe the Xhosa testimony and then to translate it into English. This process took months and included several aborted efforts. I will note that I have done similar work extensively in Ghana, a country with only one official state language, English. And yet in Ghana finding trained individuals to create African-language transcriptions and careful English translations was *much* easier than doing so in South Africa. At last, thanks to Prof. Sizwe Satyo at the University of Cape Town, I found Thuleleni Mcanda, who undertook the Herculean task of transcribing and translating the first hearing of the mothers of the Guguletu Seven studied later in this chapter. She worked from both audio and video recordings of the TRC hearings.

18.   Louis Nel at the TRC interpreters' retreat sponsored by the Colonnades Theatre Lab/*Truth in Translation* Project, March 2003.

19.   The full text of the TRC's interpretation of Nomonde Calata's testimony can be found on the TRC Web site. From the "Read More about the TRC and it's [*sic*] Committees" link on the main page (www.doj.gov.za/trc), follow these links: "Transcripts" under "Human Rights Violations Committee," then "East London," then "Nomonde Calata; Sindiswa Mkhonto; Nombuyiselo Mhlawuli" in the section labeled "1. East London—1: 15–18 April 1996" (accessed 19 December 2007).

20.   Z. Bock, N. Mazwi, S. Metula, and N. Mpolweni-Zantsi, "An Analysis of What Has Been 'Lost' in the Interpretation and Transcription Process of Selected TRC Testimonies," *Stellenbosch Papers in Linguistics Plus* 33 (2006): 10.

21.   Du Plessis and Wiegand, "Interpreting at the Hearings," 28.

22.   Kim Wallmach, "'Seizing the Surge of Language by Its Soft, Bare Skull': Simultaneous Interpreting, the Truth Commission and Country of My Skull," *Current Writing* 14, no. 2 (2002): 70.

23.   Information gathered at the TRC interpreters' retreat sponsored by the Colonnades Theatre Lab/*Truth in Translation* Project, March 2003. See also Plessis and Wiegand, "Interpreting at the Hearings," 25–30.

24.   Angela Sobrey at the TRC interpreters' retreat sponsored by the Colonnades Theatre Lab/*Truth in Translation* Project, March 2003.

25.   Sobrey, interview with the author, 26 July 2006.

26.   Annelie Lotriet, "Can Short Interpreter Training Be Effective?" in *Teaching Translation and Interpretation 4: Building Bridges,* ed. E. Hung (Amsterdam: John Benjamins, 2002), 83.

27.   Sobrey, interview with the author.

28.   Ibid.

29.   Annelie Lotriet, "Interpreter Training Needs in South Africa: Needs and Challenges," in *Language Facilitation and Development in Southern Africa,* ed. Alex

Kruger, Kim Wallmach, and Marion Boers (Pretoria: South African Translators' Institute, 1998), 83.

30. TRC, *Truth and Reconciliation Commission of South Africa Report* (Cape Town: Truth and Reconciliation Commission, 2003), 6:750.

31. Du Plessis and Wiegand, "Interpreting at the Hearings," 30.

32. TRC, *Truth and Reconciliation Commission of South Africa Report,* 6:749.

33. Ibid.

34. Du Plessis and Wiegand, "Interpreting at the Hearings," 30.

35. Lotriet, "Can Short Interpreter Training Be Effective?" 83–98; du Plessis and Wiegand, "Interpreting at the Hearings," 27.

36. Louis Nel at the TRC interpreters' retreat sponsored by the Colonnades Theatre Lab/*Truth in Translation* Project, March 2003.

37. Du Plessis and Wiegand, "Interpreting at the Hearings," 29.

38. Louis Nel at the TRC interpreters' retreat sponsored by the Colonnades Theatre Lab/*Truth in Translation* Project, March 2003.

39. Angela Sobrey at the TRC interpreters' retreat sponsored by the Colonnades Theatre Lab/*Truth in Translation* Project, March 2003.

40. Du Plessis and Wiegand, "Interpreting at the Hearings," 26.

41. Abubaakr Peterson at the TRC interpreters' retreat sponsored by the Colonnades Theatre Lab/*Truth in Translation* Project, March 2003.

42. Louis Nel at the TRC interpreters' retreat sponsored by the Colonnades Theatre Lab/*Truth in Translation* Project, March 2003.

43. Lebohang Mathibela, "Translation and the Media," in *Truth and Reconciliation in South Africa: 10 Years On,* ed. Charles Villa-Vicencio and Fanie du Toit (Claremont, South Africa: David Philip, New Africa Books, 2006), 117.

44. Sobrey, interview with the author, Johannesburg, 26 July 2006.

45. Du Plessis and Wiegand, "Interpreting at the Hearings," 25–30.

46. Sobrey, interview with the author, Johannesburg, 26 July 2006.

47. Du Plessis and Wiegand, "Interpreting at the Hearings," 28.

48. Khethiwe Mboweni Marais at the TRC interpreters' retreat sponsored by the Colonnades Theatre Lab/*Truth in Translation* Project, March 2003.

49. TRC, *Truth and Reconciliation Commission of South Africa Report* (London: MacMillan, 1999), 1:21.

50. This is the first direct excerpt of testimony to appear in the summary report, and as with most such quotations in the report, it is not contextualized and includes no information about the identity of the speakers.

51. Siphithi Mona at the TRC interpreters' retreat sponsored by the Colonnades Theatre Lab/*Truth in Translation* Project, March 2003.

52. Krog, *Country of My Skull,* 169.

53. Mathibela, "Translation and the Media," 117.

54. The ongoing play *Truth in Translation* is available at www.truthintranslation .org.

55. The phrase "parity of esteem" comes from the post-apartheid Constitution of the Republic of South Africa, which states that the official languages of the Republic are Sepedi, SeSotho, SeTswana, SiSwati, Tshivenda, Xitsonga, Afrikaans, English, isiNdebele, isiXhosa, and isiZulu. The Constitution also stipulates that "all official languages must enjoy parity of esteem and must be treated equitably." Furthermore, the Constitution recognizes that because of "the historically

diminished use and status of the indigenous languages of our people, the state must take practical and positive measures to elevate the status and advance the use of these languages." See "Constitution of the Republic of South Africa," available at http://www.constitutionalcourt.org.za/site/constitution/english-web/ch1 .html (accessed 4 April 2009).

56. Interpreter "M" at the TRC interpreters' retreat sponsored by the Colonnades Theatre Lab/*Truth in Translation* project, March 2003.

57. Robert J. C. Young, *Post-Colonialism: A Very Short Introduction* (New York: Oxford University Press, 2003), 138.

58. TRC interpreters' retreat sponsored by the Colonnades Theatre Lab/*Truth in Translation* project, March 2003.

59. Albie Sachs, interview with the author, Johannesburg, 29 June 2007.

60. Louis Nel at the TRC interpreters' retreat sponsored by the Colonnades Theatre Lab/*Truth in Translation* Project, March 2003.

61. Alex Boraine, *A Country Unmasked: Inside South Africa's Truth and Reconciliation Commission* (New York: Oxford University Press, 2000), 102–103.

62. Wendy Orr, *From Biko to Basson: Wendy Orr's Search for the Soul of South Africa as a Commissioner of the TRC* (Saxonwold, South Africa: Contra Press, 2000), 36.

63. Desmond Tutu, *No Future without Forgiveness*, 1st ed. (New York: Doubleday, 1999), 148.

64. Angie Kapelianis and Darren Taylor, *South Africa's Human Spirit: An Oral Memoir of the Truth and Reconciliation Commission*, CD (Johannesburg: SABC, 2000), track 6.

65. Philip Miller, *REwind: A Cantata for Voice, Tape, and Testimony*, live performance at St. George's Cathedral, Cape Town, 16 December 2006.

66. Krog, *Country of My Skull*, 51.

67. Ibid., 57.

68. Nomonde Calata, interview with Liza Key and the author, Cradock, 2 July 2007.

69. See, for instance, Christopher James Colvin, "Performing the Signs of Injury: Critical Perspectives on Traumatic Storytelling after Apartheid" (Ph.D. diss., University of Virginia, 2004); and Fiona C. Ross, *Bearing Witness: Women and the Truth and Reconciliation Commission in South Africa* (Sterling, Va.: Pluto Press, 2003).

70. Krog, *Country of My Skull*.

71. Yazir Henry, "Where Healing Begins," in *Looking Back, Reaching Forward: Reflections on the Truth and Reconciliation Commission in South Africa*, ed. Charles Villa-Vicencio and Wilhelm Verwoerd (London: Zed Books, 2000), 167; Krog, *Country of My Skull*, 70–73.

72. The full text of the TRC's interpretation of Yazir Henry's testimony can be found on the TRC Web site. From the "Read More about the TRC and it's [sic] Committees" link on the main page (www.doj.gov.za/trc), follow these links: "Transcripts" under "Human Rights Violations Committee," then "Cape Town," then "Yazir Henry—torture and detention by security police" in the 6 August 1996 portion of the section labeled "5. Helderberg-Tygerberg 5–7 August 1996" (accessed 19 December 2007).

73. Antjie Krog, "Last Time, This Time," *LitNet*, 20 March 2006, available at http://www.oulitnet.co.za/seminarroom/krog_krog2.asp (accessed 8 May 2006).

74. Krog, *Country of My Skull*, 170.

75. Harris, "Accountability," 31, 33.

76. Laura Moss, "'Nice Audible Crying': Editions, Testimonies, and *Country of My Skull*," *Research in African Literatures* 37, no. 4 (2006): 87.

77. Dirk Klopper, "Narrative Time and the Space of the Image: The Truth of the Lie in Winnie Madikizela-Mandela's Testimony before the Truth and Reconciliation Commission," *Poetics Today* 22, no. 2 (2001): 464–474.

78. Ibid., 471.

79. Ibid. Note that all the women appear to have testified in Xhosa. The English translation available in the transcript is likely based upon the simultaneous translation made by a TRC interpreter on the day of testimony. Clearly much more close analysis of TRC testimony could and should be conducted by consulting the original language of testimony. But as of now, the archive does not make this material available to the public. For another example of a secondary source that makes extensive use of this testimony, see Fiona Ross's analysis of Eunice Miya's testimony in Fiona C. Ross, *Bearing Witness: Women and the Truth and Reconciliation Commission in South Africa* (Sterling, Va.: Pluto Press, 2003), 38–40.

80. Krog, *Country of My Skull,* 251–255.

81. Ibid., 252.

82. Ibid.

83. The police were in a hurry to bury the corpses of the Guguletu Seven, for the dead bodies provided forensic evidence of the attack that contradicted the official police version. For an account of the TRC investigation into this case, see Zenzile Khoisan, *Jakaranda Time: An Investigator's View of South Africa's Truth and Reconciliation Commission* (Cape Town: Garib Communications, 2001).

84. For the transcript of the TRC's interpretation of Cynthia Ngewu's testimony on 23 April 1996, go to the main page of the TRC Web site (www.doj.gov.za/trc), click on the "Read More about the TRC and it's [*sic*] Committees" link in the lower right-hand corner, and follow these links: "Transcripts" under "Human Rights Violations Committee," then "Cape Town," then "Christopher Piet—killing," in the 23 April 1996 portion of the section labeled "1 Heideveld 22–25 April 1996" (accessed 25 April 2005).

85. On the role of women in the TRC process, see Ross, *Bearing Witness.*

86. George Bizos, *No One to Blame? In Pursuit of Justice in South Africa* (Cape Town: David Philip Publishers and Bellville: Mayibuye Books, 1998).

87. Cynthia Ngewu, testimony on 23 April 1996.

88. Tutu, *No Future without Forgiveness,* 115.

89. Cynthia Ngewu, testimony on 23 April 1996.

90. Thuleleni Mcanda, in consultation with Prof. Sizwe Satyo at the University of Cape Town, created fresh Xhosa transcriptions and English translations of the Guguletu Seven TRC testimony. This project was commissioned by the author and was based upon Mcanda's study of both audio and video recordings from the TRC.

91. On the concept of performance as twice-enacted behavior, see Richard Schechner, *Performance Studies: An Introduction* (New York: Routledge, 2002).

92. Cynthia Ngewu, testimony on 23 April 1996.

93. Ibid.

94. Ibid.

95. Ibid. Officer Hendrik Cornelius Johannes Barnard died several years before the Truth and Reconciliation Commission began its work.

96.   Ibid.

97.   Ibid.

98.   Translation by Thuleleni Mcanda in consultation with Prof. Sizwe Satyo.

99.   Eunice Miya provided this testimony on 23 April 1996. To see the TRC's inter-
      pretation, go to the main page of the TRC Web site (www.doj.gov.za/trc), click
      on the "Read More about the TRC and it's [sic] Committees" link in the lower
      right-hand corner, and follow these links: "Transcripts" under "Human Rights
      Violations Committee," then "Cape Town," then "Christopher Piet—killing,"
      in the 23 April 1996 portion of the section labeled "1 Heideveld 22–25 April
      1996" (accessed 25 April 2005).

100. Translation by Thuleleni Mcanda in consultation with Prof. Sizwe Satyo.

101. Sanders, *Ambiguities of Witnessing*, 12.

102. Dozens of citations exist for each of these iconic moments. I provide here just a
      few examples: on Calata's cry, see Krog, *Country of My Skull*, 57. On Mtimkulu,
      see Mark Sanders, "Remembering Apartheid," *Diacritics* 32, nos. 3–4 (2002):
      60–80; and Jillian Edelstein, *Truth & Lies: Stories from the Truth and Reconcili-
      ation Commission in South Africa* (London: Granta Books, 2001), 128–129. On
      Benzien, see, among others, Bester, "Trauma and Truth," 165–171; and Mark
      Sanders, "Renegotiating Responsibility after Apartheid: Listening to Perpetra-
      tor Testimony," *Journal of Gender, Social Policy & the Law* 10, no. 3 (2002): 587–
      595. For the press conference in which Coetzee makes the comment, "Remorse,
      I can assure you, a lot, a hell of a lot," see *TRC Special Report*, 10 November
      1996, videotape in author's possession. Dirk Coetzee formed part of the charac-
      ter study for Pa Ubu in the play *Ubu and the Truth Commission*; see Jane Taylor,
      William Kentridge, and Handspring Puppet Company, *Ubu and the Truth
      Commission* (Cape Town: University of Cape Town Press, 1998), 69. On Lucas
      Sikwepere, see Tutu, *No Future without Forgiveness*, 167. On Winnie Madikizela-
      Mandela's testimony, see Klopper, "Narrative Time," 452–474.

103. For the full text of the TRC's interpretation of Geoffrey Yalolo's testimony on 19
      June 1996, go to the to the main page of the TRC Web site (www.doj.gov.za/trc),
      click on the "Read More about the TRC and it's [sic] Committees" link in the
      lower right-hand corner, and follow these links: "Transcripts" under "Human
      Rights Violations Committee," then "Cape Town," then "Geoffrey Yalolo—
      tortured by police," in the section labeled "3. George, 18–19 June 2007" (ac-
      cessed 25 April 2005).

104. For the full text of the TRC's interpretation of Elsie Jantjie's testimony, go to the
      to the main page of the TRC Web site (www.doj.gov.za/trc), click on the "Read
      More about the TRC and it's [sic] Committees" link in the lower right-hand
      corner, and follow these links: "Transcripts" under "Human Rights Violations
      Committee," then "Cape Town," then "8. Karoo, 7–9 October 1996," then "Len-
      nox Maphalane—killing" under the date 23 April 1996 (accessed 25 May 2009).

105. For the full text of the TRC's interpretation of Sisana Mary Maphalane's testi-
      mony, go to the to the main page of the TRC Web site (www.doj.gov.za/trc),
      click on the "Read More about the TRC and it's [sic] Committees" link in the
      lower right-hand corner, and follow these links: "Transcripts" under "Human
      Rights Violations Committee," then "Cape Town," then "1. Heideveld, 22–25
      April 1996," then "Sophie Butele—killing" under the date 8 October 1996 (ac-
      cessed 25 May 2009).

106.   Wisani Sibuyi at the TRC interpreters' retreat sponsored by the Colonnades Theatre Lab/*Truth in Translation* Project, March 2003.

107.   For the full text of the TRC's interpretation of Nomusa Shando's testimony, go to the to the main page of the TRC Web site (www.doj.gov.za/trc), click on the "Read More about the TRC and it's [*sic*] Committees" link in the lower right-hand corner, and follow these links: "Transcripts" under "Human Rights Violations Committee," then "Durban," then "Day 3" in the section "8. Empangeni, 4–6 November 1996" (accessed 26 May 2009).

4. Eyes and Ears of the Nation

The first epigraph is from Daniel Dayan and Elihu Katz, *Media Events: The Live Broadcasting of History* (Cambridge: Cambridge University Press, 1992), 78. The second is from Philip Auslander, *Liveness: Performance as Mediatized Culture* (New York: Routledge, 1999), 128–129.

1.   Albie Sachs, interview with the author, Johannesburg, 29 June 2007.

2.   Ibid.

3.   Auslander, *Liveness,* 128–129.

4.   Jonas Barish, *The Antitheatrical Prejudice* (Berkeley: University of California Press, 1981).

5.   Dayan and Katz, *Media Events,* 17.

6.   Ibid., 100–101.

7.   Janet Cherry, John Daniel, and Madeleine Fullard, "Researching the 'Truth': A View from inside the Truth and Reconciliation Commission," in *Commissioning the Past: Understanding South Africa's Truth and Reconciliation Commission,* ed. Deborah Posel and Graeme Simpson (Johannesburg: Witwatersrand University Press, 2002), 34–35.

8.   Sachs, interview with the author.

9.   Max du Preez was formerly an editor of the newspaper *Vrye Weekblad* (The Free Weekly), a paper founded by Afrikaner journalists who were frustrated by the timidity of the mainstream press under apartheid. Published between 1988 and 1994, *Vrye Weekblad* was eventually bankrupted because of a lawsuit brought against it by General Lotha Neethling of the South African Security Police.

10.   Annelies Verdoolaege, "Reconciliation. The South African Truth and Reconciliation Commission: Deconstruction of a Multilayered Archive" (Ph.D. thesis, Universiteit Gent, Belgium, 2005); Annelies Verdoolaege, "Media Representations of the South African Truth and Reconciliation Commission and Their Commitment to Reconciliation," *Journal of African Cultural Studies* 17, no. 2 (2005): 181–199; Tanya Goodman, "Setting the Stage for a 'New' South Africa: A Cultural Approach to the Truth and Reconciliation Commission" (Ph.D. diss., Yale University, 2004).

11.   As a well-produced, widely circulated program, *TRC Special Report* deserves a much more detailed analysis than it has heretofore received. Fortunately, the entire series has recently been digitized by the Yale Law School Lillian Goldman Library and is now accessible via streaming video on the Internet at www.law.yale

.edu/trc/index.htm (accessed 15 August 2008). Viewers should be warned that the Yale links are not always accurate: sometimes when one clicks on a particular episode, the wrong one is loaded. Also some of the episodes are misnumbered; the content of these episodes does not correspond with the TRC summary report listing of when and where various hearings occurred, and the dates of these episodes do not correspond with the dates on videotapes I bought from the SABC of the entire series of *TRC Special Report.* When there was a discrepancy between the Yale Web site and the videos I purchased from the SABC, I followed the dates on my videotapes. The Yale digitized set is also missing some episodes. Despite these problems, the digitization of the series through Yale is a tremendous archival resource, and hopefully in time these cataloging and technical errors will be remedied.

12.   Dayan and Katz, *Media Events,* 78–118.

13.   *TRC Special Report,* 4 May 1997.

14.   TRC, *Truth and Reconciliation Commission of South Africa Report* (London: MacMillan, 1999), 6:654.

15.   For the full text of the TRC's interpretation of Evelina Puleng Moloko's testimony before the Human Rights Violations Committee on 4 February 1997, go to the to the main page of the TRC Web site (www.doj.gov.za/trc), click on the "Read More about the TRC and it's [*sic*] Committees" link in the lower right-hand corner, and follow these links: "Transcripts" under "Human Rights Violations Committee," then "Johannesburg," then "Evelina Puleng Moloko" under "Duduza, 4 Feb 1997" in the section labeled "14. Duduza, Benoni, and Vosloorus, 4–7 February 1997" (accessed 5 July 2008).

16.   TRC, *Truth and Reconciliation Commission of South Africa Report* (Cape Town: Truth and Reconciliation Commission, 2003), 7:821. Note: the spelling of "Skhosana" in the final report is inconsistent with Krog's spelling as "Skosana." Inconsistent spelling of African surnames was an endemic problem even within the truth commission, according to Nicky Rousseau, a former researcher for the Truth and Reconciliation Commission. Phone conversation with the author, 10 September 2005.

17.   Antjie Krog, *Country of My Skull: Guilt, Sorrow, and the Limits of Forgiveness in the New South Africa* (1998; New York: Three Rivers Press, 1999), 63.

18.   *TRC Special Report,* 23 June 1996, 27 October 1996, 9 February 1997, and 9 March 1997.

19.   Criticisms of television coverage of the TRC are covered later this chapter.

20.   *TRC Special Report,* 23 June 1996, starting at 19:47.

21.   TRC, *Truth and Reconciliation Commission of South Africa Report,* 7:928.

22.   *TRC Special Report,* 23 June 1996, at 21:46

23.   Michelle Parlevliet, "Considering Truth. Dealing with a Legacy of Gross Human Rights Violations," *Netherlands Quarterly of Human Rights* 16, no. 2 (1998): 163; Verdoolaege, "Media Representations," 190.

24.   Evelina Puleng Moloko, testimony on 4 February 1997.

25.   *TRC Special Report,* 9 February 1997.

26.   *TRC Special Report,* 15 June 1997.

27.   The Pebco Three were Sipho Hashe, Champion Galela, and Qaqawuli Godolozi. In 1985, they disappeared from an airport in Port Elizabeth. They were members of the Port Elizabeth Black Civic Organisation (PEBCO), and the South African Security Police are suspected as being responsible for their deaths.

28. *TRC Special Report,* 21 April 1996.

29. On the concept of media events, see Dayan and Katz, *Media Events.*

30. Joel Joffe, *The Rivonia Story* (Cape Town: Mayibuye Books, University of Western Cape, 1995), 26.

31. Ibid., 60.

32. On broadcasting and press censorship in South Africa, see Christopher Merrett, *A Culture of Censorship: Secrecy and Intellectual Repression in South Africa* (Macon, Ga.: Mercer University Press, 1995). See also Ruth Tomaselli, Keyan Tomaselli, and Johan Muller, eds., *Broadcasting in South Africa* (London: James Currey, 1987); and Keyan Tomaselli, Ruth Tomaselli, and Johan Muller, eds., *The Press in South Africa* (New York: St. Martin's Press, 1989).

33. Robert B. Horowitz, *Communication and Democratic Reform in South Africa* (New York: Cambridge University Press, 2001), 68.

34. Krog, *Country of My Skull,* 46.

35. *TRC Special Report,* 1 December 1996, at approximately 34.40. Evita is a fictional character invented by the famous drag performer, comedian, and political gadfly of the apartheid state Pieter-Dirk Uys. Evita first appeared in 1978 as the fictive wife of a National Party Member of Parliament and author of a gossip column. She gradually became a performed stage persona that Uys embodied in drag. Over the years, Evita has presented the "cactus of democracy" in Parliament and trekked all over South Africa promoting democratic elections. She has even run for president! For more about Evita, see "Tannie Evita Bezuidenhout," *Tonight* (Johannesburg), 29 October 2003, available at http://www.tonight.co.za/index.php?fSectionId=442&fArticleId=271188.

36. Priscilla Hayner, *Unspeakable Truths: Confronting State Terror and Atrocity* (New York: Routledge, 2001), 5.

37. Sachs, interview with the author.

38. Anthea Garman, "Media Creation: How the TRC and the Media Have Impacted on Each Other," *Track Two* 6, nos. 3–4 (December 1997), 36; Graeme Simpson and Paul van Zyl, "South Africa's Truth and Reconciliation Commission," *Les Temps Modernes* 585 (November–December 1995): 394–407.

39. Simpson and Zyl, "South Africa's Truth and Reconciliation Commission," 394–407.

40. Ibid.

41. On the TRC's relationship with stills photographers, see TRC, *Truth and Reconciliation Commission of South Africa Report* (London: MacMillan, 1999), 1:358. The highest level of media coverage was for high-profile hearings such as that of the Mandela United Football Club. See *TRC Special Report,* 30 November 1997 and 7 December 1997.

42. *TRC Special Report,* 7 December 1997, at 23:39.

43. Wendy Orr, *From Biko to Basson: Wendy Orr's Search for the Soul of South Africa as a Commissioner of the TRC* (Saxonwold, South Africa: Contra Press, 2000), 90–91.

44. TRC, *Truth and Reconciliation Commission of South Africa Report* (Cape Town: Truth and Reconciliation Commission, 2003), 6:30.

45. For a list of these stations, see Horowitz, *Communication and Democratic Reform in South Africa,* 162.

46. Joe Thloloe, "Showing Faces, Hearing Voices, Tugging at Emotions: Televising the Truth and Reconciliation Commission," *Neiman Reports* 52, no. 4 (1998):

53; Max du Preez, interview with the author, Napier, Western Cape, 18 December 2006.

47.   Zubeida Jaffer and Karin Cronjé, *Cameras, Microphones and Pens* (Cape Town: Institute for Justice and Reconciliation, 2004), 22; Thloloe, "Showing Faces, Hearing Voices, Tugging at Emotions," 53.

48.   See TRC, *Truth and Reconciliation Commission of South Africa Report*, 1:356. The following radio stations carried weekly TRC programs with excerpts of selected testimony: Lasedi (SeSotho) on Sunday evenings; SA FM on Friday mornings; Ukhozi (isiZulu), Umhlobo Wenene (isiXhosa), Thobela (Sipedi), Ikwekwezi (Ndebele), Motsweding (SeTswana), Munghana Lonene (xiTsonga), Ligwalagwala (SiSwati) on Friday evenings; and Radio Sonder Grense (Afrikaans) on Monday mornings after 8. These programs are mentioned at the end of the *TRC Special Report* broadcast on 19 October 1997.

49.   John Allen, e-mail correspondence with the author, 2 December 2006.

50.   TRC, *Truth and Reconciliation Commission of South Africa Report*, 1:357.

51.   Ibid.

52.   For a cinematic rendering of this, see the video *Red Dust* (2004, BBC Films presentation in association with Videovision Entertainment and the Industrial Development Corp. of South Africa; dir. Tom Hooper).

53.   Orr, *From Biko to Basson*, 173.

54.   Gillian Slovo, "Making History: South Africa's Truth and Reconciliation Commission," *OpenDemocracy*, 12 May 2002, available at www.opendemocracy.net/democracy-apologypolitics/article_818.jsp (accessed 28 May 2007).

55.   Orr, *From Biko to Basson*, 90–91.

56.   TRC, *Truth and Reconciliation Commission of South Africa Report*, 1:358.

57.   *TRC Special Report*, 21 April 1996.

58.   Ibid.

59.   This phrase comes from a summary episode that *TRC Special Report* prepared as a retrospective view of the TRC. See the 29 June 1997 episode.

60.   *TRC Special Report*, 8 September 1996.

61.   *TRC Special Report*, 17 August 1997.

62.   *TRC Special Report*, 21 April 1996 and 26 May 1996.

63.   *TRC Special Report*, 29 June 1997. This overview segment was rebroadcast several times, sometimes slightly reedited; see the episodes that aired on 29 October 1997 and 29 March 1998.

64.   Du Preez, interview with the author.

65.   Ibid.

66.   Ibid.

67.   Ibid.

68.   Hugh Lewin, "The Never-Ending Story," *Track Two* 7, no. 4 (1998): 41. New staff tended to be more racially diverse but less experienced in broadcast journalism.

69.   Du Preez, interview with the author.

70.   Ibid.

71.   See Mathatha Tsedu, "Questioning if Guilt without Punishment Will Lead to Reconciliation: The Black Press Relives Its Own Horrors and Seeks Justice," *Nieman Reports* 52, no. 4 (1998): 56; Lewin, "The Never-Ending Story," 41.

72.   *TRC Special Report*, 1 December 1996, at 34.40.

73.   Claudia Braude, "Media Should Get the Truth Out," *Mail & Guardian Online* (Johannesburg), 7 February 1997 (accessed 11 July 2006).

74. Ibid.

75. Du Preez, interview with the author.

76. On pass laws, see *TRC Special Report,* 2 February 1997, starting at 18:40; and *TRC Special Report,* 24 November 1996 starting at 29:00 (this is a segment on the colored Karoo population). On forced removals and residential segregation, see *TRC Special Report,* 24 November 1996; see this episode also for the destruction of Sophiatown (starting at approximately 21:32). On District Six, see *TRC Special Report,* 5 May 1996, starting at 3:30. On the hostel system and coerced labor, see *TRC Special Report,* 23 February 1997, starting at 16.00. On Bantu education, see *TRC Special Report,* 4 May 1997, starting at 8:53.

77. The mandate of the Truth and Reconciliation Commission was to "focus on what might be termed 'bodily integrity rights', rights that are enshrined in the new South African Constitution and under international law. These include the right to life, the right to be free from torture, the right to be free from cruel, inhuman, or degrading treatment or punishment, and the right to freedom and security of the person, including freedom from abduction and arbitrary and prolonged detention." See TRC, *Truth and Reconciliation Commission of South Africa Report,* 1:64.

78. Mahmood Mamdani, "Amnesty or Impunity? A Preliminary Critique of the Report of the Truth and Reconciliation Commission of South Africa (TRC)," *Diacritics* 32, no. 3 (2002): 37.

79. Ibid., 33–59.

80. Du Preez, interview with the author.

81. Verdoolaege, "Media Representations," 194.

82. Dayan and Katz, *Media Events,* 91.

83. Gustav Thiel, "Truth on a Shoestring," *Mail & Guardian* (Johannesburg), 1 August 1997 (accessed 11 July 2006).

84. Thloloe, "Showing Faces, Hearing Voices, Tugging at Emotions," 53.

85. Du Preez, interview with author.

86. Ibid. See also Thloloe, "Showing Faces, Hearing Voices, Tugging at Emotions," 53.

87. The length of the program changed over time. Early episodes ran about forty minutes, but the program was shortened to thirty minutes in January 1997. It was finally expanded to sixty minutes in October 1997.

88. Alex Boraine, *A Country Unmasked: Inside South Africa's Truth and Reconciliation Commission* (New York: Oxford University Press, 2000), 272.

89. Du Preez, interview with the author.

90. Max du Preez, "When Cowboys Cry," *Rhodes Journalism Review,* special edition: *The Media & the TRC* (1997), available at www.rjr.ru.ac.za/no14.html (accessed 4 August 2004).

91. Verdoolaege, "Media Representations," 191; Jaffer and Cronjé, *Cameras, Microphones and Pens,* 13.

92. Deborah Posel, "Truth? The View from South Africa's Truth and Reconciliation Commission," in *Keywords: Truth,* by Ali Benmakhalouf, Ganesh Devy, Yang Guorong, Bertrand Ogilvie, Douglas Patterson, and Deborah Posel (New York: Other Press, 2004), 17.

93. See Rosemary Nagy, "Violence, Amnesty and Transitional Law: 'Private' Acts and 'Public' Truth in South Africa," *African Journal of Legal Studies* 1, no. 1 (2004): 14. Nagy's is one of the few sources to provide demographic analysis of those who applied to the TRC for amnesty. One of the most breathtaking failures

of the TRC's truth-for-amnesty deal was that the Amnesty Committee deliberations happened so slowly that the final report in 1998 and even the codicil to the report in 2003 published little meaningful data and analysis on the demographics of amnesty applicants. It is thus not widely known that 77 percent of these applicants were already incarcerated. See "Notes on a Briefing by Advocate Denzil Potgieter, S.C., Chair of the Media and Communications Committee of the Truth and Reconciliation Commission at the Parliamentary Media Briefing, 7 August 1998," South African Government Information Web site, available at www.info.gov.za/speeches/1998/98811_trc9811098.htm (accessed 19 May 2007). For more on amnesty and the TRC, see Charles Villa-Vicencio and Erik Doxtader, *The Provocations of Amnesty: Memory, Justice, and Impunity* (Trenton, N.J.: Africa World Press, 2003).

94. Ron Krabill, "Symbiosis: Mass Media and the Truth and Reconciliation Commission of South Africa," *Media, Culture & Society* 23, no. 5 (2001): 582; Verdoolaege, "Media Representations," 190.

95. Edward Bird and Zureida Garda, "Reporting the Truth Commission: Analysis of Media Coverage of the Truth and Reconciliation Commission of South Africa," *Gazette* 59, nos. 4–5 (1997): 338.

96. Verdoolaege, "Media Representations," 188

97. Ibid.; Rory Bester, "Trauma and Truth," in *Experiments with Truth: Transitional Justice and the Processes of Truth and Reconciliation,* ed. Okwui Enwezor, Carlos Basaualdo, Ute Meta Bauer, Susanne Ghez, Sarat Maharaj, Mark Nash, and Octavio Zaya (Ostfildern-Ruit, Germany: Hatje Cantz Publishers, 2002), 169.

98. Posel, "Truth?" 17.

99. Verdoolaege, "Media Representations," 194; Bird and Garda, "Reporting the Truth Commission," 342.

100. Verdoolaege, "Media Representations," 188; Bird and Garda, "Reporting the Truth Commission," 340.

101. Posel, "Truth?" 17–18.

102. Krabill, "Symbiosis," 582.

103. For a theatre form that is more Marxist in orientation and a critique of Artistotelian theatre, see Augusto Boal, *Theater of the Oppressed* (New York: Urizen Books, 1979).

104. Du Preez, interview with author, 18 December 2006.

105. Ibid.

106. Ibid.

107. See the Afterword to this volume.

108. Among these memoirs are Boraine, *A Country Unmasked*; Pumla Gobodo-Madikizela, *A Human Being Died That Night: A South African Story of Forgiveness* (Boston: Houghton Mifflin, 2003); Zenzile Khoisan, *Jakaranda Time: An Investigator's View of South Africa's Truth and Reconciliation Commission* (Cape Town: Garib Communications, 2001); Krog, *Country of My Skull*; Piet Meiring, *Chronicle of the Truth Commission* (Vanderbijlpark, South Africa: Carpe Diem Books, 1999); Orr, *From Biko to Basson*; and Desmond Tutu, *No Future without Forgiveness,* 1st ed. (New York: Doubleday, 1999).

109. Former SABC editor-in-chief Joe Thloloe reported that *TRC Special Report* had a team of five core producers, of whom three were black and two were white. See Thloloe, "Showing Faces, Hearing Voices, Tugging at Emotions," 53. Pro-

ducers who stayed with the series were Anneliese Burgess, Benedict Motau, Gael Reagon, and Rene Schiebe.

110. The one exception to this is the veteran TRC producer Jann Turner. Her father was executed before her eyes as a child, and this story was one of the many explored by the TRC. Turner lived in exile for many years, returning to South Africa both to find her father's killers and to cover the TRC for *Special Report*. A moving autobiographical documentary by Turner aired on *TRC Special Report* on 7 July 1996.

111. Thiel, "Truth on a Shoestring."

112. Ibid.

113. See, for instance, the closing moments of *TRC Special Report,* 8 September 1996.

114. Du Preez, "When Cowboys Cry."

115. See interview with Hayner, *TRC Special Report,* 8 February 1998, at 42:00.

116. The Yale library collection of *TRC Special Report* offers finding aids developed by the library, including an index of names of cases and people who appear on the program. See www.law.yale.edu/trc/index.htm, accessed 20 August 2008. However, problems exist with this resource; see note 11 above.

5. Dragons in the Living Room

The first epigraph is from Thokozani Mtshali, "Tutu Ignores Important Role of Whites— DA," *Cape Times,* 24 April 2006. The second is from F. W. de Klerk, "'I Didn't Know of the Illegal Activities of Security Forces,'" *Sunday Independent* (Johannesburg), 30 April 2006. The third is quoted in David Welsh, "Coping with the Past Imperfect," *Business Day* (Johannesburg), 25 April 2006, 11. For more about Evita Bezuidenhout, see note 35 of chapter 4.

1. Alex Boraine, Janet Levy, and Ronel Scheffer, eds., *Dealing with the Past: Truth and Reconciliation in South Africa,* 2nd ed. (Cape Town: Institute for Democracy in South Africa, 1997).

2. "Promotion of National Unity and Reconciliation Act, Act no. 34, 1995," *Government Gazette,* 26 July 1995, 16579. Available online at www.doj.gov.za/trc/legal/act9534.htm (accessed 17 March 2009).

3. Sheena Adams, "F. W. Backed TRC, but 'It Failed' in a Big Way," *Pretoria News,* 8 April 2006, 1.

4. TRC, *Truth and Reconciliation Commission of South Africa Report,* vol. 1 (London: MacMillan, 1999), 4.

5. Tina Rosenberg, "Latin America," in Boraine, Levy, and Scheffer, eds., *Dealing with the Past: Truth and Reconciliation in South Africa,* 66.

6. Mary Burton, "Five Views," in Boraine, Levy, and Scheffer, eds., *Dealing with the Past: Truth and Reconciliation in South Africa,* 122.

7. See chapter 4 in this book for further analysis of media coverage of the TRC.

8. Lars Buur, "'In the Name of the Victims': The Politics of Compensation in the Work of the South African Truth and Reconciliation Commission," in *Political Transition: Politics and Cultures,* ed. Paul Gready (Sterling, Va.: Pluto Press, 2003), 148.

9. Yasmin Sooka quoted in David Yutar, "'Prosecute Apartheid Politicians,'" *Cape Argus*, 21 April 2006 (accessed 11 July 2007).

10. Christopher J. Colvin, "Overview of the Reparations Program in South Africa," in *The Handbook of Reparations*, ed. Pablo de Greiff (New York: Oxford University Press, 2006), 176–177.

11. "Promotion of National Unity and Reconciliation Act."

12. Howard Varney quoted in David Yutar, "Victims of Apartheid Let Down," *Saturday Weekend Argus* (Cape Town), 22 April 2006, 13; see also Piers Pigou, "There Are More Truths to Be Uncovered before We Can Achieve Reconciliation," *Sunday Independent* (Johannesburg), 23 April 2006. Even if other authors might wish to improve upon the report's uneven authorial voice, dry prose, and massive scale by writing more accessible, succinct, and compelling accounts, their ability to do so is severely curtailed by the limits currently placed on access to the TRC archive.

13. Diana Taylor, *The Archive and the Repertoire: Performing Cultural Memory in the Americas* (Durham, N.C.: Duke University Press, 2003), 20.

14. The National Prosecuting Authority called Ginn Fourie, the mother of Lyndi Fourie, who died in the Heidelberg Tavern attack, "infinitely naïve" for her decision to forgive Letlapa Mphahlele, the commander who ordered the attack. See "Victim's Mom Backs Tavern Killings Leader," *Cape Argus* (Cape Town), 17 November 2006, 10.

15. The Forgiveness Project, "Ginn Fourie & Letlapa Mphahlele," available at www.theforgivenessproject.com/stories/fourie-letlapa (accessed 21 February 2007).

16. Taylor, *The Archive and the Repertoire*, 20.

17. The phrase "living memorial of reconstruction" comes from Albie Sachs, who is quoted in Boraine, Levy, and Scheffer, *Dealing with the Past*, 130.

18. The phrase "the prosaic rooms of our later understanding" is from Walter Benjamin, "Berlin Chronicle," in *Reflections: Essays, Aphorisms, Autobiographical Writings*, ed. Peter Dementz (New York: Harcourt Brace Jovanovich, 1978), 26. Desmond Tutu said that the TRC would become "the paradigm for the rest of the world" if it "got it right" when Mandela and De Klerk were awarded the Nobel Prize for Peace in 1993. Quoted in Allister Haddon Sparks, *Tomorrow Is Another Country: The Inside Story of South Africa's Road to Change* (Chicago: University of Chicago Press, 1996), 10.

19. Nomfundo Walaza quoted in Sivuyile Mangxamba, "A Decade On, TRC has 'Unfinished Business,'" *Cape Argus*, 24 November 2006, 12.

20. Christelle Terreblanche, "'Many Still Await the Promised Land,'" *Sunday Argus* (Cape Town), 9 April 2006, 23.

21. Max du Preez, "TRC a Great Achievement," *Daily News* (Durban), 6 April 2006, 18.

22. Max du Preez, "Greig Reviewed TRC, Not the Play: Don't Miss It," *Sunday Independent* (Johannesburg), 17 September 2006, 6.

23. The three TRC conferences during this anniversary year were The Truth and Reconciliation Commission—Ten Years On, sponsored by the Institute for Justice and Reconciliation on 20–21 April 2006; Memory, Narrative & Forgiveness: Reflecting on Ten Years of South Africa's Truth and Reconciliation Commission, 22–27 November 2006 at the University of Cape Town; and Ten Years of the TRC, an exhibition and conference at the Red Location Museum in Port Elizabeth, 14 December 2006.

24. Charles Villa-Vicencio, "The Unfinished Business of the TRC," *SA Reconciliation Barometer* 4, no. 1 (2006): 3, 7.

25. See Brian Raftopoulos, "Gains and Perils of Reconciliation," *Cape Times* (Cape Town), 4 May 2006, 11.

26. "The Pain of Apartheid Still Festers," *Pretoria News,* 24 April 2006, 9.

27. Mahmood Mamdani, "The Truth According to the TRC," in *Politics of Memory: Truth, Healing and Social Justice,* ed. Ifi Amadiume and Abdullahi An-Na'im (London: Zed Books, 2000), 176–183.

28. Salaudin Majnoon, "Whites Should Be Thankful," *Weekly Mail & Guardian* (Johannesburg), 4 May 2006, 25.

29. Terreblanche, "'Many Still Await the Promised Land,'" 23.

30. Mariette le Roux, "TRC Could Have Done More to Narrow the Wealth Gap, Says Tutu," *The Herald* (Port Elizabeth), 28 November 2006, 1.

31. "The Past Will Not Be Past Until More Information on Apartheid Killings Emerges," *Sunday Independent* (Johannesburg), 9 April 2006, 5.

32. Bobby Jordan, "Mother of Slain Activist Finally Sees Justice Done," *Sunday Times* (Johannesburg), 15 January 2006, 9; SAPA, "Apartheid-Era Cops Jailed for 1987 Murder," *Pretoria News,* 26 November 2005, 3.

33. "Truth and Justice," *Business Day* (Johannesburg), 19 January 2006, 1.

34. "Tutu Laments Lack of Apartheid Prosecutions," *Independent Online* (Cape Town), 15 December 2005 (accessed 15 July 2007).

35. "Old Foes and Today's Woes," *The Citizen* (Johannesburg), 3 May 2006, 12.

36. Patrick Laurence, "Uneven Prosecutions Could Rekindle Bitter Divisions of Past," *Sunday Independent* (Johannesburg), 29 January 2006, 6; Wyndham Hartley, "Parties Warn on Apartheid Cases," *Business Day* (Johannesburg), 27 January 2006, 4.

37. "Victims' Groups Moot Challenge to 'Backdoor Amnesty,'" *Sunday Independent* (Johannesburg), 9 April 2006, 1; "Prosecution Amendment Raises Concern," *The Citizen* (Johannesburg), 31 March 2006, 10; Linda Daniels, "Offenders Get 'Another Bite at Amnesty Cherry,'" *Cape Times,* 21 April 2006, 5.

38. Christelle Terreblanche, "Lawyers Appeal Against Apartheid Amnesties," *Sunday Independent* (Johannesburg), 16 April 2006, 1.

39. Razina Munshi, "Another Chance at Amnesty?" *Financial Mail* (Johannesburg), 19 May 2006, 1.

40. Daniels, "Offenders Get 'Another Bite at Amnesty Cherry,'" 5.

41. Moshoeshoe Monare, "Vlok's Penance 'Did Not Wash Away the Poison,'" *The Sunday Independent* (Johannesburg), 27 August 2006, 3.

42. "Feet Washed in Apartheid Apology," *BBC News,* 28 August 2006 (accessed 15 July 2007).

43. Karyn Maughan, "Vlok's Foot Washing Apology to Chikane Flayed," *Pretoria News,* 28 August 2006, 2; SAPA, "Vlok Apology Is 'Not Enough,'" *Independent Online,* 28 August 2006 (accessed 15 July 2007).

44. Christelle Terreblanche, "Mbeki Hails Vlok for Repenting," *Sunday Independent* (Johannesburg), 10 September 2006, 4.

45. "Feet Washed in Apartheid Apology."

46. Angela Quintal and SAPA, "Apartheid Pains Must Be Resolved," *The Star* (Johannesburg), 28 August 2006, 3.

47. Staff Reporter, "Tell All on Killings, Vlok Urged," *Cape Argus,* 4 September 2006, 5.

48.   Max du Preez, "Why Did God Not Move You to Speak Earlier?" *The Star* (Johannesburg), 31 August 2006, 20.

49.   Monare, "Vlok's Penance 'Did Not Wash Away the Poison.'"

50.   Jacobus Du Pisani and Kwang-Su Kim argue that commissioners could control the interpretation of testimonies given by witnesses in HRVC hearings "by stressing certain topics and through elicitation. This made it possible for the TRC to impose its viewpoints, objectives and framework on participants." Jacobus S. Du Pisani and Kwang-Su Kim, "Establishing the Truth about the Apartheid Past: Historians and the South African Truth and Reconciliation Commission," *African Studies Review* 8, no. 1 (2004): 82.

51.   Max du Preez, "It Is Time to Leave the Past Behind," *The Star* (Johannesburg), 27 January 2005, 1.

52.   The Forgiveness Project, "Ginn Fourie & Letlapa Mphahlele."

53.   Angela Quintal and Linda Daniels, "Victim's Mom Backs Tavern Killings Leader," *Cape Argus,* 17 November 2006, 10.

54.   "Victim's Mom Backs Tavern Killings Leader."

55.   Richard Wilson, *The Politics of Truth and Reconciliation in South Africa: Legitimizing the Post-Apartheid State* (Cambridge: Cambridge University Press, 2001).

56.   Christelle Terreblanche, "TRC Joins Fight as Apartheid Victims and State Clash," *Sunday Independent* (Johannesburg), 22 January 2006, 3.

57.   For recent developments in the Alien Tort Claims Act lawsuit, see Simon Barber, "South Africa: Legal Journey into Historical Darkness Not a Bright Idea for Country," *Business Day* (Johannesburg), 17 April 2009, available at http://allafrica.com/stories/200904170012.html (accessed 25 May 2009).

58.   For an explanation of the legal basis upon which the TRC determined apartheid to be a crime against humanity, see the appendix to chapter 1 of TRC, *Truth and Reconciliation Commission of South Africa Report,* 1:94–102. On the duty to prosecute, see Juan Mendez, Tina Rosenberg, Aryeh Neier, and Jose Zalaquett, "Four Views," in Boraine, Levy, and Scheffer, eds., *Dealing with the Past: Truth and Reconciliation in South Africa,* 88–106.

59.   Mendez, Rosenberg, Neier, and Zalaquett, "Four Views," in Boraine, Levy, and Scheffer, *Dealing with the Past: Truth and Reconciliation in South Africa,* 101.

60.   Ibid., 106.

61.   Terry Leonard, "SA Reaction to Botha's Death 'Remarkable,'" *Independent Online* (Johannesburg), 3 November 2006 (accessed 24 May 2008).

62.   Christelle Terreblanche, "Missing PW Documents Mystery," *Sunday Tribune* (Durban, South Africa), 5 November 2006, 5.

63.   Ibid.

64.   Verne Harris, "Contesting Remembering and Forgetting: The Archive of South Africa's Truth and Reconciliation Commission," *Innovation* 24 (June 2002): 4; Zelda Venter, "The Secret Files They Don't Want You to See," *The Star* (Johannesburg), 29 January 2004, 3; Christelle Terreblanche, "Deadline Looms for Transfer of TRC Spy Files," *The Star* (Johannesburg), 22 September 2003, 3.

65.   Sipho Masondo and Louis Oelofse, "Cradock Four Film Gets Boost from Court," *The Herald* (Port Elizabeth), 15 September 2006, 1.

66.   AFP, "Mourners Gather for PW Botha," *iAfrica.com News,* 8 November 2006 (accessed 11 July 2007).

67.   Sheree Russouw, "The Earth Yields Up to the Quest for Justice," *Saturday Star* (Johannesburg), 19 March 2005.

68. TRC, *Truth and Reconciliation Commission of South Africa Report,* vol. 6 (Cape Town: Truth and Reconciliation Commission), 107.

69. "MK Graves to Be Opened Soon," *SABC News,* 8 March 2005. The NPA does not rule out the possibility that it will use forensic evidence unearthed through exhumations for future prosecutions.

70. Milan Kundera, *The Book of Laughter and Forgetting,* trans. Aaron Asher (1979; New York: Harper Perennial, 1996) 4.

71. Leonard, "SA Reaction to Botha's Death 'Remarkable.'"

72. Ibid.

73. J. H. Hofmeyr, *Sixth Round Report: The SA Reconciliation Barometer Survey* (Wynberg: Institute for Justice and Reconciliation, 2006), available at http://www.ijr.org.za/politicalanalysis/reconcbar/reports/6%20sixthroundreport/view?searchterm=Sixth%20Round%20Report (accessed 26 May 2009). See also James L. Gibson, *Overcoming Apartheid: Can Truth Reconcile a Divided Nation?* (New York: Russell Sage Foundation, 2004); and James L. Gibson, "The Truth about Truth and Reconciliation in South Africa," *International Political Science Review* 26, no. 4 (2005): 341–361.

74. Hofmeyr, *Sixth Round Report,* 46–47; Leonard, "SA Reaction to Botha's Death 'Remarkable.'"

75. Hofmeyr, *Sixth Round Report,* 69.

76. Ibid.

77. Ibid., 39, 67.

78. Gibson, "The Truth about Truth and Reconciliation in South Africa," 341–361. See also Gibson, *Overcoming Apartheid: Can Truth Reconcile a Divided Nation?*

79. Gibson, "The Truth about Truth and Reconciliation in South Africa," 344.

80. Ibid., 347.

81. *Truth in Translation* is an ongoing collaborative project. Its Web site says this about the play's authorship: "The script was developed in a collaboration over time between a collective of South African actors, director/creator Michael Lessac, and writer/collaborator Paavo Tom Tammi." See http://www.truthintranslation.org/index.php/v2/the_play (accessed 25 May 2009).

82. Albie Sachs, address to the Cape Town Memory Project, 11 June 2005, Cape Town City Hall, available at http://www.ijr.org.za/recon-recon/archives/memory-project-archives/city-meeting-june-11-2005 (accessed 24 May 2008).

83. Mary Burton, Dumisa Ntsebeza, Albie Sachs, Andre du Toit, and Wilmot James, "Five Views," in Boraine, Levy, and Scheffer, eds., *Dealing with the Past: Truth and Reconciliation in South Africa,* 130.

84. Ciraj Rassool, "Making the District Six Museum in Cape Town," *Museum International* 58, nos. 1–2 (2006): 11.

85. Ciraj Rassool and Sandra Prosalendis, eds., *Recalling Community in Cape Town: Creating and Curating the District Six Museum* (Cape Town: District Six Museum Foundation 2001). See also chapter 2 in Annie E. Coombes, *History after Apartheid: Visual Culture and Public Memory in a Democratic South Africa* (Durham, N.C.: Duke University Press, 2003).

86. See chapter 2 in Coombes, *History after Apartheid.* See also the Robben Island Web site, available at www.robben-island.org.za (accessed 4 April 2009); and Loren Kruger, "Robben Island Museum," *Public Culture* 12, no. 3 (2000): 787–791. On Freedom Park and the Red Location Museum, see Gary Baines, "The

Politics of Public History in Post-Apartheid South Africa," available at academic.sun.ac.za/history/news/baines_g.pdf (accessed 27 February 2007).

87. Mark Gevisser, "From the Ruins: The Constitution Hill Project," *Public Culture* 16, no. 3 (2004): 507–519.

88. Ibid., 511.

89. Michael Ignatieff, "Articles of Faith," *Index on Censorship* 5 (September/October 1996): 110–122; Theodor W. Adorno, "What Does Coming to Terms with the Past Mean?" in *Bitburg in Moral and Political Perspective,* ed. Geoffrey H. Hartman (Bloomington: Indiana University Press, 1986), 114–129; Alex Boraine and Janet Levy, eds., *The Healing of a Nation?* (Cape Town: Justice in Transition, 1995).

90. Ignatieff, "Articles of Faith," 110. See also Adorno, "What Does Coming to Terms with the Past Mean?"

91. Meg Samuelson, "Cracked Vases and Untidy Seams: Narrative Structure and Closure in the Truth and Reconciliation Commission and South African Fiction," *Current Writing* 15, no. 2 (2003): 65.

92. Albie Sachs, "Five Views," in Boraine, Levy, and Scheffer, eds., *Dealing with the Past,* 129; emphasis mine. A similar idea has been used in relationship to the Holocaust with the notion of *tikkun,* a Hebrew word that connotes mending rather than reconciliation. See Geoffrey H. Hartman, "Introduction," in *Bitburg in Moral and Political Perspective,* ed. Geoffrey H. Hartman (Bloomington: Indiana University Press, 1986), 10.

93. Ignatieff, "Articles of Faith," 110.

94. Philip Miller, *REwind: A Cantata for Voice, Tape, and Testimony,* live performance at St. George's Cathedral, Cape Town, 16 December 2006.

95. *The Human Rights Cantata,* written by the priest Esteban Gumucio, was first performed in November 1978 at the Santiago Cathedral for an international human rights symposium.

96. Angie Kapelianis, "TRC Experiences and Memories: Is it Art?" *SABC News,* 7 April 2006 (accessed 28 July 2007).

97. National Public Radio in the United States aired a story about *REWind* on its *Weekend Edition* program on 22 October 2006. See Charlene Scott, "Cantata Recalls Wounds of Apartheid," available at http://www.npr.org/templates/story/story.php?storyId=6362645 (accessed 22 October 2006).

98. Dimpho di Kopane's filmed version of *Carmen,* entitled *U-Carmen eKhayelitsha,* won a Golden Bear for Best Film at the Berlin International Film Festival 2005.

99. Kapelianis, "TRC Experiences and Memories: Is it Art?"

100. See, for example, TRC, *Truth and Reconciliation Commission of South Africa Report,* 1:112–113; Njabulo Ndebele, "Memory, Metaphor, and the Triumph of Narrative," in *Negotiating the Past: The Making of Memory in South Africa,* ed. Sarah Nuttall and Carli Coetzee (New York: Oxford University Press, 1999), 19–28.

101. The phrase "grain of the voice" comes from Roland Barthes, *The Grain of the Voice: Interviews 1962–1980,* trans. Linda Coverdale (New York: Hill and Wang, 1985).

102. Philip Miller, interview with the author, Johannesburg, 15 February 2007.

103. Scott, "Cantata Recalls Wounds of Apartheid."

104. Julia A. Walker, "Why Performance? Why Now? Textuality and the Rearticulation of Human Presence," *The Yale Journal of Criticism* 16, no. 1 (2003): 160.

105. Roland Barthes, "From Speech to Writing," in Barthes, *The Grain of the Voice: Interviews 1962–1980,* trans. Linda Coverdale (New York: Hill and Wang, 1985), 3–7.

106. Fiona C. Ross, *Bearing Witness: Women and the Truth and Reconciliation Commission in South Africa* (Sterling, Va.: Pluto Press, 2003), 35. In an essay analyzing another sound-based representation of the TRC, the audio documentary *South Africa's Human Spirit* produced by the SABC, Mark Libin also notes how the aural record, the voices of perpetrators and victims, seem to be conveyed without mediation. See Mark Libin, "Can the Subaltern Be Heard? Response and Responsibility in *South Africa's Human Spirit," Textual Practice* 17, no. 1 (2003): 119–140.

107. Trudy de Ridder, "'Vicarious Trauma': Supporting the TRC Staff," *Track Two* 6, nos. 3–4 (1997): 35.

108. In *The Philosophy of History,* Hegel said, "At this point we leave Africa, not to mention it again. For it is no historical part of the World; it has no movement or development to exhibit. . . . What we properly understand by Africa, is the Unhistorical, Undeveloped Spirit, still involved in the conditions of mere nature, and which had to be presented here only as on the threshold of the World's History." G. W. F. Hegel, *The Philosophy of History,* trans. John Sibree (New York: Dover, 1956), 99.

109. Luise White, Stephan F. Miescher, and David William Cohen, eds., *African Words, African Voices: Critical Practices in Oral History* (Bloomington: Indiana University Press, 2001), 4.

110. Ibid., 10.

111. On the South African historiography of oral history in relationship to the TRC, see Gary Minkley and Ciraj Rassool, "Orality, Memory, and Social History in South Africa," in *Negotiating the Past: The Making of Memory in South Africa,* ed. Sarah Nuttall and Carli Coetzee (New York: Oxford University Press, 1999), 89–99.

112. John Allen, e-mail correspondence with the author, 2 December 2006. Allen was the director of media relations for the TRC.

113. Laura Moss, "'Nice Audible Crying': Editions, Testimonies, and *Country of My Skull," Research in African Literatures* 37, no. 4 (2006): 86.

114. Philip Miller, telephone interview with the author, 15 February 2007.

115. Philip Miller, interview with filmmaker Liza Key, Cape Town, 15 December 2006.

116. Steve Smith, "Bringing Life, Death, and Sight to Sound," *New York Times,* 10 July 2007; Percy Zvomuya and Yunus Momoniat, "The Reverb of Rewind," *Mail & Guardian Online* (Johannesburg), 25 April 2008 (accessed 24 May 2008).

117. While the name "Plaatjie" is Afrikaans (and hence some might assume that the name indicates a white person), this individual is black.

118. TRC, *Truth and Reconciliation Commission of South Africa Report,* 1:147.

119. Ibid., 111.

120. Philip Miller, interview with the author, 15 February 2007.

121. Spier Arts, "The Spier Summer Arts Season Winds Up with the TRC Cantata Lecture Demonstration," press release, 2006.

122. Miller, interview with the author, 15 February 2007.

123. Mamdani, "The Truth According to the TRC," 176–183.

124. IRIN, "Violence Still Haunts South Africans a Decade after the TRC," *Daily Dispatch* (East London), 5 May 2006, 1.

125. Hugh Lewin, "Official Voices," *Rhodes Journalism Review,* special edition: *The Media & the TRC* (1997), available at http://www.rjr.ru.ac.za/no14.html (accessed 3 March 2005).

126. Ibid.

127. Miller, interview with the author, 15 February 2007.

128. Ibid.

129. Miller, *REwind: A Cantata for Voice, Tape, and Testimony,* live performance, St. George's Cathedral, Cape Town, 16 December 2006; Philip Miller, *REwind: A Cantata for Voice, Tape, and Testimony,* unpublished libretto in author's possession, 2006.

130. Philip Miller, interview with the author, 17 December 2006, Pringle Bay, Western Cape.

131. The soprano part was sung by Nokrimesi Skota in the Cape Town production and by Bronwen Forbay in the Williamstown production.

132. TRC, *Truth and Reconciliation Commission of South Africa Report,* vol. 4 (London: MacMillan, 1999), 312–313.

133. On the role of women in the TRC, see Fiona C. Ross, "The Construction of Voice and Identity in the South African Truth and Reconciliation Commission," in *Political Transition: Politics and Cultures,* ed. Paul Gready (Sterling, Va.: Pluto Press, 2003), 165–180.

134. Miller, interview with the author, 15 February 2007.

135. Ibid.

136. Miller, interview with the author, 17 December 2006.

137. "Promotion of National Unity and Reconciliation Act, Act no. 34, 1995," *Government Gazette,* 26 July 1995, 16579. Available online at www.doj.gov.za/trc/legal/act9534.htm (accessed 17 March 2009).

138. Miller, interview with the author, 17 December 2006.

139. Kapelianis, "TRC Experiences and Memories: Is it Art?"

140. Miller, interview with the author, 15 February 2007.

141. Performed on 29 September 2006 at the Massachusetts Museum of Contemporary Art in North Adams, Massachusetts. Lead sponsors included the Andrew H. Mellon Foundation, the Appelbaum-Kahn Foundation, and a grant from the New England Foundation for the Arts and the Creative Connections program of Meet the Composer, Inc.

142. Janice Honeyman, interview with the author, 17 December 2006, Pringle Bay, Western Cape.

143. Miller, interview with the author, 15 February 2007.

144. From author's field notes, 15 December 2007.

145. See "More about Cape Wine Lands," http://www.southernafricatravel.co.uk/destination.jsp?destination_id=2025 (accessed 4 April 2009).

146. Willem de Vries, "Waarheid-en-versoeningskomposisie (Truth and Reconciliation Composition)," *Die Burger,* 14 December 2006, scan of article available at http://www.philipmiller.info/images/press/42.jpg (accessed 4 April 2009).

147. Miller, interview with the author, 15 February 2007.

148. Ibid.

149. Ibid.

150. Ibid.

151.   Taylor, *The Archive and the Repertoire,* 20.
152.   Theodor Adorno, *Can One Live after Auschwitz? A Philosophical Reader,* ed. Rolf Tiedemann (Stanford, Calif.: Stanford University Press, 2003), 162.
153.   Antjie Krog, "Last Time, This Time," *Litnet Seminar Room,* 20 March 2006, available at http://www.oulitnet.co.za/seminarroom/krog_krog2.asp (accessed 5 October 2008).
154.   Yazir Henry, "Reconciling Reconciliation: A Personal and Public Journey of Testifying before the South African Truth and Reconciliation Commission," in *Political Transition: Politics and Cultures,* ed. Paul Gready (Sterling, Va.: Pluto Press, 2003), 266–267.
155.   Loren Kruger, "Making Sense of Sensation: Enlightenment, Embodiment, and the End(s) of Modern Drama," *Modern Drama* 43, no. 4 (2000): 558.
156.   Mark Sanders, *Complicities: The Intellectual and Apartheid* (Durham, N.C.: Duke University Press, 2002).
157.   Jane Taylor, William Kentridge, and Handspring Puppet Company, *Ubu and the Truth Commission* (Cape Town: University of Cape Town Press, 1998).
158.   See Stephanie Marlin-Curiel, "A Little Too Close to the Truth: Anxieties of Testimony and Confession in *Ubu and the Truth Commission* and *The Story I Am About to Tell,*" *South African Theatre Journal* 15 (2001): 77–106.
159.   For more about *Truth in Translation,* see the play's Web site at www.truthin translation.org.
160.   Miller, interview with the author, 15 February 2007.
161.   Ibid.
162.   Kapelianis, "TRC Experiences and Memories: Is it Art?" On the death of Elias Masina, see TRC, *Truth and Reconciliation Commission of South Africa Report,* vol. 7 (Cape Town: TRC, 2002), 341.
163.   Kapelianis, "TRC Experiences and Memories."
164.   Miller, interview with the author, 15 February 2007.
165.   Peter Storey, at the roundtable discussion "Lessons of Caution and Promise from South Africa and Greensboro for Durham," Duke University, 21 March 2007.
166.   Miller, interview with the author, 15 February 2007.
167.   Miller, interview with filmmaker Liza Key.
168.   Krog, *Country of My Skull,* 37
169.   Miller, interview with filmmaker Liza Key.
170.   Ibid.
171.   Miller, interview with the author, 15 February 2007.
172.   Miller, interview with filmmaker Liza Key.
173.   In deference to the confidentiality of these negotiations, I have chosen not to publish that amount here.
174.   Miller, interview with the author, 15 February 2007.
175.   Lucas Sikwepere, interview with filmmaker Liza Key, 11 December 2006, Cape Town; translated by Gcisakazi Mdlulwa.
176.   Eunice Miya, interview with filmmaker Liza Key and the author, 12 December 2006, Guguletu, Cape Town; translated by Gcisakazi Mdlulwa.
177.   Nobantu Nomsisi Ethel Plaatjie, interview with filmmaker Liza Key, 28 November 2006, Eastern Cape; translated by Gcisakazi Mdlulwa.
178.   Mrs. Edward Juqu, video interview with filmmaker Liza Key and the author, 12 December 2006, Guguletu, Cape Town; translated by Gcisakazi Mdlulwa.
179.   Miller, interview with the author, 15 February 2007.

180. Nelson Mandela, "Message by President Nelson Mandela on National Reconciliation Day, 16/12/95," South African Government Information, http://www.info.gov.za/speeches/1995/0x408c16.htm (accessed 4 April 2009).

181. The phrase "attempt to fit satisfactory alternatives" is from Joseph R. Roach, *Cities of the Dead: Circum-Atlantic Performance* (New York: Columbia University Press, 1996), 2–3.

182. See "16 December 1838: The Battle of Blood River," part of the *This Day in History* Web site, available at www.sahistory.org.za/pages/chronology/thisday/1838-12-16.htm (accessed 31 March 2007).

183. Rayda Becker, "The New Monument to the Women of South Africa," *African Arts* 33, no. 4 (2000): 8.

184. Coombes, *History after Apartheid,* 23–34. On the performance of Afrikaaner nationalism through festivals, public display, memory, and commemoration, see also Leslie Witz, *Apartheid's Festival: Contesting South Africa's National Pasts* (Bloomington: Indiana University Press, 2003).

185. Coombes, *History after Apartheid.*

186. Ibid., 25.

187. Rassool, "Making the District Six Museum in Cape Town," 127.

188. See "16 December 1838: The Battle of Blood River."

189. Nelson Mandela, "Message by President Nelson Mandela on National Reconciliation Day, 16 December 1995," available at www.anc.org.za/ancdocs/history/mandela/1995/pr951216.html (accessed 31 March 2007).

190. Ibid.

191. Desmond Tutu quoted in TRC, *Truth and Reconciliation Commission of South Africa Report,* 1:4.

192. Ibid., 22.

193. IRIN, "Violence Still Haunts South Africans a Decade after the TRC," 9.

194. Lindelwa Ngxamngxa quoted in ibid.

195. Both Gunn and Henry run nonprofit organizations dedicated to the rights of victims; Gunn works with the Human Rights Media Center and Henry with Western Cape Action Tours.

196. Ndebele, "Memory, Metaphor, and the Triumph of Narrative," 148.

197. Miller, interview with the author, 15 February 2007

198. Desmond Tutu quoted in TRC, *Truth and Reconciliation Commission of South Africa Report,* 1:4.

199. Hartman, "Introduction," 7.

200. Christopher J. Colvin, "Overview of the Reparations Program in South Africa," in *The Handbook of Reparations,* ed. Pablo de Greiff (New York: Oxford University Press, 2006), 176–214.

201. Quoted in Claudia B. Braude, "Making Art from Tribulation," *Mail & Guardian Online* (Johannesburg), 5 May 2006 (accessed 11 July 2007).

202. James E. Young, "Memory and Monument," in *Bitburg in Moral and Political Perspective,* ed. Geoffrey H. Hartman (Bloomington: Indiana University Press, 1986), 112.

203. See Fiona C. Ross, "On Having Voice and Being Heard: Some After-Effects of Testifying before the South African Truth and Reconciliation Commission," *Anthropological Theory* 3, no. 3 (2003): 325–341; Fiona Ross, "Codes of Dignity: Thinking about Ethics in Relation to Research on Violence," *Anthropology Southern Africa* 28, nos. 3–4 (2005): 99–107.

204. Anthea Buys, "A Loaf of Bread, a Choir, and the TRC," *Mail & Guardian Online* (Johannesburg), 2 May 2008 (accessed 26 September 2008).

Conclusion

The epigraph is from Shoshana Felman and Dori Laub, *Testimony: Crises of Witnessing in Literature, Psychoanalysis, and History* (New York: Routledge, 1992), 70–71.

1. Priscilla B. Hayner, "Truth Commissions: A Schematic Overview," *International Review of the Red Cross*, 88, no. 862 (2006): 295–310.

Afterword

1. Deborah Posel, "The TRC Report: What Kind of History? What Kind of Truth?" in *Commissioning the Past: Understanding South Africa's Truth and Reconciliation Commission,* ed. Deborah Posel and Graeme Simpson (Johannesburg: Witwatersrand University Press, 2002), 154–155; Richard Wilson, *The Politics of Truth and Reconciliation in South Africa: Legitimizing the Post-Apartheid State* (Cambridge: Cambridge University Press, 2001), 36; TRC, *Truth and Reconciliation Commission of South Africa Report* (London: MacMillan, 1999), 1:110–114.
2. Deborah Posel, "Truth? The View from South Africa's Truth and Reconciliation Commission," in *Keywords. Truth,* by Ali Benmakhlalouf, Ganesh Devy, Yang Guorong, Bertrand Ogilvie, Douglas Patterson, and Deborah Posel (New York: Other Press, 2004), 17. For another criticism of how the TRC defined truth, see Wilson, *The Politics of Truth and Reconciliation in South Africa,* 36.
3. Lars Buur, "Monumental Historical Memory: Managing Truth in the Everyday Work of the South African Truth and Reconciliation Commission," in *Commissioning the Past: Understanding South Africa's Truth and Reconciliation Commission,* ed. Deborah Posel and Graeme Simpson (Johannesburg: Witwatersrand University Press, 2002), 75.
4. Wilson, *The Politics of Truth and Reconciliation,* 44.
5. Ibid., 37.
6. Mark Sanders's recent book is an exception in this regard. See Mark Sanders, *Ambiguities of Witnessing: Law and Literature in the Time of a Truth Commission* (Palo Alto, Calif.: Stanford University Press, 2007).
7. TRC, *Truth and Reconciliation Commission of South Africa Report,* 1:112–113.
8. Ibid., 112.
9. Ibid.
10. Alex Boraine, *A Country Unmasked: Inside South Africa's Truth and Reconciliation Commission* (New York: Oxford University Press, 2000), 290.
11. Wilson, *The Politics of Truth and Reconciliation,* 42–43; Mansoor Jaffer, "Nationwide Statement-Taking Drive Kicks Off," *Truth Talk: The Official Newsletter of the Truth and Reconciliation Commission* 2, no. 1 (1997): 1.
12. Lars Buur, "Institutionalizing Truth: Victims, Perpetrators and Professionals in the Everyday Work of the South African Truth and Reconciliation Commission" (Ph.D. diss., Aarhus University, 2000), 66–93; Buur, "Monumental Historical Memory," 66–93.

13. Entry for 17 May 1995 in South Africa, Parliament, *Debates of the National Assembly (Hansard)* (Cape Town: Parliament of South Africa, 1995), 1346.

14. Wilson, *The Politics of Truth and Reconciliation*, 44.

15. Buur, "Monumental Historical Memory," 79; Wilson, *The Politics of Truth and Reconciliation*, 43.

16. Buur, "Monumental Historical Memory," 66–93.

17. Janet Cherry, John Daniel, and Madeleine Fullard, "Researching the 'Truth': A View from inside the Truth and Reconciliation Commission," in *Commissioning the Past: Understanding South Africa's Truth and Reconciliation Commission*, ed. Deborah Posel and Graeme Simpson (Johannesburg: Witwatersrand University Press, 2002), 21.

18. Wilson, *The Politics of Truth and Reconciliation*, 44.

19. Cherry, Daniel, and Fullard, "Researching the 'Truth,'" 35.

20. Desmond Tutu, *No Future without Forgiveness*, 1st ed. (New York: Doubleday, 1999), 120.

21. Mary Burton, interview with the author, Cape Town, 4 August 2006.

22. Wendy Orr, *From Biko to Basson: Wendy Orr's Search for the Soul of South Africa as a Commissioner of the TRC* (Saxonwold, South Africa: Contra Press, 2000), vii.

23. Yasmin Sooka, interview with the author, Pretoria, 26 July 2006.

24. Ibid.

25. TRC, *Truth and Reconciliation Commission of South Africa Report*, 1:4.

26. Ibid., 112–113.

27. Fiona C. Ross, *Bearing Witness: Women and the Truth and Reconciliation Commission in South Africa* (Sterling, Va.: Pluto Press, 2003), 27–50. A new book was released as this book was in the final stages of production that makes an extremely important contribution in this regard. See Antjie Krog, Kopano Ratele, and Nosisi Mpolweni, *There Was This Goat: Investigating the Truth Commission Testimony of Notrose Nobomvu Konile* (Pietermaritzburg: University of KwaZulu Natal Press, 2009).

28. Ibid., 35.

29. Constitution of the Republic of South Africa, 1996, Chapter 1 (Founding Provisions), section 6 (Languages), available online at http://www.info.gov.za/documents/constitution/1996/a108-96.pdf.

Select Bibliography

The bibliography on South Africa's Truth and Reconciliation Commission is massive, far too large to publish here. What follows is a select bibliography that is a general guide to the fields of transitional justice, South Africa's TRC, and texts on African history, cultural studies, and performance studies that have been particularly helpful to me in writing this book.

Films and Documentaries

Long Night's Journey into Day: South Africa's Search for Truth and Reconciliation. Dir. Deborah Hoffman and Frances Reid. Video. San Francisco: California Newsreel, 2000.

Oral Histories

Kapelianis, Angie, and Darren Taylor, eds. *South Africa's Human Spirit: An Oral Memoir of the Truth and Reconciliation Commission.* CD. Johannesburg: SABC, 2000.

Live Performances

Miller, Philip. *REwind. A Cantata for Voice, Tape, and Testimony.* World premiere performance at St. George's Cathedral, Cape Town, 16 December 2006.

Books and Articles

Arendt, Hannah. *Eichmann in Jerusalem: A Report on the Banality of Evil.* New York: Penguin Books, 1963.

Asmal, Kader. "Truth, Reconciliation and Justice: The South African Experience in Perspective." *The Modern Law Review* 63, no. 1 (2000): 1–24.

Asmal, Kader, Louise Asmal, and Ronald Suresh Roberts. *Reconciliation through Truth: A Reckoning of Apartheid's Criminal Governance.* Cape Town: David Philip Publishers, in association with Mayibuye Books, University of the Western Cape, 1996.

Auslander, Philip. *Liveness: Performance as Mediatized Culture.* New York: Routledge, 1999.

Austin, J. L. *How to Do Things with Words.* 2nd ed. Cambridge, Mass.: Harvard University Press, 1975.

Bell, Terry, in collaboration with Dumisa Buhle Ntsebeza. *Unfinished Business: South Africa, Apartheid and Truth.* Cape Town: RedWorks, 2001.

Bizos, George. *No One to Blame? In Pursuit of Justice in South Africa.* Cape Town: David Philip Publishers and Bellville: Mayibuye Books, 1998.

Boraine, Alex. *A Country Unmasked: Inside South Africa's Truth and Reconciliation Commission.* New York: Oxford University Press, 2000.

———, Janet Levy, and Ronel Scheffer, eds. *Dealing with the Past: Truth and Reconciliation in South Africa.* 2nd ed. Cape Town: Institute for Democracy in South Africa, 1997.

Bozzoli, Belinda. "Public Ritual and Private Transition: The Truth Commission in Alexandra Township, South Africa 1996." *African Studies Quarterly* 57, no. 2 (1998): 167–195.

Cohen, David William, and E. S. Atieno Odhiambo. *The Risks of Knowledge: Investigations into the Death of the Hon. Minister John Robert Ouko in Kenya, 1990.* Athens: Ohio University Press, 2004.

Cole, Catherine. "Performance, Transitional Justice, and the Law: South Africa's Truth and Reconciliation Commission." *Theatre Journal* 59, no. 2 (2007): 167–187.

Coombes, Annie E. *History after Apartheid: Visual Culture and Public Memory in a Democratic South Africa.* Durham, N.C.: Duke University Press, 2003.

Dayan, Daniel, and Elihu Katz. *Media Events: The Live Broadcasting of History.* Cambridge: Cambridge University Press, 1992.

de Greiff, Pablo, ed. *The Handbook of Reparations.* New York: Oxford University Press, 2006.

Derrida, Jacques. "The Laws of Reflection: Nelson Mandela, in Admiration." In *For Nelson Mandela,* ed. Jacques Derrida and Mustapha Tlili, 13–42. New York: Henry Holt and Co., 1987.

Douglas, Lawrence. *The Memory of Judgment: Making Law and History in the Trials of the Holocaust.* New Haven, Conn.: Yale University Press, 2001.

Edelstein, Jillian. *Truth & Lies: Stories from the Truth and Reconciliation Commission in South Africa.* London: Granta Books, 2001.

Felman, Shoshana. *The Juridical Unconscious: Trials and Traumas in the Twentieth Century.* Cambridge: Harvard University Press, 2002.

———, and Dori Laub, eds. *Testimony: Crises of Witnessing in Literature, Psychoanalysis, and History.* New York: Routledge, 1991.

Gibson, James L. *Overcoming Apartheid: Can Truth Reconcile a Divided Nation?* New York: Russell Sage Foundation, 2004.

Gobodo-Madikizela, Pumla. *A Human Being Died That Night: A South African Story of Forgiveness.* Boston: Houghton Mifflin, 2003.

Goffman, Erving. *The Presentation of Self in Everyday Life.* Garden City, N.Y.: Doubleday, 1959.

Gready, Paul, ed. *Political Transition: Politics and Cultures.* Sterling, Va.: Pluto Press, 2003.

Hamilton, Carolyn, Verne Harris, Jane Taylor, Michele Pickover, Graeme Reid, and Razia Saleh, eds. *Refiguring the Archive.* Boston: Kluwer Academic Publishers, 2002.

Hayner, Pricilla. *Unspeakable Truths: Confronting State Terror and Atrocity.* New York: Routledge, 2001.

Ignatieff, Michael. "Articles of Faith." *Index on Censorship* 5 (September/October 1996): 110–122.

———. "Digging Up the Dead." *New Yorker,* 10 November 1997, 84–93.

Jaffer, Zubeida, and Karin Cronjé. *Cameras, Microphones and Pens.* Cape Town: Institute for Justice and Reconciliation, 2004.

James, Wilmot Godfrey, and Linda van de Vijver, eds. *After the TRC: Reflections on Truth and Reconciliation in South Africa.* Athens: Ohio University Press, 2001.

Joffe, Joel. *The Rivonia Story*. Cape Town: Mayibuye Books, University of Western Cape, 1995.

Kani, John. *Nothing but the Truth*. Johannesburg: Witwatersrand University Press, 2002.

Karis, Thomas, and Gwendolen M. Carter, eds. *From Protest to Challenge: A Documentary History of African Politics in South Africa, 1882–1964*. Vol. 3, *Challenge and Violence 1953–1964*, by T. Karis and G. M. Gerhart. Stanford, Calif.: Hoover Institution Press, 1977.

Khoisan, Zenzile. *Jakaranda Time: An Investigator's View of South Africa's Truth and Reconciliation Commission*. Cape Town: Garib Communications, 2001.

Krog, Antjie. *Country of My Skull: Guilt, Sorrow, and the Limits of Forgiveness in the New South Africa*. 1998; repr., New York: Three Rivers Press, 1999.

Mamdani, Mahmood. "Amnesty or Impunity? A Preliminary Critique of the Report of the Truth and Reconciliation Commission of South Africa (TRC)." *Diacritics* 32, no. 3 (2002): 33–59.

Mandela, Nelson. "Black Man in a White Man's Court." In *No Easy Walk to Freedom*, ed. Ato Quayson, 105–142. New York: Penguin Books, 2002.

———. *Long Walk to Freedom: The Autobiography of Nelson Mandela*. Boston: Little, Brown and Co., 1994.

Marlin-Curiel, Stephanie. "Performing Memory, Rehearsing Reconciliation: The Art of Truth in the New South Africa." Ph.D. diss., New York University, 2001.

McKenzie, Jon. *Perform or Else: From Discipline to Performance*. New York: Routledge, 2001.

Merrett, Christopher. *A Culture of Censorship: Secrecy and Intellectual Repression in South Africa*. Macon, Ga.: Mercer University Press, 1995.

Minow, Martha. *Between Vengeance and Forgiveness: Facing History after Genocide and Mass Violence*. Boston: Beacon Press, 1998.

Nuttall, Sarah, and Carli Coetzee, eds. *Negotiating the Past: The Making of Memory in South Africa*. Cape Town: Oxford University Press, 1998.

O'Donnell, Guillermo, Philippe C. Schmitter, and Laurence Whitehead, eds. *Transitions from Authoritarian Rule: Tentative Conclusions about Uncertain Democracies*. Baltimore, Md.: Johns Hopkins University Press, 1986.

Orr, Wendy. *From Biko to Basson: Wendy Orr's Search for the Soul of South Africa as a Commissioner of the TRC*. Saxonwold, South Africa: Contra Press, 2000.

Osiel, Mark. *Mass Atrocity, Collective Memory, and the Law*. New Brunswick: Transaction Publishers, 1997.

Posel, Deborah. *The Making of Apartheid, 1948–1961*. New York: Oxford University Press, 1991.

———, and Graeme Simpson, eds. *Commissioning the Past: Understanding South Africa's Truth and Reconciliation Commission*. Johannesburg: Witwatersrand University Press, 2002.

Rassool, Ciraj, and Sandra Prosalendis, eds. *Recalling Community in Cape Town: Creating and Curating the District Six Museum*. Cape Town: District Six Museum Foundation, 2001.

Roach, Joseph R. *Cities of the Dead: Circum-Atlantic Performance*. New York: Columbia University Press, 1996.

Ross, Fiona C. *Bearing Witness: Women and the Truth and Reconciliation Commission in South Africa*. Sterling, Va.: Pluto Press, 2003.

Salazar, Philippe-Joseph. *An African Athens: Rhetoric and the Shaping of Democracy in South Africa*. Mahwah, N.J.: Lawrence Erlbaum Associates, 2002.

Sampson, Anthony. *The Treason Cage: The Opposition on Trial in South Africa*. London: Heinemann, 1958.

Sanders, Mark. *Ambiguities of Witnessing: Law and Literature in the Time of a Truth Commission*. Palo Alto, Calif.: Stanford University Press, 2007.

Scarry, Elaine. *The Body in Pain: The Making and Unmaking of the World*. New York: Oxford University Press, 1985.

Schechner, Richard. *Between Theatre and Anthropology*. Philadelphia: University of Pennsylvania Press, 1985.

Segall, Kimberly Wedeven. "Over My Dead Body: Trauma and Unreconciled Truths in South African Performance." Ph.D. diss., Northwestern University, 2001.

Sparks, Allister Haddon. *Tomorrow Is Another Country: The Inside Story of South Africa's Road to Change*. Chicago: University of Chicago Press, 1996.

Taylor, Diana. *The Archive and the Repertoire: Performing Cultural Memory in the Americas*. Durham, N.C.: Duke University Press, 2003.

———. *Disappearing Acts: Spectacles of Gender and Nationalism in Argentina's "Dirty War."* Durham, N.C.: Duke University Press, 1997.

Taylor, Jane, William Kentridge, and the Handspring Puppet Company. *Ubu and the Truth Commission*. Cape Town: University of Cape Town Press, 1998.

Tomaselli, Keyan, and P. Eric Louw, eds. *The Alternative Press in South Africa*. Denver: iAcademicBooks, 2001.

Tomaselli, Ruth, Keyan Tomaselli, and Johan Muller, eds. *Broadcasting in South Africa*. London: James Currey, 1987.

Truth and Reconciliation Commission. *Truth and Reconciliation Commission of South Africa Report*. Vols. 1–5. Cape Town: Truth and Reconciliation Commission, 1998.

———. *Truth and Reconciliation Commission of South Africa Report*. Vols. 6–7. Cape Town: Truth and Reconciliation Commission, 2003.

Tutu, Desmond. *No Future without Forgiveness*. 1st ed. New York: Doubleday, 1999.

Verdoolaege, Annelies. "Managing Reconciliation at the Human Rights Violations Hearings of the South African TRC." *Journal of Human Rights* 5, no. 1 (2005): 61–80.

———. "Media Representations of the South African Truth and Reconciliation Commission and Their Commitment to Reconciliation." *Journal of African Cultural Studies* 17, no. 2 (2005): 181–199.

Verwoerd, Wilhelm, and Mahlubi Mabizela, eds. *Truths Drawn in Jest: Commentary on the TRC through Cartoons*. Cape Town: David Philip Publishers, 2000.

Villa-Vicencio, Charles, and Erik Doxtader. *The Provocations of Amnesty: Memory, Justice, and Impunity*. Trenton, N.J.: Africa World Press, 2003.

———, and Wilhelm Verwoerd. *Looking Back, Reaching Forward: Reflections on the Truth and Reconciliation Commission of South Africa*. New York: St. Martin's Press, 2000.

White, Luise, Stephan F. Miescher, and David William Cohen, eds. *African Words, African Voices: Critical Practices in Oral History*. Bloomington: Indiana University Press, 2001.

Wilson, Richard. *The Politics of Truth and Reconciliation in South Africa: Legitimizing the Post-Apartheid State*. Cambridge: Cambridge University Press, 2001.

Index

absence of resolution: *REwind* and, 146; and South Africa's national memory, 157, 159

African Christian Democratic Party, 128

African National Congress (ANC): abuses in training camps of, 116; adopts strategy of making apartheid state ungovernable, 96; Afrikaner police incompetent to transcribe speeches of political leaders of, 30; apartheid state infiltrates, 98; and applications for amnesty, 114; Crown uses Declaration of Human Rights against in Treason Trial, 58; impact of state of emergency on, 43; members massacred in Bisho, 181n98; members massacred of in Guguletu, 18, 20; and National Prosecuting Authority, 127; Nelson Mandela uses Incitement Trial as platform for explaining philosophy of, 45; offers state funeral to Botha, 124; plants land mines, 107; policy of nonracialism of, 49–50; post-apartheid government of and reparations, 123 (*see also* reparations); Raymond Suttner and, 184n42; *REwind* uses struggle song of, 144–145; shift toward violence after Sharpeville massacre, 32–33, 47–48, 155–156 (*see also* Umkhonto we Sizwe)

Afrikaans identity, 154–155

Afrikaans language: and definition of apartheid, 31, 145; and hiring of translators in apartheid era, 72; mentioned, 80; number of speakers in South Africa in 1990s, 106; and "parity of esteem," 75, 191n55; and radio broadcasts of TRC hearings, 198n48; and translation at TRC hearings, 67, 70–71, 73, 160, 168; used as resistance in apartheid-era courtrooms, 36; used at apartheid-era inquests, 84; and *Vrye Weekblad,* 110–111

Alien Tort Claims lawsuit, 129

Amandla! A Revolution in Four-Part Harmony, 137

Amnesty Committee hearings: in analysis of TRC, xiv; applicants to, 114–115, 143, 145, 199–200n93; and background work of TRC, xviii, 119; Clive Derby-Lewis's testimony at,

107–108; commissioners and, 92; denies amnesty to perpetrators, 126; does not require remorse, 129, 162; effect of testimony at, 15, 66; Eugene de Kock's testimony at, 74; first of its kind, 58; functions like court of law, 4, 14, 73; grants amnesty to perpetrators, 123; hearing process described, 4, 14; initial controversy over public access to, 103–105; interpreters' difficulties at, 76; and Joe Mamsela's confession on *TRC Special Report,* 107; judges and, 14; mentioned, 66, 95; multiple languages used at, 67; and murder of Chris Hani, 108; perpetrators refuse to request, 129; physical arrangements at, 16; powers of, 14, 176n26; Promotion of National Unity and Reconciliation Act authorizes, xi, 5, 176n26; requirements of perpetrators who testified at, 4; reveals corruption of apartheid state, 18, 167, 176n28; testimony of Eugene de Kock at, 74; TRC report and, 6–7, 105, 120; *TRC Special Report* explains processes of, 95, 98, 113; voluntary nature of participation in, 5, 14, 125. *See also* National Prosecuting Authority (NPA); *Red Dust*

amnesty seekers: gender and race of, 145; portrayed in *Country of My Skull,* 81

Anglo-Boer War, 155

Apartheid Museum, 32

apartheid South Africa: absence of television in until 1976, 102; accuses activists of communism, 20, 33, 35, 38–39, 42; blocks media coverage of judicial proceedings, 102–103; and censorship, 6, 33, 35, 38–39, 51, 54, 56, 104, 197n32; and coerced labor, 112; and detention without trial, 60; and forced removals, 112; and hiring of interpreters for courts and hospitals, 72; leaves British Commonwealth in 1961, 32, 58–59; legislation of, 31–32; and mass arrests, xi, 32–33, 34–35, 44; as police state, 30, 42–43, 53; seen as a crime against humanity by South Africans, 134; sites for dissident rhetoric within, 182n4; and Special Branch secret police, 35, 40, 51; state of emergency and, 32, 43, 61, 185n69;

constitutions of Republic of South Africa, 32, 52, 57, 191–192n55, 212n29

Coombes, Annie E., 155

Country of My Skull: focuses on Desmond Tutu, 108; mentioned, 118, 134–135; and necklacing of Maki Skosana, 78–82, 97; Yazir Henry objects to artistic license of, 150. *See also* Krog, Antjie

Cradock Four, xix, 69, 131, 173n32. *See also* Calata, Fort; Calata, Nomonde

Cronje, Jack, 98

dance as resistance, 29, 56–57, 62. *See also* *toyi-toyi* dance

Daniel, John, 128, 166

Day of Reconciliation, 138

de Klerk, F. W.: belief of that purpose of TRC was to create consensus about South Africa's history, 122; claims Afrikaners created a nonracial South Africa, 121; responds positively to Adriaan Vlok's foot washing apology, 128

de Kock, Eugene, 74

de Wet, Quartus, 102

Department of Justice, xviii, xix–xx, 123

Derby-Lewis, Clive, 107

Derrida, Jacques, 32, 52, 57

detention without trial, 60–62

Dikeni, Sandila, 99–100

Dimpho di Kopane, 138

Dirk-Uys, Pieter. *See* Bezuidenhout, Evita

Dirty War (Argentina), x, 132. *See also* Argentine Forensic Anthropology Team

District Six Museum, 135, 150. *See also* living memorials; national memory

Douglas, Lawrence, 1

Drill Hall, 35, 37–38, 42–43, 53, 58

du Preez, Max: argues that TRC commissioners should be neutral observers, 23; chooses staff for *TRC Special Report*, 116–117; comments on lack of appreciation of TRC's work in South Africa today, 124; convinces SABC to make *TRC Special Report*, 110; criticizes Vlok foot-washing incident, 128; forced to recant a detail of necklacing coverage, 101; journalistic independence from TRC, 120; lures police and security operatives to watch *TRC Special Report*, 112; professional background of, 110, 195n9; provides context for necklacing in *TRC Special Report*, 99, 101; sees *TRC Special Report* as ears and eyes of South Africa, 107; uses apartheid-era SABC footage, 118; view

of truth-telling as a form of justice, 108; works to reach conservative white audience for *TRC Special Report*, 111

Eichmann trial, x, 1–5, 17, 22, 25, 67, 159, 161. *See also* Nuremberg trials

embodiment: conflation of with content in writings about TRC, 78; Cynthia Ngewu's testimony and, 84; and ethical issues related to adaptations of TRC testimony, 151; importance in conveying dimensions of human experience, 25; linked to resistance under apartheid, 26, 64; memory and, 29–30, 123, 134; need for analysis that includes, 90; reconciliation in South Africa and, 129–130; *REwind* and, 141; spoken word and, 63; transitional justice and, xx; TRC interpreters and, 66; and TRC's similarities with theatre, 13; *TRC Special Report*'s use of, 96, 106, 119; TRC testimony and, xv–xvi, 6, 11, 67, 89, 92, 161–162, 167. *See also* chanting; dance as resistance; freedom songs; gesture as resistance; traditional dress as resistance

Finca, Bongani, 24

First, Ruth, 61, 106

Fischer, Bram, 43, 102

Flame Lily Foundation, 101

Forbes, David, xix–xx, 131

forced removals: in apartheid South Africa, 111–112; and District Six Museum, 135; in post-apartheid South Africa, xiii–xiv; *TRC Special Report* covers, 111–112, 120, 199n76

Foreign Correspondents' Association of South Africa, 114

Forgiveness, 135, 137

Forman, Lionel, 34–35, 36–38, 40–41, 44

Fourie, Ginn, 129–130

Fourie, Lyndi, 129. *See also* Lyndi Fourie Foundation

Fransch, Anton, 81

Freedom Charter, 37, 41, 58

freedom songs: apartheid-era government's inability to control, 56; demonstrators use at apartheid-era trials, 29, 33, 34–36, 39, 42, 51, 55, 64, 184n37; importance in anti-apartheid struggle, 137–138; minister of justice complains about, 56–57; and national memory, 135; used in *REwind*, 137, 144, 147, 153–154. *See also* *Amandla! A Revolution in Four-Part Harmony*

"Free Mandela" campaign, 51

Fullard, Madeleine, 166

Kathrada, Ahmed, 63
Kentridge, William, 137
Key, Liza, 149
Khulumai Support Group, 142, 157
Khumalo, Sibongile, 141
Kodesh, Wolfie, 45
Konile, Elsie, 19, 82, 86, 180n86
Konile, Zabonke John, 19. *See also* Guguletu Seven
Krabill, Ron, 8, 51, 115
Krog, Antjie: advocates accessible writing in South Africa, xxi; comments on international journalists at TRC hearings, 102–103; comments on physical arrangements at TRC hearings, 16; covers TRC hearings for SABC, 80–81, 102–103, 110; does not see need to ask permission of victims to use their testimony, 153; encourages Philip Miller to compose *REwind*, 137, 139; focuses on Desmond Tutu in *Country of My Skull*, 108–109; focuses on her own psychological state in *Country of My Skull*, 97, 118; handling of Cynthia Ngewu's testimony, 82–83, 88; invisible editing of in *Country of My Skull*, 78–82; writes about necklacing of Maki Skosana, 97. *See also Country of My Skull*; Henry, Yazir
Kruger, Jimmy, 56–57, 64
Kruger, Loren, 151

land mines, 107
Language Facilitation Unit (University of the Free State, Bloemfontein), 72–73, 76
Lapsley, Father Michael, 137
Lewin, Hugh, 142
living memorials: Constitutional Court as, 136; District Six Museum as, 135, 150; Old Fort Prison as, 135; *REwind* cantata as, 136–137, 150
"Liza lis'idinga Lakho," 152–153
Lyndi Fourie Foundation, 129
Lyster, Richard, 23

Mabizela, Mahlubi, 9
Madikizela-Mandela, Winnie, 24, 48, 108, 127, 129
Magna Charta, 52
Majnoon, Salaudin, 125
Malgas, Ernest, 107
Mamasela, Joe, 98, 107
Mamdani, Mahmood, 112, 125, 142
Mandela, Nelson: accused in Incitement Trial, 44; body language of during Incitement Trial, 45; commitment of to nonracialism,

50; dances with Desmond Tutu when TRC report is completed, 56–57; jailing of after Incitement Trial, 52; prison release of, 28; as proponent of rainbow nation, xiii; Rivonia Trial of, 53–56; speech during Incitement Trial, 51–52; speech during Rivonia Trial, 54–56; tried in Rivonia Trial, 33–34; tried in Treason Trial, 33; uses clothing as speech during Incitement Trial, 45–52. *See also* "Black Man in a White Man's Court" speech; Incitement Trial; kaross; Rivonia Trial; traditional dress as resistance; Treason Trial; Xhosa clothing
Mandela United Football Club, 24, 89, 104, 108, 129, 197n41
Manthata, Tom, 101
Maphalane, Sisana Mary, 90
The Market Theatre: mentioned, xxiv, 149; performance of *REwind* at, 137–138, 147, 149. *See also* Purkey, Malcolm
Marx, Gerhard, 137, 148
Masina, Anne, 152, 154
Masina, Elias, 152
Mathabe, Paul, 50
Mathibela, Lebohang, 66, 74–75
"Mayibu'ye iAfrika," 34, 37
Mbeki, Govan, 63
Mbeki, Thabo: appealed to by various groups about amnesty policy of National Prosecuting Authority, 127; orders that cases of missing freedom fighters be resolved, 132; reacts positively to Vlok's foot-washing ritual, 128; receives TRC Summary Report, 4
Mboweni Marais, Khethiwe, 75–76
McCarthy, Joseph, xvii
McCormick, Kay, 11
Mdlulwa, Gcisakazi, 149
media coverage of TRC hearings. *See* radio coverage of TRC; television coverage of TRC; *TRC Special Report*
media events: defined, 66–67, 93–94; Rivonia Trial as, 55; TRC as, 19, 66–67, 93, 102, 106, 109, 116, 119, 177n39; *TRC Special Report* as, 113
Meshoe, Kenneth, 128
Miescher, Stephan F., 139
Miller, Philip: composes *REwind*, 124, 136; describes decision to use voices from TRC testimony in *REwind*, 140; on ethics of representing victims' voices, 151–152, 153–154; reaction to lecture demonstration of *REwind*, 152; seeks balanced representation of black and white voices, 142–145;

Miller, Philip (*continued*)
  on use of live testimony in *REwind,* 138; uses
  Eunice Miya's testimony in *REwind,* 140, 160;
  on the voice as an instrument in South
  Africa, 137–138; writes *REwind* for those
  interested in transitional justice, 146
Milošević, Slobodan, x
Miya, Eunice: Antjie Krog uses testimony
  of in *Country of My Skull,* 82, 88; identifies
  shoe-thrower at TRC hearing, 180n89;
  Philip Miller uses testimony of in *REwind,*
  88, 140, 151, 160; reacts positively to *REwind,*
  154; testimony at TRC hearing, 19,
  194n99
Miya, Jabulani, 88, 140, 154, 160. *See also*
  Guguletu Seven
Mkalipe, M., 42
Mofoking, Mduduzi, 153
Mohasoa, Thabiso, 64
Moloko, Evelina Puleng, 97, 101
Mona, Sipiti, 75–76
Mphahlele, Letlapa, 129–130
"Mrs. Plaatjie," 141
Mtimkulu, Joyce, 107
Mvinjelwa, Fikile, 144–145
Mxinwa, Irene, 19
Mxinwa, Simon, 19. *See also* Guguletu
  Seven

National Archives and Records Service:
  houses audio and video footage of TRC
  testimony, xviii–xix, 26, 158, 168, 179n76;
  and inaccessibility of TRC records,
  xviii–xix, 161, 190n17; incriminating
  cabinet minutes transferred to, 131
National Day of Reconciliation, 147, 154–155
national memory: and death of P. W. Botha,
  132–133; and metaphor of repair, 136; and
  National Day of Reconciliation, 154–156;
  REwind and, 140–141, 150, 158; and TRC,
  132–135, 168. *See also Forgiveness; In My
  Country;* living memorials; *Red Dust; Truth
  in Translation*
National Party: controls broadcast journalism,
  102; mentioned, 42; and murder of Guguletu
  Seven, 20; and national holidays, 155;
  repressive legislation of, 31–32; rule of ends,
  x; and Treason Trial, 35
National Prosecuting Authority (NPA), 123;
  announces policy of prosecuting perpetrators, 126–127; criticized for not prosecuting
  ANC members, 127; exhumes bodies of
  freedom fighters, 132; Ginn Fourie refuses

to cooperate with, 129; legal challenge to
  policies of, 127, 129; objections to its
  truth-for-amnesty policy, 127
National Women's Monument, 155
Ndebele language, 73, 198n48
necklacing, xiii, 96–100. *See also* apartheid
  South Africa; Moloko, Evelina Puleng;
  Skosana, Maki
Nel, Louis, 68–69, 73–74, 77
New Age, 45, 50
Ngewu, Cynthia: Antjie Krog's analysis of
  testimony of, 82–83; author's analysis of
  testimony of, 83–88; emphasis of on human
  rights violations, 83–85; emphasis on goal
  of justice, 86–87; testimony of, 18–19, 80–88,
  180n83; Xhosa-language translation of, 85
Ngudle, Looksmart Solwandle, 60–61
Ngudle, Maria, 60–61
Ngxamngxa, Lindelwa, 156
Nkosi, Makhosini, 132
"Nkosi Sikelel i'Africa," 36, 51
"No Greater Than," 142–143
Ntsebeza, Dumisa, 21–23, 128
Nuremberg trials, x, 2–5, 22, 25, 34, 161.
  See also Eichmann trial

Odhiambo, E. S. Atieno, xii, xvii, 26
"Offering of the Birds," 152
Old Fort Prison, 34–35, 135
Old Synagogue, 42–43, 45, 47, 49, 53, 58,
  185n67
Omar, Dullah (South African Minister of
  Justice), 165
Orr, Wendy: describes hearing preparation
  process, 8–9, 24; describes initial opposition
  to television coverage of hearings, 104–105;
  describes Nomonde Calata's testimony,
  79; mentioned, 106; states that TRC hearings
  rewrote history, 6; states that whites dismiss
  TRC testimony as overemotional, 167
Ouko, John Robert, xvii

Palace of Justice, 53–54
Pan Africanist Congress: attacks St. James
  Church, 143; banned, 32; Letlapa Mphahlele's
  presidency of, 129; popularity of in 1960s, 50
"parity of esteem" and South African languages,
  75, 160, 191n55
pass laws: Black Sash resists, 181n96; ineffi-
  ciency of, x–xi; mentioned in TRC testimony,
  xxv; protests against, x, xiv, 32, 181n96; *TRC
  Special Report* covers, 111–112, 120, 199n76.
  See also Sizwe Bansi Is Dead

victims: cameras give recognition to at TRC hearings, 108; commissioners' responses to testimony of, 23–24; Desmond Tutu sees testimony of as crucial for national transition, 24, 129; emotional expressiveness of at TRC hearings, 92, 139; ethics of representing artistically, 149–154, 157; families of at hearings, 23, 65; impact of testimony of on national consciousness, 24, 92, 94, 164–165; interpreters empathize with, 66, 74–75; NGOs advocate for rights of, 103–104, 127, 142, 157–158; reconciliation of with perpetrators, 129–130; see themselves as victimized by TRC, 123–124; TRC staff decides who will speak, 26, 92–93, 139; TRC's use of term, 115, 178n64. *See also* Alien Tort Claims lawsuit; Calata, Nomonde; Guguletu Seven; Miya, Eunice; Ngewu, Cynthia; reparations; Skosana, Maki; storytelling

Victor Verster Prison, xxiii
Villa-Vicencio, Charles, 7, 125–126
Vlakplaas: infiltrates Guguletu Seven, 19; and necklacing, 97; operative Eugene de Kock testifies at TRC, 74; plants booby-trapped hand grenades among anti-apartheid activists, 97–98; plants evidence at Guguletu Seven crime scene, 180, 193n83; and state-sponsored murder, 107
Vlok, Adriaan, 127–129
Vorster, B. J., 51, 61
Vrye Weekblad, 101, 110, 195n9

Walaza, Monfundo, 124
Watts, Hilda, 33, 36
Wessels, Leon, 128

Western Cape Action Tours, 210n195
wet-bag torture technique, 17–18, 89, 92, 104, 129, 144. *See also* Benzien, Jeffrey
White, Luise, 139
"Who's Laughing," 144–145, 153
Williams College, 138, 147
Wilson, Richard, xv, 24, 163, 166
Woza Albert!, xxii

xenophobic violence, xiii, 133
Xhosa clothing, 45, 50, 185n84
Xhosa language: Desmond Tutu uses at TRC hearings, 16, 179; difficulties with translating into English, 71, 73, 76; Eunice Miya's testimony and, 88, 193n79; number of speakers of in 1990s South Africa, 106; Pumla Gobodo-Madikizela uses at TRC hearings, 23; storytelling style of, 73; translation of at TRC hearings, 71, 193n79; translation of testimony after TRC hearings, 85, 88, 179n76, 190n17, 193nn79,90; used in *REwind,* 144

Yalolo, Geoffrey, 89–90
Yutar, Percy, 54, 102–103

Zapiro, xiii
Zokwe, Nonceba, 126
Zokwe, Stembele, 126
Zulu language: and police translations of activists' speech, 40; SABC broadcasts using, 106; and translation at TRC hearings, 67, 71, 160; use of in apartheid South Africa, 183n28; use of in post-apartheid South Africa, 73; used as resistance in apartheid courtroom, 36

Catherine M. Cole is Professor in the Department of Theater, Dance, and Performance Studies at the University of California, Berkeley. She is author of *Ghana's Concert Party Theatre* (Indiana University Press, 2001) and editor (with Takyiwaa Manuh and Stephan F. Miescher) of *Africa After Gender?* (Indiana University Press, 2006).